MW00635761

Coach and Marilyn Dunlap

THE DUNLAP RULES

Go Gats!

Jim Dunlap

ENDORSEMENTS

"Tiger Dunlap's book is a wonderful collection of stories that collectively capture the special qualities of his parents and the transformative impact they have had on so many. The values of education, work ethic, discipline, loyalty, preparation, persistence, compassion, competitiveness, family, and love are evident throughout the book and will resonate with readers irrespective of their connection to Coach or the Dunlap family. I have long recognized and appreciated that my life, life path and life's work were influenced substantially by Coach Dunlap; this reflective tribute compiled by Tiger captures the essence of why that impact was so meaningful and enduring for me and for many others. Nostalgia and humor aside, the takeaways are that living each day guided by values and principles, at home or at work, forms the foundation for a fulfilling and meaningful life, and a life that influences others by its example."

—JOE STERRETT, Dean of Athletics,
Lehigh University, Lehigh class of 1976

"Besides my own parents, no one has influenced my life more than Fred and Marilyn. I couldn't put Tiger's book down…it's about family, leadership, football, success, life and love. What more can you ask for?"

—VICKY CHUN, Vice President of Athletics,
Colgate University, Colgate class of 1991

"This book is a testament to Fred and his wife, Marilyn Dunlap, told from the perspective of their son, Fred Jr, better known as Tiger. He describes them as only a son could, yet his words resonate with those of us who Fred and Marilyn treated as if we were sons of their own. Tiger uses many of the same words and phrases to describe Fred and Marilyn that us second-tier family members would use: honest, loyal, disciplined, empathetic, tenacious...Fred's coaching and mentoring skills, as described by Tiger, are the reason so many former Colgate football players have excelled in so many areas of life...Coach brought out the best in us every day, even when we had little to play for except each other, and for our pride."

—JOHN MARZO, M.D., Former Team Physician, NFL Buffalo Bills, Colgate class of 1980

"This is a must-have (business and beyond) manual for any individual who is or wants to be a leader of people, regardless of the industry chosen...It's amazing how many leaders miss the people part of their business. Thanks for reminding me and teaching others about the 'Dunlap way' of leadership...And thank you for writing a great book with great personal meaning for those of us who know your parents. And for all the leaders and aspiring leaders out there, this book is a Success Manual!"

—ROBERT G. RELPH, JR., Colgate class of 1978

"COACH DUNLAP WAS AN INSPIRATION IN THE SPIRIT OF VINCE LOMBARDI."

—MARK MURPHY,

President and CEO, NFL Green Bay Packers

THE DUNLAP RULES

Motivational Life Lessons from an Award-Winning College Football Coach and the Inexhaustible Woman Who Inspired Him

FRED "TIGER" DUNLAP

Published by XLH Publishing LLC, a Delaware limited liability company
2220 Galloway Blvd, Trophy Club, TX 76262

Designed by Kathryn E. Campbell

ISBN 978-0-9967729-0-7

Printed in the United States of America by Gorham Printing

DEDICATED TO MY PARENTS,
MARILYN AND FRED DUNLAP
TRULY "TWO OF A KIND."

CONTENTS

"SUCCESS BREEDS SUCCESS.
IT'S THE POWER OF MOMENTUM."

—FRED DUNLAP

"Man of the Year"

Walter Camp Football Foundation

1977

FOREWORD

More than 40 years ago, long before I became president and CEO of the Green Bay Packers, I met Coach Fred Dunlap when I was a Clarence Central High School (NY) senior on a football-recruiting trip to Bethlehem, Pennsylvania, home of Lehigh University.

At the time, Fred coached there and had been highly successful. He was a serious and confident coach who, I learned later, had survived adversity before turning the program around. His son, "Tiger," presents that story very vividly in this book.

Although I liked Lehigh and was impressed with Fred, I decided to attend Colgate University since the athletic department would allow me to play both football and basketball. Colgate's schedule also featured more top ranked opponents. Little did I realize this decision would lead to a reunion with Fred three years later and a lifetime of invaluable mentoring from this special coach.

During my first three years at Colgate, located in Hamilton, New York, our football teams had been very average and inconsistent. We beat teams with more talent, and lost to teams we should have beaten. We were talented, but did not play up to our potential.

After my junior year, our previous head coach accepted the head coaching job at Holy Cross. Colgate's administration acted quickly hiring Fred as our new coach. He was a great fit, a Colgate graduate who was familiar with Colgate's players, having coached against them during several recent seasons.

When we started training in the spring, it was very clear to me that things were going to be different. Fred was very focused and organized. Every meeting was precise and well run. What Fred did reminded me of what former players from the Vince Lombardi Packer teams have told me about their first impressions of the legend when he became head coach. Lombardi was very confident and had an aura about him, and the players immediately knew they were going to be successful.

Like Lombardi, Fred came in and immediately changed the culture surrounding Colgate football, something Tiger explains well in this book. He also chronicles how involved Fred's wife, Marilyn, was in the program, something I recall so well from my days at Colgate.

When I was elected captain of the team that spring, I was very fortunate to see firsthand how Fred came in and established his own program while observing his leadership style. I learned valuable lessons from him about management and leadership, ones so well presented in this book, and have applied them throughout my varied professional career.

Tiger explains how Fred's coaching led our Colgate team to turnaround its won-lost record the very first year. With each win, we gained more confidence, and we were able to put the failures of the past behind us. As the season went along, we started to receive national attention, as well as votes for the top 20 NCAA Division I schools, and interest from representatives of bowl games—all unheard of for Colgate. Without doubt, thanks to Fred and Marilyn, Colgate football was back on the map.

One game of interest I recall so well was our match-up with Rutgers nationally televised on Thanksgiving night and played in the new Meadowlands Stadium. With the win, Rutgers completed an undefeated season, but, as Tiger explains, a controversial call that went against Colgate (and greatly benefited Rutgers) brought even further attention and recognition to the Colgate team.

After I graduated from Colgate, I was fortunate enough to play 8 years for the Washington Redskins. The lessons learned from Fred about football and life were very helpful to me during my playing career. I stayed in the DC area after that career ended, working for the NFL Players Association and then the Department of Justice. I stayed in touch with Fred, and always appreciated his advice and counsel.

As you will read, when Fred retired as Colgate's athletic director, I was interested in the position and decided to apply despite enjoying working for the Justice Department. Throughout the search process, I was in regular touch with Fred. Although I had played at Colgate, I didn't know a lot about athletics administration. Within a short period of time, my old coach brought me up to speed on all the issues facing Colgate athletics. I'm sure I would not have been offered the position without his support and guidance.

I went on to serve as Colgate's AD for more than 11 years. Fred and Marilyn had decided to stay in Hamilton after retirement, and it was great to be directly reconnected with them again. Fred was always available to discuss any questions or issues I was facing. At the time, Colgate was a small, liberal arts college (2700 students) competing without scholarships against NCAA Division I opponents. It was challenging to field competitive teams with no scholarships and high academic standards, and Fred was invaluable to me during my tenure there.

In 1996, Fred went above, and beyond, the call of duty to help out

Colgate football and me. The program was really at a low point. The head coach I had hired had just finished his third season with a 0-11 record. I knew that I had to make a coaching change, but the coach had a year remaining on his contract, and the administration was not willing to buy out the last year of his contract.

I described the situation to Fred and also told him that I really liked assistant coach Dick Biddle (a member of Fred's coaching staff in the early 1980s) and would consider promoting him to head coach. As Fred and I discussed the situation, he made a suggestion. He would be willing to serve as the offensive coordinator on a voluntary basis (no pay) in order to allow me to make the coaching change. Fortunately, the administration approved the plan.

The impact that Fred and Dick had on the program was immediate, similar to the change in 1976 when Fred became Colgate's coach. Although we lost our first four games, the team played well and continued to improve. We ended up winning the next six games and played against Bucknell for the Patriot League championship in the last game of the season. The rest, as they say, is history. The next year, Fred stayed on to coach the quarterbacks, providing continuity into a second season. Colgate won the Patriot League championship in 1997 and played in the NCAA I-AA playoffs. In 2003, Colgate made it to the NCAA I-AA championship game, posting a 15-1 record. Dick Biddle retired after the 2013 season as Colgate's all-time winningest coach.

The 1996 season was really a special one in many ways. To me, it was a vivid example of the value of great coaching. It also reaffirmed my belief in football players. Fred had been out of coaching for almost 10 years, and I was worried about how the players from the 1996 team would relate to him.

As it turned out, I had nothing to worry about. The players

immediately took to Fred. They could tell he knew so much about football, and that he was helping them improve as players. Over the previous three years, I had heard nothing but complaints from these same players and their parents about the program and the quality of coaching. It was truly inspiring to see the reverence they had for Fred. I should add that Marilyn also came out of retirement in 1996. She was at most of the practices, and helped bring together the coaches as well as the players. Marilyn, along with Dick and Fred, helped completely change the attitude and culture of the program. It was the most remarkable turnaround I've seen in my career.

After the 1997 season, Fred returned to retired life, and continued to live in Hamilton. During the rest of my tenure at Colgate, he served as a great sounding board for me as I worked through various issues.

In 2003, I had an opportunity to become the Director of Athletics at Northwestern University. I was really torn about whether to accept the position. I was excited about the opportunity, but had deep roots at Colgate, and my wife, Laurie, and I loved raising our family in Hamilton.

When I asked Fred about the move, he said that I was a young man (47 at the time), had a long career ahead of me and that the Northwestern position represented a very special opportunity. Once again, Fred's advice proved to be wise. I served as AD for Northwestern for five years, loved my time there, made a number of connections within the Big Ten and the Midwest, and my experience there positioned me well for my move to the Green Bay Packers in 2008.

As I look back on my professional career, I now have a much greater appreciation for how fortunate I was to play that one season for Fred. I also realize how blessed I have been to have had him as a mentor for all these years. Fred is remarkable, and an inspired leader. He had a distinguished Hall of Fame career as a coach. When I think about Fred, though, what stands out most to me is the wonderful relationship that he has with Marilyn. They are always together; are truly a team and continually support each other.

The Dunlap Rules will be invaluable to couples and families as Tiger takes you inside Fred and Marilyn's marriage and describes the lessons he learned from this truly remarkable couple. Those lessons extend beyond the family setting as well, to leadership and management approaches and to methods of dealing with everyday life pressures. Like Tiger, I have learned those lessons directly from his parents and applied them in my career.

The Dunlap Rules encapsulates all of the ways that Fred and Marilyn have influenced the people they have touched in their lives. I feel fortunate to be one of them.

—Mark Murphy
President and Chief Executive Officer,
NFL Green Bay Packers

PREFACE

BY DEFINITION, FRED DUNLAP ISN'T a celebrity, certainly by today's standards where everything gets magnified and exaggerated. By the media, by social networks, and by the voracious thirst our society has today for instant gratification. To quench this thirst, the media fixates on the superlative. The biggest. The greatest. The strongest. The most famous.

Size seems to matter today, doesn't it? And with that distraction toward the surreal and the emphatic, other things, very special things, can get lost or become obscured.

Most people don't know who Fred Dunlap is. His isn't a household name. Yet he was named "Man of the Year" by the prestigious Walter Camp Football Foundation. He shares that distinction with Hall of Fame NFL quarterbacks John Elway and Bob Griese, former NFL Commissioner Pete Rozelle, and Army's legendary fullback Doc Blanchard, who also received the award. This recognition was also bestowed on Coach Lou Holtz, Coach Don Shula, quarterback Roger Staubach and Congressman and presidential candidate Jack Kemp.

Now those are household names. They are famous. They are celebrities. But what then about Fred Dunlap? How did he end up in this class? What did he do to warrant such an honor?

Fred Dunlap was a small college football coach. He is regarded in those circles as highly successful, turning teams around and leading a resurgence to prominence first at Lehigh University and then later at Colgate University.

Though these were small college programs, Fred Dunlap coached more than 25 athletes who were drafted or played in the NFL. All-Pro Mark Murphy played for Coach Dunlap at Colgate, preparing him for an eight-season career with the Washington Redskins. He succeeded Fred Dunlap as Colgate's athletic director after retiring from the NFL. Mark relied on Coach Dunlap first as a coach and later as a mentor as athletic director. Today, Mark is president and chief executive officer of the Green Bay Packers.

Fred Dunlap also mentored assistant coaches to become successful college and NFL coaches—among those, Chris Palmer, who was an assistant coach for a decade before beginning a successful 30-year career as an NFL coach, including being head coach of the Cleveland Browns.

To be certain, Fred Dunlap possesses outstanding credentials as both a coach and a mentor, but these are *not* the reasons he was selected "Man of the Year." Instead, it was because of the *way* he did it—because of the unique leadership and motivational approaches he applied and the manner with which he positively influenced those around him. Nevertheless, he does not meet today's standards as being famous.

Fred's wife of 63 years, Marilyn Dunlap, is even less well known. However, she is highly regarded not simply for being Fred's spouse and a mother, but also for the *way* she did it, inspiring Fred, contributing to his career, helping his players in the classroom, and for representing Fred in the day-to-day effort of raising two children.

Fred and Marilyn Dunlap's *way* has been the singular reason why their son has been successful in life. He absorbed their methods, their approaches and their values all wrapped up in what may be called The Dunlap Rules. And while those rules were demonstrated to him through the lens of his parents' sports career, he had a hunch those values and unique approaches would transfer effectively to the business world, where he made his career. It was where he competed, similarly to how his dad had competed on the football field.

With this in mind, he committed himself to applying these approaches as management techniques while moving up the corporate ladder. This led to sales achievements and then to management and leadership roles, and to becoming CEO of a large healthcare business—a company that was recently sold for more than $2 billion.

Without a doubt, the son's success wasn't because of anything he did other than to implement special leadership and management approaches, ones bestowed on him by two people: the "Man of the Year" and an inexhaustible woman who is as unique as he is.

The reason I know this is because I am their son, the one so impacted by *my parents' ways*. This book examines their unique style and explains how their approach can lead to winning in sports and in business. And in parenting and in dealing with the pressures life presents.

So, come take the journey with me and listen to the story of Fred and Marilyn Dunlap, admired and respected by all those who know them. Reap the benefits of The Dunlap Rules, approaches that caused a true revolution in my life and ones that may be motivational in yours, as well.

—FRED "TIGER" DUNLAP

PART I

The Formation of the Team

Wedding Bells

"I first want to say that we love our son. He's *our guy* and has been so for 55 years."

He paused for a moment, standing with a microphone in one hand and some notes in the other. "And it's an honor for me to be the best man," my father said. "I am 86 years old and this is the first time I have been a best man. So this is really new for me."

The audience chuckled in response. The room at the Baltimore Country Club was full of smiling faces listening intently to his message. I was standing next to him, as I had done so many times. And I was watching him work the crowd. But this moment was different. It was not a speech in a locker room full of football players before a big game. It was not an alumni gathering filled with interest for Colgate University football. And it wasn't a high school gymnasium filled with recruits wondering whether this was the kind of coach they wanted to play for in college.

No, it was our audience and our friends, and they were here for our wedding. Sure, some of the guests had played football for my father, but for the most part, he was speaking to a group of strangers. The only thing he had in common with them was that everyone had a special connection to my bride Andrea and me.

His words were personal, spoken as a father and not as a coach. But his delivery was the same—filled with humility and charisma. It was a style with quiet confidence and a strong presence.

"I brought some notes with me," Dad said, "that I might refer to now and then, but I am really an off-the-cuff guy."

Dad then spoke of his love and affection for Andrea and me. But he didn't use the word *his*. He said *our*. The other half of *our* was Marilyn Dunlap, my mother, and his wife of 63 years, sitting in the audience admiring her guy as he spoke.

Dad talked about their happiness for us. And that they hoped we would have many years of the same kind of joy that he and my mother have had. He told stories about my childhood, filling the room with laughter. It was a receptive crowd because it was a happy moment. But as I watched Dad hold 160 people captive, I pondered troubling events from earlier that week.

It was now Saturday night, and I was at my own wedding reception. Only three days prior, I received the call that no son wants to get. Dad informed me from a Hamilton, New York hospital that my mother had suffered a stroke.

As that day progressed, I wondered whether my parents would be able to attend our wedding. Certainly Dad wouldn't leave her behind, and it seemed impossible that Mom would be able to travel. I discussed a contingency plan with my son Tyler, asking him to stand in for my father as the best man.

Concerned, I stayed close by the phone as Dad updated my mother's condition. She improved gradually as the day passed, but I still doubted she could make it for the wedding.

I should have known better. After two days in the hospital, the doctors reluctantly discharged her to go home. As she settled in, my mother Marilyn again began to be *Marilyn,* insisting she could still travel to Baltimore. Then she changed *could* to *would*. Mom was 84 years old, but she always thought age was a state of mind. I remember as a young boy, when she turned 36, she stood in the kitchen trying to convince me that she was a "36-year-old kid." She always said, "Overcoming obstacles is my favorite sport." She was unrelenting to her core.

Now, 48 years later, and only three days after her stroke, I stood watching as she listened to her husband tell their story. She looked tired that Saturday evening and was clearly not feeling well. But being at our wedding was what she was going to do. To her, there was no other option.

My father's approach to life has been the same, one of the reasons they make such a great couple. Both are passionate. Both are tenacious. And above all, both have always been in pursuit of the best things in life for those around them.

As I reflected on that, Dad continued. "Our son, Tiger, has always been a hard worker," he said, "and he's been dogged and relentless. Marilyn and I used to call him a badger."

Everyone laughed at this depiction and at discovering that my childhood nickname was Tiger. "And although he was such a badger," Dad said, "he's always been a dreamer, wanting to do amazing things in life."

"Marilyn used to dance with the kids and dance with the cat. She sang "Moon River" to them as she danced around the kitchen," Dad said, before he surveyed the room and paused. "And when we were reminiscing the other day about that, for the first time, I actually looked at the lyrics of "Moon River." As I read them, I thought about how much those words signify how our son has spent his life."

My father pulled out his notes. And then he read the lyrics rhythmically.

The words spoke of a dreamer and an explorer, filled with optimism and looking to see the world. While Dad believed those words symbolized my life, I was certain that the song exemplified my parents' life. The lyrics described their pursuit of great things and their love for people.

These are my parents, Fred and Marilyn Dunlap. They are timeless, and they have impacted the lives of countless people who have known them. For 55 years, I too, have been impacted by their presence. I have learned many lessons from them, shaping how I have lived.

Those lessons have been indelibly etched into my very fiber. The motivational lessons are applicable in leadership and in management. They are lessons in parenting and in coping with life's challenges. And they are lessons in how to treat others.

My parents' influences on me, and on everyone else they have touched, have made all of us better parents, better leaders and better managers. They have made us better people.

With this in mind, this is the story of Fred and Marilyn, told from a son's perspective. A son who on his wedding day was a 55-year-old kid.

Getting Started

I DID NOT GROW UP in a log cabin. I did not walk five miles to school in the snow. And it wasn't uphill both ways.

I was Tiger Dunlap. But that wasn't my original "handle." In fact, when I arrived home from the hospital a couple weeks after my birth, following an operation for a strangulated hernia, I was undernourished, basically skin and bones. My parents remained worried after my surgery, but in an attempt to infuse some levity, they called their emaciated boy, "Turkey Bone." As months progressed, they shortened

Turkey Bone to "T-Bone" and then to "T." My grandparents rescued me from this verbal abuse and convinced my parents that "I deserved a much less dubious nickname." So my parents chose to call me "Tiger," a nickname remaining with me to this day.

I did not grow up poor or rich. I grew up in a middle-class environment where people worked hard for a living and saved what they could. It was the 1960s, a time when it was customary for the husband to work and provide for the family while the wife stayed home and raised the kids. Like most families, we fit that mold.

My father was a college football coach. When I was six years old, we moved to Bethlehem, Pennsylvania, after Dad accepted the head coaching position at Lehigh University. I was in the first grade at the time and my sister, Jessie, was in second grade. We lived in a new house in a new development. Our address was 1 Willowbrook Drive. Though I didn't know it at the time, I would call that address my home for the next eleven years.

While we were in many ways a classic 1960s family, there were a few unusual differences with the Dunlaps due to Dad being a football coach. It is a different kind of job—and it's stressful. There is a lot of travel. And most of all, it is a highly visible occupation. If you win, everybody knows it. If you lose, ditto.

The hours that a football coach spends working are massive, no nine to five. It's a busy time during football season but after the season ends, months are spent recruiting new classes of players or meeting the requests/demands of alumni yearning to spend quality time with the coach. There are also demands from the college administration officials. And many mandatory meetings with the athletic director and other university dignitaries who need to see the coach for a variety of reasons.

At six years old, I didn't know exactly what Dad did each day, I just knew he was busy. "Your father wishes he could be here with us," my mom told us, "but he has a very busy job and he is out there working hard so we have a house, clothing and food to eat." Mom added, "But we are the Dunlaps. We are a team, and we look out for each other at all times."

That was the code, recited to us weekly, if not daily. Mom was immensely loyal, which in turn made us loyal. We didn't question why; we just trusted it to be true.

Jessie and I revered our father. And loved him. I don't ever remember wondering why Dad wasn't around as much as the "other dads." I just remember how thrilling it was when he was around. He was our dad and every time he was home, he made us feel like we were the only thing in life that mattered. Because we had so little time as a family, we cherished each moment that the four of us were together.

Dad's free time with the family happened only during June and the first half of July when recruiting season was over and the fall football season hadn't yet started. During the football season, the only family time we had was immediately after the Saturday game until Sunday noon when Dad had to go into the office to start scouting the next opponent. That involved reviewing game films and building a unique set of strategies for the following game.

When Dad was in town, he often worked late each night, arriving home after our bedtime. Jessie and I would catch him for a minute in the morning before school and before he left for work. But that was pretty much it.

With Dad's work demands being so consuming, Mom supported everything else. She was the ship captain, and Jessie and I were the mates. When I was a child, I didn't grasp some of the pressures and challenges my mother must have faced being alone a great deal of the time. As kids, we didn't see anything unusual about "dinner for three" every night.

The 1960s was a period before nannies and cleaning ladies were fashionable. It was before the Internet and before pizza delivery. But even if that had existed, we didn't have the money to afford that kind of help or that type of food service.

Mom cooked every meal and did the dishes. She did the house cleaning and the laundry. She did the shopping. She bathed each of us until we were self-sufficient. I was a late bloomer with bathing. Sure, I was capable enough, but I would rather run around as a soiled mess; "Pigpen" of *Peanuts* was my role model. Yet Mom would find a way to corner me like a good hoops team would run a half-court trap, and get me into the tub. Damn! Eventually I developed skills with a bar of soap and a brush, a huge relief to my mother.

Since Dad was so busy, Mom did it all. Or so it seemed. But I am sure we didn't fully appreciate how great she was at it. As a parent myself, I have a much stronger appreciation now for the task Mom had and for how well she performed it.

When her daily duties ended, Mom even found time to review our homework with us. At six years old, that didn't involve editing any term papers, but she helped with all my schoolwork. Her guidance on term papers came later.

Mom graduated from St. Lawrence University as an English major at the top of her class. She also worked as a high school English teacher when we were very young. It was therefore compulsory in the Dunlap house to learn the proper use of the English language. There were no split infinitives, no sentences that ended with a preposition. None of that.

When we made mistakes, Mom corrected us. It wasn't nagging and it wasn't abusive. She just reminded us of the correct usage. It was coaching, not chastising. Mom had a way of explaining how valuable it would be for us to master the English language—how beneficial that would be for us later in life.

Mom's instruction always came with an incentive. Not a gift. Nothing involving bribery. There was no "I'll give you ice cream if you do your homework." Her incentives came in the form of a promise that we would become more successful if we followed through. It was a promise not from her, but rather a prize we would earn. "If you don't do it," she would say, "it will hurt your future." The fulcrum thus became our own accountability.

Jessie and I had other areas of accountability, too. Mom created her own Molly Maid service. The maids' names were Tiger and Jessie. By the time I was eight years old, Mom sat us down and explained the concept of an allowance and the concept of services rendered. Jessie and I were each given a list of chores for each day of the week. This initially seemed ominous, but boy, did I want that allowance. There was a penny candy store down the street and I saw myself sauntering up to the counter ready to make my own contribution to the U.S. Gross Domestic Product. Gum balls. Sour balls. Ooh baby!

What kind of chores were we assigned? Cleaning the dishes, taking out the trash, mowing the lawn, dusting, vacuuming. Sweeping out the garage. Shoveling snow in the winter. And the worst: cleaning the toilets. Yuck! I needed Hazmat gear for that.

Aside from chores, there were the standard laws of the house: keep a clean bedroom, make our beds, and always pick up our toys after playing with them. Jessie and I were meticulous in our care for the house. Mom would remind us that the house was *our house* and therefore part of the Dunlap Team.

At Mom's insistence while Dad was at work, Jessie and I began systematically doing our chores, and earning an allowance. If IRS agents reading this book wonder, I can assure them that my weekly wage wasn't above the minimum taxable threshold, since we earned 15 or 20 cents a week. At the time, that seemed reasonable to me. But as charter members of the *Twerp Union*, Jessie and I thought we might need to renegotiate that each year.

After a few months of earning our allowance, the piggy banks Jessie and I had were becoming heavy. Mom took us down to the local bank to set up savings accounts. As I cautiously handed my life savings (a pile of nickels and dimes) to the man behind the counter, I looked him in the eye and asked if my money was going to be secure. He pointed to the safe behind the counter and I began to understand how banking worked. I learned the phenomenon of deposit interest: if you deposited money, your money began to work for you.

Mom talked to us on the way home, reinforcing many of the things we learned that day. As I listened, I concluded that I had a good job. And I had a good boss. I figured if I kept that garage spotless, I would make more money. And though it was a bit early to start thinking about a 401(k), I began to estimate how large my savings account might become with compounded interest if I resisted spending what I earned.

These were valuable lessons learned at a young age and they shaped much of how I handled my finances later in life.

This was how I grew up on Willowbrook Drive. I was part of the Dunlap Team, a mix of fun and accountability. And while that mostly involved time spent with Mom and Jessie, it was like Mardi Gras when Dad could be with us.

On the Other Side of South Mountain

WILLOWBROOK DRIVE WAS LOCATED IN Saucon Valley, a suburb on the south side of Bethlehem. Between Saucon Valley and Bethlehem was a big hill that the local folks called South Mountain.

On the other side, on the edge of Bethlehem, stood Lehigh University where Dad coached football. It was only five miles from the house, but back then, when I was standing a mere four feet, two inches tall, it seemed like a long way away. With Dad's long hours keeping him at work, it seemed even more distant.

Mom, Jessie and I would occasionally make the trip into Bethlehem, driving past the Lehigh campus. On a rare occasion, we stopped and visited him in the office. The football offices were located in a very old building called Taylor Hall.

As we walked through the lobby, trophy cases were displayed along the walls from floor to ceiling. They were filled with photographs of teams and game balls of past lore. I remember how dank things smelled and how dimly lit that lobby was. I didn't know the word *dank* at the time, but that's how things smelled.

The memorabilia was old, some of it dating to the late 1800s. The game balls from those days looked more like pillows, round and puffy, safely stored behind the vaulted cases. *How long had these balls and trophies been there*, I wondered. Did they ever clean them? Or did they leave them untouched out of respect for the heroes of the past?

I stared at the faces of the players in the photos—they looked so young. When I did the math, however, it occurred to me that the players on the 1890 team, for instance, though youthful in appearance, were probably all dead. Taylor Hall was impressive, but it felt more like we were walking through a museum.

Dad's office was on the second floor and his assistant coaches had offices next to him. I didn't really understand the significance at the time, but Dad was the only coach who had his own office. The assistants were packed into the other offices, two or three coaches to a room. That seemed cozy at the time, but in hindsight, I can appreciate it was evidence of the size of the football budget—or lack thereof.

After we greeted the coaches, Dad took us on a tour of the athletic facilities. Intramural basketball courts. Weight rooms. The swimming pool. Grace Hall, where the wrestling and basketball teams competed. And then the biggest thrill of all—walking into Taylor Stadium where Dad's team played their games.

It all seemed so impressive. The truth was that Taylor Stadium was an old stadium with a lower level constructed of cement with seats also of cement. It met the definition of "original construction" in the most emphatic way.

There was nothing symmetrical about the shape of the stadium and the only apparent enhancement since it was originally built was an upper level set of bleachers on the home side, spanning the full length of the field. On each row of the stands were aluminum benches. Hard aluminum benches. In November: cold, hard aluminum benches!

This was not the age of seat backs and seat cushions. It was the age where spectators stood and cheered sometimes just to get the blood flowing again.

Taylor Stadium also served as the baseball stadium so it was open-ended in one of the end zones. I didn't sense it at the time but it was clear that the Lehigh athletic department was getting the most out of a limited number of facilities and resources.

No matter, to a young kid, this was the big time. Mom, Jessie and I walked onto the field in the off-season and stood at the 50-yard line gazing at the scoreboard in the end zone. And then we looked straight up at the home stands that towered above us. And at the press box located above the home side bleachers. It looked like it was on top of us. Across the front of the press box was painted in huge letters: LEHIGH.

I don't remember how many times we actually visited Dad at the office, but each visit usually included a tour like this, and a trip into Taylor Stadium where I raced my sister up and down the stadium steps. When we were older, we sometimes brought our swimsuits or played basketball in the gym.

Trips to Lehigh and Taylor Hall were always fun. Although we didn't really spend much time sitting with Dad in his office, it made us feel more connected to what he was doing on the other side of South Mountain.

Waste Not, Want Not

ON WILLOWBROOK DRIVE, ANOTHER THING eluding me as a young pup in a new neighborhood was the broader concept of money and financial security. As a six-year-old, my keen intuitive skills were limited to comparisons at the lowest end of the food chain. From my observation deck, we looked like everyone else on Willowbrook Drive. We had a house—they had a house. Check. We had a yard—they had a yard. Check. We had two cars—they had two cars. Check. We went to school—they went to school. Check.

Any scrutiny beyond that was out of my reach as a first-grade twerp. I just assumed everything and everyone was pretty much the same, that the rules in my house were the same rules in any house, and that we could afford what anyone else could afford.

What I didn't realize was that my father's job was not the most lucrative. Lehigh was a Division II football program and the 1960s an era before the likes of Nike and Adidas began paying teams to wear their uniforms and paying coaches for shoe contracts.

Don't get me wrong—my Dad's job was highly prestigious. It seemed interesting and exciting to everyone around me. People didn't gather around to talk about our neighbors' jobs. After all, with all due respect, how interesting could it be to talk about business or managing a steel factory? But a football coach? That's worth curling up on a couch and jawing about the prospects for next season. Or Saturday's game. So how's the team look this year? What do you think about that new running back?

My Dad's job was much cooler than some of the banal factory or business pursuits, but compared to jobs at Bethlehem Steel Corporation, it wasn't financially comparable. As mentioned, I didn't grow up poor or rich. We were middle-class. What I didn't know was how much of a financial high-wire act it was for my parents to raise us in that middle-class setting.

To be certain, we were pinched financially, much more than I could comprehend at the time. My parents were born in 1928 and 1930. That made them children of the Great Depression. The despair around them when they were kids had left a residue of conservatism in their minds. Frugality, therefore, came to them naturally. You could say they were well-trained for the challenges of managing on a tight budget.

As economically tight as it was for my family in the 1960s, from a kid's perspective, it was our *normal*. We didn't have an alternative basis to appreciate how austere things were. Jessie and I assumed it was normal to turn lights off every time we left a room. We assumed it was natural to have the heat set at 63 degrees throughout the winter and that wearing a sweatshirt indoors all the time was common. And we didn't find anything peculiar about taking three-minute showers or turning the water faucet off while we were brushing our teeth only to turn the water back on to rinse our mouth.

All of this was explained to us as "doing the right thing" to conserve water and electricity. I realized much later that these steps, while possibly beneficial to the environment, were essential to meeting the family budget.

Jessie and I didn't think we were missing out on better options when we always shopped at K-Mart. We just assumed that K-Mart was where you went when you needed to buy something. K-Mart seemed to have everything—at least that is what I had concluded.

Back at home in our small kitchen, Mom was a great cook. That was good, because I was a very hungry kid. She always said she hated to cook, but the truth was that she was good at it. We had a "food schedule," or so it seemed. It was like there was a rotation of dishes for each day of the week.

There were also hybrid meals. My mother was a genius at managing and optimizing leftovers. The refrigerator was her science lab for a confluence of dishes showing up on our plates. On "leftovers night," there might be one spoonful of baked beans (from three nights earlier), one chicken drumstick (from two nights earlier) and some potato salad from yesterday's lunch. All rolled up, it was a meal.

"Waste not, want not," my mother used to say. She would tell us that the key to protecting the Dunlap Team was to never waste anything and be thankful for everything. "We are SO fortunate," she said. "We have each other. We have our health. And we are a great team who sticks together!"

In addition to all of the things Mom managed, she made many of our Christmas and birthday gifts. That included sweaters, mittens and hats under the tree. Sure, there were Hot Wheels and Barbie dolls she bought, but it didn't occur to us that making gifts was unique. We assumed that was normal.

Discreetly throughout the year, Mom made these gifts in order to make Christmas more plentiful in the absence of having the money to do it differently. My sister and I fondly remember those many Christmas mornings. Neither of us can ever recall feeling as if we didn't get all the presents we wanted.

Understanding My Dad

Dad grew up in Carbondale, Pennsylvania, as the third son of a coal miner. His parents (Homer and Mildred Dunlap) raised four children there. They were a relatively poor family but they somehow managed to put all four kids through college.

I never knew Dad's father. He died six months before I was born. But I knew my grandmother well, and we visited her in Carbondale often when Jessie and I were young.

The Dunlaps were a conservative family. I think growing up in such humble circumstances was partly the reason, but the Scottish and German heritage of the family also contributed to their demeanor. They were soft-spoken and warm by nature but they were reluctant to communicate openly, either verbally or physically. This didn't leave me wondering whether my grandmother and other relatives loved me. It's just that they weren't comfortable being expressive with that affection. They were more *violin* and less *trombone*.

That measured humility was abundant among the Dunlap clan. After leaving Carbondale, Dad carried that humility with him to college and into his adult life as a football coach.

Understanding My Mom

My mother was the daughter of Bill and Violet Clark, my grandparents. By the time she went to college, my grandfather and grandmother were living in Utica, New York. Grampa (as I called him) was a doctor by training but he finished his career as the chief administrator at the Masonic Home, located in Utica.

My mother's family had far more means financially. Later in life, Mom would often tell Jessie and me how much harder Dad's family had it. She actually felt guilty about what her family enjoyed compared to how my father grew up.

The striking contrast I noticed between my parents' families was how outgoing and openly affectionate the Clarks were. It's not that I felt any more love from one family than the other, but the difference was the manner in which they each expressed it.

My mother's family was outwardly expressive. My grandmother constantly hugged and kissed me. Frankly, as a small boy, I could have gladly taken a smaller dose of that but the spirit behind her affection was what really mattered.

Grandma's affection for my grandfather was similar. They were two birds in love, albeit that they were Medicare-eligible birds. They never hesitated to show it or share it.

Grampa was a really funny guy, a prankster who related well to his six grandchildren. He loved to play hide and seek. When he did, he took on the role of Mr. Monster. He hid and pounced on us when we found him, saying, "I'm going to eat all of the small children. Munch! Munch!"

Grampa also taught us how to fish, and he played baseball with us in the back yard. He was like a camp counselor, always making up games and finding activities that were great fun. He was like a kid himself and used to tell us jokes, most of them somewhat off-color and told with a dry sense of humor.

When I was about eleven, I visited his house. He and I sat alone together and he asked me if I had any big, exciting things coming up that summer. I told him I was starting Little League football practice the next week. Grampa gave me a serious look and said, "Well, Tiger, I always say that when you've got something big coming up tomorrow, it's best to go to bed early, and then go straight home and get some sleep." It took me a couple more years of adolescent growth to appreciate what Grampa was talking about.

That was Grampa. Always the clown, always playing tricks, and always in search of levity, even when circumstances might dictate otherwise. His light-hearted spirit permeated the Clark family culture.

And it was always apparent that Bill and Vi Clark were a team. They celebrated openly their love and affection for each other and that permeated the Clark family culture, as well.

Understanding Mom and Dad—Together

So how does a somewhat reserved young man meet up with an outgoing, expressive young woman?

Dad went to Colgate in the fall of 1946. He played football for four years as a fullback and a linebacker. Dad said he was never a star and was more of a journeyman, but his former teammates have told me otherwise. When he wasn't playing football, he was captain of the wrestling team and in his sophomore year, as a boxer, was campus light heavyweight champion.

Since Dad came from humble beginnings, the family didn't often eat at restaurants. When he was a freshman football player, Dad traveled with the Colgate team to a game at Army. On the return trip, the team stopped at a restaurant for dinner. While Dad sat with other players and reviewed the menu, the waitress took orders. When she looked at Dad, he ordered his dinner but no appetizer. When the waitress asked him if he wanted a shrimp cocktail, my father responded, "No, thank you, I don't drink." The players around him nearly fell over laughing. They kidded him about that for years.

Dad loved athletics, but he was also a conscientious student, wanting to make his parents proud of their decision to send him to college. In order to accomplish all of these activities, he didn't spend much time socializing during college. For sure, he didn't drink any shrimp cocktails. But he did manage to join a fraternity, Alpha Tau Omega (ATO).

In early 1948, while in his sophomore year, my father bumped into Bill Clark, my future uncle. Bill was a Colgate baseball pitcher and a basketball player. He was an engaging guy, full of energy and a catalyst for fun.

Bill was smart and could have been a great student, but a year earlier, as a freshman, he determined that the library and classroom activities were in direct conflict with his goal of having a good time. A sensible man, Bill decided to remove those impediments to focus on his pursuit of more enjoyable activities. To that end, he became popular with the local bartenders.

Unfortunately, Bill's fun during his freshman year caused academic difficulties. His unhappy father pulled him off campus during his sophomore year to eliminate social distractions and to improve his grades. Bill moved back home to Utica and commuted to Colgate each day for class.

Bill had a friend who was a fraternity brother at ATO and he spent time with him between classes at the fraternity house. Since Dad was an ATO, he became acquainted with Bill Clark.

Over time, the two men became good friends. They saw each other during the day but Bill returned to Utica in the evenings. There, Bill had two younger sisters, one of whom was Marilyn Clark.

When spring arrived, Bill invited Dad to visit Utica for a weekend. Dad was aware of Marilyn since Bill had talked about her for quite a while. "You've got to meet my sister Marilyn," Bill said. "I think you two would like each other."

When Dad agreed to visit Bill's home, he didn't know Bill had been talking to his sister about him. Bill had told her, "I am bringing home the guy you are going to marry."

The story isn't totally linear from there. When Dad arrived, Marilyn had already committed herself to a date that weekend with another young man. But she was nice enough to call one of her girlfriends and ask her if she would like to go on a blind date with her brother's friend.

Though they didn't go on a date together that weekend, Mom and Dad admitted later that there was a strong attraction between them. Mom even said she didn't try *too hard* to get Dad a really good date.

Two weeks later, Bill brought Dad home again. This time, Mom and Dad had their first date, and it went very well.

In 1948, it wasn't easy to stay connected. Email, texting, Facebook and Skype were several decades away, and the two didn't see each other that summer. Dad returned to Carbondale and worked for a local dairy. He drove a dairy truck, delivering milk to Jewish summer camps located in the Poconos. He worked from midnight to 8 a.m., seven days a week, driving 150 miles a day into the mountains. He arrived at the camps while it was still dark and drove back to Carbondale as the sun rose.

As the summer neared its end, Dad prepared for his return to Colgate and fall football camp. He contacted Marilyn, letting her know he would be back in the area soon. Then, when he had a free night, he borrowed a car from one of the Colgate players and drove up to see her in Utica. The second date went just as favorably as the first.

In September, Dad began his junior year at Colgate and Mom started her freshman year at St. Lawrence University. They didn't see each other for quite some time because as Dad said, "In those days, nobody had cars and the roads weren't good. It wasn't easy to maintain a long-distance relationship. We mostly communicated through letters."

Over the next nine months, my parents saw each other four times: Fall Party Weekend at Colgate; Winter Carnival at St. Lawrence; Spring Party Weekend at Colgate; and then Dad traveled to St. Lawrence since Colgate's football team played a scrimmage against the St. Lawrence team.

Following the scrimmage, Dad's coaches allowed him to stay at St. Lawrence so he could spend the weekend visiting with my mother. Dad did more than that—he gave her his fraternity pin. For younger folks who may not understand the significance of his doing so, giving a fraternity pin to a girl in 1949 was analogous to pre-engagement. Or as my mother described it, "It meant that I was TAKEN."

Bill Clark wasn't the only guy promoting this new love relationship. His father (my grandfather) also began courting my father to spend the upcoming summer working as a camp counselor at the Masonic Home. As head of that organization, my grandfather was responsible for overseeing the Masonic Home Camp located in the Adirondacks about an hour's drive north of Utica. Each summer the Camp opened its doors to orphan children who lived in the Masonic Home. The orphans spent the entire summer there under the supervision of camp counselors.

Dad accepted the offer and he and Mom worked as camp counselors for the summer of 1949. It was the first time they spent concentrated time together. The relationship quickly blossomed.

That summer was Dad's first real exposure to the Clark family and to their expressive nature. Dad really liked the Clarks but it took some time for him to get comfortable with their affectionate manner.

Initially, there were some tense moments. When Mom tried to hold Dad's hand in public, or wrap her arm around her bashful boyfriend, he struggled with her doing so. And a kiss in public? At those early stages? No Way!

Dad really loved Mom, but he wasn't comfortable expressing it publicly. She was a bit frustrated, but confident he would adjust over time. Mom was unrelenting and Dad realized that ultimately he would just have to get used to it. Fortunately, Dad had a flexible, accommodating way that proved valuable with Mom.

They joke about it to this day. He attributes to her the renaissance of "bringing him out of his shell." To that, my mother usually smiles. "I couldn't help it. I am a hugger," she confesses, while imploring to anyone around her: "Isn't he cute?"

When that summer ended, Mom and Dad returned to their respective colleges. The following school year went by quickly and in June 1950, Dad prepared to graduate from Colgate. He had accepted an offer from Magnolia Petroleum to become an oil scout. That meant he'd travel throughout Texas and New Mexico combing the terrain for attractive sites to build oil rigs.

Those plans were interrupted when the Korean War broke out. The Army draft was in full swing, and like other young men, Dad took a required physical. Tests showed he was quite fit and he was given a I-A Classification, making it very likely he would get drafted.

Upon hearing this news, Dad's Magnolia Petroleum bosses suggested he postpone his hire date. His boss told him there would be a job waiting for him when he got out of the service, and he wished Dad good luck.

With the job on hold and his military start date unknown but potentially imminent, Dad decided to work another summer with the orphans at the Masonic Home Camp. That meant he was able to spend time with my mother, who was also working there as a camp counselor.

When fall arrived, Dad hadn't yet been called for military service. He accepted a job in Hudson, New York, working at Hudson High School. Dad taught math and coached the junior varsity football team.

Meanwhile, Mom started her junior year at St. Lawrence. She and Dad saw each other when they could, but the distance between Hudson and St. Lawrence was great and their meetings were few.

As the football season ended and Thanksgiving approached, Dad received his military orders. He was required to report to Fort Jackson in South Carolina for infantry training with the 8th Army.

Prior to his departure, Dad drove to Utica during the week before Thanksgiving to spend his few remaining days with my mother. He secretly planned to give her an engagement ring. Dad had earned the money for the ring that fall by playing semi-pro football for the Hudson Falls Green Jackets. Their games were played on Sunday afternoons and Dad earned $40 per game.

During that weekend, Dad and Mom took walks, strolling through the grounds of the Masonic Home while revisiting many of their memories from the past two years. Of all the different sites within the complex where Dad could have taken my mother, he chose the farm area where they had a piggery. It was used to feed those working at the Home.

As Mom and Dad stood among more than 200 squealing animals, Dad somehow thought this might be a good time to propose. My mother sensed his mood change and upon seeing Dad start to pull the ring out of his pocket, she stopped him and said, "Fred, if you are going to do this, it's NOT going to be in front of a lot of pigs."

Later that weekend, when Dad and Mom were at Colgate, he took her to nearby Lake Moraine and proposed in style. It was a great setting for their special moment. Mom said, "It was even better because we weren't surrounded by pigs."

Bill Clark was right. She was going to marry him.

Ultimately, Bill Clark became my "Uncle Moose." Like his father (my Grampa), Uncle Moose was a fun-loving guy. And over the last 50 years, he has become more of a friend than an uncle to me.

Dad's "Other Love"— The United States Army

With his Army duties before him, Mom and Dad had no idea when they might actually marry. She needed to return to college and he had to report to Fort Jackson, South Carolina.

Dad departed Carbondale on the Monday after Thanksgiving. He traveled by train to Scranton, then to Harrisburg, and then to Fort Meade, Maryland. There he spent a week at the Induction Center going through a battery of tests and physical exams. Dad also received the requisite number of shots according to Army regulations.

During the first week of December, Dad and the rest of the enlisted men traveled by train from Fort Meade to Fort Jackson. "The Army was short on supplies in 1950," Dad told me. "They didn't have uniforms for us at Fort Meade—we wore corduroys and saddle shoes on the train to South Carolina. We didn't get uniforms until we got to Fort Jackson." He then added, "But we got something *else*, a preview of Army life, when we arrived. It was the middle of the night and pitch black outside. There was a sergeant there to greet us. He barked out orders as we disembarked from the train, and we were immediately rushed into formation."

"The sergeant yelled, 'You boys don't need to think anymore. Leave that to me! I am now your momma and your daddy, and you will do whatever I say,'" Dad said with a smile. "The sergeant was the epitome of hospitality."

This was Dad's indoctrination into Basic Training at Fort Jackson. He was in K-Company, part of the 61st Infantry Battalion. When I asked Dad if he was given the rank of private, he laughed and said, "Hell, I was lower than that! I was called a recruit! They didn't make us privates until they found out if we could survive Basic Training."

The weeks progressed, and Dad coped with the rigors as well as any soldier could. But he was surprised by something after the first week. While the recruits ran through rigorous drills, he noticed that Captain Patrick Morgan, the company commander, was constantly observing them as they trained.

Captain Morgan closely watched the soldiers during drills. He observed his next in command as they performed their duties. He spent time with his direct reports, mentoring them and discussing procedures. He also spent time with the recruits. When there were breaks, he introduced himself to them and asked questions about their experience at Fort Jackson.

Dad was surprised that Captain Morgan was such a hands-on leader. He asked the soldiers specific questions about their hometowns and where they went to school. Except, Dad recalled, Captain Morgan didn't actually ask them where they were from. Instead, he asked questions like, "How do you like the weather in Carbondale? Is it cold up there right now?" to gain more information about the soldiers.

It was evident that Captain Morgan had been reviewing the soldiers' files in the evenings to get acquainted with their backgrounds. He then used that knowledge to build a rapport with them. Dad hadn't expected this, especially after the surly reception he and the other recruits received from the sergeant upon their arrival.

To be certain, Captain Morgan showed a personal interest in the soldiers. That, in turn, made the soldiers feel more connected to the base leadership.

My father continued to observe Captain Morgan as the weeks continued. Dad was impressed by his demeanor and professionalism. "He was always neat and polished—he walked and carried himself like a soldier," Dad said. "And he led by example—he wouldn't ask anyone to do something that he wouldn't do himself. He was highly organized at all times and he had a special way of communicating to us. He didn't scream at soldiers—he *instructed,* using a very even delivery. His tone was controlled, but he still commanded his troops because there was immense respect for him."

Dad said that while Captain Morgan demanded discipline, he wasn't afraid to show his human side. He sat with the troops and talked about his experiences as a way to mentor the young soldiers. "And he wasn't afraid to lighten things up," Dad explained. "He used to organize wrestling matches between soldiers during breaks. He read my file and found out I was a college wrestler, and he set up a match between me and this huge guy from Alabama who was 30-40 pounds heavier than me." Regarding the outcome, Dad said, "I think it was pretty much a draw; we were both exhausted at the end."

Over the years, Dad described to me many times the impact Captain Morgan had on him and his peers. "He was the finest example of a soldier (and a manager) I have ever witnessed," Dad said. "I always thought Captain Morgan would have made a helluva football coach. He wasn't afraid to get to know his soldiers *or to let them know him.* He made you feel special because he knew who you were and showed an interest in you. And the net result was that it made everyone want to work harder for him."

Dad added, "I've seen a lot of bosses and leaders try to intimidate their people. With Captain Morgan, we didn't fear him. Rather, we had great respect for him. And it was because of the way he handled himself, the way he handled his men, and the way he treated his men."

Under Captain Morgan's leadership, Dad persevered through Basic Training. Nearing the end of the three-month schedule, in the final few days, Captain Morgan asked Dad to come to his office.

After Captain Morgan told Dad he could expect to be sent to Korea soon, he praised him as a natural leader with strong future potential. He suggested that Dad stay at Fort Jackson to participate in a six-week Leadership School, after which he would receive a promotion to the rank of sergeant. Captain Morgan thought Leadership School and the upgraded rank would put Dad in a better position in Korea where he could serve in a leadership role, by commanding a platoon as compared with being a private.

Dad took Captain Morgan's advice. Five weeks later, toward the end of Leadership School, Captain Morgan checked in with him again to see how he was progressing. Following the short discussion, Captain Morgan invited Dad to come to his house and spend a day with his family for a Sunday picnic. "Being with his family," Dad told me, "I

Sergeant Dunlap at Leadership School in Fort Jackson, SC—March 1951

got to know him personally and see how he interacted with his wife and children. He took a special interest in me and I trusted his advice."

During the picnic, Captain Morgan broached the idea of Dad staying in the United States and going to Officer Candidate School (OCS). Dad agreed. After he completed Leadership School and graduated as a sergeant in the summer of 1951, Dad headed to Fort Riley, Kansas, for OCS Training.

Two More Army Forts and One Air Force Base

My father loved the Army and it shaped him into the man he became. Certainly Captain Morgan had made a huge impression, but Dad also loved the discipline, the organization and the sense of order that came with being in the military. He looked forward to the next six months in Officer Candidate School.

OCS was challenging. It had been described to him as similar to being a plebe at West Point except that OCS was only six months long.

During that time, Dad got used to being repeatedly called what every OCS soldier was called: Candidate. "It was never said with care—it was said with disdain," Dad recalled with a smile.

In December 1951, Dad graduated from OCS as a 2nd Lieutenant. He had a week's leave before being shipped off to Fort Knox, Kentucky. He spent that week in Utica, getting married to my mother.

Leading up to the wedding, it had been seven months since my parents had seen each other. She had been in college and he had been in OCS training in Kansas. Their only methods of communicating during that time were letters and the rare phone call when Dad could use the pay phone in the PX (Postal Exchange). He wasn't the only soldier who wanted to call home; there was only one pay phone and there was always a long line of soldiers wanting access to it.

Mom and Dad only spoke five times by phone in the seven months they were apart. As they neared the wedding date, they wondered whether they would even recognize each other.

On December 22, 1951, the "hugger" and her "captive" were wed. That was followed by a short honeymoon at the Masonic Home Camp. It was a fitting place because of the history they shared there.

Wedding Day—December 22, 1951

A few days later, Dad headed to Fort Knox and she returned to St. Lawrence to finish her last three months of college. He rented an apartment in Louisville because his new bride would be arriving in March. Mom, always determined and relentless even then, had taken an accelerated course load in order to graduate early since she wanted to be with her husband as soon as possible.

At Fort Knox, Dad enrolled in the Basic Armor School for officers. During those six months, he learned every aspect of tank training. He learned how to operate them, how to fire the weaponry, and how to maintain and service the machinery.

Upon completion of his training, Dad (with Mom) was shipped to Gary Air Force Base in San Marcos, Texas. Dad was still in the Army but had been assigned to Gary AFB for flight training, which was not uncommon for Army officers. He spent the next six months in Primary Training.

While there, Dad advanced to flying solo flights in Piper Cubs. They were single-engine canvas-covered airplanes used to operate recon missions to identify the location of the enemy. These planes flew slowly and very low to the ground. The pilots practiced forced landings on uncertain terrain such as choppy roads and fields. Dad said the planes were so small and light that the cruising speed was barely faster than a car.

Dad completed Primary Training in December 1952. His (and Mom's) next stop was at the 4th Army Division at Fort Sill in Lawton, Oklahoma. They arrived there just before Christmas.

Living in the southwestern United States was new for my parents. Even though the Army moved them every six months, they really enjoyed military life. They were experiencing living in Texas and Oklahoma, and they were doing it together as a young married couple.

Many times over the years, I listened to my parents talk about this time in their lives and how special it was for them. They were in their early 20s, and it was the first time they had ever been away from home, away from their parents, and away from any relatives. That separation allowed them to build their own foundation and their own relationship, and, at its infancy, what they called, "The Dunlap Team."

Dad's transfer to Fort Sill permitted him to participate in Tactical Flight training. He no longer flew Piper Cubs but a faster, larger aircraft, *the L-19*. "They were called 'Bird Dogs,'" he recalled, "...fixed-wing aircraft with a lot more power than the Piper Cubs."

"Tactical Training was much more demanding on pilots and much more risky," Dad said. "We practiced contour flying where the goal was to fly as close as possible to the ground below us. The training was intended to make pilots and their planes more elusive in the event they were confronted by enemy ground-fire. If we flew at 500 feet, we were vulnerable to small arms fire but if we stayed right above the trees, we could fly over them so fast that the enemy couldn't get a shot at us."

Dad continued, "So we would skim the tops of trees and dive into valleys, flying just above the rivers below. We'd practice short field landings and maximum performance take-offs. We'd practice landings on roads and fields, and then takeoffs from that same terrain. With short-field landings, we needed to put down on a steep decline, barely missing the treetops below us and then hit the brakes as quickly as possible, so as not to run out of runway."

Waving his hands like they were wings, Dad said, "We'd *slow fly* on approach. That meant that we'd slow the plane down almost to a stall, then put the nose of the plane up and glide on the air, risking a stall, in order to get our ground speed as slow as possible. On takeoffs, we'd push the plane as far back into the woods as we could to give us the most available runway. We'd set the flaps at 45 degrees and rev the engine while holding the brakes. Then we'd release the brakes and take off, trying to jump the plane up in the air before we got to the trees on the other end of the runway." He smiled. "If it wasn't done right, you could crash into the trees."

By the end of March 1953, Dad had completed Tactical Training and graduated from Flight School. "I got my wings," he said proudly. With that graduation, Dad prepared to be deployed to Korea. "Back then, soldiers were to report to San Francisco," he told me. "It was the staging site for Korea."

Dad had no qualms about what was supposed to happen next. "I was really excited to go to Korea. It was my turn to serve my country. Your mother and I were teenagers during World War II, but we knew how important that period of time was to United States history, and we knew the sacrifices others had made for our well-being. And Korea was, for me, a chance to make my own contribution."

Dad's brother had served in the U.S. Navy during World War II on a ship stationed in the South Pacific. Many of Dad's high school and college friends were already in the Korean battle. He wanted to join the fight.

Unfulfilled Dreams—
A Soldier's Plea Gets Denied

DURING THE WEEK BEFORE DAD was to travel to San Francisco, he and my mother returned home to see their parents. He was there to say goodbye. She went there to live while he completed his tour in Korea. My mother was braced for his departure, which was expected in days.

During the trip home, Dad received an unexpected telegram advising him that he would not be deployed to Korea. Instead, he was selected to become a flight instructor at Fort Sill. He would train other pilots on Tactical Skills. My father was shocked and angered by this sudden change of plans. He immediately tried to appeal the decision: he wanted to go to Korea. After being denied, he even called Army officials at the Pentagon directly and made another appeal. No matter, the decision was final. Dad was told to drop his appeal and return to Fort Sill immediately.

Predictably, my mother had mixed feelings about Dad staying Stateside. She was as patriotic as he was and could appreciate his sense of responsibility, but she was a newlywed and she knew Fort Sill was a safer place than Korea.

Deeply disappointed, Dad returned to Fort Sill and began his tenure as a flight instructor. He taught single-engine/fixed-wing aircraft for the next 18 months. While he was instructing, Mom worked for the Provost Marshal, a colonel who headed up the 4th Army's law enforcement division.

That job was offered to Mom after she earned the highest score on the Civil Service Exam, a prerequisite test for prospective Civil Service employees. After hearing of her accomplishment, the colonel hired Mom to be his secretary. Dad said, "Your mom had the high profile job, not me. She worked with the highest ranks in the 4th Army as they dealt with criminal matters involving Army personnel." Mom added, "Yes, the officers were nice. But I had to go into the jails and meet with the criminals, too. That wasn't so glamorous."

While Mom worked as a secretary, Dad was busy with flight training. He was an Instructor Pilot (IP), and his days consisted of 1:1 training. Dad said, "The newer pilots spent most of their day in ground training before meeting with me for two hours of flying. I flew with four pilots each day, every day—two in the morning and two in the afternoon. We worked on maneuvers, implementing the things they had learned in ground training."

Dad had a few risky episodes as a flight instructor. "I was given some pretty green pilots, and they made their share of mistakes," he told me. "Our goal with Tactical Training was to push the limits and to put the pilots in stressful situations. Contour flying. Short-field landings. Max Performance take-offs. All of this was done in windy weather. That Oklahoma wind could really blow!"

One story Dad told was unsettling. He had a young pilot with him one day and the wind was howling when the pilot tried to land in a field. "We were practicing a touch and go," he recalled, "a maneuver where the pilot comes in for a landing but right after touching the ground, he hits the throttle to take off again. Here, the field looked large enough for us to land, but what we couldn't see from the air was that the field was filled with barbed-wire fences."

Dad continued, "We didn't hit the fences on landing. But when the pilot tried to take off again, he hesitated. I told him to hit the throttle and as he raced the engine, the nose of the plane lifted but because of the brief hesitation, the landing gear under the tail of the plane caught the barbed wire fence."

Fortunately, the story had a happy ending. "We didn't crash," Dad said with animation, "and the pilot got the plane to a safe altitude. He was rattled by the experience but we flew back to the base and landed safely." Dad paused and smiled. "What we didn't know was that we had dragged about a hundred feet of barbed wire with us, all the way back to the base."

Flying planes under pressure, just like being subjected to Army discipline and order, was preparing Dad for a career choice that would encompass all he was learning. He just didn't know it yet.

The Emergence of a Football Coach

During his days at Fort Sill, Dad continued to refine his flying skills while being promoted to 1st lieutenant. He also was selected for helicopter training, and he became a certified pilot in both fixed-wing and rotary-wing aircraft.

During the summer of 1953, Dad played on the base softball team, which was being coached by a colonel in charge of the aviation unit. The colonel mentioned that the 4th Army was starting a football team for the coming fall. Since he knew Dad played football in college, he asked if Dad was willing to be a player/coach.

Dad jumped at the chance, and with that, his schedule changed. He spent mornings as a flight instructor and afternoons coaching and training the base football team. An added bonus was a chance meeting with a true legend, University of Oklahoma football coach Bud Wilkinson, whose Sooners won three national championships. "We were given leave to go for a few days to a coaching clinic at the University of Oklahoma," Dad recounted. "Bud Wilkinson and his staff met with us for a couple days, talking nothing but football. We discussed offensive and defensive plays. We discussed blocking techniques and special teams and we learned how they set strategy depending on what type of offense or defense they were facing. What an education it was."

Dad and the other Army coaches incorporated many of the concepts they learned from Wilkinson into their own team strategies. "We had a good team that fall," Dad said. "It was really an odd assortment of players from different backgrounds, but as the season progressed, the team really came together."

Meeting and learning from Wilkinson caused Dad to recall how much he enjoyed his first coaching assignment three years earlier with the Hudson High School junior varsity team. More important, it opened his eyes to the possibility of a career coaching football.

Meanwhile, as the summer of 1954 dawned, the conflict in Korea was starting to subside. Dad's commitment to the Army was ending and he had to make a decision. "I needed to re-up for another two years or get out. With the war ending, I didn't feel that my role in the Army was as essential."

Dad and my mother discussed the options. "If I left the Army, I really had three choices. I had my commercial licenses to fly, so I could get a job flying planes or helicopters. I also had that standing offer from Magnolia Petroleum to go be an oil scout. And I had been contacted by Hudson High to teach math and be an assistant coach for the varsity football team."

One consideration was the different compensation levels. "The job at Magnolia Petroleum included a $5,000 salary, a car and an expense account," he shared. "That was *real money* in those days. And the job at Hudson High had a salary of $2500. Period. The pay wasn't even close."

Dad was conflicted. Mom was not, telling him, "I don't care about money. What is it that you *really* want to do?" Dad thought for a moment and said, "I want to coach football."

The decision was made and in August 1954, after Dad was discharged from the Army, my parents moved to Hudson, New York.

Curious about the decision when I was in my 20s, I asked my father why he decided to go into coaching. "I always loved football," he said with a sparkle in his eye. "I loved the strategy and the complexity. I loved how tough the sport was, both physically and mentally." He thought for a moment. "In many respects, football is like the Army. Setting a strategy. Going into battle. Overcoming obstacles. So, leaving the Army to become a football coach didn't really feel like I was leaving the Army. Football was just a different version of it."

He continued: "By 1954, I had played four years of college football and two years of semi-pro football. In the course of that time, I'd been exposed to a number of different football coaches, each with a different style—as strategists and as leaders. And I guess I was observing and learning which methods were more effective."

Regarding the coaching profession, he added, "I had also been a coach, first at Hudson High and then at Fort Sill. And when I was at Hudson, coaching the JV team, I was a *lousy* coach. I made all kinds of mistakes. Gosh, I was awful!" He paused. "But then I went into the Army and I had the chance to observe more "coaches"—meaning the officers who were in charge. I got to watch their leadership styles, their attention to detail and their sense for organization. And then I got to be a football coach at Fort Sill where I tried to emulate their approaches and implement many of the good things I had learned."

Dad referred to his days at Basic Training in Fort Jackson, South Carolina. "The best leader I ever worked with was Captain Morgan," he said. "He was everything I thought a great football coach should be. He was a great soldier, and I always thought a great soldier would be a great leader, and that a great leader would be a great football coach."

Keeping Captain Morgan in mind, Dad recalled, "When I played college football, our coaches were all technically sound. They understood the game very well. They knew football. But they didn't know how to handle people. They didn't know how to get the best out of their players...or how to connect with them. Some were weak and unprincipled, and the programs lacked discipline. Some were sarcastic and biting, which created a chasm between them and their players. Others were overbearing or uncaring, or oblivious to the possibility that they may have some players who needed more support. Another one of my coaches was aloof. He never took the time to get to know his players or to let them get to know him. That created a communication gap."

One example was front and center for Dad. "I had one head coach who got angry at a player during practice and called him 'gutless,'" he said, throwing his hands up in the air. "Gutless! Who the hell was he to call that kid gutless? And more importantly, after calling him that, how was he *ever* going to get that kid to play hard for him? All of these mistakes in judgment led to an overall performance less than what it could have been. The results were sub-optimal."

Watching other coaches made a real impact on Dad. "I often wondered how much better those coaches would have been and how much more successful they could have been," he said, "if they had been better managers and leaders, like Captain Morgan. More than anyone else, I patterned my leadership style after his, since he was the consummate professional in the way he handled himself, the way he handled the men and the way he treated the men. And that's what I was determined to do as a coach."

1954 to 1964

When Mom and Dad arrived in Hudson in August, football season was about to begin. Dad was the lone assistant coach, reporting to the head coach, so the two split the duties.

The head coach was an affable guy, who, according to Dad, "didn't know a helluva lot about football." So he delegated the coaching to Dad. "I ended up running everything," he said, "which was good experience. And we won almost every game that year."

During the winter, the high school principal asked my father what he wanted to do with his career. Dad was surprised by the question. He thought the principal might be asking him to become the head coach. When Dad told the principal he wanted to be a college football coach, the principal said, "Well, if that's the case, you're wasting your time at the high school level. You should get into college coaching as fast as you can."

Heeding that advice, two months later, Dad accepted a graduate assistant coaching position at Colgate University, working in that role for the 1955 season. After the season ended, Dad applied for a number of coaching positions. Some of them were head coaching assignments at high schools (Herkimer, NY and Corning, NY). He also interviewed for a college assistant coaching job at St. Lawrence University.

While Dad considered his options, he called a friend, Dick Offenhamer, to get his perspective. Dick was the head coach at the University of Buffalo. The two spoke at length, and as the conversation neared an end, Dick asked him how soon he needed to make a decision. When Dad told him "a week," Dick responded, "Well, see if you can stall them. I'll meet with our president and see if I can add another coaching position to our staff. If we can, I want you."

Two weeks later, Dad accepted the position at the University of Buffalo and became receivers coach.

Dad coached at Buffalo for three seasons under Offenhamer. By the third season (1958), he was responsible for the offensive and defensive backs. Also during those three years, the Dunlap Team grew: Jessie and I were both born in Buffalo.

Following the 1958 season, Dad received a call from Lefty James, head coach at Cornell University. Lefty wanted to hire him to coach the defensive backs. Cornell was a much bigger football program than Buffalo and the lure of the bigger program was great. Dad accepted the assistant coaching position at Cornell, and the Dunlap Team moved to Ithaca, New York.

The days in Buffalo provide no memories for me since I was only a year old at the time. My sister and I were like intelligent pets, except that we didn't wear flea collars and we didn't eat dog food. Wherever our parents went, we went, too.

Time spent in Ithaca was more memorable to me since I was more aware of our surroundings. We were there for six years. While Dad coached, Mom taught high school English. Ithaca was also where my parents taught us to ski when we were four and three years old. I can remember them taking us on the snowy hills at Greek Peak ski area. We were small, the skis were short, and the rope tow was heavy. But we learned to snow plow and learned how to avoid frostbite.

Meanwhile, Dad coached the defensive secondary in 1959, and the offensive backfield in 1960 and 1961. In 1962, he was promoted to defensive coordinator, a role he served in for three seasons.

During the three years at Buffalo and the six years at Cornell, Dad continued to hone his coaching skills. Those nine years were also formative to his style as a leader. He continued to learn from the good and bad things that he witnessed from coaches around him. The more he coached, the more he could see lost opportunities through the mishandling of players and personnel. He grew frustrated by the policies and cultures that were being controlled by his head coaches. And he yearned for an opportunity to be in charge where he could regulate and foster a different, more positive culture.

On a snowy evening in January 1965, my father arrived home and asked my sister and me to meet with him and Mom. We were only seven and six years old at the time. Dad talked to us in the kitchen and told us that we were moving to Pennsylvania since he had accepted the head coaching position at Lehigh University.

The Dunlap Team was moving again.

PART II

Learning from Early Lessons—The Lehigh Years

Taking a Shot—
Coaching at Lehigh in the Early Years

As a 55-year-old kid, I have a lot of perspective now looking back on that move to Bethlehem, Pennsylvania. But as a six-year-old twerp, I was just part of a four-animal pack migrating to a new state. My life revolved around my parents and my sister, and our black cat named Slippery.

As intelligent pets, Jessie and I followed our parents like a gaggle of geese, except that our poops weren't quite as offensive. Well, at least we didn't deposit them on sidewalks.

We relied on our parents for the core essentials—food, water and an affectionate stroke now and then. Hey, maybe I *was* a pet?

Moving was exciting but a bit scary, too. Amid all of the new things I'd encounter, I had certain forms of security. My mother promised that when the moving van arrived, I'd still have my toy box and that Crock, my stuffed alligator, was safely inside. So I was somewhat secure, or at least I had convinced myself of that.

Jessie and Tiger (with Long-Neck Kitty, my *somewhat distressed* stuffed animal).

Lehigh was Dad's first head coaching job, and like first jobs for most people, uncertainty prevailed as to how good the job really was.

Lehigh was a Division II football program with a spotty past. The prior head coach had been there for only three seasons before being fired. During that coach's tenure, Lehigh had won only five games, and only two of which were during the final two seasons. There were reasons for the weak results and the quality of athletes was one of them. It's fair to say that Lehigh football in 1965 was a real rebuilding project.

Regardless, Dad had been a college assistant coach for nine years and he wanted very much to have an opportunity to be a head coach. He realized that Lehigh's program was down, that success wasn't guaranteed, and that it would take a lot of hard work to rebuild it. But he thirsted for that challenge.

While the program was depressed at the time, Dad was optimistic that he could revive it and return it to the top Division II program that it had been in the 1950s. Like most of us, Dad didn't know what he didn't know when he started something new. This was the case with Lehigh, as Dad would learn.

In college football, there are several factors that can impact the success of a head coach. The coach himself needs to be organized, a good communicator, a good leader and a knowledgeable football guy. Outside of these personal requirements, there are environmental factors that can enhance or detract from the potential for success, no matter what the qualities of the coach. They are:

- Inheriting a talented group of athletes from the preceding coach
- Having a realistically ample budget—to hire qualified coaches, to cover travel expenses for recruiting, and to be sure that the team is outfitted with good equipment

- Having a school that "sells well" so athletes can be successfully recruited. Things like:
    - An attractive campus
    - Reasonable tuition costs
    - Athletic scholarships
    - An accommodating admissions committee in the case of an athlete who is marginally qualified academically
- Having a supportive administration that recognizes and embraces the needs of the program (including facilities, recruiting budget and equipment)
- Having a supportive alumni following

Lehigh was an excellent academic institution, but that academic prowess cut both ways. On the positive side, Lehigh was an attractive university to high school athletes who were good students seeking a quality education. On the negative side, Lehigh had very high admission requirements. That made it difficult to get recruits with marginal grades accepted by the admissions committee.

Another hurdle to attracting good athletes was that Lehigh's tuition costs were much higher than many competing private colleges and far higher than state-funded institutions.

To make matters more challenging, Lehigh was not a scholarship school. There were no free rides (code for being on full scholarship). Financial aid was only available on a needs basis, so families only received tuition breaks if they were lower income. Summing up, recruiting athletes to Lehigh was challenging. It was only easy to recruit to if:

- The recruit had great academic qualifications, and
- The recruit's family had enough money to afford tuition, or

- The recruit's family was poor enough to qualify for financial aid

Unfortunately that described only about 15% of the attractive athletes Dad tried to recruit. The other 85% of attractive recruits fit the following description:

- Middle class—good student athlete but the family was not eligible for need-based support and not able (or willing) to pay Lehigh's high tuition costs, or
- Eligible for need-based support, but not capable of meeting the academic admission standards, or
- Able to pay, but not able to meet the academic standards, or
- A great athlete recruited by bigger programs (like Penn State and Temple) and given a free ride by those full-scholarship schools.

Beyond these limitations, there were other reasons why Lehigh football had not been prominent. Lehigh was respected as having a nationally ranked wrestling team. The alums and the local fans were rabid wrestling followers and Lehigh (in the 1960s) was known more as a wrestling school than a football school. This over-shadowed Lehigh football, making it less visible to potential recruits.

There was one other notable limiting influence. His name was Bill Leckonby, the Lehigh athletic director. He had been head football coach in the 1940s and 1950s and was the head coach during the only undefeated season (1950) in Lehigh football history. Based on that accomplishment, Leckonby was considered the greatest football coach in Lehigh's history.

After the 1961 season, Leckonby had relinquished the football coaching position to become the athletic director. He promoted his top assistant coach, Mike Cooley, to become his successor. Cooley lasted only three seasons.

Now there was a new head coach, Fred Dunlap, reporting to a man who would end up more foe than friend.

Entering the Fray—January 1965

My recollections about Dad's days as coach of Lehigh football are a blend of two things: my direct experiences as a kid interwoven with the perspectives I gained later in life from countless discussions with my parents about the Lehigh years.

In January 1965, Dad left to begin his new job in Bethlehem. It was a busy time. He needed to hire and quickly assemble a coaching staff and also meet the returning Lehigh players. Beyond that, as the new head coach, he was in demand from alumni groups and university administration officials.

After the assistant coaches had been hired, the entire staff hit the road to recruit players in earnest. Because of the coaching transition, Dad and his staff were late getting out to recruit; other programs had been recruiting since the end of the last season (November). Even with this late start, the Lehigh coaches knew they needed to bring in a strong, talented class of recruits. That would be essential to turning the program around in future years.

While the coaching change (Dad's arrival) brought a certain level of excitement, Dad and the rest of the coaches were also part of an unproven program. Without any collective track record, they were essentially selling futures, selling what they *could be*. And selling what they were striving to accomplish. There was no past season record corroborating their sales pitch. There were also no current Lehigh players who could vouch for their coaching abilities.

Recruits thus needed to buy in to the idea of what Lehigh was going to become as opposed to choosing a school and a coaching staff with an established track record. That ambiguity and uncertainty created some reluctance with certain recruits.

While on the road, the coaching staff couldn't focus solely on recruiting. They also were planning and preparing for spring football practice beginning in late May. It would be the first chance for the coaches to institute a new offense and defense, and it would be the first opportunity to evaluate the current players and to assess their talent level.

Lehigh football was not replete with talent in 1965. Dad had just come from Cornell and the comparison of talent between the two schools wasn't a favorable one for Lehigh. But it was what he inherited and he had to make the best of it. He began to plan his offensive and defensive plays and slot his players in a way that gave them their best chance for success in the fall.

Beyond player talent, Dad was struck by a few things organizationally. As he neared the beginning of spring practice, he learned more about the prior coaching regime. It was apparent that there had been very little emphasis on off-season training, so the players didn't collectively come to spring practice ready and in good shape.[1]

---

1 Spring practice is a maximum of 20 practices (governed by the NCAA) usually spread out over five-six weeks, and culminating in a spring football game (scrimmage) between and among the team. That game is usually the 1st Team Offense and the 2nd Team Defense against the 2nd Team Offense and the 1st Team Defense in an attempt to create a fair contest.

Another concern Dad had was discipline. There had been little structure and very few rules instilled in the program under the previous regime. Dad was a *rule guy*. He had been that way as a kid with strict parents, and that sense of structure and discipline became even more ingrained from his Army experiences. To Dad, effective discipline needed structure and could not be effectively enforced without it. He strongly believed that human beings performed best within a structured environment where they were given clear direction.

With this mindset, Dad set out to create "Team Rules" by which the Lehigh football program would be governed. He met with the team and coaches to communicate those rules fully. To Dad, the test of a team was whether the entire organization could adhere to (and respect) them. It was a litmus test as to whether people were committed to the cause.

The Team Rules were not just about conduct at practice or with coaches, but also included conduct *outside* of football. There were rules concerning academic performance and rules about conduct in social circles, including the campus fraternities. Dad's belief was that *doing the right thing* was a 24/7 commitment. To him, any break from that, even if it happened outside of football-related activities, was a warning sign about a person's character. This then presented a question about that individual's ability to act in a disciplined way on or off the football field.

Dad talked often to the Lehigh players about the importance of character. He renounced the common cliché "Character is built in a crisis," countering with "Character is not *built* in a crisis. Character is *exhibited* in a crisis." And, "How we (the team) conduct ourselves 24/7 is how our character gets built and how our character gets defined." And, "Without strong character, we will never be capable of doing special things." And, related to character, "Special things define greatness."

Dad believed "respect was essential to building a real bond across all of the troops. It was about having respect for yourself, but also feeling an obligation to respect others and ultimately the team."

Dad also emphasized to the Lehigh players the importance of preparation—for a game, for a season, for a huge upset over a team that, on paper, might be far superior in talent. He told the players, "Preparation has to be a way of life. It's not something you begin doing when something big is coming up. It's something you do habitually, as a way of life."

Dad spoke to the team about one of his personal postulates: "If you take care of the little things, the big things will take care of themselves." The little things centered around preparation and discipline. Preparation couldn't be sporadic. It was essential for the team to exhibit the discipline to continually prepare for battle...and to be ready at all times.

As with any new program with new rules, there were times in early 1965 when players stepped over the line, whether obliviously or consciously. When this occurred, Dad and the coaches would re-clarify the Team Rules. If the infraction was clearly not out of ignorance, he enforced the rules by delivering penalties such as running laps.

Dad's view was that in order to have a winning program, it was necessary to build a winning culture—and culture is something intangible. It's something, he told the players, you can't touch. It's something you feel, something you sense. And winning cultures are those that accentuate the positive. They foster openness. They are based on trust, and that trust comes from discipline and respect, best measured by the adherence to Team Rules. "Trust," he added, "comes from selflessness where an individual understands that the interests of the team outweigh the interests of the individual. A winning culture creates its own magnetic field, drawing the participants to it in a very committed, loyal way."

These messages were recited to the team continually in order to create an ingrained mindset across five coaches and eighty players. It took time and persistent monitoring, but Dad felt that the football program at Lehigh could not be rebuilt unless, at the core, there was a winning culture.

It was early in Dad's tenure as a head coach in 1965. What he didn't know was that one of his greatest leadership tests would happen early, too.

A Challenge to the Culture

THE FIRST FEW MONTHS AS Lehigh's head coach were frenzied. When not on the road recruiting the next fall's freshman class, the coaches met with upper-classmen players, among other things, communicating the Team Rules while initiating off-season training in advance of spring practice.

While the pace was hectic, Dad could feel a certain excitement building with most of the upper-classmen. Admittedly, his new Team Rules and their requirements seemed a bit overwhelming to most of them, given the sharp contrast from the lax culture of the previous coaching staff.

Most of the players began adapting to these rules. As certain players broke rules, penalties were issued. When those players paid the penalties, other players observed the enforcement. This helped validate that Team Rules were firm and applied to everyone. At the infancy of Dad's tenure as a head coach, this helped to establish a platform for the discipline and structure he felt were so essential to real success and a winning culture.

One player became the exception to an otherwise cooperative team. He walked into Dad's office a week before the start of spring practice and told Dad he didn't want to participate. He didn't ask his head coach—he notified him, as in, "I'm not going to attend spring practice." This player claimed, "I don't think I need to participate because I'm already one of the best players and I don't need the extra work."

The truth was that this kid *was* one of the most talented players on the team. And there weren't that many talented players on the 1965 roster.

During the previous month, this player had also been less supportive of the Team Rules. When they met, he told Dad, "I think some of your rules aren't helpful. If you ask me, I think they're a waste of time."

Dad looked at the disgruntled player for a moment before telling him that spring practice was mandatory for all players, that Team Rules applied to all players, and that consistency was important. Dad explained that the coaches had a lot of work to do getting new plays instituted and assessing the talent in order to put together the best lineups. Spring practice was the chance to do that. And besides, Dad said, "I'm not going to treat players unevenly."

The player paused before saying, "Coach, I'm *not* going to play spring ball." Dad peered at him for a moment and then replied, "Anyone who doesn't participate in spring ball won't be invited to fall practice and won't be on the team."

The young man sat up and asked in an animated way, "So you're going to kick *me* off the team if I don't play spring football? If you kick me off the team, you can't win without me. I'm your best player." Dad confirmed his position and that was the end of the conversation.

A week went by. The player didn't show up for the first practice. Given his boycott, Dad communicated to the team that the young man had been kicked off for violating Team Rules. The news of this dismissal drew concern from some of the players since they knew they lost a valuable player. Their initial reaction was that his departure was a setback to their chances for the upcoming season. But the more important reaction was that the team now saw very vividly that rules did matter and that there was a firm hand leading the Lehigh football program.

Looking back, Dad considers that incident to be a critical time, a defining moment in his coaching career. It confirmed that the team is more important than the individual. Dad made an unpopular decision but one that earned him the team's respect. It was based on structure and discipline, the foundations for rebuilding the Lehigh football program.

That September, Lehigh began its 1965 football campaign. They played nine games that year and lost the first eight. They weren't a good football team, but there were some positive moments to remember. In the opening game, the team played a much more talented Rutgers team to a scoreless tie heading into the final minute of the game. With seconds remaining, Rutgers scored and won the game 6-0.

Another limiting factor for the 1965 team was that they played the entire season without Bobby Draucker, their starting quarterback. He had been out with an injury all season, and it wasn't until the final game of the year that he was healed and could return to the starting lineup.

That game was against Lafayette, Lehigh's archrival. In fact, the Lehigh/Lafayette rivalry was then (and is still now) the most played football rivalry in NCAA history.

In the game, with a strong performance by Draucker, Lehigh upset a heavily favored Lafayette team by a score of 20-14. It was Dad's first win as a head football coach and a great send-off for the senior players on the team. When the game ended, the players carried Dad on their shoulders across the football field. It was a very special moment for him.

One win and eight losses didn't reflect what happened during the 1965 season. Amid the losing record, a team had come together under a new head coach. And, more important, a healthy, disciplined culture had been established.

Developing a Winning Culture on the Other Side of South Mountain

THE DEMANDS ON MY PARENTS were significant in the mid-1960s, which caused them to split the duties, each working primarily on opposite sides of South Mountain. While that was the case, their connection to each other and to the family union was firmly sealed. What Mom told Jessie and me was true, "the Dunlap Team sticks together," and while we saw much more of my mother than my father during our upbringing, my father still had a very strong influence on how we were raised because Marilyn and Fred as a couple were merged as one.

This meant that all of the covenants to the family culture descended from both of our parents. These beliefs were the basis for what made a strong Dunlap Team and, inherent in them, a winning family culture similar to what Dad was creating at Lehigh.

My parents love each other very much. Their affection for and devotion to each other remains quite evident today and it was fully apparent throughout my childhood. Perhaps even more important than love and devotion, they have always had an immense respect for each other. They also had respect for the *potential* of great parenting and their first and only stab at it was with Jessie and me. We were their guinea pigs.

Anyone who knows Mom and Dad realizes they are strong people. They are decisive, guided by solid principles. This might cause some to wonder...wouldn't two strong-minded people make for some serious fireworks? Wouldn't there be incidents of harsh disagreement? That happens every day, in private and in public, especially when there is an unhappy marriage. Even with a relatively happy marriage, parents can have major differences of opinion.

Since Mom and Dad both had strong personalities, some may

speculate that I grew up as the referee for an Ultimate Fighter cage match. That didn't happen. I didn't grow up in the Octagon.

Why not? My parents, while decisive, had immense respect for each other and carefully observed the roles in life they each played. They also benefited from growing up in healthy family environments. While there were style differences between my parents' families, the point of consistency was that both home environments were harmonious. Moreover, there was trust and respect among family members.

Did my parents ever disagree? They must have. You can't have two powerful people finding a way to agree on every important thing. But as a kid, I didn't see it. And neither did Jessie.

Later in life, I learned that my parents had a pact with each other: never show a break in ranks in front of the kids. They felt that open discord would be harmful to what might be called "the mission of Dunlap solidarity." They felt it would hurt the Dunlap Team and detract from our winning family culture.

Whether Dad developed this approach in the military or through his coaching experiences, I am unsure. But I discovered that their trick was to set aside any difference they may have had until they had a chance to discuss the issue in private. And when in a private setting, they would reach a decision and both would embrace it. And then the commanders (parents) would deliver the plan to the infantry (the kids) in a unified manner.

We were then left to believe that what was said by one would certainly be confirmed by the other. That simple concept was the primary reason that my sister and I felt completely secure within our family unit, as I believe Dad's players did with him at the team's helm.

To pull this off, what were their "tricks of the trade?" Here's a hypothetical example. If I asked my father for an opinion on a snowy day,

"Do I really need to go out now and shovel the snow?" He'd respond with the question, "Did you ask your mother? What did she say?" I'd answer, "She wants me to go do it now, before it gets too deep." And he would reply, "If she said that, then that's what you should do."

For years, I wondered why I couldn't catch them with even a little difference of opinion. This was the 1960s and it was well before text messaging hit the scene. *How the heck did they stay so seamless?* I asked myself.

The staple to their parenting regimen was something I'd call the "The Dunlap Code of Ethics" or perhaps better said, "The Dunlap Rules," the tenets by which Jessie and I were raised. My parents never formalized such a thing, being far too humble to emblazon or promote such a doctrine.

Regardless, they mentored us about certain things, recalling examples from their own experience. These sessions were like a history lesson about the future. They gave countless examples, but presented each as being a valuable perspective to help us make better decisions when we got older. They established rules for us, just as Dad was establishing rules for his football team.

What made up the Dunlap Rules? The first one was "Conduct Yourself in an Exemplary Way at All Times." To illustrate, my parents provided examples of good behavior and bad behavior. They weren't religious in their sermons. Frankly, they had *their own religion.* It was a religion about how you should treat people. Mom said, "Treat people as you want to be treated. And try to appreciate how the other person feels."

Dad would then follow that with, "And if you do so, you should expect that the other person will return the favor." He meant that mutual respect was critical to any good relationship. He'd say "And if you are caring to another, but find that the person is not meeting your care with the same, then it's time to move on to other, better people."

Dad, on and off the football field, was all about accountability. Not that Mom wasn't, but Dad didn't want us loving everybody and getting compromised.

Understanding this concept was complex, and I didn't quite get the subtlety he was referring to when I was a child. But that became more apparent to me in later years.

A second Dunlap Rule was "Embrace Loyalty and Honesty." (Though Dad used nicer words above, he was basically saying: "If the other guy treats you like shit, blow him off.") Therefore, the second rule needed clarification and my parents handled the chore. They spoke about relationships and time, and how time and good deeds can establish equity in a relationship. They said that every relationship goes through ups and downs. And while a friend might treat you poorly one day, "This might be a person who is going through a tough time."

Mom also said, "This might be someone with whom you have a lot of trust established. If so, before you abandon him, consider the wealth of good experiences you have had with that person and treat this aberration as just that, an aberration."

Mom and Dad were big on trust. It came from their core as honest people. They told us, "Trust is established inch by inch, over time, as a result of honesty between parties. Your friends, Tiger, aren't perfect and neither are you. But if you and they are honest with each other, when you make mistakes, you can then trust each other, because you aren't being deceptive."

Respect was certainly important to my parents. They told me that true respect, when you are speaking about your closest allies, comes from loyalty and honesty, the building blocks of trust.

A third Dunlap Rule was "Work Hard and Be Committed to a Goal." Mom and Dad were driven people in whatever they did. Their screening method for whether they were going to take on a new task required that it be something they were willing to pursue *all out*. If they couldn't agree on that, the task was discarded.

Whether as a parent or a coach, Dad always talked about commitment. He told us, "Nothing exceptional can be accomplished unless you are committed fully to it." I was a young kid, and like a lot of kids, I was prone to being distracted by the *fun thing du jour*. As I got older, Dad continued to ask me, "What is it that you really want to do?" His filtering process was measured by *which thing is it that you are willing to throw yourself at with full force?* Gradually, as I matured, I recognized that it might be better to focus my efforts on fewer things so I could become better at those chosen pursuits.

Dad said, "Pursuit of an important goal is a real privilege. It's something you have decided is important, and if you are successful in your quest, the reward is lasting satisfaction."

At 15 years old, I didn't fully appreciate that. But later, after I went to college and then into the business world, this concept really resonated. Much of my business success, while running large corporations, was based on Dad's philosophy as a grounding for the challenges I accepted and the things I accomplished.

"Respect the Inner Circle (The Safe Zone)" was a fourth Dunlap Rule. We have all heard "You can pick your friends, but you can't pick your family members." That is true. Unfortunately, there are many instances of dysfunctional families. In those cases, it can cause discourse, even long after family members have grown and moved away.

To be certain, these relationships can be comical or quirky aberrations to a family's structure. But there can be harmful and hurtful cases too.

Why is it that when you can't pick your family, and the circumstances are dysfunctional, you are still expected to be loyal to family members? It's as if there is a magnetic force compelling people to protect and support family even if the years spent with them were dysfunctional. It doesn't make sense. And yet many families, like homing pigeons, migrate back to that dysfunctional circus several times a year. Is it to pay homage? Is it out of guilt?

Fortunately, I grew up in a functional house with functioning family members. At the core of our family was treating family members with respect at all times. That led to being in the "Safe Zone." That is my term, not my parents', but it makes sense. It's not something that is limited to family members but can also include very close friends, business associates, and in Dad's case, members of his football coaching family.

Simply put, the Safe Zone is a carefully chosen collection of people who can be trusted. These are people who are loyal and to whom there is loyalty. As a youngster, my Safe Zone included my parents and my sister. My parents were strict—my sister will attest to that. But they were especially adamant when it came to the Inner Circle and what I call the Safe Zone. For this important area, my parents emphasized what I will call "subset rules within the Dunlap Rules" including:

- Respect your parents, because they love you unconditionally. Never raise your voice to them.
- Treat your sibling with respect.
- Respect your belongings and treat them with the utmost care.
- Respect your elders and conduct yourselves in public with the decorum expected by society.

- Treat other kids, schoolmates, and playmates with respect, the way that we deserve to be treated.

While I was a D student at #2 above (you know, the typical sibling strife), I generally adhered to Rules 1, 3, 4 and 5. Why? Without question, our parents loved us. They supported us, especially when we were struggling with problems we couldn't handle by ourselves. All they asked of us was that we recognized their love by being respectful of their role (and seniority).

Our parents believed that *words mean things*. They thought that harsh tones and harsh words could threaten the closeness of the family unit. And the same should apply to relationships with close friends.

How many times do people get mad at someone and then haul off and give them an earful—only to call them back later and say, "I didn't mean what I said"?

Did those words do damage? Did the person yelled at really forgive what was said? Or did those words linger in the friend's mind long afterwards?

My parents demanded that we be civil with them. And in turn, they were civil with us. We didn't yell and scream in our house. Sure, we disagreed on some things, but we discussed them civilly. Why? Because we recognized that the people we were interacting with were in our Inner Circle, part of our Safe Zone.

Words mean things. My parents reinforced this point from the time I was a toddler. And they established a culture in our home where love and security were paramount and where acrimonious bickering was not allowed. They did so because they felt that such drama wasn't needed in order to make a point. They further believed that emotional outbursts could lead to exaggeration, bringing into question the degree of the person's honesty. And finally, they believed such acrimony could threaten the very love and security my parents had worked so hard to instill.

A fifth Dunlap Rule was simple: "Establish High Standards While Planning for the Future."

While my parents were strict, they were also optimistic, positively charged people. They celebrated the hell out of anything good that we did. Looking back now, they may have overdone it with some things like "Yay, Tiger has learned to brush his teeth!" (Really?) While sometimes overblown, their adulation was always directed at how important these "accomplishments" would be to our future.

One day they said they wanted to talk to Jessie and me. Mom took the lead. "Kids, your Dad and I are having several parties at the house this summer." she said. She stood like she was making a proposal. "We'll have different types of people visiting our home. There will be Lehigh alumni, professors and administrative officials. And there will be many neighbors who will attend." She paused and looked at Dad. "It's time we included you in these gatherings."

Jessie and I looked at each other tentatively. "Dad and I thought we should start to teach you how to handle yourselves with adults," Mom said, "and we think these parties are an excellent opportunity to learn." Following that discussion, we spent the next day practicing things like how to deliver a firm handshake, how to say "How do you do," how to say "It's nice to meet you," and how to defer to an adult under the rule of "respect your elders."

Learning proper manners wasn't actually that hard, since Mom had been coaching us during the past year. With Dad's job, Jessie and I were already quite visible, and it was incumbent upon us to make a good first impression. Mom always reminded us that this was "good training" and "it would pay off for us later in life." She said, "The impression you make is a reflection on the whole Dunlap Team."

Taking the teaching to heart, we practiced quite a bit and we made good impressions at the parties. As the next couple years unfolded and we were increasingly involved in more adult settings, it became natural and we got good at it. We developed an advanced level of social aplomb. I could notice the difference when I encountered other kids my age. They weren't as aware of what to do or what to say—and I was proud to have made a better impression.

Mom and Dad always congratulated us after the parties. Mom might say, "Mrs. Smith said you were a delight to meet" or "The Baxters said you are very mature for your age." This was typical of our parents—providing positive reinforcement all the time.

Mom and Dad were preparing Jessie and me for the future, for when we were adults. They talked to us about skills and capabilities they thought would be good to master as we approached adulthood. They taught us to ski. They taught us to play tennis. They taught us to play golf. And they taught us to play bridge. As Mom said, "If you learn these sports and card games, they will serve you well with adults in later years."

But tennis, golf and bridge were an unmitigated disaster. I give Mom credit—learning these games was a great idea. There was only one hitch.

Jessie is a loveable girl. She loves her mother, her dad, and even her brother. But she didn't want to be competitive with any of us—EVER. So she participated—grudgingly.

Our family had great fun skiing—because the sport of skiing *wasn't* directly competitive. We took family trips each week to Big Boulder, a ski area in the Poconos. Mom and Dad pulled us out of school each

Tuesday and we skied all day long. All four of us enjoyed it, especially Jessie, since it wasn't her against us, or against me.

Both Jessie and I are glad we learned to ski. But with bridge, golf and tennis, Jessie didn't care for any of them.

Regardless, these Rules and activities were our family's points of emphasis. For Jessie and me, this was our normal. After having met hundreds of families over the years, it has become more apparent how uniquely conscientious our parents were as we were growing up and how large a work project they had initiated with us.

"Trouble" on Willowbrook Drive

MY PARENTS INVESTED TIME AND energy educating and nurturing our understanding of the Dunlap Rules. Predictably, one question to ask is how quickly and consistently did Jessie and I comply with the rules? Or, more broadly, how quickly are other parents able to reign in their children to act responsibly as they grow up?

Can parents flip a switch one morning and their kids suddenly become model children? No. Can parents send them to be trained at an obedience school, only to have them delivered back to the owner, capable of lifting a leg and hitting a shrub? No. Compliance happens by way of trial and error. Or in my case, error and error!

My parents never posted the Dunlap Rules on the walls and they never acted like dictators enforcing them. The Dunlap Rules were, especially for Mom, more of an evolving, morphing range of expectations. It's not that she pulled a "bait and switch" on us. Rather, it is that she continually "process improved." Her menu of child improvement opportunities were an ever-emerging list.

Since Dad worked a great deal, Mom and Dad decided that she

should take the role of rule enforcer. She was the game warden but the spirit of her tutelage was always about improvement, and we took it as such.

These rules (another word might be "goals"), were explained to us by Mom, and she used the same strategy as she did with the topic of proper English. She said the Dunlap Rules were the right ways to behave, that following them would make us more responsible people, which would prepare us for life as an adult. That was the carrot: she always emphasized the positive and hung that *future promise* out there.

Mom was a cheery and expressive sort most of the time. However, that was only as long as we adhered to the rules. Jessie and I understood the messages she conveyed, but that didn't mean we bowled a 300 game every time. And when we threw a gutter ball...OUCH! If we ever broke a house rule, a Dunlap Rule, or anything resembling a rule, there were consequences.

We were not perfect kids. We tried to be, in order to please our parents, but we fell short a few times. Jessie was better at behaving than I was. But she had an advantage—she didn't have to live with HER as a sister! I did. I therefore rationalized that I had a higher degree of difficulty with *being good*.

What were the penalties for misbehavior? My parents were opposed to harsh bickering and emotional discourse. As an effective alternative, they developed skills far more insidious. Mom never yelled at us. She did worse than that. And it usually happened when I was causing trouble with my sister.

Jessie was one of my finest targets for teasing. And I developed covert skills at a young age to execute my plans for pestering. But sometimes my methods were not covert enough.

In a *highly rare situation* where I might have been bothering my sister, Mom would growl, "Tiger!" That sound usually made my heart stop. Then she would lower her voice to almost a whisper. But it wasn't a loving whisper. It was more like the sound that a Cobra made when someone got too near to it.

"Tiger, you know better than that." She'd say in a low tone. "Were you taught as a child to do that kind of thing?"

I'd think, *Hey, I am a child. What the heck do you mean by that?* But I never said it. Instead I might defend myself by replying, "No, Mom. But Jessie deserved it! She's sitting in my seat."

Then came the reminder, again in the low tone, "Tiger, Jessie is part of the Dunlap Team and she has every right that you have." My mother would then stare (or I should say glare) at me. Saying nothing. And I would slink away, back to whatever I was doing, not knowing if any of my privileges were suddenly in jeopardy.

Mom was the pro at "Less Is More." And Dad was just as adept this way with us, and with his players and coaches. My parents understood that it was more effective to send a message by saying fewer words. It made each word they said more potent.

"Less Is More" was my mother's fastball, and her change-up pitch was the "Marilyn Cool Treatment." She could become aloof, unengaged and un-warm, it seemed. Boy, I hated that. Let's face it. I *knew* I screwed up—I knew it was my fault. I was ready for the parental scolding and I deserved it. But instead of getting a dose of "What the heck is wrong with you, Tiger?" I got a few even-keeled (albeit visceral) whispers…which left me unsure if I was then in the clear.

The cool treatment only extended my agony. Was Mom still mad at me? Was she still disappointed? Did she still love me? OF COURSE she loved me. But I wanted her to *like* me, too! *Heck,* I wondered, *what did I have to do to get that positively charged, happy-to-see-me mother back?*

Reflecting back, I imagine that in those moments, Mom must have discretely watched me squirm. She must have known that the cool treatment was smothering me. But she also knew that "Less Is More" was then sending me a much more efficient and more lasting message.

Confrontations like that with Mom were relatively few. Why? Because Jessie and I hated to disappoint her or Dad. Admittedly, it was largely because we hated the cool treatment. It was like being banished to the Gulag with no assurance of parole. So my sister and I got pretty good at following the rules and toeing the line.

The Dunlap Rules and their offshoots covered many areas. They included completing our chores, treating our parents and belongings with respect, treating each other nicely (which was challenging at times), and treating other people outside of our house with compassion and care. The third one was tough, as my sister and I were often at odds. We were kids who were vying for an advantage in the land-grab for territory within the household.

With the perspective of an adult, my sister, Jessica, was a really sweet kid. She's 56 now, and she's a great person and I really appreciate her. But my affection for her back then was, shall we say, sporadic? That changed when we went to college. I realized that we weren't really in competition with each other—we were actually wanting the best for each other.

But as a kid, I had an alternative opinion of her. She was *in my way.* She was a year older than me. She liked to do girly things. YUCK! And she presented a competitive threat around the home. *This town ain't big enough for the two of us!* I often thought. Don't get me wrong—I understood that Jessie was part of the Dunlap Team. But I was convinced that she must be the water boy.

So, while Dad readied his Lehigh players for the coming season, and Mom continued to handle the home front, Jessie and I fought (or I should say that I fought with her?). Given the rules of the house, however, I needed to find a way to mount my offensives like a stealth fighter: delivering my blows in the dark or undercover.

I wasn't as crafty as I thought. And as a result, I found myself at times on the wrong side of the law (Mom). My punishments ranged between the "Cobra" and the "Cool Treatment," with loss of privileges, or groundings. And if privileges were taken away, the sentence never got compromised. If I lost my privilege to play outdoors for two days, it was for two days. Exactly.

During the penalty phase, I might wish or hope for leniency, but down deep I knew it would be two lost days sitting in the house. And I wasn't just sitting. My mother modeled herself after Franklin Delano Roosevelt: there were work projects associated with the punishment. At times, I felt like I was a contributor to the Tennessee Valley Authority. Or a member of a chain gang—except that I didn't have to wear an orange jumpsuit.

My parents were maddeningly consistent. If they said, "Don't do it," they meant it. As an adult, I can see how important this was; that consistency provided clarity and structure. It reinforced the strength of their leadership.

Meanwhile, playing in the neighborhood was our primary source of fun. But we needed to be home when Mom and Dad had indicated. If Mom told us to be home by 6 p.m. for dinner, then we better be within eyesight, running toward the door. I was always cutting it close, trying to stay for that one last pitch in our pick-up baseball game. I remember the Se-Wy-Co Fire Department had a siren that sounded off at exactly 6 p.m. each night. The siren lasted about 10 seconds and I had it pretty well gauged to know how long it would take to get from the field to the house. When that siren started to blare, I took off.

When dinner was other than 6 p.m., Mom had an old cowbell she would ring from the front porch. That was our signal to get our butts home. Sometimes when I walked through the door, I'd "moo" at her. She'd smile at my attempt at humor. Unless of course, I was late getting there. Then my mooing was less appreciated.

Were my parents' methods extreme? I might have thought so at times when I was young. But in hindsight, Mom's consistent, unwavering administration of the rules reinforced to us that rules are important...and that they matter. My story about dinnertime may seem like an extremely strict example. But the size of the issue wasn't mine to debate. And the reinforcement of rules (big or small) set expectations for us. It provided structure. And that framework proved valuable in my teenage years. As I grew older, my freedom to make my own decisions increased. But the discipline around the Dunlap Rules helped guide me in situations where I might have considered taking much more risky liberties.

Did that discipline ever include physical punishment from our parents? I think Jessie escaped childhood unscathed. I, on the other hand, remember one incident when the punishment probably fit the crime.

On this one particular day some 50 years ago, this *really nice* 7-year-old boy (he was a model citizen, in my view) got in a pinch. It was summertime, and most of his friends (Did I mention that this boy was a really great kid?) were away on vacation and he was bored. He/I didn't have many options in the way of entertainment. And one of those few options was Jessie, generally my last choice.

Regardless, on that day, Jessie was already deeply involved with playing with her dolls. *Who would squander their time on this earth doing that*, I muttered to myself. Particularly when there are more worthy pursuits, such as kicking the ball, playing catch, or looking for field mice in the back yard. And what about catching tree toads? Now that's REAL fun!

Having no success cajoling Jessie to do *real* activities, I decided to go outside and make my own fun. Just me and the field mice.

Like Tom Sawyer, I surveyed the back yard for rodent playmates. I couldn't find any. Maybe they were on vacation, too. So I resorted to other fun activities. I picked up twigs and threw them. I climbed a couple trees. I even ran races with myself back and forth across the yard, imagining that I was in the Olympics. It was a humid August day and I was getting hot and sweaty.

Since we lived in a new house in a new neighborhood, there were home lots all around our house that were undeveloped. Those lots were filled with weeds, trees and vines—great for playing hide and seek where kids could camouflage their whereabouts. If we were playing Combat, we could coil in the brush planning our next attack.

Some of these idle lots were in the early stages of construction where a bulldozer had cleared the brush in advance of the construction or where early construction was already underway. We liked those lots, too, because we could climb on the cement foundation or climb up the temporary staircase and weave between the 2x4 studs.

When those new homes were being constructed, the ground around them had been excavated. This was the best part, because it would unearth rocks or even create dirt bombs!

Dirt bombs were a kid's best friend. We would play war and use dirt bombs as our ammunition. Dirt bombs were just that—dirt that was caked together. They had been created by the bulldozer when the land was cleared. Dirt bombs ranged in size from a golf ball to a loaf of bread. The latter were too heavy to throw more than a few feet but the golf ball or tennis ball-sized dirt bombs were ideal for our war games.

The cool part of a dirt bomb is that when you threw it at a rock or another hard object, it would explode on impact into little dirt fragments. Hence the name "dirt bombs."

Why all this background information? Well, on that hot, sweaty, boring day in August, I decided to throw dirt bombs. I imagined myself a big league pitcher. I threw them hard. I threw them far. And then I looked around and saw our house...and, I bet myself...that I was strong enough to reach it.

The first volley came up just short. *I didn't throw that one well. Surely I can do better.* A second one was launched and...BANG! It hit the house. What a great throw! And the coolest thing about it was that the dirt bomb didn't just explode, it made a loud noise when it hit the aluminum siding.

The sound on impact was deafening. It was like a real bomb. I was enthralled with this.

I launched another. Direct hit! And another. Blamo! Dirt was flying everywhere with the crashing sound of the impacts. This was *so* cool! I couldn't wait to show my friends how fun this was when they returned from vacation.

And then...the Cobra appeared.

Yes, she stood in the doorway just as I launched another dirt bomb. And together we watched the arching volley descend on the house in a mighty crash.

"Hey!" I heard, a sound that scared me so much I suddenly jerked around.

It was then that I realized my dirt bomb attacks on our house might not be such a good idea. I don't remember much of what Mom said after that first stern word. I only remember running at her command at warp speed to where she was standing. She must have given me some directive that amounted to something like, "Get the hell over here, you brain-dead kid." She never would have used those words, but I can tell you that I felt that sensation.

And then it hit me. What was I thinking? Firing dirt bombs *at our house?* Was I nuts? When I reached her, huffing and puffing, she asked me a question that I couldn't answer: "Why did you think it was OK to throw things at the house?"

A good question, I thought. *Gosh, Mom really had a way of stumping a guy...*

"I don't know," I said, staring at my feet.

"You have been told before NOT to do anything like this," she growled. "And yet you did it anyway." I kept my gaze low and nodded.

Mom was more upset than I had ever seen her. Then she started in. "You know our rule about taking good care of your belongings." I nodded. "Well, this house is OUR belonging." She paused. "The Dunlaps *respect* our things and take care of them. We don't throw dirt bombs at them!"

To put it mildly, Mom was really angry. She ordered me to get inside the house while she walked over to inspect the aluminum siding. I hustled inside while she started toward where my dirt bombs had been hitting the house. I was in a panic, running room to room to get a peek at her through the windows as she surveyed the damage. Boy, was I in trouble. This was not my usual dose of trouble. We were in new terrain. I had never seen her so mad.

After what seemed like an eternity, Mom came in and found me in the kitchen. She was seething. She told me to go to my room. Then she looked at my condition, all sweaty and dirty, and said gruffly, "No, get upstairs and get into the tub."

I scampered up the stairs, figuring the faster I moved, the more she would appreciate my sudden obedience. And maybe forget the fact that I had been attacking the house with dirt bombs, ones being thrown at the new aluminum siding. *What was I thinking? How on earth did I think that was a good thing to do?*

I got undressed and turned on the water. I didn't care if it was cold or hot—I jumped right in. I just wanted to comply as fast as I could in the hopes that it might assuage Mom's anger at least a little bit.

And then I sat there. In the tub. In the middle of the day. For what seemed like hours.

I couldn't hear her. *She must be downstairs*, I thought. *But why wasn't she still scolding me? Surely, there was more that I would hear about this.*

The water in the tub was getting cold, and I was beginning to shiver. And then I heard it—the methodical, rhythmic sound of footsteps coming upstairs. My heart raced.

Mom stopped in the doorway and glared at me. I looked down, thinking contrition was my only sensible strategy. She then moved into the bathroom but stood above me. Staring at me. Saying nothing.

And then she began, in that steely whisper that I had become accustomed to hearing whenever I would find myself in one of life's ditches. "You disappoint me, Tiger," she began. I looked down again. "This is the *worst* thing you have done. Do you understand?" I nodded with an *about to sob* look. I was still looking down at the chilly water.

"Why did you think it was OK to do that?" she asked. I shrugged my shoulders. I kept my eyes down, thinking that if I looked at her, it would only incite her more. "Look at me!" she said, in a tone that was a bit more stern. *So much for that strategy*, I thought.

"Do you know how much this disappoints me?" she asked. I

nodded again. "What are we going to do about this?" She paused and I shrugged.

I *knew* a punishment was coming, but I couldn't imagine what it would be. And I thought it best *not* to contribute to the *creative phase* of this discussion.

"You will be punished," she said. "But this one is different. It's worse."

Bingo! I knew we were in uncharted territory.

Suddenly, as my eyes widened, Mom pulled something out of her pocket: a hairbrush. She told me to get on my knees and bend over the side of the tub. And then she kneeled over me.

I had heard about kids getting hit with a hair brush before. There were war stories told by kids after they had really been bad. Unlike today, in the 1960s, the weaponry of choice by parents was usually a belt, a paddle or...a hairbrush. So here I was, about to join the dubious club of kids who got whacked.

Frankly, of those three choices, the belt and the paddle seemed a lot more frightening. If I was going to get hit, I figured that I got a good lottery pick with the hairbrush. *After all, it's just a hairbrush*, I considered, *used to comb hair! How bad can that be?*

Mom paused above me. As I braced for the whack, I thought, *Come on, Mom, get it over with. I know I goofed up. I know I was wrong. This delay stuff is killing me.*

"Tiger," Mom said, "I have never hit you kids before. And I was hoping I would never have to."

At that moment, I decided that this was *not* the time to remind her that she just finished her sentence with a preposition. I crouched silently instead.

Mom's voice began to quiver. "But this is for your own good," she said softly. "And it hurts me more to do it, than it will hurt you."

Mom hit me a couple times, not even too hard. And then she stopped. She was now crying. She stood up, saying nothing more, and walked out the door and back downstairs.

I didn't move...still leaning over the wall of the tub. My butt was stinging for sure. But all I could think about was the shock of seeing my mother cry. I hadn't remembered ever seeing her cry before—she was such a strong person. I stayed there by the tub for a few moments. Though my butt was burning, I didn't cry. I was upset though. I was upset that *I made her this upset*. I had made her cry and made her so disappointed in me.

Later, I walked downstairs. Contrary to my expectations, she wasn't in cool treatment mode. I had expected her to be.

Mom's voice was soft when she asked me to sit down at the kitchen table. Then she sat down next to me. "I spoke with your father just now," she said. "And I explained what happened today." She spoke deliberately with a measured tone. "And he and I have decided that you will spend the rest of the week indoors doing some chores that I will assign you. The only time you will be allowed outside is to do some of the chores." She looked at me firmly. "Do you understand?"

"Yes, Mom," I said in my bravest voice. "I know I was wrong. And I am not sure why I did it. But I know it was wrong."

Mom nodded hesitantly and got up from the table.

The incident was over. I had had my day of reckoning with the hairbrush. And I still needed to serve my time indoors doing chores. The crisis had passed.

There was something empathetic about my mother's tone as she punished me. It was almost like she was sorry or that she felt sorry for me. *Why is she not still mad*? I wondered. *Why does she look sad, sorry or even guilty? And why did she cry?*

Years later, Mom and I discussed what had happened. And we could laugh about it. The answers to the questions I had back then provide insight into her expectations of herself as a mother.

Mom explained to her then 20-year-old son that what became known as the "dirt bomb incident" was complicated for her.

First, Mom loved me and it hurt her to inflict pain on me.

Second, she had never needed to hit either Jessie or me until that day. She had prided herself that, until that day, she had successfully been able to instill so many values in us and also enforce the family rules without ever having to use physical force.

In some respects, she admitted, by needing to use the hairbrush on me, she saw that as a reflection of her failure as a mother. This gives you a sense of the high standards that she set for herself.

Third, Mom said she was angry that I defied the rules. And while she could see that I immediately recognized my mistake, she felt she needed to follow through with the spanking because we had been led to believe that if you broke the rules there were consequences. For her, it was more important to maintain consistency in how she managed the children. If she had not followed through with the punishment, it might have given me a mixed message.

On that day, as I sat in the lukewarm water of the bathtub, the hairbrush incident was the one and only time my parents ever hit us. I guess you could say that they and we both managed to navigate our upbringing without the need for a second event.

Obediently, I served my sentence that week and we moved forward. I still loved to throw dirt bombs, but I learned to choose my targets… more selectively.

The Dunlap Rules and Their Applications

THESE GUIDEPOSTS AND CORE FAMILY tenets were not imparted on Jessie and me all at once. They were taught to us gradually by our parents, as core values for how to live in the world. They were broad rules designed to address many challenges we might face.

Life isn't black and white. Issues require judgment. The Dunlap Rules don't, by themselves, satisfy every problem and every issue. Rather it is the application of them, titrated appropriately to each situation that makes for 'good judgment.'

The lessons learned from my parents as I matured, were, therefore, less a sterile use of the rules, but more the judgment and leadership they exhibited, in applying the rules in unique ways and unique degrees. The most impressive thing about my parents was their *consistency* in applying them. As I grew older, I realized that the Dunlap Rules would come in the form of lessons learned by watching my parents navigate their world.

The 1966 Season—A Few Friends and a Bunch of Enemies

HEADING INTO THE 1966 SEASON, Dad discovered that the rebuilding process at Lehigh was more involved and more difficult than he had expected. He also realized it would take longer to complete, but the team had been making gradual progress. While they won only one game in 1965, the organizational continuity between the players and coaches was significantly improved in a number of ways and after the 1965 season, the returning players worked hard in the off-season with strength and endurance training.

The coaches also had a more productive off-season because they had been together for the past year and were a much more cohesive group. They were able to hit the road immediately after the season ended to capitalize on the recruiting season.

Like any new organization, it took time to develop systematic approaches. And the coaching staff was becoming more effective with every passing month.

Unfortunately, there was still the shortage of talent on the 1966 team. While the coaches had recruited some good players the previous spring, the NCAA rules at the time prohibited teams from playing freshman on the varsity. So 1966 was another year where the new staff had to make the most of the talent that had been recruited to Lehigh before their arrival.

The 1966 team was improved and they were competitive in most of the games they played. "There were bright spots," Dad told me years later, "where had we won a game here or there, the season would have turned out differently."

One of those games was the season opener against Penn. Lehigh was ahead 21-7 at the half, clearly outplaying the stronger Penn team. But in the second half, Penn got the upper hand and forged ahead in the fourth quarter. Lehigh lost 38-28.

Later that season, Lehigh played Colgate, one of the strongest teams on the schedule. Dad remembered Jon Rushatz playing a great game at running back. He was a local kid, having grown up in the Bethlehem area. He was a nationally ranked wrestler at Lehigh, and he played football as his second sport. Although Jon had an exceptional game, Lehigh lost by the score of 21-15.

Lehigh was improved in 1966, but they didn't win a game. To this point, Dad's two seasons had delivered 1 win and 17 losses.

This period of time was frustrating for my father. Lehigh was his debut as a head coach. He and his staff had worked tirelessly for two years, but they didn't see the results in the form of wins.

As a football coach, your performance and results are displayed on Saturdays in front of thousands of fans. Many of them are alumni who are proud of their school and want their team to be a standout. Beyond that prism, in the 1960s, the newspaper reporters wrote about the results every week in the Monday edition. In the case of Lehigh, that came by way of the *Allentown Morning Call* and the *Bethlehem Globe Times*. And if the results weren't good, it wasn't easy to be a football coach.

At 7 years old, I remember going to games and listening to some fairly disenchanted fans. They yelled at the players. They yelled at the coaches. And they said things about my dad.

When I went to school on the following Monday, some kids teased me. They'd say, "What happened this weekend?" and then gloat at me. They knew we had lost another game.

At that ripe age of a second grader, I didn't have a heavy social calendar. No hot dates. No disco dancing. My weekend nights were spent at home with my mother and my sister. And the closest glimpse I got to the pressure that my father felt was when I answered the home phone during the early Lehigh years.

Like most people during that era, we had our phone number listed in the phone book. A typical call went like this:

"Hello?" I answered.

"Hey, is Fred Dunlap there?"

"Yes, this is Fred Dunlap." (That was my real name, but most people called me "Tiger.")

"No! No! I want to speak with your father, the coach." There was loud noise in the background as the caller yelled into the phone.

"I'm sorry, but he's not here. He's staying tonight with the players before tomorrow's game."

"Hey, Kid. Sleeping with the players isn't going to make any difference. Lehigh can't win, no matter what they do. And Kid, your Dad is a lousy coach!" The caller then hung up.

This was my experience as the 7-year-old son of a college football coach. The guy was probably sitting in a bar (loud noises) and getting blitzed with some buddies. And then one of his friends put him up to it. They probably thought it would be funny to call the coach and give him a piece of their mind. Dumb fans. Stupid drunk alumni. The cruel side of the human race.

No matter, at 7 years old, it upset me to hear someone say such awful things about my father. Sadly, this type of thing happened on a frequent basis.

My parents considered getting an unlisted phone number to help shield Jessie and me from calls like that one. But my mother was against it for a number of reasons.

After all, so many of the people we knew already had our number; changing it would be a big inconvenience. More importantly, she felt that changing our number was analogous to running away from a fight. She sat us down and apologized to us for having to hear harsh things about Dad—on the phone, in the stadium and in the classroom. She said that cowards made phone calls like that: they aren't courageous enough to say it to our faces. They'd rather throw word bombs and run, she explained.

Ever the inspirational one and defender of Dad, Mom talked about how things were going to get better. She said, "Your dad is a great man. He needs our love and support." And then she pointed at the ceiling, as if it were the sky. "That's what the Dunlap Team does," she told us. "It sticks together."

Then Mom stood up and shook her finger at us. Her eyes grew intense. "I am looking forward to the day when we can laugh in the faces of people like that," she said with force, "because Lehigh will be a great team. Then the rest of the world will know how great a person your father is."

Of course, I loved my father and idolized him, despite a lot of fans and the general public who might not have appreciated his coaching. I was never embarrassed that he was losing most of his games. Each week we rooted hard for him and the team, and the only pain I felt (when we lost) was for my father and his disappointment. But I will admit that I dreaded going to school on Monday after the team lost a game, where I would again face the jeers from other students. In hindsight, I regret that I let that bother me. But at the age of 7, I'm not sure my feelings were all that unnatural.

The 1966-67 winter went by quickly. And similarly, the spring and summer passed. Autumn had arrived, and with it, the start of the 1967 football season.

I always looked forward to the start of another season. It was exciting, and I could sense my father's anticipation. I also loved watching Fall Camp preceding the season. The players arrived three weeks before the first game to participate in double sessions, two practices per day during the dog days of a Bethlehem summer. These practices were always held at Saucon Valley Athletic Fields, a huge parcel of land owned by the university. There were baseball fields, football fields, a track and some tennis courts. It was a great place for an 8-year-old boy to hang out.

My mother dropped me off in the morning and I stood on the

sidelines and watched practice. I got to watch my father at work. Dad ran the practices like military exercises. (No surprise there—they were run on a tight schedule.) As one activity ended, the players quickly ran to another station to begin another activity. The players were marshaled into certain drills by the sound of the coaches' whistles. You could hear that shrill sound continually as if there were a flock of birds overhead.

Those days were long that summer, particularly for an energetic 8-year-old. When I got tired of standing, I sat on some of the blocking dummies if they were not in use. I arranged a few together and plopped myself on top of them. They were so soft. It was like having my own La-Z-Boy out in a field!

During that summer I had my first exposure to Gatorade. The equipment manager mixed the magical yellow powder with water in huge jugs. Then he would stir it vigorously with a huge ladle while pouring ice cubes into the jugs. In a few minutes the magical powder was converted into a delicious lemony, salty drink. Tasty!

Gatorade restored the fluids the players were losing during practice. He served it to them when they were taking breaks. I, on the other hand, was *always* on break. So I drank a ton of Gatorade that summer.

Another favorite of mine was salt tablets. They were provided to the players as another precaution against heat prostration. I didn't sweat and I wasn't overheated, but that didn't stop me from eating them like candy. I wasn't aware of the two-per-day adult dosage. Between the Gatorade and the salt tablets, I shudder to think what stress I put on my digestive system that summer. But I lived to tell about it.

Watching Dad in action was exciting but one of the really fun things about being at all of those practices was that I got to know the players and coaches better. On those hot summer days, they ran by me saying,

"Hi, Tiger!" Or they kidded me by saying, "Why don't you get a helmet and shoulder pads and get in here, Tig?" That made me feel like I was a part of the program, which in turn made me more emotionally invested in it. By the way, "Tig" (pronounced like Tiger, but without the 'er') was the *nickname for my nickname.* When they called me Tig, I felt even more accepted.

The downside to August's arrival was that it was followed by September. That meant going back to school. And with the start of school came the potential for more of the classroom chatter that I had dreaded in past years. It was the start of another season, and because Lehigh football was very visible, everybody in the Lehigh Valley was focused on how the team was doing.

When I showed up for the first day of school, I was again exposed to some remarks from schoolmates. "What's the team look like? How good are they going to be this year? Are they going to win *any games* this year? Ha ha!"

At that age, I wasn't aware that there was another agenda brewing at Lehigh surrounding the football program. My father had spent two years trying to win games and that hadn't worked out very well. There was growing disenchantment among alumni and fans, and Dad was undoubtedly under a certain level of pressure to keep his job. However, what he didn't realize during that effort was that he was continually gaining support from some alumni factions and also the university administration for the "kind of person" he was and the "kind of organization" he was building. I learned about this a number of years later.

At Lehigh, it was important to win football games but it was also very important to run a program meeting the highest ideals. Those ideals included good conduct by players and coaches, on and off the field. They also included a strong commitment to academic excellence and an ability to interface effectively and positively with key alumni groups. While the wins were few, Dad was excelling in these areas.

Dad was the consummate professional in all areas of his life. He didn't consider that to be anything special. In fact, he took that for granted because it was the only way he would allow himself to be. The rules he established about how he conducted his life were also instilled into his football team. And while those rules weren't exceptional to him, they were nonetheless distinguishing in the eyes of those who closely followed the football program, particularly in comparison to how the football program had been managed under previous regimes.

Two seasons in, public opinion on my father's job performance was split. There was a broad contingent who thought he was a nice guy, but they were still unhappy that Lehigh was losing. These non-supporters were impatient and were beginning to suggest that a coaching change was needed.

There was another (albeit smaller) contingent, however, that understood the challenges of rebuilding Lehigh. They were more patient and supportive, and they believed that with enough time, Dad would bring Lehigh back to prominence. There were some notable people within this group who were instrumental to my father keeping his job. Most important were Pat Pazetti and Corky O'Keefe.

Pat Pazetti was a very influential alum who played football for Lehigh in the early 1900s. He was an All-American who competed against the legendary Jim Thorpe. Pazetti was subsequently inducted into the Football Hall of Fame.

After Pazetti graduated from Lehigh, he went to work for Eugene Grace, the CEO of Bethlehem Steel Corporation, but it was a unique assignment. Grace asked Pazetti to work for the company throughout the year except for the fall, at which time Grace asked Pazetti to coach the Lehigh football team. Like Pazetti, Grace was an alum and a staunch supporter of Lehigh football.

Eventually, Pazetti elevated to the position of General Manager at Bethlehem Steel. He was one of the most respected people there. Even the union workers liked and respected him. Pazetti was famous for crossing the picket lines during disputes and corralling union leaders in order to work out reasonable resolutions.

By the time Dad arrived at Lehigh, Pat was not only a leader at Bethlehem Steel but was also a leader among Lehigh alumni organizations. He was also prominent at Saucon Valley Country Club, an expansive golf and tennis club owned by Bethlehem Steel. Pazetti was so prominent that they named a building after him. The Villa Pazetti still sits today on the Grace Course in recognition of Pat's contributions over the years.

Corky O'Keefe graduated from Lehigh in the 1920s and became a talent agent in the entertainment industry. His list of clients included Bing Crosby, the Tommy Dorsey Band and the Glenn Miller Band. Corky was a soft-spoken man, kind and humble. One would never suspect that he spent leisure time playing golf with Bing Crosby and Bob Hope.

Corky was close friends with Pat Pazetti and they both were close advisors to Dr. Deming Lewis, Lehigh's president for several years before Dad's arrival. He had graduated from Georgia Tech and prior to taking the helm at Lehigh, was head of Bell Laboratories.

Dr. Lewis had a strong respect for the importance of athletics at Lehigh, if for no other reason than its ability to rally external interest in the university and keep the alumni connected with the school. President Lewis was a soft-spoken, somewhat shy man, a thoughtful person and a good listener. And he sought out my father at the suggestion of Pat and Corky.

Dr. Lewis was responsible for the entire university, including upholding a positive image with alumni and future students. Academic performance was certainly important to him, but student conduct was equally important for the type of image he wanted to project. Deming Lewis saw Dad's Team Rules as being very much in concert with his own objectives.

Many years later, Dad told me that Corky and Pat were critical to his keeping his job "because President Lewis knew them well and respected them." Dad said Corky and Pat advised Dr. Lewis that, "in spite of the losing seasons, player morale is strong, the team is making progress, and they felt that good things would happen if they remained patient."

There were many other people who were also supportive of Dad during those first two years. But these three gentlemen were instrumental in rallying support for my father at a time when a larger contingent wanted him fired.

When Dad took the job at Lehigh, he was given a three-year contract. Now, two years into his tenure there, he had only one win and only one more year left on his contract.

The army of non-supporters was growing. One of the non-supporters was his boss, Bill Leckonby, Lehigh's athletic director. During the interview process in 1964, Leckonby seemed likeable at first. But when Dad arrived on campus, he found that his boss had a more aloof demeanor.

After he took the job, Dad noticed a dearth of quality equipment and the shabby state of the football facilities. When Dad asked about purchasing new equipment or getting some basic renovations done to the facilities, he was met with a less than accommodative response. "We don't have the money for that in our budget," Leckonby countered.

"Actually, that brings up another issue," Dad said. "I asked you for the football budget last month and never got a copy. Can I see it? Maybe there are some things we are buying that I could cut out in order to create money for new equipment and some improvements to the locker room."

"You don't need to see the budget—that's my job to manage," Leckonby replied with some impatience. Being in his first few months on the job, Dad chose not to push the issue further.

Without any sense for his budget, how could Dad possibly plan for recruiting trips if he didn't know what he was allowed to spend? As time passed, Dad found Leckonby to be equally evasive when he met with him to discuss other requests for improvements.

When Dad requested money for one of his coaches to travel to a certain region, Leckonby might respond by saying, "We've never gotten any good athletes from that part of Pennsylvania. That's a waste of time and money to go there."

As Dad instituted his Team Rules, he felt it appropriate to advise his boss about them and update him on the progress of the football program. "You will never get the players to comply with that," Leckonby scolded. "You will end up running off your best players: they'll quit on you." Leckonby added, "Look, you don't have that many good players. If you mandate that they attend spring football, they will quit. And you can't afford to cut them."

Dad looked at Leckonby and responded, "The way I see it, I can't afford *not* to cut them. We need to build a program that has a foundation, and where players adhere to fundamentals."

Leckonby recounted how he had done it when he was head coach. He explained how his methods had delivered the only undefeated season in Lehigh's history. Leckonby exuded an air of superiority in those sessions. When he wasn't criticizing my father's approaches, he generally maintained an aloof rapport with Dad. But while he was aloof with Dad generally, he was far from silent in alumni circles.

Despite having two losing seasons, Dad had made enough allies to receive feedback from those alums regarding what Leckonby was saying about Dad and his staff. It wasn't favorable. Dad quickly concluded that Leckonby was not to be trusted.

At one point many years ago, Dad told me another story about his time with Leckonby. For some reason, Dad rode with Leckonby to an alumni function. This was unusual, as Leckonby liked to travel alone. But on this ride, Leckonby was in a jovial mood so they talked extensively.

Leckonby began talking openly about Mike Cooley, the head football coach before Dad. He said, "Mike was a great assistant coach, but I never thought he would be a good head coach." Dad wondered, *"Then why the hell did you put him in the job?"*

Leckonby continued. "It was apparent that he wasn't the right guy pretty early on. He was actually a bit of an embarrassment to me, but I figured I didn't need to shoot him, because he was going to take care of that himself. You see, Fred, Mike can't handle his drinks. He has a problem with that. And when he drinks, he likes to chase women." Leckonby smiled with a sense of self-satisfaction. "So I figured it would only be a matter of time before he would hang himself. Which he did."

When Dad told me this story years later, he was still incredulous. He couldn't believe Leckonby left a friend exposed that way. He couldn't believe (out of respect) that Leckonby wouldn't have confronted Cooley in an attempt to correct the situation rather than laying a trap for him.

That evening's ride was revealing about his new boss. Dad wondered, *"Why wouldn't Leckonby step in and address the situation, if for no other reason than for the benefit of the football program...unless he didn't want the football program to get better."* Maybe, my father thought, "he didn't want another coach to ever meet or exceed his own coaching record."

In Dad's short time at Lehigh, he found Leckonby to be a consistent obstructionist. Leckonby micromanaged him, withheld access to the budget, and turned down most of Dad's requests.

Toward the end of the 1966 season, after losing all of the games, it was also clear that Leckonby was mounting support among alumni against my father. Leckonby had cronies—and the coolness that those alums projected toward my father left him with no ambiguity as to their allegiance to Leckonby and their lack of support for Dad.

Dad was now entering the third year of his three-year contract. Disturbingly, he knew he didn't have the support of his boss.

The 1967 Season—
Losing More than a Football Game

EVER THE OPTIMIST, DAD LOOKED forward to more improvement from the team in this third season. The opening game was against Ithaca College at Taylor Stadium. Lehigh played well and dominated their opponent, winning 50-20. It had been 21 months since its only other win, and everyone close to the football program was relieved.

I remember my mother rushing Jessie and me home after the game so she could paint, in big block letters, the word "HALLELUJAH" across our large garage door. She wanted that message to be the first thing Dad saw when he arrived home after the game.

We celebrated that night, and again the next morning at breakfast, before Dad needed to leave for the office to prepare for the next opponent, the University of Pennsylvania. Lehigh was a decided underdog, and to make matters worse, it was an away game played at Franklin Field in Philadelphia. Lehigh played hard, but lost 35-23.

Coach Dunlap on the sidelines—1967

Following that loss, Lehigh ran a six-game gauntlet against superior teams. Losses were to Rutgers by a touchdown (14-7), Bucknell by a point (14-13) and Gettysburg by a touchdown (14-7). Great efforts were made by many individuals in those close games, in which Lehigh was predicted to lose badly. Against Rutgers, for instance, tight end John Miller totaled 13 catches in the losing effort. Lehigh was now 1-4 going into the last four games.

Up next, Lehigh faced a strong Furman team. It was a night game being played in Greenville, South Carolina, in front of a raucous Furman crowd.

That evening, tragedy struck the Lehigh football program. After trailing at halftime, the team left the locker room to return to the field for the second half. Jim McConologue, one of the assistant coaches and one of the most popular on the staff, headed for the press box. He was a talented coach, and he also had a very funny, endearing personality.

As Jim climbed the steps of the stadium toward the press box, he collapsed from a massive heart attack. He died immediately.

The second half had started before anyone on the field was aware of what had happened. And it was a while before the news of his death reached the coaches and players on the sidelines.

In those early Lehigh days, the budgets were so tight that Dad could only afford to travel with a limited number of players to away games, and he could only bring half of his coaching staff. Dad was the only coach who traveled on the flight with the team for the game.

John Whitehead and Jim McConologue were the only two assistant coaches who traveled to Furman. They left Bethlehem by car on Thursday with two players in tow, driving 10 hours to the game in South Carolina in order to add staff and players to the roster for the game.

As a result, there was no other Lehigh coach in the press box that night with Jim McConologue. Whitehead was on the sidelines with Dad, communicating with McConologue in the box. When he couldn't reach him at the start of the second half, Dad asked Whitehead to climb up to the press box and find out what was wrong.

Whitehead left the sidelines, but before he did, he handed the headphones to back-up quarterback Jimmy Baxter. He was asked to handle the headset until Whitehead found out what was amiss. At that point, Dad and Whitehead thought there was a technical problem with the headphones.

While Whitehead climbed the steps toward the press box, Baxter was finally able to reach someone in the press box. Dad remembered vividly the image of being pulled away from the game by Baxter, who informed him about what had happened. Within minutes, the news spread throughout the Lehigh sideline. The game was ongoing, so the news was delivered to a limited few in an attempt to keep the team focused on the game. Nevertheless, the news made its way gradually through the players.

Lehigh lost the game by a score of 38-15. The team was devastated by the loss of their coach. Because the game was so far from home, the team stayed in a hotel that night before returning to campus on Sunday. Dad recalled being awake all night, sitting with the players and talking about the tragedy, since nobody could sleep.

Following that game, the team was defeated by Colgate and Delaware. "The loss of Jim took the air out of the team," Dad said. "Everybody prepared hard and played hard, but our hearts were broken, and we were in no position to win a football game."

As Lehigh approached its last game of the season against archrival Lafayette, the team was 1-7. The game was very close throughout, but Lehigh lost 6-0.

The off-season became a time of healing for the players. They were still reeling from the loss of Coach McConologue.

An Uphill Fight

Thanksgiving weekend was a favorite for the Dunlaps. The football season was over and recruiting season had not commenced. I looked forward to spending time with Dad so we could sit, talk and watch football on TV.

As a youngster sitting on that couch, I really had no understanding of how unsettled Dad must have felt. The 1-8 season in 1967 meant his record through three years was 2 wins and 25 losses, and his contract was up.

The following Monday, Dr. Lewis asked Dad to meet at the president's office. Years later I would learn that Dad figured the meeting was to notify him he was being fired.

Dad and Dr. Lewis discussed the season, and how Dad thought the program was progressing. Dr. Lewis acknowledged that Athletic Director Leckonby wanted to fire Dad. This explained why the meeting was with Dr. Lewis and not Leckonby.

Dad presented data that Dr. Lewis had requested. Dr. Lewis had heard Dad's concerns about the lack of funding for the football program, and asked him to provide comparative data for budgets for teams Lehigh played, including Colgate, Penn and Lafayette. Dr. Lewis was obviously privy to Lehigh's football budget, given that Leckonby reported to him, but he had no understanding of what other schools spent.

With Mom's assistance, Dad compiled the football budgets and financial aid allowances for all of the teams Lehigh competed against. Dr. Lewis found the data to be enlightening. The meeting was an important milestone…eventually leading to more appropriate financial support for the football program.

To Dad's relief, Dr. Lewis granted him a one-year extension while admonishing him that the team needed to start winning. Dad expressed his gratitude for the support and pledged to keep making progress.

Dad was certain that Pat Pazetti and Corky O'Keefe had played an instrumental role in getting Dr. Lewis to extend Dad's contract. Both of these gentlemen had been consistent supporters since his arrival at Lehigh, and they recognized that, while Lehigh was still losing most games, the team was far more competitive than it had been in the past.

As Dad drove home, he replayed the meeting in his mind. He wasn't surprised by the news about Leckonby's opinion; he had expected it. His agitation with Leckonby was balanced by his satisfaction in knowing that he had President Lewis' support. But by the time he arrived home, neither of those emotions mattered. They had been replaced by urgency and the need to get on the road quickly and recruit a new class of athletes.

The following day, before Dad sent his assistant coaches on the road to recruit, he had to meet with Leckonby to get approval for the travel expenses. That meeting was awkward, given each person's feelings for the other. When asked for the funds to begin recruiting, Leckonby allotted the few dollars needed but again was unwilling to share the scope of the football budget. Dad departed the meeting and set out to recruit high school football players.

As Dad traveled, he considered where his program stood and about how hard it had been to turn it around. He thought about how little support he was getting from his boss and how many fans and alumni were against him. With Leckonby in charge, he concluded, winning was going to be even more difficult than it needed to be. His boss was uncooperative, and it didn't help that he was openly critical of Dad's staff when he met with key alumni groups.

The most maddening thing was that Leckonby wouldn't give Dad access to his own budget. He had never heard of such behavior before. No matter what Dad's request, Leckonby's stock line was, "there wasn't any more money available."

Leckonby's personal actions didn't match that description. Leckonby often stayed in the finest hotels when he traveled, and he often flew first class.

Contrastingly, the football coaches stayed in cheap hotels when they traveled and weren't allowed to fly. "That's too expensive," Leckonby argued. This meant the coaches had to drive for all recruiting trips.

One story best illustrates the austerity Leckonby inflicted on the football program. When I was much older, Dad told me that in 1967, Lehigh played an away game at Bucknell. On the opening kickoff, starting running back Mike Leib was kicked in the kidney. It appeared that he was bleeding internally and was rushed to the local hospital in Lewisburg, Pennsylvania.

Since Dad's budget allowed for only so many traveling players for away games, he had brought only two running backs. With Leib's injury on the first play of the game, Frank Cavagnaro had to play every offensive down for the entire game.

When the game ended, the team left Mike Leib in Lewisburg. He stayed in the hospital for several days until he was stabilized. Meanwhile, Dad and the team traveled back to campus to prepare for their next game. By the middle of the week, Dad received a call from a doctor at the Lewisburg hospital. Mike was ready to be discharged, but he was too weak to walk and couldn't travel in a sitting position. The doctor said he could only travel if he were in an ambulance where he could remain in a lying position for the entire trip. It was a three-hour ride.

With this news, Dad visited Leckonby's office to request money to have an ambulance drive the injured player back to Lehigh. Leckonby dismissed the request, saying there wasn't enough money in the budget to pay for an ambulance.

Dad's concern was for the injured player. With no other viable options available, Dad asked John Scibble, one of his assistant coaches, if they could borrow his old station wagon. Dad and Coach Scibble threw a mattress in the back of it. On that Thursday, they headed to

Lewisburg to pick up Mike Leib and bring him back to campus.

Instead of being able to focus on strategies and preparation for the next game two days later, Dad and his assistant coach spent an entire day driving up to Lewisburg and back. Having a player with a kidney injury ride on a mattress in an old station wagon with bad shock absorbers was hardly ideal, but it was the best scenario Dad could create. He wasn't going to leave the player in Lewisburg.

This story gave a revealing picture of life with Leckonby. As Dad drove that day, he thought: *It's wrong to treat an injured player that way. And it was wrong to cause the head coach to miss a valuable preparation day for the next opponent...unless the athletic director didn't care if he caused hardships or didn't care if the team performed poorly.*

Second Thoughts

IN THE WEEKS AFTER HE met with Dr. Lewis, Dad reflected on how difficult the previous three years had been, about how few wins there were, about the continued lack of funds to travel to recruit the best players, and about how difficult his rapport was with his boss.

In January, Dad attended the conference for the American Football Coaches Association (AFCA) held each winter. It was a chance to reconnect with many of his friends who had coached with him at other schools. During the three-day meeting, Dad bumped into Vic Fuscia, the University of Massachusetts head coach. Fuscia had an opening on his coaching staff and he was looking to hire a defensive coordinator. Fuscia asked to meet with Dad in private.

In the course of their meeting, Fuscia offered my father the high-level coaching position. "UMass was a really BIG program back then," Dad recalled later. "They had a lot of money and they were building a bigger stadium. And the whole university was behind the football program."

Fuscia made his pitch. "Fred, we all know you inherited a can of worms there at Lehigh," he said. "The program was in shambles before you got there. And even though you haven't been winning, we have watched how competitive your team has become against some of the tougher opponents. You clearly are making a difference there."

Dad thanked him for his comments as Fuscia continued. "But Fred, that place is set up to fail. Everybody knows what Leckonby is like. It can't be easy to work with him. Let's face it. He doesn't want you to succeed. It would threaten his own legacy." Dad nodded his head and agreed that it hadn't been easy.

"How much are they paying you, Fred?" Fuscia asked. Dad told him. "Shit, that's less than I pay most of my assistant coaches!" the coach exclaimed, waving his arms. "How are you going to be able to keep good coaches and hire better ones if that's all they are paying you?"

"Fred, you are a damn good coach," he said. "We all know that." Fuscia gestured around the hotel. "But if you don't have a realistic budget to get the basic things you need, your team can't be successful, no matter how talented you are." Dad smiled and said, "Hell, I don't even know what my budget is!"

"You're kidding me!" Fuscia shouted. "That's ridiculous! See, that's what I mean. Leckonby doesn't want you to succeed."

Dad remained silent. "Fred, how long is your contract?" Fuscia asked.

Dad explained that he had just gotten a one-year extension following the initial three-year contract.

"What are you supposed to do with a one-year contract?" Fuscia asked. "You aren't going to suddenly have a winning season there next year; there is more rebuilding to do." Fuscia shook his head. "Did Leckonby give you that extension?"

Dad laughed and said, "No, I had to meet with the president. Leckonby wanted to fire me."

"Fred, that's a bad situation," Fuscia said. "You deserve to be in a better environment. We can win with you on my staff. And I can pay you 30 percent more than you are making as head coach there."

The meeting concluded with Dad thanking Fuscia for his time. Dad agreed to consider the offer and to call him the next week.

When Dad returned home, he discussed the job offer with Mom. They talked for a long time. They talked about the frustrations of the last few years, about Leckonby, about the prospect of leaving Bethlehem, and about the implications of giving up the head-coaching role.

To be clear, my parents didn't exactly talk. My mother has a different approach. Today, they call it the "Socratic method," which is interacting with someone by asking questions. I guess my mother was ahead of her time because that was her style, long before Socratic even became a commonly used method.

What did that mean? Well, Mom asked questions to drive the discussion. Of course, she was a strong woman with fairly healthy perspectives of her own on these subjects. But she withheld her opinions and deferred to Dad with questions like:

- "How did you like the UMass coach?"
- "Didn't you know him before the AFCA meeting? How well do you know him?"
- "Do you think he would be a good guy to work for?"
- "How do you feel about leaving Lehigh?"

- "How do you feel about losing the head coaching position?"
- "Do you think things with Leckonby will get better or easier?"
- "What do you think the team will be like this year? Do you think we will win more?"

With each question, Dad answered Mom dutifully. Though she asked those questions, his responses weren't newsworthy to either of them. They both knew the answers but this was Mom's way of helping Dad sift through the points of consideration. It was how she helped him separate the big issues from the less important ones.

"Marilyn," he finally said, "maybe it was a mistake to come here to Lehigh. Maybe it is destined to fail. Maybe we should have stayed at Cornell a little longer and waited for a better head coaching job where the limitations weren't so great." Dad paused. "Maybe if I went to UMass, I could help them win. And if they won, then I would have other chances to become a head coach again."

Mom then asked Dad two big questions. "What will happen to your assistant coaches if you take the job at UMass?" and "How would you feel about leaving Lehigh after you have recruited three classes of players here? You *know* that they came here to play for *you*."

These two questions tripped up Dad. He had been cruising, seemingly driving toward a predetermined conclusion. Though unsettled by the two questions she had just asked, he dodged them and regrouped. Then Dad stood up and began pacing in front of her while resuming his pitch.

"But think about how strapped we are right now," he began. "We are living paycheck to paycheck. The UMass salary increase would give us a cushion and allow you to buy the things we need but haven't been able to afford."

Mom never said a word. "And think about the kids and you," he continued. "You guys are catching so much flack from fans. It's not good for the kids to hear bad things about me. I am an adult, and I can handle the guff. But they are *just kids*. They don't deserve that." He paced. "If I were an assistant coach, there would be none of that. When fans complain, they complain about the head coach, not about the assistant coach."

Mom continued to be silent. She had lobbed a bunch of questions and he had responded to most of them. The conversation continued for a while, and Dad realized that Mom hadn't shared *how she felt* about what he was presenting. "Well, Marilyn, how do you feel about all of this?" he finally asked.

I mentioned that the Socratic approach was my mother's style. I have seen it many times over the years, when I was in Dad's seat, discussing some of my own dilemmas with her. Along with Mom's Socratic style, she had also developed a style for this transition moment in the discussion.

During my discussions with Mom, when we reached the "what do you think, Mom" phase, she had a style that was uniquely *Marilyn*. She was like a relief pitcher who had just been called up to the mound. She would straighten up, grab her glove (figuratively), slap it and start strutting to the mound with a determined intensity on her face. And with Dad that day, that was exactly what she did.

"Well, Fred, since you are asking, I do have some opinions about what you have told me." She paused for effect. "You know best if UMass is a good job or not. And you know if the coach would be a good guy to work with. But how do you feel about leaving Lehigh, after all the work you have put into it?" she asked. She was being rhetorical. So he stayed silent. "And while Leckonby has been difficult, you have had to contend with jerks before. You overcame them each and every time. And you don't know that there won't be another jerk in Massachusetts."

Mom was now on a roll, and Dad knew it. We *all* grew to know it when we had a session like this with Mom. It was as if her Socratic segment was her giving phase, and the segment she and Dad were now in was when she collected the debts. We all knew not to interrupt her in this phase for two reasons: first, Mom deserved her moment for having patiently listened, and second, because there was usually a special insight that she had, making it worth the wait.

"Fred, for me, it's not about the money," Mom said. "We are tight, yes, but we are doing okay. It really comes down to what you want. Would you miss being a head coach? Would you miss the players and coaches that are part of your team?"

Dad interjected, "But we aren't a good team yet. And with only a one-year contract, if we don't win more games, we might be out of a job in November. And if we have another losing year, you and the kids will have to put up with more negative comments from the public."

Mom winced at his comment and lurched forward on her chair. Her butt was on the edge of the cushion as if she were poised to pounce. "Now, wait a minute!" she said. "Is *that* what this is all about?"

Given the severity of Mom's look, Dad knew this was not the time to answer her question. "Who cares about those jerks?" Mom shouted. "People will say what they say, and we can handle it." She stood up, shaking her finger at him. "I am tough, Fred! And the kids are tough! We can handle anything. We are part of the Dunlap Team and we stick together. *Nobody can hurt us!*"

Dad sat silently with his indignant wife standing above him. He looked down, like a kid who had been scolded. And after a momentary pause, he quietly asked, "So what do you want to do, Marilyn?"

Mom didn't answer him immediately. She looked around the room for a moment (perhaps for dramatic effect) and then sat back down. "I know this job has been hard," she said in a measured, thoughtful tone. "I know you are trying to do this with little or no support from Leckonby. And I know you are frustrated by not having had more success to this point. But do you think your program is better than it was in 1965?" He nodded. "And do you think your program is better than it was last year?" Again, he nodded. "And do you think you are on the *right track* to become better next year and the year after?" Dad nodded again.

Mom sat forward like a prosecuting attorney about to make her closing argument. "Well, then you *are winning*. Sure, the number of games won may be few. But the things you believe in—the things that you think are essential for winning—are taking hold."

Dad started to speak but Mom kept on going. "Fred, we don't know the future, but we do know the present. And at present, you are the head coach at Lehigh University, and you are making undeniable progress. You know that you have another year to make *more* progress. And I know that's what you will do. We don't know if you will keep your job next year; fate will determine that. If they decide to remove you, they would be fools in my opinion, but that's their decision." Then Mom peered at Dad with a solemn look. "But if we make the decision to leave, that feels like we are running away from a fight. It feels like a retreat. And I have never known you to retreat from anything."

Dad soaked in those words as he sat quietly.

"And besides," Mom said as she lightened up, "I want to be here several years from now when we are a winning football program and be able to sit in the stands and smile at those opinionated jerks sitting around me! And see the looks on their faces when we win." She laughed defiantly. "We'll show 'em who's right! We'll show them how wrong they were to doubt Fred Dunlap!"

Mom's wisdom prevailed and Dad decided not to accept the job at UMass. He was more determined than ever to improve the Lehigh football team.

Don't Mess with Marilyn Dunlap

I HAVE SHARED MUCH ABOUT my mother. Her staunch support for her husband and her kids is well documented. Much of the description has been told through stories occurring within the family unit, and in most cases, inside our home.

However, you should not conclude that her reach was limited to the family and the home. Simply put, the Cobra went where the Cobra needed to go.

During the first few years at Lehigh, fans were harsh toward my father and the team. As Mom, Jessie and I sat in the stands watching the team lose, we endured harsh bellowing around us.

Mom had prepped us in 1965 that "some fans may say dumb things." She added, "They don't really mean what they are saying—they are just excited about the game. If they say something mean about your dad, don't pay any attention to it." We were pretty young, and this took some adjustment for Jessie and me. The three of us rooted for the team. We clapped when good things happened. We sat quietly (almost invisibly) when bad things happened. And when bad things happened, caustic remarks from the crowd prevailed.

Because we kept a low key in the stands, most people around us didn't know our affiliation with the team or the head coach. But all of that changed during one game at Taylor Stadium. It was a hot day and it was crowded around us in the stands. Lehigh, a heavy underdog, had difficulty moving the ball against the opponent's defense.

As the game progressed, Lehigh fell behind by a big margin. Sitting a row in front of us, there was an alum who was especially loud and outspoken. Because we were losing, his opinions were negative and cutting. He had a friend who was sitting behind us, and throughout the game, the alum had carried on a discussion with him about his displeasure with the team. A few examples included:

- "We can't do ANYTHING right!"
- "We can't even hold onto the ball!" he yelled when we fumbled.
- "This quarterback is terrible! Don't we have ANYBODY who can throw the ball?"
- "These players don't know what they are doing! Don't we have any coaches for this team?" he bellowed with sarcasm.
- "Dunlap, what do you do all week? I can see that you aren't spending any time coaching!"
- "Why do we even have coaches? Give the money to the wrestling team. At least they are worth watching."
- "Dunlap, you are a bum!"

All the while, Mom whispered to us, "Don't pay any attention to that guy. He doesn't know what he is talking about."

Jessie and I sat there inconspicuously, braced for the next volley of mean words. The man continued his rants, and the accumulation of comments was starting to take a toll on Jessie. She began to sob. And then she sobbed more. I looked across Mom's lap at her, and Jessie was now in full-sob mode. Her shoulders were shaking and tears streamed down her cheeks.

Mom put her arm around her to console her. I, on the other hand, just sat there quietly, trying not to be noticed. I was curious who this guy was, but I wasn't going to ask, for fear of blowing our cover.

As the game neared its end, the unruly alum became even more vocal and more sarcastic, causing the people around him to laugh at his jokes. The three of us were sitting in an *invisible Hell*, listening to a pack of abusive people. They had no idea who we were, or what kind of impact this complaint-fest might be having on us.

At one point, the woman next to Jessie noticed her crying. She asked my mother if Jessie was okay. My mother smiled at her and assured her that Jessie was fine.

As the clock wound down, fans began to leave the stands. When the man in front of us got up to leave, Mom suddenly lurched forward into his row and cut him off. She looked at him directly and stuck out her arm, as if to shake hands with him. She was standing in his way and he was startled by her advance. Again, she reached out for his hand and the man instinctively shook it.

"I'd like to know who you are?" she asked, in a firm, measured tone, as she gripped his hand tightly. Her tone seemed really familiar to me. *Heck*, I thought, *that's the same tone I heard whenever I had done something wrong.*

As the man's face froze, she repeated the question. "I would like to know WHO YOU ARE."

The man looked at her nervously, surprised by this sudden overture. He stuttered and then told her his name.

With the Cobra glare and the Cobra whisper, Mom said "Well, my name is Marilyn Dunlap and my husband is Fred Dunlap." The man's jaw dropped. And the reaction was similar among the group around us. The man tried to free his hand, unsuccessfully.

My mother smiled at him and at the other startled people. "And these are my two children. And for the last three hours, we have had the pleasure of listening to your football wisdom." The man looked at me and then at Jessie, who was now weeping openly. He began sputtering, trying to produce some form of an apology, but my mother cut him off by saying, "I just want to be sure I knew who you are, so that when Lehigh football is successful, I can remember this day and think of you."

Mom's words cut holes in the alum's chest. The man stammered and tried again to explain himself. Mom cut him off again. She looked at the scoreboard and then back at him. "Oh, I see the game has ended. It's time for me to get these kids home now," she said. Still holding his hand, she added, "But it's been a *real pleasure* meeting you."

Mom ushered us to the aisle and we started down the steps of the stands. The group we had just left was still there standing in shock.

When the next home game took place a couple weeks later, we sat in our usual seats. Not surprisingly, the crowd around us was a polite, fairly appreciative group of people.

That episode was vintage Marilyn D.!

It was another lesson for me about "Less Is More." I had watched my mother surgically eviscerate another adult, and she did it without losing her cool or being impolite. Wow! What power! Sure, Mom had done that with me, *but I was a kid!* Now I was seeing how effective her approach was with *any* person.

The alum was so upset by that exchange that he called Dad at the office on Monday and explained what had happened. He apologized to Dad, and asked if it would be okay for him to drive out to our house and apologize to Mom.

Later that week, while Jess and I were at school, Mom had a visitor at the house. And an apology. And over time, the alum actually became friends with my mother. And a fan of my father.

A few years later, Mom once again had to put a Lehigh alum in his place. Details to follow, but once again the Cobra defended our team, this time a player, in a tone that was more pointed than when she defended Dad and the program.

Living on a Shoestring

While Dad continued to improve the Lehigh football program, we enjoyed living in our house in a middle-class neighborhood. Doing so was symbolic of the high-wire act necessary to keep the family's finances afloat. High-wire acts require great balancers, and my mother was an Olympian.

In order to keep our costs down, Mom took on many trades. Not only did she make gifts and manage all of the household activities without hired help, but she performed the role of architect when our house was built. I am sure that might have been an awkward situation at times for the builder, but it saved on the cost of the home.

She made every rug in our house. By hand. Mom collected old garments wherever she could find them. Then she tore them into long strips of material. After tastefully matching certain colors with other colors, she began to braid them together. She created a long braid that looked like a serpent made of cloth. For big rugs, the serpent might be more than a hundred feet long.

Next, Mom began at the center, coiling and sewing the long sinewy snake into a spiraled pattern. We had braided rugs everywhere. And the cost to make them? Nothing but the cost of the thread and a lot of sweat equity.

While Dad spent his days at the Lehigh football field or at his office, Mom single-handedly remodeled the entire basement when we were older, relying only on a plumber and an electrician where necessary. All of the stud work, the drywall, the paint, the lighting, the flooring—installed by Marilyn D.

Mom also built a tree house for Jessie and me. Was it small and crude in structure? No, it had a spiral staircase and a railing! We couldn't have any unnecessary accidents, she was certain.

Mom always had some kind of project going. It could be reorganizing the attic. Or doing spring cleaning on the house—top to bottom. Or replacing the shrubs or pruning the trees. Or clearing the vacant lot behind our house so we had that "back forty" look.

But the most extreme example dealt with her rock walls. Mom decided the house and lot would look prettier if rock walls were constructed along the street and around the flower beds. In total, she built more than 200 feet of rock walls. We had rock walls everywhere. They weren't small walls: they were two to three feet high!

Where did Mom get the rocks? She walked the wheelbarrow around the neighborhood, picking up rocks from vacant lots. And when the wheelbarrow was full, she wheeled it all the way back to our house. This project took her *two years* to complete. After it was done, I noticed a surprising scarcity of rocks in the neighborhood.

The common thread regarding all of her activities is that Mom did it herself, or with the help of us kids. Mom wasn't bothered by how little discretionary money we had. Her goal was to make the most of what we had and to make her house and yard look as good as they could look. Why? Because our house was a symbol of the Dunlap Team. And a team sticks together.

Dad was certainly dedicated to his job but Mom was inexhaustible. Her enthusiasm and pride supplied the fuel for whatever challenge she attacked. She was a spirited lady. Jessie and I got to witness first-hand how nothing was impossible…and how anything can be accomplished if you commit yourself fully to it (one of the Dunlap Rules).

She and my father were very similar people that way, though they worked on opposite sides of South Mountain. My father believed that no hill was insurmountable with the right amount of effort and conviction. It was about *willing it to happen* and doing whatever it took. Both my parents were captivated by envisioning how something might be improved. Even after they had improved something, they continued to study it to see if there might be some way to make it even better. They were both driven and both perfectionists, though their trades were substantially different.

One of the things Mom is most remembered for by the neighborhood kids and parents on Willowbrook Drive was her Track & Field Day. We were seven or eight years old when Mom decided to organize this event. She had observed the kids sitting around, somewhat bored, as the summer dragged along, and she decided that some fun needed to be injected into the neighborhood.

To publicize the event, Mom created a flier and sent a copy to each of the homes, announcing that a Track & Field Day would be held in early August at the Dunlaps' house. The positive response was overwhelming—so strong that she elected to break the kids into age groups: 5-7 years old, 8-10 years old, 11-13 years old and 14-16 years old.

The events included:

- 50-yard Dash
- 200-yard Run
- High Jump
- Obstacle Course
- Three-legged Race
- Wheelbarrow Race
- High Hurdles

Mom organized every event. She even used one of Dad's stopwatches to time the races. How she kept 20+ kids under control during the day-long event is hard to imagine. But she seemed to do it effortlessly.

At the end of the event, there was the Treasure Hunt. Mom enlisted the support of other parents to hide the clues. There was a different hunt for each age range, and the degree of difficulty was geared accordingly.

Mom blew the whistle and the kids took off, running from station to station to find the clues. Each clue was a poem my mother wrote (there's that English major again) and each clue directed the kids toward the next clue, which was another poem.

The last clue directed the kids to a treasure. Upon finding the treasure, that group of kids brought it back to our house where they got their prize. The prize was always a big pile of cut-up watermelon—one pile for each age group.

After a full day of races and other events, the kids were hot and sweaty. To cool us off, Mom turned on a sprinkler, and we ran under the water to cool down.

When all of the treasure hunters had returned from their hunt,

Mom held the awards ceremony. Each age group winner received a small trophy. The trophies weren't anything expensive or special, but everybody wanted to win one.

The 1st Annual Track & Field Day was such a hit that there was a second one. And then a 3rd annual event.

Older kids who aged out of the 14- to 16-year-old class pleaded with my mother to add a 17- to 19-year-old class. She decided against it, but instead enlisted their support to help her run the Track & Field Day in following years.

This event was so popular that my mother began receiving calls in May from neighbor parents who were planning their summer trips. They said, "We are going out of town on vacation, but our kids wanted to make sure we weren't gone when the Track & Field Day was taking place. Have you picked a date yet?"

Of everyone involved, I think my mother had the most fun with this event. In many ways, she was carrying the legacy of her father by being the camp counselor for the neighborhood.

The Track & Field Day was a huge undertaking, requiring weeks of planning. For a woman who was living on a shoestring, the costs were an extra expense we really couldn't afford. Years later when I asked her about that event, she smiled and shrugged. "It wasn't all that much," she said. "You can get a lot out of a little money, if you put your mind to it."

Heartbreak Hill—The Fall 1968 Campaign

DAD'S 1968 SEASON BEGAN JUST like the year before, with a big opening game win against Drexel (59-21). The enthusiasm for that win quickly faded, however, as Lehigh lost the next four games, each by a fairly wide margin.

During the sixth week of the season, Lehigh won convincingly against Gettysburg (34-14) but the following three games were lost, with only one of the games being close.

Lehigh had two wins and seven losses, and the only remaining game was the annual rivalry against the Lafayette Leopards, who came into the game with a record of 7-2 for the season. The game was held in Easton, Pennsylvania, 10 miles from Bethlehem.

Due to Lehigh's losses, the fans and media in the area were calling for my father's head. Lehigh had only four wins in nearly four complete seasons, and the newspapers and the radio pundits were predicting there was no way Dad would keep his job. "It's just a formality at this point" one reporter suggested. "Dunlap will be removed next week after the season is over."

When I arrived home after school on Wednesday that week, Mom told me my father had some exciting news for me when he came home later. That piqued my curiosity. I ate dinner and finished my homework, essentially clearing my schedule for whatever news Dad was going to bestow on me.

Dad arrived home right before my bedtime and sat down with me. He asked, "How would you like to come down on the sideline this Saturday and watch the game with the players and coaches?"

"Wow!" I said. "Really?"

"Yep," he replied. "Your mother and I talked about it, and we thought you were old enough now to do this. Plus, it's the Lehigh/Lafayette game. What better time to have your first game on the sidelines?"

Holy cow, I thought, *I'm going to be right in the middle of the action.* That had only happened previously during practice. But this was a *game*. This was huge! I was in the *big time*.

I couldn't contain my excitement. The two days couldn't have gone by fast enough for me. For my parents, however, those two days could not have been more excruciating. What I didn't know was that my parents had decided to let me be on the sidelines because they thought it might be the last game Dad coached at Lehigh. And they wanted me to have the experience of being right next to him for his final game if that's what it was.

With the rumors swirling earlier that week, my parents had quietly talked about what might be in store for them. They discussed the distinct possibility that Dad would be fired. And then they discussed their options, which apparently was an unsettlingly short conversation.

If Dad got fired, he didn't even know if he would still be an attractive candidate as an assistant coach at another university or whether he would want to be. He could always get a job in business, he believed. He had offers before but had never acted on them.

Dad faced the prospect that this might not just be his last game as a head coach. It might be his final week of coaching. On the Friday before the game, I was blissfully oblivious. I was as stoked as I could be, totally unaware of the anguish and uncertainty that was consuming my parents.

That evening, Dad and Mom were expected to attend a reception held every year on the night before the Lehigh/Lafayette game. But on that Friday, amid the headlines of his impending firing, this would be a far more difficult affair to attend.

During the festivities, Dr. Lewis approached my father and said hello. As they shook hands, Dr. Lewis leaned in and discreetly said, "I know you have probably seen the headlines in the newspaper this week." He paused and winked. "Don't believe every word you read..."

Boom! Dad didn't expect that.

The next day I had my first experience on the sidelines. It was like being in battle and being on the firing lines. From where I stood, I watched a Lehigh team dismantle a very talented Lafayette team. The final score: Lehigh 21, Lafayette 6.

The Lehigh fans were so charged up that they stormed the field at the end of the game and tore down the goal posts. Lafayette fans were angry about the upset and tried to stop them. An open brawl ensued. Police were everywhere, trying to control the crowd. It was mayhem and a lot of fans got hurt. Billy clubs were flying everywhere.

I stood near my father and we both watched the fray. It was a scary sight. While watching, I also reflected on the game and the unexpected result. At the age of nine, even I could appreciate the magnitude of the day, and I was so proud of Dad.

The upset win (and the brawl) made the front page of the paper the next day. The *Bethlehem Globe Times* reporter had taken a picture of my father's reaction to the brawl. That picture was next to the article. Also in the picture, standing near to him, was me, his 9-year-old son. Our facial expressions were the same—our minds looking seemingly identical. But each of us had quite different emotional weeks leading up to this moment.

1968 Lehigh/Lafayette Game. Two Dunlaps pictured.
Two different generations, but the same expression.

Driving out of Easton that Saturday afternoon, I realized that another Thanksgiving weekend was upon us. This one was made more special by the big upset win over Lafayette. We celebrated it as we always did, the best weekend of the year!

My parents waited 5 years before they told Jessie and me the full story about that week in 1968 and about why I was invited to the sidelines that Saturday. Instead of telling us at that time, they chose to keep their drama concealed—for our benefit, they reasoned.

On the Monday after Thanksgiving, Dad drove to the Lehigh campus and met with Dr. Lewis. The president gave him another one-year extension.

Puberty—What in Blazes Is That?

During the spring of 1969, I started to become curious about more personal things. I was 10 years old, which was still a naïve age. But the thing about being 10 and at the end of 4th grade is that some of my classmates had older brothers who were in 7th and 8th grade and going through puberty. Nobody in 4th grade knew or used the word puberty. We were still pretty much in the Crayon Battalion.

With the influence of certain 7th and 8th graders on their younger siblings, primitive forms of sex education got spread around the 4th grade, and with that, our innocence started to be replaced by more adult concepts. Our vocabulary expanded to include words like "boner," "boobs" and "pussy."

I also learned about peer pressure that spring. Two kids in my grade had older brothers, and they had learned some interesting things from them. They talked about it in the cafeteria and on the playground. It sounded crazy to most of us, but they spoke to the rest of us with such authority that we figured it *had* to be true.

On the playground, Johnny would throw a football at another kid's crotch and yell, "I hit you in the BONER!"

And the other kid would run around calling others names. "You are nothing but a big fat fort!" I looked at those kids: they didn't look overweight. In fact, they were kinda skinny. I was confused.

There was no question teasing was on an uptrend that year on the playground, and the rest of us didn't like being teased. What do you do when you are being teased and you don't have a clue what the heck the bullies are saying? You jump on board and start doing it, too.

So across the playground there was a siege of 10-year-olds throwing balls at crotches (and boners) and accusing others of being big fat forts.

My joining in only meant that I was being a follower and succumbing to peer pressure. But the alternative was to become the target of the abuse, and I was convinced that wasn't the better option.

I sat in class one afternoon, bewildered as to what a *big fat fort* was. And by the way, what the heck was a *boner?* The boys had been throwing the ball at my ying-yang. Yes, I had a ying-yang, and I had enjoyed a certain fascination with it over the years in the bathtub, but there was nothing boney about it.

When I rode home on the bus that day, I was convinced that I must have some physical impairment. If all the other boys had a boner, why was mine like a Slinky? I had seen their Slinkys in the school bathroom: did they have a second one? Did they have *something* I didn't have? Holy cow, was I deformed?

By the time I got home, I had worked myself into an emotional wreck. My mother greeted me as I came through the door, and I decided it was time to ask her. After all, I couldn't bear the thought of having to go back to school the next day—especially as a deformed kid. At least I wanted to understand my non-conformity.

Mom could tell I was bothered by something. The conversation began almost immediately. I explained what had happened at school. She listened intently. Then she began to grin. And then chuckle.

Why was my usually empathetic and supportive mother laughing at me, amid my very serious plight? Here was her son, discovering he was missing a bone in his anatomy, and to make matters worse, he found out that he was a big fat fort.

Over the course of the next few minutes, I discovered it wasn't the *fort* that was big and fat, but rather...*the fart.*

In our house, we had always used the word "toot." And as a gassy kid, I was an accomplished tooter. When I inquired why we used "toot,"

Mom replied that she just thought it was a nicer-sounding word than fart.

Okay, that cleared that up. But what about my crotch problem? Was I destined to become a circus spectacle?

Mom paused and then looked me in the eye. "Tiger," she said, "you don't have anything wrong with you. You are *just fine.* You are a normal, healthy 10-year-old boy."

"But Mom, I don't have a boner. And it sounds like all the other boys do."

"Yes you do. It's right there." She pointed to my crotch. I wondered: *What is it with everybody's fixation with my crotch today?* I looked down and then back up, even more bewildered, asking, "Where?"

Mom paused again. I couldn't remember her ever being at this big a loss for words. I thought, *Come on, Mom, spit it out! I need to know what every other 4th grader seems to know!*

I sat there as she carefully began to explain what was eluding me. I knew I was on to something REALLY BIG when she began by saying, "I didn't think we would be having this discussion when you were this young."

Great, I thought, *I am ahead of my time—I am on the cutting edge. This must be good! Or...this might be bad.*

"You see, Tiger, when a man loves a woman..." She fidgeted in her seat. "And when he's with her..."

I was tracking Mom so far. Man loves woman. Check! *That's like my mom and dad,* I thought. And when he's with her? Check! *Mom and Dad are together when we visit Grampa and Gramma,* I thought. *Now we are getting somewhere!*

"And when they touch..." she stalled.

I was still tracking. Mom and Dad touched a lot. Check!

"When that happens," she continued, "the man's ying-yang gets hard like a bone."

Mission Control, we have a problem! I thought, before I interrupted her. "Mom, I touch Jessie and you all the time. And mine doesn't get hard."

"That will change when you get older," she said. "When you meet a girl you are attracted to."

Hold on a minute, I thought. *Girls? Attracted to? Yeah, when the sun stops shining.*

"Mom," I said, "girls are yucky. Look at Jess. She's really yucky. All they ever do is play with dolls. Why would I want to get close to that?"

Mom struggled with my lack of comprehension. "Like I said," she resumed, "that will change."

I asked a few more award-winning questions, like, "Once it gets hard, will it stay hard forever?" Mom replied, "No, just for a while."

And then I asked a good one: "*Why* does it get hard?" And then the breakthrough question, "Mom, the guys are also calling me a pussy. Slippery is a pussy, not me. Why do they think I am a cat?"

Another big pause, from the woman I have never known to lack for comment.

"A pussy is a slang term for the vagina," Mom said.

What in blazes is that? I wondered. It sounded like a southern state.

Mom then began a lengthy, meandering, borderline-technical discussion that left me wondering where this was headed. After all, I just needed a quick explanation, not an educational certification.

"Tiger, women have babies," she explained. "You know that." She pointed out the window. "The mother next door is pregnant right now. You can see how big her tummy is." Again, she pointed across the street. "She is having *his* baby," she said, referring to the husband.

"But Mom, what does that have to do with boners and pussies?" I asked. "Er, I mean, Virginias?"

"It's vagina, not Virginia." She laughed.

And then my saint-like mother, who I thought was wonderful in every way and could do no wrong, started to complete the final phase of the explanation.

Gross! I thought. *GRRrrrooossssSSSSS.*

Yuck.

Bleccch.

My mouth was agape and I couldn't even close my eyes to blink. My mind raced. Visions of my mother. And then visions of my dad. And, oh God, visions of them *together.* Doing *that.*

These were upstanding people, my parents, whom I admired greatly. And I thought they stood for the greater good. And all the while, they were...GHACK!

This was my indoctrination into a whole new world. I sat still at the kitchen table as she finished, and Mom, seeing me in my frozen state, got up to start cooking dinner. I wasn't doing a very good job of taking this in stride.

Just then my sister came in the door. Mom looked at Jessie, and stepped away from her dinner preparation. "Jessica, we need to talk," Mom said. I looked at my sister and she looked at me. You see, the "Jessica, we need to talk" line was something we had heard before. It usually meant we were in some degree of trouble. And as my sister glared at me, she probably assumed I had ratted her out on something.

But she wasn't in trouble, and I hadn't ratted her out....this time.

It's just that we were both pretty much the same age, only ten months apart. Because of that, Mom was consistent in her dealings with us. We were held to the same standards and we learned lessons together. So Mom probably thought Jessie deserved to hear our earlier conversation, too.

I was still sitting at the kitchen table in my fairly nauseated state. But I perked up to watch what was going to happen. I already knew the punch line, and now I had a ringside seat to a show I just had to see. Jessie, on the other hand, had no clue what she was about to learn. And I found it very entertaining to watch her expressions as each layer of the discussion sunk in.

Mom marched forward with her explanation. Jessie was quiet, still not sure if this was going to end in some form of punishment. But as they got closer to the highlight of the story, and Jessie started to visualize what I had spent the last hour getting my arms around, she looked at Mom in shock and then looked at me. And then she started crying.

It should be noted that Jessie was a professional crier. Not just your average crier, but a real pro. And her skill came with practice. She cried at almost everything. Bad things. Joyous things. Frustrating things. Everything.

The tears started streaming down Jessie's face. And she sobbed. It was kind of like a snorting, choking sob. Like she was suffocating. Or like she was crying while a towel was being stuffed down her throat.

Mom tried to console her while I tried not to laugh at her. Mom explained that this *was just part of nature.* But to us kids, it was a horror flick.

When Mom served dinner that night, I couldn't help but keep looking at her crotch—a crotch that had a whole new meaning.

When Dad came home, my eyes were again crotch-bound. Especially when he kissed Mom and hugged her. *Where is the boner?* I wondered.

For the next week, I couldn't concentrate on anything but that. I was consumed with thoughts and questions about this whole world of indoor Olympics. When I walked into a neighbor's house and saw the parents, I fixated on the fact that "they did it, too!" The neighbor lady was nice but she was out of shape and chunky. Rubbing up against her? Naked? Disgusting!

Gradually, I got more used to the idea of this nighttime sport. I was thankful for my mother taking the time to explain it to me. I could now confidently go to the school playground knowing that I didn't have a deformity, and that my ying-yang didn't need to be a boner just yet.

Why do they refer to that lesson as the "birds and the bees"? As a naïve 10-year-old, it sure seemed more like the worms and the snails. Or the aliens and the aliens. I thought it would just be better if parents simply called their kids into a room, sat them down and said, "Your mother and I would like to totally take away any respect you might have for us. We haven't seen you sick to your stomach in a couple of weeks, and it's high time that you puked again!"

Growing up had its surprises, but in 1969 the surprises kept coming.

Later that summer when Dad could take time away from his football coaching duties, we went on our family vacation, a trip from Eastern Pennsylvania to the Jersey Shore. We loved the beach and we spent a few days there each summer.

We spent the days at Island Beach State Park, with miles of white sandy beaches. Mom packed peanut butter and jelly sandwiches for lunch. We ate them sitting in the sand while we took a break from riding waves. After a long day in the sun and salt water, we drove back to where we stayed, which was a nearby campground. We had a tent, and we pitched it on our campsite. It wasn't a tall tent; even I had to bend over inside. It fit the four of us...snugly.

Mom prepared meals on a portable Coleman stove. She cooked baked beans right in the can, and she grilled hot dogs to perfection over the Sterno flame.

If we had to go to the bathroom or take a shower, there was a community bathhouse with one side for the girls and the other side for the boys, located about a hundred yards away.

Jessie and I thought camping was fun. We didn't mind tent lodging. We had sleeping bags, and Mom bought inflatable mattresses so we didn't have to rest on the hard ground.

I was tasked with blowing up the four mattresses. Boy, did that make me light-headed. We were roughing it, like pioneers. Going on vacation to the beach was a time for the four of us to be together, and spending time in the woods, camping after a full day in the sun, was a delight, too.

The tent was small and the campsites weren't much bigger. There were tents all around, pitched very close to us. On our first night there, I woke up in the night to the sound of howling. I woke Mom up. She was sleeping next to me. It sounded like wolves. "Mom, what's that?" I asked. More howling ensued. And then there was grunting. Were there wild boars out there, too? Grunting and howling. Howling and grunting. It continued as Mom and I lay frozen, listening. But then the wolves said words. A wolf howled "Yes!" And then "OH!" And then a boar grunted and cried, "Amy!"

And the wolf howled, "Don't stop!"

Wait a minute, I thought. *Amy? Don't stop?* Then I thought, *Okay, my education that year was continuing.*

In the morning, we rose and went outside the tent. Dad and I headed to the community bathrooms. I hadn't woken him the night before during the wolf and boar episode, but I wondered, as we walked, if he had heard it, too. And I wondered *if he wondered* if I knew what really was going on in the tent next to us. He didn't give me any indication.

We returned to the tent and I saw my mother working her Sterno magic. She looked up at me with a knowing smile and said, "The wild animals are gone."

That was probably the first time I had been included in a sophisticated inside joke. I just smiled back at her and asked, "What's for breakfast?"

The Turning Point—The 1969 and 1970 Campaigns

The 1969 Season

The dawn of the 1969 football season brought a couple of notable changes.

First of all, I was a fixture on the sideline for every Lehigh football game. My experience back in November at the Lehigh/Lafayette game was just too much fun. I had spent the off-season lobbying for a permanent position. Lobbying very successfully, I might add.

Best of all, I was given a job, assigned to be the ball boy for home games, assisting the officials when they needed a fresh ball. That was pretty much every other play.

During away games, I was in charge of running on the field after kickoffs to retrieve the kicking tee. Let that sink in for a minute. I was running *on to the college football field.* In front of *all* of the players and fans! I was a rock star. Or at least that's what my 10-year-old brain had concluded.

It was a blast. It made me feel a part of the effort and a part of the team.

Other notable changes in 1969 had nothing to do with me. With the advent of Dad's fifth season at Lehigh, he was fielding his first team completely composed of his staff's recruits over the previous years.

The NCAA had previously prohibited any freshman from playing at the varsity level, but that changed in 1973. In the 1960s, only sophomores, juniors and seniors could play varsity.

In 1969, the seniors on the team were players who had been recruited by Dad's staff in the spring of 1966. Keep in mind that the 1965 recruiting season was essentially lost, because of Dad's transition to Lehigh and the need to hire coaches, develop systems, and organize the program.

The 1965 recruiting hadn't been easy because Lehigh was losing and the newly hired staff was unproven. Gradually, however, the cohesiveness of the coaching staff and the reputation of the program were starting to build a following. As they opened the 1969 season, players like Don Diorio, John Hill, Rich Revta and Jack Rizzo were now eligible to play varsity.

The coaches arriving at Fall Camp were filled with optimism that this could be a better year than the previous one. They had three wins in 1968, which was an improvement on the initial three seasons. And Dad felt that they would be more competitive in 1969 than in any previous year.

Lehigh's toughest opponents each season were Penn, Rutgers, Colgate and Delaware. I will call them the "Big Four." Though Lehigh was improving, these teams still were decidedly better. When we played them, Lehigh was a heavy underdog.

There were usually a couple other games scheduled against very tough opponents, but those weren't perennial matchups. In 1969, these games were against The Citadel and Wittenberg.

Other perennial matchups were teams like Gettysburg, Bucknell and, of course, Lafayette. These teams were good, but we were reaching a point where we were becoming competitive and had a realistic chance to beat any of these opponents if Lehigh played well.

Lehigh opened the season in 1969 with an away game at The Citadel. Lehigh was no match for them, and we lost 41-16. The following week Lehigh played at home against Ithaca and defeated them 55-7. The third game was at Wittenberg and Lehigh lost a close one, 21-13.

The record at this point was 1-2 and Lehigh faced a five-week stretch when four of the opponents were the Big Four.

The team first headed to New Brunswick, New Jersey, to face Rutgers. The Scarlet Knights were undefeated coming into the Lehigh game. During 1969, the NCAA celebrated the 100th anniversary of the first college football game, played between Rutgers and Princeton in 1869. As a result of the anniversary year celebration, Rutgers played all of its football games in their home stadium.

Rutgers had a strong team and Lehigh came into the game as a huge underdog. The players knew that Rutgers was really good, but there were other reasons why this game was significant to the Lehigh players.

Over the years, Dad had recruited many players from the northern New Jersey area where Rutgers was located. Justin Plumber was from South Plainfield, New Jersey. John Hill was from New Brunswick. And there were many more.

For several of the Lehigh players, playing at Rutgers was like coming home. And in a lot of cases, many of their high school teammates were playing for the Scarlet Knights. The players on both teams, therefore, knew each other well, which gave extra meaning to players of both teams.

In the days leading up to the game, my father learned another reason why this game had significance. Dad got a call from one of his players who asked to meet with him. Defensive end Danny Hoerig was playing second string. He hadn't gotten much playing time that season, and Dad wondered if that was why he wanted to meet. It wasn't unusual for players to ask what they needed to do to get into the starting lineup. As it turned out, Danny was there to discuss something else.

Danny was a soft-spoken kid, and he wasn't there to complain about playing time. He was one of the players who hailed from the area near Rutgers, and he wanted to let my father know something else about the upcoming game.

"Coach," he said, "this game has a lot of meaning for me." Danny was slow to start his explanation. "You know the Rutgers quarterback, right? Well, I went to high school with him and I played with him." Dad was already familiar with the quarterback and had tried to recruit him to attend Lehigh.

"Well, Coach, there's one other thing," Danny continued. "Last summer, he stole my girlfriend. I know I'm not your starting defensive end, and you may not be planning to play me on Saturday, but I wanted you to know that if I got in the game, *I'd kill* that quarterback! I want to get back at him, and I will make you proud of me if you put me in."

Dad was learning that the Rutgers game had many forms of significance. He knew his team was predicted to lose by a wide margin, but he also knew Lehigh had a solid defense. While developing the game strategy that week, he thought that if the team could somehow find a way to stay in the game and keep the score close, anything could happen late in the fourth quarter.

As Dad related the story over the years, the Lehigh coaches instituted a new defensive scheme in practice during the week before that game. "Because Rutgers had an excellent passing offense," he told me, "we put in a defensive game plan that only rushed four linemen. We also intended to play a two-deep safety, with five other players playing *under man*. This meant that those five players would cover each of the receivers (man-to-man coverage) from the start of the play and on short yardage pass routes. The two safeties would need to cover center field. They would be responsible for the deep pass, while the other five flowed underneath, covering their respective pass receivers." He concluded, "The defensive plan was a blend of *man-to-man coverage* and *zone coverage*, which we thought might confuse the hell out of the Rutgers coaches and quarterback."

"To change things up, we planned to blitz our linebackers on some plays to put more pressure on the quarterback. We figured our defensive linemen would be no match for their talented offensive line. And if we didn't blitz, the quarterback would have "all day" to throw the ball, which wouldn't be good." Dad intended to rush two or even three linebackers when they blitzed.

In the locker room before the game, I remember the message my father gave to the team. "Men, their passing game is very good, but I want to shake the quarterback up early in the game and see if we can rattle him." He implored the players, "On the opening defensive play, we are gonna blitz our linebackers. We're going to *sell out* to get back there and knock that quarterback on his ass!" He turned to the safeties. "Now you safeties! We can't afford to get beat deep early in the game, so if you have to, I want you to hold the receivers. You just can't let them catch the ball."

Following the speech, the Lehigh team took the field to conduct pre-game warm-ups. What they didn't know was that Rutgers' players had a little pre-game surprise for them.

In an attempt to taunt the Lehigh players, Rutgers took the field that Saturday by running out of the locker room and right through the area where Lehigh was conducting its pre-game warm-ups, disrupting the team's drills. The Rutgers players had attempted to intimidate the Lehigh players, but it angered them instead.

On the opening defensive play, Lehigh brought seven players on the rush and they sacked the quarterback for a 15-yard loss with multiple Lehigh players piled on top of him. But there was a flag on the play. The officials promptly marched off the penalty for defensive holding. As Dad recounted later with laughter, "Our safeties practically tackled the receivers. They weren't gonna get beat deep."

Dad's goal had been achieved. The Rutgers quarterback learned early what it felt like to have his shoulder blades embedded in the turf.

"Early in the game, I could see that our defensive line couldn't beat their offensive line," he confirmed, "and when we weren't blitzing, the quarterback had a lot of time back there. But our hunch was right: our pass defense did confuse him. And with seven guys back in the secondary, we were able to cover the receivers well and break up a lot of plays."

The first half was a war, but Lehigh held its own and Rutgers only led at the break, 7-3. In the second half, the teams traded possessions. As Dad had hoped, the defense kept the game close. Only trailing by four points, he knew anything could happen.

Late in the third quarter, when Rutgers was driving down the field, the defensive scheme paid off. The Rutgers quarterback threw the ball and Lehigh's Denny Clayton picked off the pass and ran it back for a touchdown. Suddenly, Lehigh led by a score of 10-7.

Rutgers pressed forward on the next drive, but Lehigh's defense held and Rutgers was forced to punt. Again, possessions traded hands. With only a few minutes left in the game, Rutgers again got the ball. After a few downs, the defense came up with another interception when

Chuck Lieb, a linebacker from Beaver Falls, Pennsylvania, jumped in front of the intended receiver and returned the interception to the Rutgers nine-yard line.

Lehigh had the ball and the lead, and we were deep in Rutgers' territory. The Lehigh sideline was bedlam—players, coaches, trainers, equipment managers and a 10-year-old, all were jumping around over the sudden turn of events.

Over the years, Dad told me that he had wanted to call timeout to get everybody settled down, "but we had burned all of our timeouts earlier in the half. Our defense had been on the field all day and they were exhausted. So we used all of our timeouts to give the defense a rest."

With no timeouts, the offense took the field. Dad called their stock play, off tackle on the right side, giving the ball to the halfback, with the fullback, Justin Plumber, leading the way.

Three yards gained on first down. The clock was still ticking, devouring the precious time remaining.

Four more yards on 2nd down, using the same play, following Plumber's excellent blocking. Lehigh was now on the two-yard line and it was 3rd down. The clock was still ticking.

In the Lehigh huddle, everyone was anxious as they began to realize what was about to happen. They had been a four-touchdown underdog on that day, and they were about to beat Rutgers!

The same play was called on 3rd down—off tackle, right side. The ball carrier pierced the goal line and scored. With the extra point, Lehigh now led 17-7 with only seconds remaining.

After the touchdown, the Lehigh sideline erupted with jubilation. As the offensive players came off the field, they were met with hugs and screams. But the players coming off the field weren't jubilant. They were laughing. While my father congratulated each of them, he wondered, *Why are they laughing at a moment when they should be celebrating their accomplishment?*

Dad cornered a couple of them and asked what was so funny. The players couldn't stop laughing to answer him clearly. It wasn't until a bit later that Dad got the full story.

During those final offensive downs, the players were getting nervous, given what was at stake. In particular, Miles Belic, the right guard from Steelton, Pennsylvania, got very nervous.

The team had called the 1st and 2nd down plays to Belic's side, and after 2nd down, he returned to the huddle and complained he was feeling sick. The other players around him told him to suck it up.

On third down, as they again ran to the right behind Belic, he exploded into the Rutgers defensive lineman and drove him onto his back to clear the way for the touchdown run. As he lay on top of the Rutgers defender, Belic lost control and threw up all over the guy.

The sight of a Rutgers player lying on his back with vomit all over him was what set off the laughter. The moment became famous to anyone closely connected to Lehigh football. It was and will forever be remembered as the "Barf Block."

The game ended. Lehigh completed a huge upset.

As for Danny Hoerig and his vendetta with the Rutgers quarterback, Dad decided to play Danny in that game. He actually played a lot. Dad told me, "Danny made some great plays. But then again, he had some 15-yard penalties too, for roughing the passer."

The Rutgers win in 1969 made a huge statement for the Lehigh football program. It put them on the map. Nobody cared what the 1969 record was: everybody just wanted to know *how the hell did you beat Rutgers?*

Adding to their credibility, the team that year also managed to tie Colgate (14-14)—another of the Big Four.

At the end of the season, Lehigh finished with a win against Bucknell and then a convincing win over Lafayette. They finished 4-5-1. It was technically a losing season but it didn't feel that way, given the great performances at Rutgers and Colgate. Those two games were critical to the program and to future recruiting.

The 1970 Season

Lehigh football—1970 Coaching Staff (Dad is bottom row, second from the left).

THE FOLLOWING YEAR, I STILL had my job on the sideline. The wages were slim, but I loved the connection to the team.

One of the greatest experiences was being with the team in the locker room before the game, during halftime and after the game. It wasn't that it smelled good after the game; it actually didn't. It was the smell of hot leather and perspiration. While that was a little funky, I looked forward to eating the postgame snack with the players. That amounted to drinking cans of Coke and eating slices of oranges from the heaping piles the managers had prepared.

But what I appreciated most about the sessions in the locker room were the emotions that were palpable, consuming every cubic foot of the room. There were moments of tenseness before the game, as each player sat silently, preoccupied with the impending battle. There were frustrations at halftime as they discussed what wasn't working or what strategies needed to be altered in the second half. And there were joyous (or disappointing) moments that came from the game's ending.

Over the years, I watched the jubilation and the heartache, and through both, I learned to appreciate the intensity that came with the team's commitment to what they were doing.

Amid all of that intensity stood the head coach, my father. I could see it in his eyes as he paced before games, as he ardently worked to make adjustments at halftime, and as he searched for the right words to convey to the players to give them perspective after wins or losses.

Dad's pre-game talks were epic—everybody yearned to hear what he might say. There were no two pre-game talks the same. I have listened to more than a hundred of them and I can tell you that they were all different.

What I also found to be fascinating, especially in the earlier years when I was younger, was that Dad talked to the players with the same tone and same cadence that he used when he spoke to Jessie and me at home. When I first was invited to attend these intimate moments, I didn't know what to expect. I had seen movies where generals would shout to their troops, "Get over that hill, men!" I assumed I was going to witness an altered version of my father in that setting. Something like "Kill 'em! Beat 'em! Eat 'em!"

There was none of that. Dad was always soft-spoken and, at a relative level, a man of few words. That made each word more potent.

For each game, Dad addressed the team a few minutes before they took the field. You could hear a pin drop, as every player was filled with tension, most of them staring vacantly at the floor, consumed by the uncertainties before a battle...until Dad started.

Their coach tended to pace at first, looking at the floor as he walked. It was his own authentic way of getting going. Like a wind-up for a pitcher or a pre-shot routine for a golfer, Dad paced. He would look up briefly and intensely at a few players. He would look down and pace some more. Then he began. With his first word, every head that had been staring at a floor tile with a vacant expression would suddenly jerk up and fixate on their coach.

"Men (he began every speech by addressing the players as *men*), we have spent nine months preparing for this day. Nine months of training and nine months of thinking and planning, knowing that this day would come."

Dad's message addressed things unique to the team we were playing or unique to something our team was doing or had accomplished. It was always topical and never the same.

Dad spoke in a measured tone. He was a master of it. It was a low tone. Not somber, but almost foreboding. It was a tone and cadence filled with determination. A tone almost subdued, but the pacing and the piercing look in his eyes left no question that right below the surface lay the potential for volatility and ferocity. He was like a volcano that steams, threatening to erupt.

Dad was *controlled fury.* And yet it was contained, leaving the degree of ferocity to the imagination of the players around him. As he neared the conclusion of his speeches, while his tone remained the same, the artful delivery of his words almost wreaked of indignation. Leaving the throng with emotions like, "Why don't we deserve to win?" Or, "Who the heck are they to think they can play with us!" And, "We owe it to ourselves to play great and control the outcome!" He rarely said those words directly, but he had a way of sending them telepathically to his troops.

I have heard hundreds of ex-players tell me over the years that they have never been more motivated in their lives than in a pre-game talk with Coach D. "I would run through a wall for your father," I heard some say.

Dad was a master at getting the most out of his players. It didn't mean that they won every game, but his goal was to have them in a mindset that ensured peak performance.

No matter how skilled an orator Dad might be, the reason his talks were so memorable and had such great influence on the players was really a function of what he stood for as a person and as a leader. He had built a program grounded by deep respect and deep commitment. The culture of the program, at its core, was driven by a man who treated people well, treated them fairly and established a consistent management style that could be counted on and trusted.

By 1970, that culture was firmly engrained in everyone who was a part of the organization.

The fall campaign started with a win but was followed by two losses.

Lehigh found itself with a 1-2 record before playing Rutgers in their fourth game. Rutgers was again heavily favored, but Lehigh defeated them 7-0. This win was validation for anyone who viewed the previous year's result as a fluke.

One thing that was quite different in 1970 was Lehigh's style of offense. As a philosophy, Dad felt that coaches needed to be sensitized to the talent on the roster, *not* the offenses and defenses they had historically used. Rather than force their players to adjust to the coaches' schemes, Dad firmly believed that the coaches needed to assess their player personnel and ask the question, "What style of offense would get the most out of the talent we have?"

This was an unusual approach to football coaching, but Dad was convinced that the coaches needed to be realistic with their talent and try to put the players in a formula that was most conducive for them to be successful. He preached, "We need to employ systems that allow our athletes to use their athleticism."

In 1970, Lehigh's starting quarterback was Jerry Berger. Jerry was not a strong passer, but he could really run. Jerry was 5 feet, 6 inches tall. So Dad felt it would be difficult for him to see over the linemen in front of him, which made pocket passing impractical.

The coaches therefore scrapped their previous offense and inserted a Split-T Option scheme focusing on the running game and the run/pass option. The change took advantage of Jerry's quickness and featured more effectively the talented running backs: Jimmy Petrillo, Don Diorio and Jack Rizzo.

With this new offense in place, Berger attacked the corners. Because of that, when he passed, he didn't have to look over the top of the lineman; he was in the open field. This change took several weeks to refine, but by the middle of the season, the offense was starting to really produce and score points.

Three games later, Lehigh was 3-4, heading into a home game with Delaware, one of the Big Four. Delaware was a state school, which gave it some significant advantages. They granted free rides to their football team and were much more lenient with their academic standards, both of which made them formidable with recruiting. They had no trouble competing with Pitt and Penn State for recruits: they successfully brought in excellent talent.

Most people who closely followed college football regarded them as a Division I–quality program. While they were technically a Division II football program, they were a powerhouse, beating some big Division I programs routinely.

Delaware was on Lehigh's schedule every year. In his five previous seasons, Dad had never beaten them. Moreover, each of the losses were by 21 or more points.

With Delaware coming into town, the coaches studied the films of the Blue Hens' previous game against Rutgers. Dad knew Rutgers well, from having played them three weeks earlier, and wanted to see what Delaware's defense had done to throttle Rutgers' offense.

What Dad and his coaches created requires a bit of a technical explanation, but it vividly shows the degree of engineering that went on every week as the coaches altered their strategies for each opponent.

"Against Rutgers," Dad told me, "Delaware ran an Offset Wide Tackle Six defense. They put a defensive lineman or a linebacker in each gap. And because Delaware's players were really talented, they throttled Rutgers in the previous week."

With this in mind, the coaches needed to find some offensive scheme that would be more effective against this defense. And then they noticed something.

It seemed that Delaware used that defense incessantly *unless* the offense put more than one wide receiver in a split formation. When an opposing team did that, Delaware reverted to a 4-3 defense, which was a defense the Lehigh coaches thought they could exploit. It would force Delaware into a three-deep zone instead of man-to-man pass coverage, and Jerry Berger (Dad thought) might be able to pick apart their pass defense as he attacked the corners.

The Lehigh coaches changed every play in their playbook to include two wide receivers. (For the old Lehigh players who might be reading this, we played the A-3 and B-3 formations all day.) But the remainder of Lehigh's offensive scheme stayed the same.

The other change Dad made was to increase the size of the splits between each offensive lineman: they moved to 4- to 5-foot spreads. Delaware had such strong talent on their defensive line that Dad figured it might be hard for our linemen to create holes for running. He wagered that if his team set the spreads really wide, there might be holes for the running backs to get through, even if the offensive line wasn't able to move the defenders out of the way. Further reinforcing his decision, the best Lehigh offensive lineman that year, Thad Jamula, had broken his arm that week in practice. He was replaced by Howie Harmatz, and it was Harmatz's first game as a starter.

On defense, as Dad describes it, "We needed to stop their running game and their short passing game. So we put nine defensive guys on the line of scrimmage and *walked* our cornerbacks up to the line, so they could cover the short pass better. We had a two-deep zone with the safeties, which made us vulnerable to the deep pass. But Delaware hadn't shown much in films that said we needed to respect their deeper pass routes. So we took a chance that, because they were heavily favored, they wouldn't take the time to change their offense just for Lehigh."

When the game began, Lehigh's offense took the field. When they came to the line, two receivers were split out. And sure enough, Delaware adjusted into the 4-3 defense. And Lehigh ran the option, attacking the corners and sprinkling pass plays periodically.

On defense, our nine-man attack throttled Delaware's offense. By halftime, Lehigh led by a score of 21-7.

Quarterback Jerry Berger (#17) passing against Delaware.

In the locker room at the half, players were filled with enthusiasm. The atmosphere was electric. Lehigh had a two-touchdown lead on Delaware—a team they hadn't been able to be competitive with in the last five years.

I watched and listened to the chatter as the coaches conferred on any needed changes. And then the most memorable speech I can ever recall was presented to the team.

"Let's pull it together here, men," Dad said. He raised his voice to temper the noise. He was standing in the middle of the locker room, which got immediately quiet. He allowed the silence to permeate the group for a moment, while his eyes danced from player to player. He looked solemn and intense. By his exterior, you couldn't tell that he had a 14-point lead on the toughest opponent they would play.

"I want to conduct a quick review of things before we retake the field," Dad continued. He glanced up and down from the notes he held. "On offense, we are getting good results on a lot of our option plays and our run/pass option, and we are going to try to exploit that further in the second half. But we're getting penetration from their linebackers too often—we need you guys on the O-line to be talking to each other, so that we pick up those blitzes when they are coming, OK?" A lot of the heads nodded. "And on defense," he said, "we're doing a good job against their inside running game, but on the corners, we need to come up aggressively when you see the tailback go wide." Dad paused to look at the group for agreement. Then there was a moment of silence, as he lowered his notes to his side. He never took his eyes off the team.

"Men, look," he said and then paused. "I don't need to tell you what this moment means." He paused again, as heads nodded. "We have played a great half of football. But there's another half to play, and you gotta expect that they are gonna come back out and make a run at us. And try to take *this* away from us." More heads nodded.

"You are 30 minutes away from rocking the world," he said boldly. "Thirty minutes away from what might be the most memorable moment of your lives." All eyes were on him as he spoke evenly. "In life, you only get so many chances to do something really special. And you have a chance today to pull this off in front of your home crowd and in front of your family and friends. *Don't lose* this opportunity for immortality." He paused and looked for consent. And upon immediately getting it from every person in the room, he yelled "Okay, then let's go DO it!"

The room erupted and the team re-took the field. After the defense throttled Delaware again on the opening possession, the Lehigh offense cut through their defense like a knife and the lead was extended.

Lehigh played with the same or greater intensity that second half, and won the game 36-13. Like the Rutgers game the year before, this win shocked the college football world.

Lehigh lost the final two games and finished with a 4-6 record, yet the focus by recruits and alumni was only on the wins that year over Delaware and Rutgers. Nothing else seemed to matter.

Respect and Gratitude

THAT THANKSGIVING WEEKEND WAS DIFFERENT, but I guess in some ways it was the same, as Dad received another one-year contract extension, his fourth in a row.

But *Dad was different* as I observed him during the weekend. He had a different perspective—almost serene. Perhaps reflective.

We talked about the season. That wasn't different. We talked about what next year might be like. Dad had a strong freshman group in 1970 that would now be eligible to play on the varsity in the fall of 1971. But he was less interested in talking about the coming prospects for winning. He passed that off as, "We are gonna be *a lot* better." He seemed pretty sure where the program was headed.

The conversation reverted continually back to past seasons and past players. Dad talked to us about how hard the early years were. I guess he thought Jessie and I were old enough then to appreciate and handle it. He mentioned players who were instrumental during those early years. And though those were losing years, he spoke of each player as if he were the most important one he had ever coached.

I listened to him talk about players like Art Renfro and Hal Yeich, leaders on those early teams at Lehigh. He felt so privileged to have coached them, and he was so thankful for their commitment to his program and the Team Rules he had presented to them in 1965 and 1966.

Dad talked about Bobby Fonte and Paul Koepf, two defensive linemen from the 1967-1969 era, two players who made big contributions in those tough years. And then we discussed Mike Leib, who Dad felt contributed every ounce of his soul to the betterment of Lehigh football (and a portion of his kidney, I might add).

Rich Miller was mentioned. He was a tight end during Dad's first three years. Rich was the captain of the team in 1967 and a huge supporter of Dad's program. And guys like Jerry Berger, who was barely taller than the head coach's 11-year-old son. But, as Dad said, he played his heart out to make Lehigh the best it could be.

Dad talked about the team, but he referred to it as "the culture we were trying to foster." He was appreciative for how hard his past players played. He respected them as men, for how they were willing to adapt to the demands placed on them.

"I wouldn't do it any other way," Dad said. "But I recognize that the changes I made in 1965 were a shock to a lot of the players—a shock to their system. And I am gratified that they had the intestinal fortitude to embrace the changes I imparted, and to be leaders of those around them."

These were reflective discussions on that Thanksgiving weekend. It is anyone's guess as to how much of the gravity of his comments I was able to subsume at 11 years old. Years later, after he retired, Dad and I spoke many more times about the same people and his unwavering respect for them. With my personal maturity years later, I could certainly appreciate better what he was describing.

Dad said, "Those were hard times for all of us—players, coaches and families. And years later, it's sometimes the *hard times* that are remembered as the most special times...because you can appreciate the sacrifices that were needed and made to overcome some very daunting obstacles."

Well said, I thought.[2]

When the Dunlap Rules Don't Work—Fall 1971

AT THE START OF FALL 1971, as Dad looked forward to another football season, I was back on Willowbrook Drive where my life was growing in complexity.

Growing up can be hard, right? I think it depends on the age—some parts of growing up are harder than others, I would contend.

The period from birth through elementary school (6th grade) is relatively simple. For the most part, we are still intelligent pets during that time. We aren't old enough to be on our own. We follow the rules, whether they come from parents or teachers. It's because we lack independent thinking and independent resources to do otherwise.

Drawing a metaphor using mathematics, the complexity of life from birth through 6th grade is comparable to simple math—adding,

2 In 2014, my father received an email from Greg Zern, a running back for Lehigh from 1966 to 1968. Greg had decided to contact Dad and congratulate him for his accomplishments at both Lehigh and Colgate. In the course of his email, Greg apologized for the results during the time he played. He wished that he and his fellow players "had made Dad as successful as the players in later years had done."

Dad replied to Greg's email in a way that Greg may not have expected. Dad thanked him for the great things he and his contemporaries had done for Lehigh football. Dad told him, "You guys were there at the beginning, to help establish a tradition and a platform that then led to a resurgence of Lehigh football. Without that support, nothing of substance could have been built."

Greg and Dad had a good exchange over several emails, and Dad was touched that someone like Greg would take the time to reach out to him after 46 years.

subtracting, basic multiplication and simple division. Perhaps a little algebra. But that's about it.

However, on one September morning in 1971, when an intelligent pet showed up for 7th grade in the junior high school, it was instantly different. It was a leap to calculus in a blink.

The reasons for this instantaneous change are many.

First, we are thrust into a new and unfamiliar school with kids who are two years older. We aren't top dog anymore, like we were in 6th grade.

Second, we don't have one teacher—we have a different teacher every hour, and we need to find our way to a different room. We have lockers (that's nice), but we have to manage which books to hold when, or we end up late getting to class. And that's never good.

Outweighing both of these reasons is the one, largest, most preoccupying reason: girls.

Junior high is "Puberty Central." Each youth wandering the halls is a two-legged volatile chemical lab of exploding hormones. Only weeks before, I never even considered girls as worth watching. But these girls were different—they were 8th and 9th graders. They were very...how shall I say...sophisticated.

And I, too, was in the midst of the "Puberty Sweepstakes." That summer, I finally discovered my boner, and with that revelation, my latent worries over my potential non-conformity had finally abated.

Though I had located my boner, I was still in search of the pussy. But as I gazed at some cute 8th and 9th graders walking by me in the hallway, I was pretty sure I was closing in on it.

Another thing that became suddenly important on that first day in junior high was the word *cool*. In May of that year on the 6th grade playground, I don't ever remember that word being used. But now in

7th grade, it was everywhere.

"That's not cool," I heard someone say.

"That's so cool!" someone else said.

"He's really cool," some girls said, as they watched a 9th grader walk by.

What about the most popular teacher? Well, of course, he was the "coolest teacher."

Not only did that word get overused, but everybody had an opinion about everything. *Why, all of a sudden, is the world so judgmental,* I wondered.

Then rumor mills heated up. Heck, I didn't even know what a rumor mill was. People gossiping about each other. People picking on each other. Saying mean things. And people acting generally…weird.

Even my friends. They were suddenly different. They were still my friends and we got along well, but they were preoccupied with all of this as if nothing we did before mattered.

I began feeling insecure in this new world. Was I cool? Did girls like me?

Wait a minute! Why would I *even care* if girls liked me? They were from Yuckyland, right? I had confirmed that years ago.

Pretty quickly that September, I concluded that I wasn't all that happy about the transition from 6th to 7th grade. Just months before, the only thing that would qualify as *cool* was how far and hard you could throw a football. And now, all of my playground pals were fixated on which girl they were going to ask out on a date.

Did I miss an orientation meeting or something? Where did the fun world of balls, dirt bombs and pick-up games go? That had been the center of my world, the world of Mom and Dad and fun stuff at home and fun at the Lehigh football games.

Why is everyone focused on what they are wearing? I wondered. *And critical of what someone else is wearing?*

Overnight the world had become harsh. My parents had always told me to treat others the way I wanted to be treated. But these kids sure weren't acting that way. They were mean, and everybody was on edge because of it.

Kids craved attention, as if there was a "Coolness Meter." Everybody was trying to figure out how they rated and how they could *increase* their rating.

Worst of all, kids bullied other kids. Some kids got into fights. It was like watching *Wild Kingdom,* where the lions were having a field day chasing and catching the helpless gazelles. Those gazelles looked a lot like 7th graders.

I wanted to lead a life according to the Dunlap Rules, but I was discovering that there was a pack of lions that didn't give a damn about those types of guiding principles.

I kept a low profile at first, particularly while I was trying to figure out the freakin' rules of this game—the one I now found myself playing. Fortunately, most of my classes were with other 7th graders. The gazelles were safe there. The only time we mixed with older kids was in the hallways between classes and on the bus rides to and from school.

That's where I ran into trouble.

My bus was filled with kids from our neighborhood. One of them who lived on my street was Billy. He was two years older than me, a 9th grader. Billy and I played together quite a bit when we were younger and had gotten along well. But that was back when we were intelligent pets. Now we were in junior high and things were different.

Billy was interested in a girl who also rode on our bus, but she didn't seem too interested in him. In order to get her attention (and confirm to her his primal prowess), Billy began picking on other kids.

He didn't have the courage to pick on other 9th graders: he went after the younger kids. And one day I found myself in his crosshairs.

We rode home after school and he sat behind me. The girl he was sweet on was sitting across the aisle from me. Billy started to flick my ears, which really hurt. I told him to stop it, but that just increased his pestering.

Then Billy knocked my books on the floor (there were no backpacks in the 1970s). I began scrambling to pick the books up as the bus bumped along. By the time I managed to collect them, Billy knocked them on the floor again. This time, when I had my head down looking for my things, he kicked me in the face, causing my nose to start bleeding. I was really upset.

As I bled all over my books and clothing, I looked across at the girl. She had been watching me struggle to pull my things together and was smiling at the scene. She evidently was impressed by what Billy was doing, I concluded.

The truth was that I had a bit of a crush on her, too. And now it seemed that she was enjoying watching what was happening to me. I was hurt and humiliated.

The bus arrived at our stop and I jumped off. Unfortunately, so did Billy. He cat-called me all the way home, but he didn't hit me anymore. Perhaps it was because the girl wasn't there to watch.

When I burst through our front door, Mom looked at me in shock, since I was covered in blood. Being in the safety of my house, I broke down and started to cry.

I explained what had happened, and I could tell Mom was angry about it, but she began to counsel me about bullies and show-offs, telling me that they were *going to get theirs* in the long run. I remember thinking, *I don't give a damn about the long run. I've got to face Billy on the bus in the morning!*

I didn't absorb much of what she said. I was too distracted by the clear and present danger named Billy. After I settled down and got cleaned up, all I could think of was the image of *my girl* smiling at me during my compromised moment. Rather than think poorly of her, I wondered, *what was wrong with me, that she didn't come to my defense?*

There was no question I was having trouble with the calculus course. I didn't know what to do, since the Dunlap Rules weren't working.

Dad was out of town that night, meeting with alumni. I didn't get a chance to talk to him about it.

The next day was the same on both bus rides, to and from school. More pestering, more books flying, and more taunting. No bloody noses this time, but Billy's bullying seemed to be growing more intense with each trip.

That next night, Dad returned. He came home right after dinner and wanted to meet with me since Mom had apparently told him what happened. At that point, I was pretty worked up about this new threat to my world. Dad listened quietly as I told the two-day story. I pleaded, "Dad, what am I doing wrong to deserve this? Why is he doing this to me?"

Dad sat back, summing up his thoughts. I could tell he was mad, but he didn't say anything. I decided to throw out one more comment. "Dad, you and Mom always told us to treat people right according to our rules," I said. "And I have *always* treated Billy right. Why isn't he treating me the same?"

Dad then cut in. "Well, Tiger, the world isn't always fair. It isn't that you have been doing anything wrong. He's just being a bully and picking on you because he thinks he can get away with it."

Billy was a lot stronger than I was, and the only thing I could think was that Dad was right: Billy *could* get away with it.

"Tiger, he will continue to do this to you and make your life miserable," Dad said. He hesitated before adding, "Until you do something about it." Those words hung in the air, as I absorbed what he was inferring. "Sometimes, Tiger, you have to *meet fire with fire.*"

I sat there, wondering when this rule got developed. "What does that mean?" I asked. "I never heard that rule before."

"It means he will continue to pick on you as long as he can get away with it," Dad said. "The only way to stop it is *to stop him.*"

We sat silently for a moment as I pondered what he was saying. He was telling me that I needed to fight Billy, to get him to stop picking on me. *But Billy is bigger than me,* I thought. *What if I lose?*

"Dad, if Billy beats me up, then he will know he can keep picking on me," I said. Dad smiled and said that he didn't think so. "Tiger, at the end of the day, a man has got to stick up for himself. And no matter what the outcome, the wrong thing is to avoid the conflict and run from the fight."

Dad shared some stories of his similar experiences when he was a kid. That made me feel a little better but it didn't solve the problem I was going to face in the morning.

I asked Dad for some advice on how I should deal with it if Billy approached me again. Recall that Dad was light heavyweight boxing champion at Colgate in the late 1940s—so I asked him for some tips. We talked for a while that night until I went to bed. In the morning, he gave me a short pep talk before I headed toward the bus stop. He told me to "give it my all." It was reminiscent of another Dunlap Rule, but this sure wasn't how I imagined it would be applied.

As I walked to the corner, I could see Billy waiting for me. He was wearing a sinister smile. He made a few teasing remarks. But when the bus came, the only open seats were in the front of the bus, close to the driver. He couldn't do anything up there, but he whispered, "You got lucky this time. Wait until tonight on the ride home!"

I was full of butterflies all day. I didn't remember a single thing my teachers said. In each class, I sat staring at the blackboard, imagining the possible scenarios that might befall me after school. Would this crisis pass if Billy found someone else to pick on? Or would the threat stay with me?

That afternoon, when the bell rang, I headed to my locker to get my things, and then I started toward the line of buses. I stood in line waiting to board my bus. It pulled up with a screech and the door opened. I grabbed a seat near the front, and as I turned to sit, I noticed Billy was already sitting in the back. A mile or two later, he had managed to move up behind me and began flicking my ears. I told him to stop it, but he kept it up.

Dad had told me not to fight Billy on the bus, but to wait until we got off. As I fended off his slaps, I wondered how I was going to keep him off me *during* the ride. I quickly realized that we had a little gap in last night's strategy session.

Just then, the bus driver saw what was going on and barked at Billy to stop. Billy leaned forward and told me, "Just wait 'til we get off the bus, asshole."

When the bus stopped at Willowbrook Drive, I stood up. At the door, Billy pushed me hard, thrusting me off the bus. All of the kids on the bus were aware of the trouble brewing, and I could see them looking out the windows as the neighbor kids got off. I could even see *my girl* watching.

Billy was right behind me and was hurrying toward me, saying, "I'm gonna get you, asshole!" As he approached, I turned and punched him as hard as I could. It caught him by surprise and he went down.

Billy got up and we began to brawl. First we were standing, but it quickly turned into a wrestling kind of battle. We were kicking, scratching, throwing fists and throwing elbows, rolling around on the street.

I could say that I dominated the fight, but the truth is that I lost. However, in the course of losing, I gave Billy a bloody nose and I landed a few other good shots.

I'm sure the fight was shorter than it seemed. The last thing I remember as I kept swinging was a father from the neighborhood pulling us apart. He had gotten out of his car to break up the fight. After all, we were rolling around in the middle of the street, blocking traffic, and the man needed to go somewhere.

As he separated us, we were both breathing heavily and our adrenalin was at a boil. Billy and I walked home on opposite sides of the street, each nursing our wounds and not talking to each other.

When I got to our house, I was met at the door by my mother. I was just as bloody as the first day, except this time I wasn't crying and I wasn't upset. I was pumped up! I had worked up so much nervous energy that day, dreading the confrontation, that I now felt relieved. I had fought Billy, and although I probably didn't get the best of it, *I did survive it.*

Mom cleaned me off, as I gave her the blow-by-blows. She listened. Smiling, she told me how proud she was of me. I headed upstairs to shower as she reminded me that *bullies will get theirs* in the end.

Dad arrived home a bit later and we talked. He was serious as he listened, but he had an unmistakable twinkle in his eyes...like he was fighting a grin.

Dad asked me how I felt about everything. I told him I was sore, but somewhat relieved. Except, I said, that I still didn't know if this would change any of the bullying, to which Dad just smiled.

The next day, I was braced for more trouble from Billy. Would he try to retaliate? Would my bus rides continue to be a living hell?

As I walked out of the house, I noticed Billy coming down the street. I turned my eyes toward the bus stop, intent on minding my own business. Billy called out, "Tiger, wait up." He ran over to me. *Was this going to be an attack*, I wondered. I was ready for it, if it was.

"Hey, how are you doing?" he asked.

What did he say? How am I doing? This couldn't be Billy.

He slowed as he approached. "Hey, about yesterday...I, uh...I'm sorry that I've been bothering you. I have been trying to impress Julie and it got out of hand. I'm sorry."

I looked at him, trying to comprehend what was happening. I nodded.

He said, "It won't happen again."

I replied, "It better not."

That was the end of my troubles with Billy. He didn't bother me again. And there was a bonus. Word had gotten around that I bloodied Billy's nose. And because of that, nobody wanted any trouble with me after that.

The Dunlap Rules, I learned, have exceptions in certain circumstances. And while they should be adhered to when possible, there are alternative steps that needed to be taken if confronted with trouble.

On the night before the fight, I really didn't understand what my father meant when he said, "I don't think so" to my question of "What happens if Billy beats me up? Won't he keep teasing me?"

After Billy's apology, I realized that respect comes from standing up for yourself. I had lost the fight but had gained Billy's respect for having the courage to fight back. Dad was right.

As for Billy, he didn't stop bullying people. I guess it was his perverse method of delivering a mating call to the rest of the junior high girls. Though I am not sure it ever got him many dates.

"Bullies get theirs in the end," my mother had said. Five years later, we learned that Billy died in a head-on car crash. He had been drinking and lost control of his car. Mom was right, too.

Having a Really Good Wing Man (or Woman)

Too often people give lip service to parents, family, and especially spouses.

How important is it to have a supportive spouse? On *ESPN*, we hear "Thank you, Honey, for believing in me" when the winner gets interviewed after an event. When a golfer wins a tournament, he (or she) says in the interview, "I'd like to thank my wife (or husband) and family for the support they have given me."

During my 30+ years of business experience, I have attended many annual award ceremonies where a similar thing has happened at a Salesman of the Year Award or a Leadership Award.

In the early 1990s, when I was a healthcare executive, the Salesman of the Year Award was bestowed on that year's winner. He said, "All of this wouldn't be possible if it weren't for my loving wife and her devoted assistance."

I knew a lot about this guy, perhaps more than he would have liked. And as I gazed over at his appreciative wife, I looked just past her to the table behind her, where another woman sat, who, among other things, was sleeping with the Salesman of the Year. His unknowing wife smiled proudly at her husband, unaware that only a few months later, divorce papers were coming her way.

A few years later, while I was working at a different healthcare company, I attended a similar meeting where a buddy of mine got an award. When he accepted it, he launched into a similar set of thank-you comments, and his wife was prominently featured.

I knew my colleague well and I also knew his wife well. She was a real pain in the ass—arrogant and domineering toward her husband. Her poor comportment wasn't restricted to him, either. She exuded an air of superiority toward everything and everyone as if she were entitled to anything she wanted. As for her lifestyle, she just expected him to keep making a lot of money to ensure that she could still sit at the pool at their country club.

After my colleague stepped down from the podium, he passed me on the way to his table—a table where his wife sat gloating from the limelight of his speech. As we shook hands, I pulled him in close. I whispered, "You're a liar." He smiled, and responded, "What was I gonna say? That she's a miserable bitch?"

Examples of speeches where the wife thanks the husband happen as well, and the "great spouse, great support" speech has become cliché. Usually only those who are really close to the people know if it's genuine or deserved. Even if it is true, just how supportive is she or he? The degree of support, like all things in life, is relative.

The question surrounds the definition of "phenomenal support" and "undying loyalty to the cause." A perfect illustration is my mother, but understanding the degree of her support and loyalty also requires inspecting what my dad was doing for the partnership.

Mom singularly managed the home, including all of the business aspects of the household such as insurance, legal analysis, and handling the tax filings. She was also very involved in Dad's work life. He confided in her most things about his job, keeping her connected to the ongoing pressures and evolving issues he was facing.

Dad didn't believe his work with the team had set hours but rather that it was a 24/7 responsibility. He also believed it extended beyond campus to the players' families, girlfriends, and, in some cases, to their complicated and sometimes dysfunctional upbringing.

With each year's arriving recruits, Dad essentially inherited a new crop of 18-year-olds. He called them "men" when he spoke to the team. But he told me many times in later years that he knew they were really just kids, and that he, as their leader, needed to anticipate there could be complications with their departure from home and arrival at Lehigh. The issues might relate to homesickness or problems with the hometown girlfriend. Or they may be having trouble managing their schedule, now that they were away from their home support system. The players could be failing a class, or having trouble resisting the temptations of the Greek system where party options were plentiful.

For any of these reasons, Dad felt the first fall semester was the most fragile time for most incoming freshmen. He reminded his coaches that it was their job to stay close to the players to ward off any potential issues that could develop. This fell under Dad's philosophy that *you can't be successful unless you understand and manage all of the potential variables.*

This philosophy actually began with the recruiting process. He felt that it was important to get to know the parents and siblings of each recruit. When high school players took their recruiting weekend visit to Lehigh, Dad invited the parents and family members to come along. He met individually with the player, but he also met separately with the parents. It was customary that he and Mom hosted a cocktail party at our house on that Saturday evening for all of the visiting family members. There were six to eight recruiting weekends each year, and they hosted a party during each one.

In many ways, Dad was a psychologist. He realized he could improve his chances at convincing the athlete to come to Lehigh if the parents bought in. Most mothers and fathers worry about their kids going away to college. Dad felt that by inviting the parents and letting them get to know him and Mom better, it might increase their comfort level that Lehigh (and Dad's program) was the best place for their son.

Another benefit to this strategy was that it also allowed him (and Mom and the coaches) to get to know the parents better. Not every 18-year-old comes from a stable, healthy, well-functioning home environment. When there was any degree of dysfunction, it often became apparent during those recruiting weekends. If the parent was a jerk, Dad and the coaches didn't stop recruiting the kid. But the knowledge of the problem made them better caretakers when he arrived on campus.

Without question, Dad's strategy was sound. But to make it all work, he needed his wing man to help in many ways.

That wing man, or perhaps better said, wing woman, was Mom. For instance, regarding the parties, Mom didn't have a caterer make the food (we couldn't afford that). She didn't have waiters serve the snacks (we couldn't afford that, either). Instead, Mom made all of the food and bought the drinks and served them, and she did that for the six to eight weeks straight during recruiting season.

Being a fanatic about preparation, Mom also asked Dad for a list of the recruits, including their playing position, their hometown, their parents' names, and what other colleges they were considering. Dad gave it to her on Thursday nights, and she studied it so it would be memorized by the time of the party.

Mom felt it was important to know every parent's name and to know something about them. That, she said, was what would make her feel welcome if she were visiting. Mom believed it was a sincere way to make people feel important and valued.

Between the two of them, Mom and Dad were trying to create a differentiated approach to recruiting, one where they could build enough trust and confidence that it might ultimately be the tipping point on a recruit's college decision. I remember hearing many examples over the years of when a top recruit had been offered a free ride to a big university but decided to attend Lehigh (and pay the high tuition costs) because the parents wanted their son to play for Fred Dunlap. That positive impression came from their exposure to both of my parents.

Mom was the wife of the head coach, but her *job description* didn't require her to do all of that. She wanted to do it. When it came to supporting her husband and the Lehigh football program, Mom was ubiquitous in other ways, too. Because she and Dad knew the parents from before the player got to college, she maintained a rapport with the parents in order to reassure them their son was doing well.

If a player caught the flu, Mom might visit his dorm room and bring soup, or go get a prescription filled for him. One player got pneumonia and was sick for weeks. Bedridden, he missed many classes. Mom attended his classes and took notes and then tutored him bedside so he wouldn't fall behind.

Mom was an English major in college and an English teacher when I was young. Through the years, countless players asked Mom for assistance with their English courses. I remember them sitting at our kitchen table with her while I was upstairs in my room doing my homework.

Students had to write term papers at Lehigh for other courses, too, but before the players submitted them, they brought them to Marilyn

D. so she could edit them. Mom didn't turn anyone down, but she did have one rule. She'd only edit the term papers with the student athlete present. Mom was glad to help, but she felt that it was important for the student to learn during the process.

The players weren't the only people Mom helped. Dad solicited her assistance in many different ways. Dad was asked to speak at events to many groups such as alumni, administration officials, university professors, and the general media. Dad asked Mom to write his speeches. All of them.

Mom was a great writer, and therefore, fully capable of doing it. But she needed input for each speech so she could craft the message appropriately to each unique group. Dad sat with her and described the audience, touching on any sensitive points that needed to be addressed. Mom took notes and wrote a draft for his review. They then refined it together.

Because Dad shared nearly everything about his work with Mom, those prepping sessions weren't lengthy. She already had a strong familiarity with the expectations of each audience and an intuitive sense for the messages Dad wanted to convey.

When Mom wasn't tutoring players, attending their classes, throwing recruiting receptions, editing term papers or writing speeches, she attended football practice during the week. She showed up as often as she could.

Watching practice is not the most exciting experience if you aren't directly involved in it. And October and November evenings get chilly while standing on a muddy practice field. But Mom did it anyway.

I remember asking Mom one time why she was going to practice. I was a young adolescent at the time, having a self-centered moment, and I was probably impatient about when she was going to serve dinner. Her idea of going to practice was only going to delay the special date I was planning with a juicy hamburger.

As she walked out the door into the garage, Mom turned and said, "I have to go. The players are expecting me to be there. It's important that they know I care. And it's just as important that your Dad knows I care." I got up quickly, grabbed my jacket and jumped in the car with her. She was right. And my date with a hamburger could wait. The points she made were more important.

The players *did* expect her. You could hear "Hi, Mrs. D.!" as they ran by. And she knew everybody's name. Some of that familiarity came from tutoring and editing, but she made it a point to know everybody's name and what position they played.

Mom even grilled Dad each week on who was hurt and how long they would be out of the lineup. She also got a briefing on the game plan each week after the coaches had reviewed the films of the upcoming opponent.

Because Dad shared everything with her, Mom knew if the other team had a weak pass defense and how Dad planned to exploit it. She also knew if he had put in any new plays, and she knew what Lehigh's chances for winning were. Mom conveyed the game plan to Jessie and me on Friday nights at the dinner table. She talked about the big game the next day and we listened intently.

My mother had a playful, mischievous side, too. Since she was a mainstay at football practice, the players began to kid her if she ever missed a session. "Hey, Mrs. D.! Where were you yesterday?" they'd ask. Mom decided to turn the tables on them during a Wednesday practice on Halloween night. She had spent the previous week creating a costume. Lehigh's arch-rival, Lafayette College, had a leopard mascot that the Lafayette students affectionately called "Spot."

For fun, Mom sewed together a leopard costume, including a tail and a mask, and she put a sign around her neck that said "Spot."

It was dark when Mom arrived at practice, and the team was busy practicing under the lights. She parked out of sight so no one could see her car. Then she crept toward the team. Within minutes, she was spotted. She could see players talking to each other and turning their helmets to look. They seemed confused at first as to who this might be.

Mom had brought with her a clipboard, paper and a pen. As she moved closer to the action, she play-acted like she was scouting and taking notes (on behalf of Lafayette, of course). She even slinked up behind the huddle but didn't say anything.

The players finally figured out who Spot must be. She could hear them laughing. But she still said nothing.

At one point, Dad told the team, "The Lafayette Leopard is here to steal our plays! Let's get him!" The team rushed toward Mom, laughing. It was good fun for Mom, for the coaches, and for the players.

SPOT! Equipped with a mask and a tail…and a clipboard.

The visit by Spot became an annual tradition after that Wednesday night.

Mom was truly more than a coach's wife. She was like a mother to many of the players. She did so many things for the team, and she did them because she cared. That's what she tried to explain to me that one evening in the garage.

I don't think my mother fully realized the impact she made. She did so many things that weren't expected of her. But it was the *extent* of her commitment that, I believe, sent a unique message to anyone associated with Lehigh football. The example that Mom made with each gesture reinforced what my father had been preaching to his team about "Commitment to the Cause," and a sense of "It's us against the world."

The players and the coaches saw that if a coach's wife was willing to extend herself to this degree on their behalf, then there was no question that everyone should be "all in." Even that wonderful, crazy coach's wife, who liked to run around in a leopard suit.

The Little Things Took Care of the Big Things—Lehigh Football in 1971

Six football seasons had passed since Dad pulled the family together in the kitchen to announce our move to Lehigh. Those years had not been easy for him. And when Lehigh lost games, it had not been easy for Mom, Jessie or me, either. However, during those six years, Dad and his coaching staff had consistently made progress, and he acknowledged to me in later years that he became a better coach with each year of experience.

The program then was better each year as well, if only for the precision with which they went about their work. Better practice methods. Better scouting practices. Better off-season training programs. Better, more trusting relationships with the admissions office and the faculty. Better alumni support. Better recruiting relationships with high school coaches. And an ever-increasing mystique surrounding the Lehigh football mission. This created momentum with the quality of incoming freshman players.

These elements were hugely important to the revitalization of Lehigh football. But Dad considered them to be the *little things*, which were important ingredients for success. "For if you execute well on the little things," he would say, "the big things take care of themselves."

During the sixth year, Dad had gotten a glimpse of the quality of athletes that played on the freshman football team. And now, 9 months later, those freshman players were coming to Fall Camp as sophomores to join the varsity.

This incoming sophomore class included Kim McQuilken at quarterback, tight end Bill Schlegel, offensive tackle Dan Mulholland and linebacker Roger McFillin. They joined upperclassmen like Jack Rizzo, John Hill, Donny Diorio, Jim Petrillo and Blake Johnstone. Entering his seventh year as head coach, Dad was bullish about Lehigh's chances.

The 1971 Lehigh football team

With Jerry Berger having graduated and the promising young quarterback McQuilken eligible, Dad had to rethink his offensive scheme. Berger's skills could best be featured in a run-style offense, but McQuilken was a terrific passer and tall enough to throw effectively over the offensive linemen.

To give the team their best chance for success, he again designed the offensive scheme to accentuate the capabilities of his players. Dad therefore discarded the 1970 offensive scheme and replaced it with a Pro-Style offense, which involved more drop-back passing, with play-action to set up the running game.

Lehigh expanded its schedule to 11 games in 1971. They opened against Hofstra and the following week played C.W. Post. Lehigh dominated both teams and was 2-0 for the first time in Dad's tenure. After a loss to Penn in the third game, Lehigh ran off three more wins against Vermont (49-8), Rutgers (35-14) and Drexel (48-20). The team was 5-1 through the first half of the season and they had scored a lot of points. The offense was potent and balanced: McQuilken was flanked by a strong offensive line and some talented receivers and running backs. The team was really starting to hit their stride.

Lehigh's next opponent was Gettysburg, a team they were expected to beat. Expected to beat? Lehigh was favored? That certainly had a different sound than only a few years earlier.

During the week leading up to the Gettysburg game at Taylor Stadium, my mother quietly told Jessie and me that if Lehigh won, it would be Dad's sixth win of the year. With an 11-game schedule, that meant that the Gettysburg win would assure a winning season. Mom had been waiting for years to reach that moment, as she reminded us continually, "to show those naysayers that they were wrong. We'll show 'em who's boss!"

On that Saturday, Lehigh beat Gettysburg, 50-0.

Without Dad's knowledge, Mom had created a big sign that week and hid it in a closet. When Dad came home that evening, he saw the sign on the garage door, which read, "We always knew you were a winner! Now the WHOLE WORLD knows!"

Unfortunately, Lehigh lost their next two games to Colgate and Delaware. The Big Four were still pretty good. With a record of 6-3, Lehigh faced Bucknell and Lafayette to complete their season. We beat both teams convincingly, and in the Lafayette game, Jack Rizzo ran wild, setting a single-game rushing record with 313 yards. (A Lehigh record that still stands today.) Lehigh finished the season with an 8-3 record. It was the first winning season for Lehigh in 10 years.

Thanksgiving weekend didn't disappoint. The family had a great time together as we always did. And on that next Monday, Dad met with Leckonby and Dr. Lewis. And he was given a three-year contract.

Progress. In many respects.

An Entrepreneur Is Born

I WAS ALWAYS FASCINATED WITH math. When I was young, I counted everything. I had also figured out how to multiply at an early age. I was so fixated on numbers that my parents called me *The Number Nut*.

Riding in the backseat of the car, when we would pass a 35-mph sign, I thought to myself, *3 times 5 is 15* and *3 minus 5 is negative 2*. And if we passed a sign that said "84 miles to Harrisburg," I did the same ritual, all in my head. Was that weird? Yes, I suppose so.

But with that anomaly, you can bet I was doing the same thing with my bank account. I became very familiar with the concept of compound interest, and frequently sat down and figured out how much my account could grow in the next year, anticipating more allowance and more compounded interest. I'd proudly present my analysis to my mother so she could praise her budding tycoon.

When I was about 10 years old, I realized I could accelerate the growth of my bank account if I got another job in addition to my weekly chores. I talked to my parents about it, and they were very supportive of the idea. Dad said, "The best things in life come from working hard," and "True satisfaction in life comes from accomplishing things well."

That sure sounded like the Dunlap Rules to me. *But what kind of job could a 10-year-old get?* I wondered. There was really only one option: a newspaper route. So I did that for a couple years. And I was excited to see my bank account grow.

As I approached the age of 12, I heard about a job that youngsters like me could get: working as a caddy at Saucon Valley Country Club. I liked golf, and caddying seemed like a lot more fun than the paper route. I asked my parents for permission, since I needed them to drive me back and forth. They were supportive. In fact, Dad was quite enthusiastic, telling me, "Saucon Valley's a great club. Many Lehigh alums belong and a lot of Bethlehem Steel executives play there, too."

As a family, we couldn't afford to be Saucon Valley members. When Mom and Dad took us to play golf, it was at public courses like Wedgewood or Bethlehem Municipal, or we'd go to a small nine-hole course called Tumblebrook.

In truth, these courses were *cow pastures* with limited maintenance budgets. Nevertheless, amid the shaggy greens and the weed-filled fairways, we had great times there.

But caddying at Saucon Valley? Wow! This was the big time. There were three 18-hole courses and each was beautifully manicured. And the clubhouse was impressive, as well.

I had been there only once when my friend Tyler McCann and his father took Dad and me to play. Tyler's dad was a Lehigh alum and also an executive at Bethlehem Steel. They had been members at Saucon

Valley for years, and we had gotten to know them very well.

One cool thing about being a caddy, I learned, was that the caddies were allowed to play for free on Mondays when the club was closed to members. What a treat!

As the summer approached, my mother drove me to the club to apply for a position. I met Pinky, the caddymaster. I signed up and he suggested that I return the following week to complete orientation training. That night, Dad talked to me about the job. "Tiger, you already know how to play golf, so the caddymaster's orientation shouldn't be too tough. You remember playing there with the McCanns, so you are already familiar with one of the courses." I nodded. "But there are some *other things* I want to talk to you about."

This sounds serious, I thought.

"You will see a lot of things in this job," he said and then paused, wrestling with how he was going to make his point. "Golf is a funny game." He paused again. I was clueless as to where he was headed. "Golf brings out the best and worst in people.... What I mean to say is that you can and will learn a lot about people in this job."

In a serious tone, Dad continued. "You will see good golfers and you will see bad golfers. But what you will mostly see is how they handle it." My blank stare must have indicated I needed more. "You are going to be spending four hours in the company of people each day carrying their golf bag. And they may be having a good day or a bad day, and depending on which, you may see them behave well or poorly."

"However, no matter how they behave, your Mom and I are expecting you to *always* handle yourself in the manner that you have been taught. Do you understand?"

"Follow the Rules, right?" I asked. He nodded.

My caddy orientation was easy and I began working the next

weekend. As a first-year caddy, I was only allowed to carry one bag, which meant I received half the pay a senior caddy made carrying two. Still, I made $7 on my first day (a $5 bag fee, plus a $2 tip), and that was way more than the rate of my allowance. I was in Fat Cat City!

I caddied four/five times a week that summer, and the money I made went straight into my bank account. During that time, I refined my knowledge of the courses and honed my skills as a caddy. There weren't any measuring devices in the 1970s, so I had to memorize the distances to each green from the sprinkler heads in the fairways. I wanted to be the best caddy at Saucon Valley. So I studied everything. I got proficient at reading greens and began advising players on their putts.

I hustled all the time. I ran everywhere. I ran to get the right yardage. I ran to rake the bunkers and I ran to get refreshments for the players. I had convinced myself that, by making a superior effort, I could influence the size of the tip I received. But that wasn't always the case.

When the next spring rolled around, I was ready to start carrying two bags. It was twice the work, I realized, racing back and forth across the fairway to each golfer, but the pay was twice as much, too. For 18 holes, if the players were good tippers, I made $16, and if they were cheap, I made $14 for a *loop* (slang for carrying two bags for 18 holes).

If the golf courses were really busy, Pinky sometimes ran short of caddies and asked me to caddy a second round. If I got two loops in a day (36 holes), I could earn $30. I was exhausted going home on those days, but that was big money in the 1970s.

In the midst of my second summer of caddying, I was beginning to understand what my father had intimated about "learning a lot about people" on a golf course. I caddied for both lousy golfers and good golfers. I didn't mind the lousy golfers, as long as they played quickly. But the good players were admittedly easier to caddy for because there were fewer errant shots to chase and fewer sand bunkers to be raked.

I knew that wasn't part of the point that Dad was making. He was referring to what I saw those first two summers: people losing their cool. I saw them throw their clubs. I saw them take their anger out, inappropriately, on another caddy who was carrying the other two bags in our foursome.

I also saw some golfers cheat. Here they were, supposedly playing golf with friends, but they were cheating them.

Another revealing part of the human study happened when it came time for the gratuity. The tips I received were never consistent. It wasn't that bad golfers gave bad tips and good golfers gave good tips. Sometimes it was the "pissed off/played shitty guy" who gave a bad tip, just because he was in a bad mood. Other times a golfer who played well still didn't tip me well.

My work product didn't vary; I tried to outperform any other caddy every time I got a loop. It was how I was raised. I worked my ass off, and I took pride in my efforts.

One of the fascinating things I found with my new job was that I could listen to conversations between the golfers. It was funny how they played along and talked to each other and almost forgot that caddies were in attendance. It was like we were invisible. We were hired help, lugging golf bags over miles of golf holes, and there were times when the players didn't even acknowledge our presence. And sometimes they'd discuss some pretty confidential stuff.

Ladies' Day was every Tuesday morning. An army of women arrived each week prepared to play. No matter how many there were, they always played in twosomes. I quickly learned that cliques were in abundance at Saucon Valley Country Club and that, for women on Ladies' Day, playing golf was secondary to a steamy conversation.

I'd walk along with them quietly listening to the gossip, hearing nasty things about people who I might have caddied for just the day before. I might hear about secret affairs. Or about someone's illness, which was supposed to be kept confidential. But now it wasn't so confidential, because the 13-year-old caddy was now well-informed.

There were business outings where I would listen to deals that were happening but hadn't yet been made public. I might hear that an executive was about to get fired—a poor unaware guy, who happened to be playing in the foursome ahead of us.

As my father forecasted, I learned a lot about people as a caddy. Not all of it was positive, but it sure was educational.

I also got my *business degree* as a caddy. It was perhaps the best education I ever got, one that directly affected my business acumen years later.

I was one of about 200 caddies at the club, and each of us had a Caddy Badge with a unique number on it. There was no requirement to work every day—each caddy showed up when he wanted to work, but we needed to be there by 7 a.m.

Pinky collected the Caddy Badges and put them in a bucket, pulling them out one-by-one like a lottery. The first badge picked was the caddy to go with the first golf group that day. If yours was one of the last badges picked, you might have to wait 4-5 hours to get assigned to a loop. Everybody wanted to get lucky with the lottery, so they didn't need to sit around all day.

The caddies sat in the Caddy Pen and killed time until they were called. The Caddy Pen was a small building with a fence around it. It had a basketball hoop and some picnic tables. Caddies ranged from high schoolers like me to 70-year-old men. The guys over 25 all looked a bit ragged. I didn't know about substance abuse at that age, but these guys could have been the poster children. Er...poster adults.

Caddies played poker or shot hoops to pass the time. One of the older caddies was named Shaky Bernstein. We called him Shaky because he had an uncontrollable tremor. He was a good guy; it was almost like hanging out with someone's grandfather. He took a liking to me and told me stories about things that happened years ago.

Some of the other guys were pretty crude, so I kept a comfortable distance from them. I was also exposed, for the first time, to open prejudice and bigotry. Among some of the older guys, nothing was sacred. People's heritage and race were slighted. They would throw around words like "Spics, Dagos, Pollocks, Krauts, Gooks, Kikes"...and of course, "Niggers."

I had been raised to treat everybody the same. It hadn't even occurred to me that religious differences mattered to anybody. That was each person's choice, I always thought. Though I didn't voice it, I was horrified by how these guys spoke. It was a completely different culture from mine and I didn't like it. I therefore tended to hang out with the younger kids until my badge number got called.

Sitting idly in the Caddy Pen wasn't easy for me. I thought about all the things I could be doing with that wasted time. But when I got called, I always worked hard. And gradually, after caddying for so many members, I got to know which assignments were the best loops.

Each time my badge number got called on the loud speaker, I ran over to Pinky's office, full of anticipation regarding which members I would be walking with that day. When Pinky gave me the names, my heart would either explode with excitement or sink with disappointment.

It wasn't always about the money and avoiding overly thrifty tippers. Mostly it was about not having to spend four hours with someone who was a complete jerk. One day, I was assigned to caddy for a man named Bruce Davis. He was a really classy guy. I liked him very much. He was also one of the best golfers at the club. And if that wasn't enough, he was a great tipper and was always appreciative of my work.

As we played that day, Mr. Davis asked me how I liked being a caddy. I told him that I liked the work but didn't like sitting around in the Pen waiting for a loop. I also carefully logged the point with him that some members weren't as much fun to work with as others were. Mr. Davis smiled and said, somewhat out of character, "Yeah, there are some real pricks around here, aren't there?"

I smiled and took a bit of a chance. "Yeah, and there are some cheap pricks, too."

Mr. Davis asked me why I didn't caddy for him more often. "You're the best caddy I have ever had out here. You hustle and you know what you are doing." I told him about the lottery and that the only way I could jump the lottery is if a member asked for me specifically.

Mr. Davis said, "Well then, that's exactly what we will do." He then asked me who else I liked caddying for. And he tossed out a bunch of other names while asking, "Is he good to work with? Does she tip well?"

I answered as delicately and honestly as I could. By the end of the day, I had given him my home phone number, and he agreed to call me whenever he planned to play so I could be there to caddy for him.

Mr. Davis also called some of the other people we discussed and asked them to request me as their caddy. Suddenly I had been liberated from the caddy lottery, at least a few times a week. On the days when I had a scheduled loop with Mr. Davis or one of his buddies, I didn't bother coming in at 7 a.m. Instead, I just showed up at their tee time.

I told Mom and Dad about this development. They were excited for me and praised my ingenuity. While we talked, another great idea came to mind.

On other days, when I got assigned to golfers I didn't know, I observed them throughout the round. If they behaved well and tipped well, I'd ask them if they would like to have me again as a caddy. I knew the answer, because I had just worked my butt off for four hours, reading every putt and estimating yardages, both done accurately.

When these players responded *yes,* I'd suggest they ask for me specifically, whenever they planned to play. Gradually, I built a full caddy schedule, filled only with quality people who paid well. And the Caddy Pen was then a thing of the past for me, for the most part.

The business lessons I learned from this experience were two-fold:

That differentiation is critical to any form of business success—Had I not dedicated myself to becoming a superior caddy, I wouldn't have created the demand for my personal services. And to be sure that I was better than any of the other very capable caddies, I worked harder, running from shot to shot, showing a vigor that other caddies weren't willing to expend. This approach made a lasting impression on my clients. I remember a new client meeting me at the first tee one day and saying "Hey, you're the caddy that runs, aren't you?" That was differentiation—and it was not too different from how my parents approached the recruiting process.

That I had the guts to ask for the sale—Had I not had the gumption to confront certain members about requesting my services, I never would have been able to recruit them to *my business.* They would have just followed the standard method of working through Pinky and his badge lottery. *Asking for the sale* took guts, because I was putting my reputation on the line. What if they said, "You weren't that good—we don't care if we get you again"? Since I had just provided a product that I was sure was exceptional, asking for the sale became easy.

At 13 years old, I was learning valuable fundamentals for how to succeed in business. And I used those fundamentals for the next 40 years.

Respect, Personal Accountability and the Gift of Tolerance— The Passage from a Kid to a Young Man

Camping at the Jersey Shore wasn't our family's only experience with camping, and the Jersey Shore wasn't our only choice for vacations.

In 1973, Jessie was 15 and I was a year younger. Mom realized her chickens were getting close to leaving the coop. She often said, "You kids are growing up quickly and it's important that we make the most of the time we have remaining as a family."

With this in mind, Mom planned a big family vacation—a trip to the northern Rocky Mountains where we could visit various National Parks. To do that, the trip had to be in the summer, and Mom needed to make sure that Dad, Jessie and I were available for an extended time. Jessie and I didn't attend school in the summer and our social calendars weren't full yet. Dad was another story, always so busy with things that came up, even during the summer months.

Regardless, Mom somehow convinced Dad to take four weeks off. Four weeks!

Mom mapped out our travel and planned all the logistics. And she made an upgrade. While we'd be camping during the trip instead of sleeping in hotels (according to the Rule of "Waste Not, Want Not"), Mom rented a tent trailer. It was hitched to our Ford XL convertible and after we parked at each campsite, it popped up into a roomy tent.

We were really livin'!

The trip involved driving from Pennsylvania across the Midwest to the eastern foothills of the Rocky Mountains. We drove through South Dakota, visiting the Black Hills and the Badlands. We then crossed into Wyoming to visit the Grand Tetons and Yellowstone. Next, we headed north to Montana where we spent a week at Glacier National Park. We even traveled up to Alberta, Canada to see Banff National Park and Lake Louise.

Ever the planner, Mom procured a TripTik from AAA, a guidebook featuring a detailed map that also provided information on sites of interest, where to purchase gas and where to locate campgrounds. I was fascinated by the TripTik. I quickly commandeered it and elected myself navigator.

Our first days of travel were long; we drove 500-600 miles a day. That was tedious, especially given our excitement to see the Rocky Mountains for the first time. As I peered over my father's shoulder to look at the speedometer, I politely notified him that if he could drive five miles per hour faster, we could get there an hour sooner. "Ever the Number Nut!" he laughed, not heeding my request.

We pitched our tent trailer at campsites along the way. It was high-class living compared to the tiny tent and blow-up mattresses of the Jersey Shore. There were fewer wolves and boars, too!

Wildlife was spotted along the way, particularly when we took hikes in the national parks.

For 26 days the four of us were inseparable. That was the most concentrated time we had ever had with Dad and it led to some memorable discussions. There were no TVs, no friends, no calling alumni: all of the normal distractions had been removed.

Each night, we played bridge in the tent trailer—Dad and me

against Jessie and Mom. Jessie wasn't a fan of the game. Moreover, as previously noted, she wasn't as naturally competitive as our mother was. As Dad and I leapt out to a commanding lead, the stress level on the other side of the table became elevated. Poor Jessie. She just wanted to hang out and sing songs, or go for a hike. And yet she was trapped in a 26-day grudge match over a complicated card game that got more confusing to her as the tension in the tent increased.

Mom was determined to win; it was part of her highly competitive nature. She was goal-oriented with everything she did, and her tenacity was evident in any form of competition. When I was a single-digit-age youngster, Mom played "Candy Land" with us. It was a simple game, oriented for young kids. And we played it incessantly. What I most remember was Mom's determination to beat her two twerps.

Sitting in the Rockies, we had now advanced from a simple kid-oriented game to a very adult card game (bridge). The sophistication demands were quite different than Candy Land, but the one common characteristic was that our mother wanted to beat us badly.

Except this time, Jessie was on Mom's team. She coached Jessie on strategy during the daily hikes, hoping to enhance her understanding of the game. But then at night, Dad and I somehow kept winning. Maybe it was because we were dealt better cards. When it wasn't the cards, but rather a missed strategic play by my sister, a sudden silent pause would descend on the tent. It was an exaggerated pause, lasting as long as it took for my mother to examine the incorrect card that had just been played. And then the silence was broken. "Jessica," Mom would begin. That was never good, if you were my sister. It meant that you had played the wrong card or made the wrong bid. It wasn't the beginning of a warm series of accolades.

As that one word ("Jessica") pervaded the air in the tent amid the silence surrounding it, Dad and I sat demurely, talking only through knowing glances and a few winks. A smile or a snicker from me would have been dangerous at such a moment. Instead, I bit my lip and waited for my walk with Dad at the end of the evening's play when we headed to the campground bathrooms to brush our teeth.

During those walks, Dad and I giggled as we replayed the awkward, tense moments of the previous hours. Jessie had to take the same walk each night to the ladies' room and it was with her bridge partner. There is no way to know what Mom said to Jessie during those walks, but my hunch is that it was a less festive stroll and probably served as an extension of the coaching sessions Mom had been giving her on the hikes. After all, Mom's goal was to help Jessie become a good bridge player. Aside, of course, from Mom's greater goal, which was to win.

Jessie didn't like bridge. She dreaded it. For her, it was like a proctology exam with playing cards.

Jessie wasn't amused by what happened during our bridge games on that trip, but years later we all laughed about it.

By the end of the trip, Dad and I were the winners. By a wide margin. We didn't stop playing bridge after the trip to the Rocky Mountains. The game was always a prominent part of family activity on any trip when the four of us were together. Mom kept her score sheets—all of them. And she tracked the scores, cumulatively, over many years.

Years later during a short vacation, we again sat at the bridge table. It was late at night, and we had just completed our last hand of cards for the evening. I began putting the cards away and picking things up. Across the table from me, Mom added up the score. Then she reached into her purse and pulled out some crumpled pieces of paper. And she added some more.

Suddenly, Mom stood and proclaimed, "I have an announcement!

Jessica and I have caught up with you guys! We are now in the lead! It's taken us five years, but we finally did it!" Mom grabbed Jessie and hugged her. "We did it, Jessica!" Mom yelled. "We did it!" Competitive to her core, Marilyn D.

Back in 1973, sitting in the tent, Jessie and she weren't feeling that level of jubilation. Fortunately for Jessie, we spent most of our vacation time hiking, far away from the bridge table.

The Rocky Mountains were more impressive and beautiful than I could have imagined. Ahead of the trip, I had pored over books and pictures, trying to satisfy my curiosity. But seeing the majestic peaks above me was much more illuminating than any textbooks could portray.

As our family walked through the National Park trails, the mountains towered above us in solemn silence. I felt more alive that trip than ever before. I was seeing the world—a world that was far more impressive than the Poconos or the Jersey Shore. It made me wonder what else there was to see, even beyond the contiguous United States.

Each day also brought new discoveries. And each discovery left an indelible mark on my memory.

Each day brought other awakenings, too. Without life's usual distractions, we engaged in a number of unusual discussions. We talked about things that took a lot of time to discuss—things we had never talked about before. Perhaps it was that we had never before had that much time to dedicate to it.

Jessie and I learned stories about our parents' childhoods, about great-aunts or great-uncles we never heard about before, and about distant cousins. Maybe it was because we were so far from home, or our parents' recognition that we were older (and perhaps more mature), but our parents talked more openly about things that had previously been off limits.

Mom and Dad spoke about some of the dynamics at Lehigh, the good and the bad. While mentioning the hard times during the first six years, they admitted that my first game on the Lehigh sideline in 1968 was because they didn't believe there was going to be another chance due to Dad's losing record.

Jessie and I were shocked. I guess we knew it was possible for Dad to lose his job; we just didn't know what it would take for that to happen. We knew how angry the fans were in those early years, but we didn't think his job was at risk. That was a sobering conversation.

Jessie and I learned some sensitive information, and were sworn not to disclose it. Some of it was pretty alarming, but I still found it fascinating to hear it and be in the family inner circle. Heck, I didn't even know such a circle existed.

Mom and Dad shared insights about certain alumni whom we had met, which gave us a much better perspective on the kind of people they were. The things our parents disclosed weren't necessarily bad things—it's just that they were adult things. And we were now being introduced to a world that had greater issues and greater sophistication.

Mom and Dad asked us questions about our school experiences. We talked about things like the Billy problem. We talked about the awkwardness of being teenagers. And they gave us their perspectives from their own childhoods. From that, we learned about their old girlfriends and boyfriends. Until then, it never occurred to me that there might have been people they dated before they got together.

These conversations were sprinkled in parts or in total across 26 days together. It was like an open forum, and that month changed how I interacted with my parents from that point forward. By their openness, they were now defining us as young adults, no longer as children. They used that summer as a time to begin mentoring us for the adult world. And the only obligation that came with it was that we needed to respect the sensitivity of some of the subject matter.

My parents' openness spurred more questions from us. Jessie and I saw it as a new sport, a new activity, and we instigated more discussion every evening. We even talked about these things during our hikes.

Jessie and I felt like astronauts, riding in a rocket, exploring new and uncharted planets. There were a relative few topics that Mom and Dad resisted discussing while we talked late into the evenings. For Jessie, this was great fun, especially since our talks prevented more bridge games!

On one evening, the subject of Saucon Valley and my caddying job was raised. They asked me how it was going, whom I had caddied for recently, and what were my general impressions.

I started to talk about the personalities in the Caddy Pen. Pinky, Shaky Bernstein, and a few others. I started recounting the nasty things that were being said by some of the caddies. My mother's reaction was strong. She suggested, "Maybe you need to consider looking for a different summer job." Dad interceded and disagreed, saying, "No, Marilyn, he's going to run into that eventually, no matter where he goes."

When Mom and Dad asked more questions about my caddying, I told them about the racism and the bigotry. They asked if that was just at the Caddy Pen or whether I was encountering it at school, too. "I hear it at school, too," I told them, "but not as much as over at the Caddy Pen."

Mom shook her head in disgust and looked at Dad, anticipating his reaction. My father's face was reflective for a moment. Then he began a long delivery. He said that there is a lot of ignorance in the world. He talked about life and how, by definition, it wasn't always fair. And about how people, when they get setbacks in life, want to blame something or someone else for their problems. "People have a habit of rationalizing away their troubles," Dad said. "It's the easy way out. It's the cowardly way out. But people succumb to their own weaknesses, and in a weak moment, it's easier to blame someone else than to look inwardly at how they may have been wrong or how they might have failed.

"Human beings have a tendency to feel inadequate. We all have that tendency to some degree. It's a part of our make-up to feel some level of insecurity. But strong people channel that emotion and try to use it and learn from it. They use it as a teaching tool to evaluate how they need to improve. Weak people don't do that. They avoid that kind of reflection, and would rather deflect their own weaknesses by blaming their issues on other people."

Jessie and I watched him as he spoke. We were glued to his every word. His message fit with the Dunlap Rules we had heard before, but there was more analysis to this, with more subtle application than the basic tenets that had been explained to us in the past.

We discussed racism and some of the hurtful names that were being tossed around in the Caddy Pen. "Tiger, that's directly related to a person's own sense of inadequacy," Dad said, "and their sense of insecurity. And insecurity makes people feel bad about themselves and bad about their station in life."

Mom nodded as Dad continued. "There are two ways people can improve their station in life and deal with their insecurity," he said. "Strong people deal with their issues directly and overcome them. Weak people put other people down. They do that in order to then make themselves *appear better*." He looked stern, as if he were visualizing such a person. "And I have no respect for people like that."

There was that "respect" word again. I asked Dad what made weak people do that, and why they didn't just focus on making themselves better.

"It's really two reasons: A lot of people are just plain lazy—they know they have work to do and they know there are things about themselves to improve, but they put off their issues because they don't have the work ethic to truly address them. The other reason is that humans are rationalizing animals. They are afraid to admit their faults. They are afraid to admit to another person that they are wrong. So they rationalize that they *aren't wrong*, and that they *don't have weaknesses*. They deceive themselves by trying to convince themselves that they are right."

Dad switched subjects and asked, "Do you remember the recent strike by the union workers at Bethlehem Steel?" I nodded. I had read about their anger in the newspapers, but I told Dad that I didn't understand the reasons for it. "Well," Dad explained, "the unions thought management was underpaying them. But do you know that the line workers there make 25 percent more than Lehigh coaches do? Now I know that comparing what our coaches do with blue collar workers on the front lines in a steel mill with blast furnaces in their faces and danger all around is probably unfair, but there's a point I want to make.

"Listen, I don't fault them for making more money than we do. I fault them for believing they are underpaid and worth more, without first appreciating the good things they already have.

"Even though they sweat and toil in a hot factory, they have some good benefits, too. They only have to work eight hours a day, with negotiated breaks every two hours, and they get home by 3 p.m. to see their kids come home from school. They get to have dinner with their families." He stood up. "That's a real plus for them since management many times works much longer hours and rarely see their families except at breakfast and sometimes in the evening. When the workers openly criticize management, I don't believe they realize the challenges management people face. They don't know that management might not be able to afford their contract demands. They don't know what management goes through each day as they do their jobs. But the unions aren't hesitant to criticize and put other people down without really knowing whether the criticism is deserved." Now I saw the connection to our earlier discussion.

"Kids, unions run in packs," he said sternly. "They represent their masses and try to raise the pay for all union workers. Do they have talented people within their ranks? Of course they do. Many of them have special skills, and I admire that. But should we be led to believe that every worker in that union is talented and hard working?" His question was rhetorical. "So why should the weak performers get the benefit of the efforts of talented workers?

"If Lehigh athletics were a union, and I were part of the athletic department union, then should I have gotten a big raise in the 1960s just because the wrestling team was nationally ranked, even though the football team wasn't winning? No, I shouldn't have.

"Each person should have his own accountability in the workplace and in the community," he explained. There was that "accountability" word again. "And rewards should be commensurate with the results that are delivered. When people don't deliver results," he added, "they have a tendency to deceive themselves. It's easier for them to rationalize that their performance wasn't bad, or if that's impossible to do, then the next best option is to blame someone else for why they weren't able to do better."

I wondered if Dad would speak about his relationship with Bill Leckonby, and he did. "Given our confidential discussions on this trip, you guys now know that I don't have a good relationship with my boss, but I don't blame our losses on him. Would it have been easier to rebuild the Lehigh program with a more cooperative boss? Sure it would have. But my job was to overcome obstacles, no matter how many or how large. And to succeed in spite of any limitations.

"So I don't like Leckonby and I don't respect him. But I don't blame him for our losing seasons—it was my job to change that."

It was evident he had done that, having delivered an 8-3 record in 1971. Yet I still wondered how much faster he could have turned the program around and how much better the program could have been if he had had more support from his boss.

The subject once again turned to my summer job at Saucon Valley. We talked about the nice people I worked for, some of whom my parents knew from their connection to Lehigh. We also talked about some people who were not so nice. They were snobby and they didn't treat the caddies or other service workers with respect.

Dad shared some thoughts on this subject. "Tiger, that's connected to what we talked about, too. It's a way for them to make themselves feel better and more important. If they can put someone down, then essentially they think they have raised themselves to a higher level. People like that view others as beneath them and not worthy of their time or respect. That's kinda what those caddies are doing when the call somebody a Spic or a Dago. It's a demeaning thing to do, and it's a generalization—as if being Puerto Rican or Italian is a curse. People come in all shapes and forms," he said. "There are good people and bad people. There are hard-working people and lazy people. It's wrong to generalize and you kids should never do that.

"Your mother and I are humble people at our core. We are thankful for what we have, and we appreciate those around us. We have had the dumb luck to have been born in the United States. And we have had the dumb luck to have been raised by good parents in a supportive family environment."

Mom continued to sit patiently, listening to Dad. She wasn't the kind of person to be shy about presenting her views, so I took her silence as a sign of her being in full agreement with what Dad said.

"But not everybody gets that lucky," Dad explained. "Lots of people haven't had the benefit of being born a United States citizen, or haven't had a supportive upbringing. Or haven't had the benefit of a college education." He looked at us with purpose. "Does that mean they are bad people? No. Just because they didn't get *our* head start, does that make them less than us? And not worthy of our time and attention?" We knew the answer was no—he didn't have to say it. "There are some members at Saucon Valley who probably have never worked a day in their life. Those people have had everything given to them by their wealthy parents. They are very fortunate for that." I nodded at that statement. It made sense to me. "But if they look down on others as being less quality people than they are," Dad explained, "that's not right. They have no idea what hurdles others might have faced—real life obstacles that are difficult to overcome."

Dad and Mom were always friendly and outgoing with everybody. They had been that way with a store clerk earlier that day. They were nice to gas station attendants, asking them questions about their lives or about the area. I remembered my father touring us around the Lehigh facilities and stopping to talk to everyone along the way. The equipment manager. The janitor. The security guard.

My father had a high profile job, and these people had less significant positions in life. But my father treated them as equal. He didn't act like he was superior to them. *Treat people equally*, I thought to myself. *That's not too different from treat people the way you want to be treated.*

"Dad, I've noticed you always talk to the workers around Lehigh and call them by name," I said. He smiled. "That's because they are good people," he replied. "They are nice, hard-working people." He brought up a few of those people by name. "Jose is an immigrant and he lives in a small apartment on the south side of Bethlehem with his wife and four kids. He works three jobs and his wife works, too. They have to do that in order to pay their bills. Neither of them finished high school. But they are good people and they are good parents.

"I watch a lot of people at Lehigh walk past them like they are invisible. They are real people," he said. "Some people may think they are better than they are. But the vast majority don't acknowledge them or take the time to get to know them, because they are too busy or too self-absorbed. Guys like Jose spend a lifetime being ignored or underappreciated."

"So you make a special effort to talk to them?" I asked.

"Yes, I know that by showing Jose and others some genuine interest that it makes a world of difference to them. And it takes so little time and energy to extend yourself to others when it can mean so much to them when you do."

While Dad spoke, it became easy to see how divergent the paths could be between adults, depending on how they chose to conduct their lives. The snobs from Saucon Valley started to seem very small. Only a year earlier, I looked up to them with awe because they were members of the country club. That appraisal was now being replaced by a more analytical assessment, based on the adult lessons I was learning from my parents.

"One of the things that differentiates great people from others," Dad said, "is their wisdom to be tolerant. Great people *think* before they jump to conclusions. Great people *appreciate* the good fortune they have had, and are *patient and tolerant* of those who haven't had the same benefits." More Dunlap Rules, I was certain.

Dad held his arms up, as if to summarize everything we had discussed. "Just because someone is different from you, doesn't mean they are bad people. We all come from divergent backgrounds and experiences, and for that reason, our methods of living our lives may be different. So it's important to be tolerant of those around you, and to look for the best in people."

With that, Dad had completed his sermon. Mom had remained quiet throughout. I think the reason she stayed so reserved during that discussion was to give him a chance to deliver *his* message. Since she was always around us, she had plenty of access to bestow life lessons on us. But on this 26-day intimate family retreat, she saw this as Dad's time to teach us some life lessons. It was *his moment*, and she wanted him to have it.

It was late in the evening. We scampered down the path in the dark to the community bathrooms where we brushed our teeth and prepared for bed. I lay awake in the dark that night, taking in the sounds of heavy breathing from my sleeping parents. I replayed that discussion in my head—which took quite a while. I thought about the people at the club, the caddies, our neighbors, the alumni we had discussed… and I also thought about some of the kids in school. I analyzed each in light of the points I had just heard. It was a lot to ponder.

This trip has changed my life, I thought. Through all of the talks that month, I now saw the world through a different prism. A more sophisticated prism. And that would be a permanent change, I was convinced.

Dad had spoken of tolerance that evening, and being tolerant was how he lived. But tolerance did have its limits. He was tolerant in all ways, provided that the person: 1) Was trying his or her best, which included being a good person, being a hard worker and never being lazy; 2) Showed courage amid difficult challenges; and 3) Was not doing something destructive to others, including him. Regarding #3, Dad never looked for trouble, but if trouble came to him, he was a confrontation animal. He would address the problem quickly and decisively. He never hesitated.

My father had the greatest respect for people who tried to make the most of themselves. It didn't matter from where they started—he admired people who showed they wanted to improve. For those who didn't, Dad was still tolerant, but he didn't respect them.

During our cross-country trip that summer, Jessie and I became young adults. Like me, she never saw the world through a child's prism again. The mentoring sessions administered by our parents were carefully dispensed over those special 26 days. They have stayed with me for a lifetime, and shaped how I think and treat other people.

The Momentum Effect— Lehigh Football—1972 through 1975

"Winning makes everything easier," Dad told me many times. "It's when your reputation and accomplishments start to sell themselves."

He said that about a lot of things over the years, but certainly one of the points of reflection was the environment at Lehigh from 1969 through 1971.

Dad regarded the 8-3 record in 1971 as being very important to the reputation of Lehigh football, but he would never leave that alone in his description. "The change in the mystique of our football program really started with the '69 Rutgers game and the Barf Block," he professed. "And then the tie against Colgate...and then the wins in 1970 against Rutgers and Delaware. And then beating Rutgers again in 1971—that's three years straight—that did so much for our image in the Northeast when it came to alumni support and recruiting."

But what did Dad mean when he said everything becomes easier? "It's not that we worked less hard," he told me. "It's just that we didn't need to work as hard convincing others.

"With each success, our team was regarded and respected more. It's like making deposits in a bank account that start to earn interest by themselves. As we won, more kids wanted to come to Lehigh, to be affiliated with a program they felt was headed in a good direction. When we had positions come open on the coaching staff, more quality candidates wanted to be considered. They were less worried about the salary amount, because they wanted to be a part of us: they believed that being affiliated with our program could be helpful to their resume.

"When we needed more money for the football program, we had a more supportive university. Even if we weren't getting the support from them, we had enthusiastic alumni who might pressure university officials to change their minds."

Dad provided words that stayed with me throughout my adult life. "Success breeds success," he said, "It's the power of momentum."

The 1972 Season

IN 1972, I WAS GIVEN a job promotion on the Lehigh sidelines. I was no longer the ball boy, and I was no longer the kid who ran out onto the football field to retrieve the kicking tee. Instead, I was asked to manage the offensive clipboard.

As each game began, I stood on the sideline holding my clipboard. My job was to write down the offensive plays we ran and note the amount of yardage gained per play. I received the description from the back-up quarterback, who was watching the action. Upon recognizing it, he told me the play. It might be "B-3, Right 46." The "B-3" was the offensive formation and the remainder was the play itself.

On cue, I'd record the plays throughout the first half. Dad and the quarterbacks reviewed the results intermittently to determine which plays (in which formations) seemed to be working more effectively. And that knowledge might dictate which plays to call later in the game.

In 1972, Joe Alleva was the quarterback who communicated the plays to me. I stood next to him when we were on offense and listened to his calls. It was a cool job for a 13-year-old, and Joe was very patient with me as I learned the process.

In 1972, the team compiled a 5-6 record. On the surface that looked like a setback from the 1971 season. The '72 season was frustrating in many respects. When Lehigh won, they won big. And when they lost, it was by a tight margin. Five of the six losses were by eight points or less. One of those losses was to Gettysburg, an upset. Lehigh gave up a late touchdown to lose by two points.

The opportunities lost were many in 1972. Certainly the players and coaches felt that way. But upon closer analysis, the losses were to some high quality programs: Delaware by six points, Army by five, Penn by three, and Colgate by eight.

Dad and the team were frustrated with the final record, but even with those losses, Lehigh was very competitive, and they were beginning to realize they were good enough to beat anybody.

The 1973 Season

THE NCAA MADE A LANDMARK change in 1973 to allow freshmen to play on college varsity teams. This was good news to many schools, including Lehigh, and the 1973 Lehigh freshman class made some notable contributions that season.

The 1973 Lehigh football team

The 1973 team opened with a win over Hofstra. The following week they traveled to Storrs, Connecticut, to play a heavily favored UConn team. The game started poorly. Lehigh wasn't performing well and UConn played great in front of their home crowd.

UConn was a good team, but Lehigh's performance was making them look like a great team. As the Lehigh team headed to the locker room for halftime, they trailed UConn by a score of 20-0.

Predictably, my father had some sharp words for the team. They were scolding words. I don't remember exactly what he said, but he was clear with the team about a few things:

- They were playing sloppy and making too many mistakes
- They were making UConn look like an NFL team
- They looked scared, like they were afraid to play the opponent
- They weren't playing aggressively—they weren't *taking the game to them*

There might also have been an inference or two where Dad questioned the players' manhood. And I remember hearing more foul words come out of my father's mouth than I had ever heard before. The look on the faces of the players as Dad barked at them let me know they agreed with my perception.

Lehigh took the field in the second half and, almost immediately, I could sense a different, more intense effort. The defense stopped UConn. Then the Lehigh offense scored on the next possession.

Following the kickoff, the defense stopped UConn again. A few plays later, the Lehigh offense scored again. The team was still behind at this point, but the game momentum had swung. It was at that moment that Dad came to appreciate the value of being able to use freshman players in 1973.

UConn had the ball and was driving deep in Lehigh territory. The game was in the fourth quarter, and Lehigh couldn't afford to give up another score. The UConn quarterback threw a pass into the Lehigh end zone toward one of his receivers, and freshman Jimmy Dutt leapt in front to intercept the ball. Jimmy was a diminutive player, standing only 5 feet, 7 inches tall, and he *might* have weighed 150 pounds. But he was extremely quick and had won the starting position at cornerback. Though he was probably six inches shorter than the intended receiver, he skied up to intercept the pass and stopped what would have been UConn's game-clinching score.

Quarterback Kim McQuilken and the offense then took the field and drove the length of the field to score. Lehigh now trailed 20-19, but there were only a few minutes left in the game.

Again the defense made a stop, and UConn punted to Lehigh. With only seconds remaining, McQuilken quickly engineered a drive to UConn's 20-yard line. The clock had nearly expired—leaving only time for one more play. Dad sent in the field goal team.

There was only one catch: Placekicker Bruce Crystal was also a freshman and this was his first college field goal attempt. He had kicked in high school in Bronxville, New York, but he confessed later, "All I ever kicked in high school were extra points."

The ball was placed on the right hash mark. The kick would be at an angle, which I knew would make the attempt more difficult. From where I stood on the sideline, I was almost directly in line with the intended flight of the kick. I figured I would be able to tell the outcome of the kick the instant the ball was struck, long before the officials would give their signal.

The teams lined up as the nervous home crowd tried to distract us. The snap was accurate and the blocking was reliable. The holder placed the ball on the spot with precision. Bruce Crystal stepped toward it and coiled to attempt the first field goal of his life.

We watched from the sidelines as the ball exploded off Bruce's foot. Clearing the scrum at the line of scrimmage, the ball rotated end-over-end as it sailed toward its intended destination. Was it accurate? *Yes*, I thought. Was it long enough? *Yes*, I was sure. I smiled for that instant, knowing what the officials would signal. And then hands and arms went up. First, it was the officials. Then it was the hands and arms of the players on the field and on the sidelines as reality set in.

The comeback had been complete. Lehigh upset UConn 22-20. On their home field. After spotting them a 20-0 lead in the first half.

I can't remember a more raucous bunch than the Lehigh players in the locker room after that game. The look on my father's face was emblematic of a warrior who had conquered something great. It was a look of pride and satisfaction.

We had a happy ride back to Bethlehem that night. Winning was great, but doing it in that fashion was special. On that day, the team had moments of self-doubt, but they learned how to overcome them quickly and show their worthiness as a winner. It was a win, and more than that, it was a maturing, seasoning experience for the football program.

The following two weeks, Lehigh lost to Rutgers and Delaware, and then played a sloppy game against Cornell, resulting in a 7-7 tie. The team's record was then 2-2-1.

Fortunately, at that midpoint of the season, another freshman player, Rod Gardner, emerged from the shadows of the locker room. He became a valuable running back for Lehigh for the rest of his career.

The season continued and the team prepared for each game in their systematic fashion. A win against Bucknell was followed by a loss to Penn, and the team was 3-3-1.

Amid a losing effort in Philadelphia that day, the Cobra emerged once again. I learned this story second-hand, because I was on the sidelines during the game. My reliable source was Jessie.

Lehigh was playing at Franklin Field against the University of Pennsylvania. Mom and Jessie were in the stands that day. With each away game, the location of their seats varied by stadium. And because of that, the crowd around Mom didn't always know who was sitting within earshot.

That year, our recruiting success was flourishing and we were getting a stronger class of players with each passing year.

To that end, Lehigh had recruited a talented quarterback, Joe Sterrett, then a sophomore. Since we already had Kim McQuilken and Joe Alleva on the squad, Sterrett would need to wait for his chance to be the starting quarterback after they graduated.

Because Sterrett was a great athlete and very fast, the coaches asked him to play in the backfield during his sophomore season. Joe willingly accepted, seeing it as a way to contribute sooner to the team. In this role, he ran pass routes out of the backfield and helped the team in long yardage situations.

Unfortunately, the week before the Penn game, Joe got hit hard in the Bucknell game and his jaw was broken. In the days following that game and leading up to the Penn game, Joe had an operation to repair it. To speed the healing, the doctors wired his jaw shut.

After the surgery, Joe couldn't move his mouth. This meant he couldn't chew solid food. My mother loaned Joe our blender so all of his food could be pureed and he could "sip" meals through a straw.

In spite of the injury and surgery, Joe insisted on playing that following week at Franklin Field. The team trainer reluctantly agreed to let him play but he brought a pair of wire cutters in case there was an emergency. If Joe injured his jaw again, the trainer was concerned they would need to cut his jaw free so he could breathe.

Though he realized he wouldn't be able to perform at his best, Sterrett was intent on playing. And because Penn was a tough opponent, the coaches felt it was worth the risk to let him play.

As the game progressed, Joe had dropped a couple passes and also missed a key block on a running play. We could only imagine the pain he felt in that game whenever he got hit. It was apparent his injury was affecting his play.

Throughout the game, a fan was sitting behind Mom and Jessie, criticizing the Lehigh team. On that day in Franklin Field, the *dumb fan du jour* came in the form of a small, wiry man with a loud obnoxious mouth. Mom could tell he was a Lehigh alum because of his chatter with the people around him. But as she always did, she kept cool and didn't react to the man's comments. Mom and Jessie just whispered to each other about how stupid the fool was, those whispers being their form of catharsis.

During the fourth quarter, Lehigh ran a pass play, and the ball was thrown in Joe's direction. He didn't make the catch. Immediately, the man behind Mom yelled, "Get that guy off the field! He's terrible! He hasn't caught a pass all day!"

On that day, Mom chose to abandon her techniques of "Less Is More." Irate, she jumped up and hurried toward the man. "Who do you think you are?" she yelled. The man was startled. "Do you know who *that kid* is?" Mom added.

Mom isn't a short woman. She stands 5 foot, 9 inches tall. At that moment, she was toe-to-toe with a guy who was looking up her nostrils.

"Is he your son?" the man stammered.

"No, he is not my son! He's JOE STERRETT!"

The man looked confused.

"Do you have any idea what he has been through in the last week?"

The man's face still reflected confusion.

Mom explained about Joe's injury and having his jaw wired shut. "You tell me what kind of kid would go through that surgery and still try to play a week later! A tough kid, that's who! A really courageous kid, that's who! And then you sit up here criticizing him!" Mom took a breath. "I have been listening to you all game long. Who the heck do you think you are?"

The guy was panicked, backing away as Mom continued to stalk him. "You are a coward, that's what you are!" Mom said. "You sit up here and take pot shots at players and coaches without ever having walked in their shoes.

"I am going to go down now and sit in my seat." She pointed to Jessie. "And I don't want to hear another thing come out of your mouth! Do you hear me? If you don't like that, then move to another section of the stands."

Mom turned to walk away, but looked back. "And if you want to register a complaint," she said directly, "Tell 'em to come see Marilyn Dunlap!"

My sister reported to me later that the crowd behind them was quite silent for the rest of the game. As for me, I saw a great game from the sideline. But I wished I had been in the stands to witness that one.

Marilyn D.!

With seven games completed, it was now late October. As had become the tradition, during the following week, Spot made his (her) appearance on Halloween night, sneaking behind bushes, hiding behind blocking dummies as he (she) seemed to be scouting the team's practice for the Lafayette game later in the season.

There were four games remaining on the schedule: Gettysburg, Colgate, Rochester and Lafayette. Lehigh crushed each of these teams, beating them by 28 or more points. Particularly satisfying to my father was the 58-26 win over Colgate, his alma mater.

Lehigh's record at the end of their season was 7-3-1. Its strong finish to the season, along with the high quality wins against UConn and Colgate, resulted in Lehigh being awarded the Lambert Cup, established in 1936 to recognize supremacy in Northeastern college football for Division II.

Lehigh was ranked nationally in Division II and received a berth into the NCAA Division II Playoffs, which included 16 teams, and a four-week playoff to determine the Division II National Champion.

Lehigh was invited to play the following week against Western Kentucky. The team was excited, and so was the Dunlap family. The team flew to Nashville, Tennessee, later that week before being bussed to Western Kentucky's campus. Mom and Dad decided that Jessie and I should come along. It was the first time she and I flew on an airplane.

One amusing story came from the experience. I dubbed it the "17 Pollocks."

On that Friday, the team prepared for the game on foreign soil. After practice, Dad was obligated to attend a reception including media and both head coaches. At some point in the discussion, the subject of scholarships was raised. The Western Kentucky head coach explained that they were a state school and that all of their players were on full scholarship.

Dad was asked how many free rides Lehigh provided. He told reporters Lehigh didn't have any scholarships. He explained that tuition assistance was only provided on a needs basis, meaning that the family of the athlete had to have some degree of financial hardship to get any financial assistance.

The Western Kentucky coach looked stunned. He asked, "You mean you don't have *any* scholarships?"

Confirming this was true, Dad went on to explain that most of the players were paying some or the majority of their college expenses. "And we even have 17 players who are paying the full cost of college," he said, "with no financial assistance whatsoever."

The meeting adjourned and Dad returned to the team to prepare for the game. When the Lehigh players ran onto the field the next day, Dad walked along the sideline observing their warm-ups as he usually did. As he strolled over to where some of the Western Kentucky coaching staff were standing, he was soon within a distance to hear them talking.

"I wonder which of the players are the 17 Pollocks?" one of the Western Kentucky coaches asked. Another coach laughed and said, "Yeah, you'd have to be as dumb as a Pollock to play football for free!"

Lehigh lost to Western Kentucky that day, 26-16. But it had been another successful season followed by another successful recruiting class.

The 1974 Season

Enhancing Lehigh's profile as a strong football program, Kim McQuilken graduated and was drafted by the NFL Atlanta Falcons. Though he would be missed, Lehigh had Joe Alleva ready to step in and lead the offense. He had been waiting patiently for three years for the opportunity and was determined to make the most of it. With his elevation to starting quarterback, Joe Sterrett, the back-up, helped me track offensive plays on the sidelines.

"One of the luxuries of having established a winning tradition," Dad later recounted, "was that high school players began to *recruit us.* Good quarterbacks, good passers included. They assessed the possible schools already running an offense that was favorable to their skills and then they pursued us with interest."

Dad had good examples to choose from. "Joe Alleva and Joe Sterrett liked the offense we were running with McQuilken," he said, "and it suited their talents well." This meant Dad didn't need to change the offense to fit the athlete; the athlete already fit by his own choice of football programs.

The 1974 Lehigh squad won the first two games but lost the next three. With a 2-3 record at the mid-point of the season, the team elevated their play and ran off five straight wins. Their performance was so dominant that they defeated the last four opponents by a cumulative score of 157-26!

In the annual Lafayette rivalry, Lehigh demolished them, 57-7. Even with Spot's covert scouting mission on Halloween, Lafayette was no match for Lehigh.

One game that year is worthy of a special mention—not because it involved a thrilling comeback and not because it was an upset victory.

It was actually an easy win happening late in the season. The opponent was Davidson, and the game was played at home in our Taylor Stadium.

No matter what the outcome of any game, Dad's requirement of himself and his team was to be classy in victory and classy in defeat. During his coaching career, he had seen other coaches run up the score on teams (unnecessarily). He had experienced being on the winning and losing end of that kind of behavior, and he didn't approved of either. As a head coach, it was not his style to do that—ever.

To be certain, the Davidson contest was never competitive. Early in the game, Lehigh began to dominate. By halftime, Lehigh led by more than three scores. On its first possession of the second half, Lehigh scored again. At this point, Dad concluded that the outcome of the game was no longer in question. To avoid any injuries and to avoid running up the score any higher, Dad pulled the first team offense out of the game.

After Lehigh's defense stopped Davidson again, the second team offense took the field. It was also capable of beating the Davidson defense, so in order to limit more scoring, Dad elected to curtail the play calling by instructing the QB to only call conservative running plays. Dad figured that would run the clock out faster and would (hopefully) keep the score from getting more embarrassing for Davidson. Even if Lehigh scored, Dad concluded, each drive would take time off the clock.

In spite of his efforts to control the score, the second team scored two more times in the 3rd and 4th quarters. The score was then 45-6 and Davidson seemed incapable of stopping Lehigh's most basic, conservative running plays.

One other problem was developing. Even though they were being trounced and the game was nearly over, the Davidson defensive players started to commit late hits and cheap shots. Things were getting pretty chippy after each play, with players on both sides taunting each other.

Dad was worried some players might get hurt given some of the flagrant fouls he was witnessing. He began yelling at the officials to get the game under control. They hadn't thrown penalties on most of the stuff Dad was seeing.

On the sideline, Lehigh players were also getting angry. They didn't like their teammates getting treated with disrespect. Overall, tempers were heating up.

College football coaching is a small world. Dad knew the Davidson coach and didn't respect him. From across the field, he watched that coach urge his kids on, applauding them as they took cheap shots at Lehigh players. All the while, I was standing near Dad with Joe Alleva. Joe had not been in the game since the early part of the 3rd quarter when he was replaced by Joe Sterrett and the second team offense.

Dad was as upset as I had ever seen him. He yelled on the headset to the Lehigh coach in the press box. "That coach is instructing his kids to do that! And the refs aren't doing anything about it!"

With only a minute left in the game, Lehigh had the ball. From midfield, Dad called another running play. Joe Sterrett handed the ball to a running back and watched his teammate carry it. Out of nowhere, a Davidson player raced up from behind and leveled Sterrett. He and the guy who tackled him started fighting and then a short brawl ensued.

Officials broke it up but both Sterrett and the Davidson player were ejected from the game. Dad was furious over the cheap shot by the Davidson player, and I heard him bark, "Okay, that's it! First team offense, *GET IN THERE!*"

On the field they went, including Joe Alleva. The rest of the players on the Lehigh sideline were up now, angry about the fight on the field, but also very curious about why Dad had ordered the entire first team on the field with only a minute to play.

I had worked the clipboard long enough by then to know the plays. Before Alleva left the sidelines to go onto the field, I heard Dad give him the play. Alleva was surprised at the call (and so was I) but he headed for the huddle. As Alleva ran out, I heard my father talk on the headset to his assistant coach in the press box: "Let's see how they like this," he said with a bit of a devilish smile.

On the next play, Joe Alleva faked the handoff and dropped back as two receivers headed downfield. Alleva threw the ball to one of them. It was a perfect strike for a touchdown.

Lehigh players on the sidelines went crazy. The frenzy reminded me of the 1969 game when Lehigh upset Rutgers but this moment was even more raucous. Was it because the touchdown was crucial to the win? No. Was it because the players were already riled up after the fight on the field? Somewhat. Or was it that they had never seen their head coach do this kind of thing before?

What Dad did next surprised them even more. He told the Lehigh kicker to stay on the sideline. Instead, the call was for a two-point conversion and it was successful. The players and fans were in disbelief. But Dad wasn't yet satisfied.

Following the score, Lehigh prepared to kick-off to Davidson. It was an on-sides kick. And Lehigh recovered the ball. The sidelines and the stands were bedlam.

Without hesitation, Dad ordered the first team back onto the field even though there were only seconds remaining in the game. Again, Alleva faked a handoff and dropped back to pass. The same play had been called. The receiver caught the pass but was tackled at the five-yard line as time ran out.

It is customary for head coaches to meet in the middle of the field after games to shake hands. On that day, Dad sprinted toward the

Davidson coach. When the two met, there was a heated exchange. Threats were made by the Davidson coach about his team "kicking your ass next year when you come to North Carolina." Dad yelled back at the coach, reminding him that he had instigated it by encouraging his players to play dirty.

I had never seen my father get in someone's face like that. It was AWESOME.

In the locker room, the noise was deafening. The excitement wasn't about the win. It was about the way the game ended. Dad talked to the team about it. "Men, great win. We looked good on both sides of the ball." Then he paused and looked a bit sheepish. "What happened just now was uncharacteristic of me—it's not something I am proud of. Sometimes, when somebody brings a fight to you, you need to stand up and fight back. And that's why I did it."

The players tried to look serious as he spoke, but they couldn't contain their grins. They were proud of Dad's actions. He had stuck up for them.

As the players continued to celebrate the win, Dad approached Joe Sterrett. Sterrett apologized to Dad for getting kicked out of the game. Dad dismissed the apology and told him that he was proud of how Joe stood up for himself. Sterrett had been getting pummeled throughout the second half. Dad told him he did the right thing by fighting back.

Dad's actions against Davidson after he and Joe had been challenged by dirty play reminded me of how I had been challenged by the bully, Billy. As I had done, they each stood up to the bully and clobbered him. The Dunlap Rules were alive and well in the Lehigh locker room, I concluded.

Final score: Lehigh 53, Davidson 6.

Lehigh finished the 1974 season with a 7-3 record. As for my original clipboard comrade, Joe Alleva graduated the next spring but he didn't venture far from athletics. Today Joe is the Vice Chairman and Director of Athletics at Louisiana State University (LSU).

The 1975 Season

THE 1975 SEASON WAS JOE Sterrett's coming-out party. After having been the back-up quarterback to Alleva and McQuilken and playing other positions in previous years, Joe was now the starting quarterback. To assist on offense, he had Rod Gardner in the backfield providing a great balance between Joe's passing and Rod's rushing.

After losing to Army in the second game of the season, Lehigh's record was 1-1. Following the Army loss, the team won seven straight games, including against Penn, Rutgers, Delaware and Colgate. Lehigh had beaten all of the Big Four.

Of interest is what happened when Lehigh played Davidson in North Carolina. In spite of the Davidson coach's threat about delivering an ass-kicking, Lehigh beat Davidson 37-19. Joe Sterrett didn't get kicked out of the game, and Dad didn't call for any late-game on-sides kicks.

Having compiled a record of 8-1, games with Bucknell and Lafayette remained. Lehigh played poorly at Bucknell and was upset, but then beat Lafayette, 40-14.

The 9-2 record was the best since my father had arrived at Lehigh. It was also the first time Lehigh had won nine games in a season, dating back to 1950.

Lehigh once again was awarded the Lambert Cup and invited to play in the Division II Playoffs. This time the game was played at home against New Hampshire. The result was a 35-21 loss.

That game marked the final one for the seniors, including co-captain Joe Sterrett. During his football career, Joe had been willing to play any position the coaches had asked him to play. He played hurt, even with the pain of a broken jaw.

Joe chose to go to work for Lehigh after graduation and within 12 years was named to Lehigh's athletic director position. That was 26 years ago, and Joe Sterrett continues in that position today as Dean of Athletics.

Radio interview—Friday night before the 1965 Lehigh/ Lafayette game (Coach Dunlap at left).

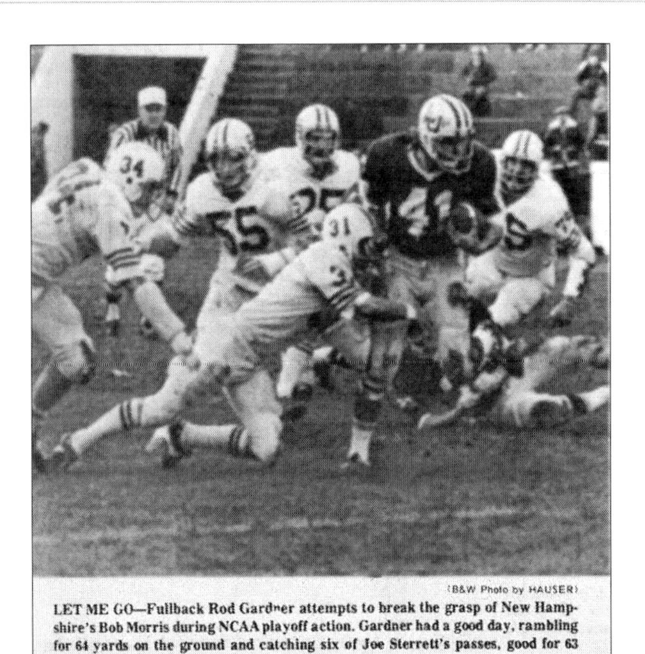

Rod Gardner runs hard against New Hampshire in the 1975 Division II Playoffs.

Award Ceremony for the 1975 Lambert Cup. Dad (second from the left) was flanked by co-captains Jerry Mullane (far left) and Joe Sterrett (far right).

Lehigh Coaching Staff (1971 and 1972)—(Dad standing front row, middle).

FREDERICK H. DUNLAP
Head Coach of Football
Eleventh Season

Fred Dunlap, Colgate '50, is in his eleventh year as head coach of football at Lehigh and the recent success he and the Engineers have enjoyed can only be described as a tribute to patience and perseverance.

The 47-year-old native of Carbondale, Pa., has completed two contrasting five-year plans. His first, 1965 through 1969, produced a 9-37-1 record during a period of painful rebuilding.

His second, 1970 through last fall, found the team posting a 31-21-1 mark, smashing Lehigh records, winning a Lambert Cup in 1973 and earning an invitation to the first NCAA college division national championship tournament.

It's been Success in the Seventies for the Engineers as they fashioned three winning campaigns in the last five years. Previous to 1971, the first of those winning seasons, Lehigh hadn't finished above .500 for 10 years.

Patience and perseverance? How about Dunlap's first three seasons, 1965 through 1967, when the record was 2-25 as the squad struggled to regain some sort of respectability? Lots of patience was needed, all around, and lots of perseverance.

Dunlap came to Lehigh after six years on the Cornell University staff. Prior to that he coached at Hudson, N.Y., High School, at his alma mater, Colgate, at the University of Buffalo and at Ft. Sill, Okla., where he helped develop a title-winning Army squad.

He is married to the former Marilyn Clark, of Utica, N.Y. They are the parents of a son, Fred, and a daughter, Jessica.

Feature article in the 1975 Lehigh game programs. Gone are the losing seasons. Also gone is his military haircut. But hey, it was the '70s!

September 1975

(B&W Photo by BLOOM)

BACKFIELD—Engineer head coach Fred Dunlap talks to his offensive backfield in fall practice session. The backfield is being indoctrinated into an entirely new offensive set-up, the Wing T. Under this set-up two halfbacks and a fullback will be in the game at the same time. The gridders will be seeking their third consecutive winning season this fall.

November 1975

(B&W Photo by HAUSER)

(B&W Photo by HAUSER)

WORDS OF WISDOM—Head coach Fred Dunlap works hard every Saturday despite the fact that the Engineer mentor never steps onto the field. Dunlap is seen talking over game strategy with Joe Sterrett. The strategy probably worked, for the gridders have reached an 8-2 record under Dunlap's leadership.

A newspaper feature article discusses Dad's success, highlighting his style as a coach and mentor.

Life's Options and Hard Decisions

AFTER THE 1975 SEASON ENDED, Thanksgiving weekend permitted time for us to sit around the house with Dad. We ate turkey and watched every possible minute of football on television.

That weekend Dad received a telephone call informing him there had been a coaching change at Colgate University, Dad's alma mater. Neil Wheelwright had resigned, and a search for the new head coach had commenced. The caller asked Dad to be a candidate.

Even though Lehigh had beaten Colgate each of the last three years, it was a Division I football program. Its football budget was much larger and it had better facilities than did Lehigh.

Dad was certain Colgate's budget was bigger, even though he still had no idea of the exact amount of Lehigh's. Dad was sure that the support for football was stronger at Colgate. He was definitely interested in the job.

The interview process ran from December through January, during which Dad advanced to one of three finalist candidates. While it was being conducted, the Colgate Athletic Director suddenly resigned. There was now a vacancy at both the football coach and AD positions.

In the meantime, Dr. Lewis, aware Colgate was pursuing Dad, began scrambling to find a way to keep him at Lehigh. Dr. Lewis knew Dad had difficulties with Leckonby and thus decided to create an Associate Athletic Director role. Dr. Lewis' hope was that this new position might allow Dad some freedom from dealing with Leckonby.

A week later, an administrative official at Colgate called and offered my father the head coaching position. Dad explained that Lehigh had just expanded his responsibilities with the associate athletic director position. Because of that expanded position, Dad thanked the Colgate official for the offer, but declined the position.

During the following week, Dad met with Leckonby to discuss how their interface might change with Dad now also being associate athletic director. Disturbingly, he found Leckonby to be just as unyielding as he had been in the past. When Dad left the meeting, he realized the expanded role was more theoretical than real, and that Leckonby would still have a strong influence on his world.

That evening, the Colgate official called again and offered my father both jobs—head football coach and athletic director. Still stinging from his meeting with Leckonby while learning of the enriched deal being presented by Colgate, Dad accepted the offer.

Mom and Dad called Jessie and me into the kitchen that evening and told us the news. It had been 11 years since the last time we had one of those meetings. And after this one, I learned we would be moving to Hamilton, New York.

For Jessie, it wasn't as big a change. She was graduating from high school in June, anyway. But I was in my junior year, meaning I'd be changing schools and hometowns for my senior year of high school.

The next day, Dad informed his coaches that he had accepted the Colgate job. He explained to me later that it was one of the hardest decisions of his life. He had invested a decade into making Lehigh better, and he was now leaving that behind. He knew his players had chosen to come to Lehigh because they wanted to play for him. He balanced those feelings by knowing he wasn't abandoning Lehigh, leaving it in the ruinous state it had been in eleven years before.

Dad had built a strong program. Now the test was whether it could thrive perennially, even after the leader had departed.

One of the positive developments of the change was that John Whitehead was selected to be Dad's successor as Lehigh head coach.

Whitehead had been the offensive coordinator on Dad's staff for many years and was well respected by the players. That news was reassuring to the players, because there would be program continuity with that change.

Dad left for Hamilton immediately to begin his new assignment. Once the newspapers reported the story, I was free to tell my friends I was leaving Bethlehem.

Through the years, people were sympathetic to my having to move before my senior year in high school. They said things like, "Couldn't your parents have arranged for you to live at a friend's house for that last year, so you wouldn't have missed out on your senior year there?" I always found that peculiar because I never thought about it. Not once.

I was part of the Dunlap Team, and I was actually excited about Dad's new opportunity. I was also excited about moving to a new place and meeting new people. I knew I'd miss my friends, but I was sure I'd make some new friends, too.

Dad was gone all of February and March except for every other weekend when he returned home. I recall taking a trip to Colgate with Mom to do an initial house hunt. We also got to see the new athletic facilities and attend a Colgate hockey game.

Mom took me to Hamilton Central School where I met a few people. Most interesting was that Central meant *central.* There was no separation between high school, junior high and the elementary grades in Hamilton. They had one building for kindergarten through 12th grade.

Hamilton was a small town and Hamilton Central School was small, too. There were only 70 students per grade, much smaller than my school in Saucon Valley where there were about 300 students per grade. Hamilton was in Upstate New York, in a remote, rural area. It was farming country; cows outnumbered people by a wide margin.

I came back from that weekend with a good, but brief, sense for our new world. I had some apprehension, but overall I was excited about it. I had only played football and golf at Saucon Valley High School. With Hamilton being a much smaller school, I wondered if I might be able to play some other sports, too.

A couple months later, my high school spring break arrived and Mom asked if I wanted to ride with Dad to Colgate and spend the week in Hamilton. I jumped at the idea and Dad and I left Sunday evening to drive four hours to Upstate New York.

Being with Dad during the trip was great. We talked about everything, most of it centering on Colgate and what life was going to be like when we moved. He reassured me that I'd like living there. Now that he had been working there for more than two months, he had gotten acquainted with many people—coaches, professors and faculty. He had learned that many of them had kids my age.

Dad had arranged for me to meet some of them during that week. On one night, we all went to Ye Olde Pizza Pub. The kids seemed really nice and made me feel welcome. I spent time that week on Colgate's campus and at the high school. I even sat in a few classes and met more of my future classmates.

Being a high school athlete, I also spent time at Huntington Gym and Reid Athletic Center where the Colgate students worked out. I got pulled into a few hoops games and chatted with some of Dad's football players.

Another treat was playing golf at Seven Oaks Golf Club later that week. Colgate owned it and it was a huge upgrade from Wedgewood and Tumblebrook.

The week went by quickly, and as Dad and I drove back to

Bethlehem on Saturday morning, I felt much more grounded with my new environment. We talked about all of the people I had met, and then he quizzed me on which of his players I had met. From there, the discussion turned to Colgate football.

Dad was really excited about the prospects for his Colgate team. He couldn't believe how talented the players were. "I know we beat Colgate the last three years," he explained, "but on paper, we had no business winning." He was upbeat and animated as we drove down the road. "These athletes are really good. I don't know what the guy before me was doing, but he squandered his chances. I would have drooled to have this much talent."

As Dad drove, he was bullish about the future and he rattled off many names. Pat Healy. Gary Hartwig. Mike Foley. John Gibney. Henry White. Jim Comforti. Bobby Relph. Mark Murphy. Keith Polito.

Dad mentioned other players as we rolled down the highway. Kenny Ebeling. Doug Curtis. Ed Argast. Paul Lawler. Ray Linn. Rick Dole. Bruce Malverty. Carl Padovano.

I had met a few of them that week, but most of these names were foreign to me. It felt odd not knowing all of the players. I knew every one of them at Lehigh. The Colgate players' names were unfamiliar to me, but I would learn them soon enough, I figured.

Leaving Willowbrook Drive—The Summer of 1976

Mom worked feverishly to get our house ready to sell. She was already cleaning out the attic and boxing things for our eventual move.

Mom (and Dad) had decided not to buy an existing house in Hamilton. Rather, she thought it was better to build another house. As she had done 11 years earlier, she took a major role in designing the floor plan of the home. There were blueprints piled up on the kitchen table when we came through the door.

The remaining months of my junior school year sped by, and in June the moving truck arrived. Over the course of two days, I watched my childhood get boxed up and loaded on the truck. The house was barren with all of our belongings removed.

Another thing different was that Jessie had started college early. She departed right after her graduation. It was just Mom and me living there.

On the final day of the move, I made my rounds to some houses in the neighborhood to say goodbye to families that were close friends. It was a poignant moment for me, as the reality hit me that I was really leaving. With each visit, it was like I was closing the book on my life to that point. After walking back from the last family I visited, I went into our empty house. Only a few boxes were sitting in the hallway waiting to be loaded onto the truck.

I went up to my bedroom and stood silently, taking in the emptiness that had been my Safe Zone only a few days before. It was where I had lain awake at night so many times, thinking about girls, thinking about bullies, and thinking about my dreams for my future. My room always felt warm and secure, quite different from the stark appearance that day.

I needed to take one last walk around my yard. I walked past the mulberry tree we climbed every summer. I went past the rock walls my mother had built so many years earlier—walls we used to jump off of, like Apollo astronauts, to imagine the weightlessness they felt. And I walked out into our back forty where we built tree houses and played war games. I stood in the spot where I got the crazy idea to throw dirt bombs at the house so long ago.

Those were warm memories (except for the dirt bomb episode), but they now seemed like they were somebody else's memories. Distant memories.

I was melancholy over the prospect of leaving and the finality of the moment. "You can come visit your friends, Tiger," Mom said, trying to reassure me. "They will still be your friends." But I knew this was really an end, and that things wouldn't be the same.

As evening approached, the truck was ready to depart. Mom and I got in our car and started to leave the neighborhood. As we pulled away, I heard that old familiar sound—the siren from the Se-Wy-Co Fire Hall. I counted the 10 seconds in my head and then the siren stopped. Silence followed the sound of the horn, signaling to me that, with our leaving, things on Willowbrook Drive would continue normally without us. We would have to develop a new sense of normal in our new lives in Hamilton, New York.

PART III

The Product of a Decade of Work— The Colgate Years

New Beginnings

When Mom and I arrived in Hamilton, the Land of "Waste Not, Want Not" arrived with us. Our new house wasn't ready to inhabit yet. We rented a house on Colgate's campus, where we lived that summer while our home was being completed.

My summer job that year was to work with Mom to complete the home. In order to reduce builder expenses, Mom had negotiated for certain parts of the job to be performed by the two of us. My list included planting and seeding the lawn, painting all of the rooms and ceilings in the house, and varnishing all of the woodwork.

When I wasn't working on the house, I managed to play golf at Seven Oaks and meet with some of the Hamilton kids. They were great. I felt very much included right from the start. They invited me to parties and we also spent a lot of time out at Lake Moraine where we swam and paddled canoes.

I quickly noticed how different the Hamilton kids were from my classmates in Saucon Valley. During the previous year, temptations for under-age drinking were growing in Saucon Valley. It was quite common and I was getting lured into it.

Up in Hamilton, the kids threw parties at their houses, which included dancing and drinking soda pop. Hamilton was a much more wholesome community in that respect.

Months later, I had an opportunity to visit my friends in Saucon Valley. By that time, many of them had progressed from alcohol to marijuana and even cocaine. I was shocked. When I drove back to Colgate, I was relieved to be in the healthier environment of Hamilton, New York.

Living in Hamilton that summer was also good because we got to see more of my father. He was busier than at Lehigh, since he had two jobs, coach and AD, but we got to see him in the evenings.

As the new head coach, Dad needed to start over with the process of building expectations for his football program. As athletic director, there were needs to be met with other sports, too. Dad wanted to use that June and July to address all of the pressing needs of the AD role so that in August he could focus fully on football and the upcoming season.

One of the things Dad really liked about the AD role was that he could be his own boss for football. As the AD, he could control budgets across the whole athletic department. This allowed him to make sure the football program was adequately funded.

Dad could also control the scheduling for future football games, and he had a unique approach. Many football coaches don't want too hard a schedule. They think their job is safe as long as they are winning. My father had a different view. He wanted *really* tough games on the schedule. He realized this would make an undefeated season harder to achieve, but he believed that a tough, competitive schedule was critical to upgrading the quality of the recruited players. He had seen the benefits of that in his later years at Lehigh.

Dad negotiated with other big schools to play Colgate in upcoming seasons. He secured games with Penn State, Rutgers, Army, Villanova, Syracuse, Duke and Temple. Why did he do that? Because he wanted to compete for the same talented players that these schools wanted to recruit.

Colgate was similar to Lehigh in that Colgate didn't offer free rides, and the tuition costs were expensive. That put Dad at a disadvantage, but he thought that if he upgraded the schedule to include these big programs, it gave him a unique selling feature. Each of these big schools had a finite number of free rides that could be offered to their incoming freshman class. These football programs were impressive, so there were more quality recruits pursuing the schools than there were free rides to award. Any of these recruits could upgrade the talent pool at Colgate, my father thought.

Dad's recruiting pitch went something like this: He touted Colgate's academic reputation. The other schools couldn't compete with Colgate on academics. Then he pitched to the recruit that they had a choice. The player could accept the free ride at Penn State, but Dad asked the recruit how long he thought it would take before making the starting lineup. He would contrast that by explaining to the recruit that if he came to Colgate, he could probably make the starting lineup in his freshman year and be on the starting lineup for his entire career (and reset Colgate's record book!) and *still* get to play against teams like Penn State.

Dad's selling method worked, and he began attracting better talent to Colgate. The other positive to scheduling major college opponents was that it brought much more revenue into the athletic department. Dad could use it to support any sports requiring more funding.

Dad's strategy wasn't common. But he and Mom always sought a challenge. It was in their DNA—it was how they behaved. They were fascinated with the task of devising tactics to overcome obstacles. And I suppose it was inevitable then, after observing them closely while growing up, that I would be similarly inclined. Their example caused me later in life to always take on tough obstacles in the business world rather than take the easy way out. I suppose the Dunlap Rules can be *behavioral*, as well.

Colgate Football—The 1976 Season

SEPTEMBER ARRIVED, AND I BEGAN my senior year at Hamilton Central School. It was the beginning of two football seasons—mine at Hamilton, and a mile away, Dad's at Colgate.

Because it was a small high school with a limited number of players, the Hamilton Central coach asked me to play every play of the game. Offensive Guard. Defensive End. Punt team. Punt return team. Kickoff team. Kickoff return team. When I took the field at the start of the game, I didn't come off until it was halftime. It was the same in the second half, unless we had a big lead. If that was the case, the coach pulled me out in order to give younger players some experience.

Across College Street, Colgate was off to a fast start with their season. Dad had been right: his team did have a lot of talent. They won every game in September.

Colgate had a strong defense. They held four of the first five opponents to a touchdown or less. The offense, on the other hand, sputtered. There was good talent, but the players had been recruited to Colgate based on the previous coach's offensive scheme. Wheelwright ran a Wishbone offense, which was almost singularly focused on running plays. Though Dad's philosophy was to build the offense around the talent, he thought that the Wishbone was too limiting. It lacked the ability to make big plays, which would be required if the team fell behind by multiple scores.

Same coach, new uniform—1976 Colgate football.

On the job in 1976.

Dad had instituted the Wing-T offense at Lehigh. It was a more balanced offense (pass vs. run) and it used running plays to set up passing plays. Wishbone wasn't an option for Dad, so he decided to transition Colgate to the Wing-T and try to find the best athletes who could effectively adjust to it. The change wasn't easy; the blocking techniques were different. And for the quarterback, passing skills were more important with the Wing-T than with the Wishbone offense.

While Colgate won its first five games, Dad grappled with finding a quarterback who could meet the needs of the Wing-T offense. Out of that search emerged Bobby Relph. Despite being recruited to Colgate to play the Wishbone offense, he adapted quickly to the offensive scheme of his new head coach.

Throughout that season, I watched the Colgate games from the sidelines (as I had done at Lehigh), helping the quarterbacks track the offensive plays. The great thing about Hamilton Central School's football schedule was that almost all of the games were held on Friday evenings. That allowed me to be available for the Colgate games, even if they were away contests. After my games ended, I would take a shower, then hustle to the parking lot to meet my mother. She would have the car stocked with food and drinks and we would drive late into the night to the location of the Colgate away game. I hadn't missed one of Dad's games in seven years and I wasn't about to stop that streak.

October was another strong stretch for Colgate. They remained undefeated going into the November games. For the most part, the games were very close, but the team found a way to win in the fourth quarter. The offense played solidly, but the key to most of the wins was the strength of the defense. During this eight-game stretch, Colgate held all but one opponent to 14 or fewer points.

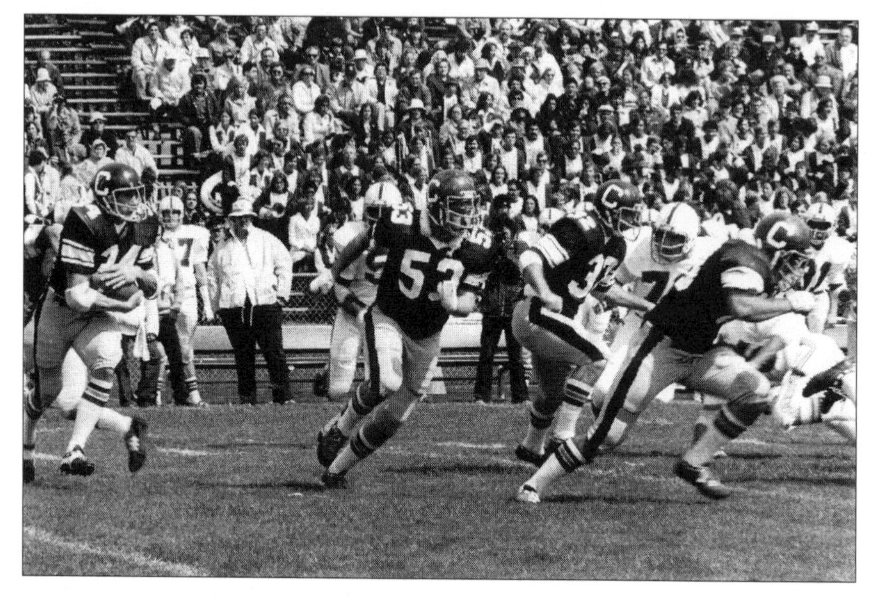

Action from the 1976 UConn game.

1976 Boston University game—QB Bob Relph on the move.

With two games to go, Colgate was undefeated, 8-0. It had been ten years since Colgate had eight wins in a season. The alumni and the town fans were ecstatic. Colgate football was the buzz everywhere.

The final two games were against two of the toughest opponents on the schedule: Army and Rutgers. Both games were played at the opponent's stadium. Colgate didn't play well against Army and lost 29-13 to a very good Army football team.

Coach Dunlap with QB Jim Russell at the 1976 Army game.

The team was now 8-1, with one game remaining. And that game was against Rutgers, which was undefeated coming into the final game against Colgate. On the Monday before the Saturday game, Fred Grunninger, Rutgers' athletic director, called Dad. ABC Sports had called Grunninger over the weekend to ask about televising the Rutgers/Colgate game.

With Rutgers being undefeated and Colgate having only one loss, the network wanted to carry the game on Thanksgiving night on national television. Grunninger wanted to do it, and he called Dad to see if he would be willing to move the game from the next Saturday back five days to Thanksgiving.

Also, ABC Sports wanted the game moved from Rutgers' stadium in New Brunswick, New Jersey, to the New York Giants' stadium in the Meadowlands.

Dad was in favor of the idea, but he needed to get permission to move the game from Tom Bartlett, Colgate's president. Dad liked President Bartlett. He enjoyed the same level of support from him that he had with Dr. Lewis at Lehigh.

Dad met later that day with Bartlett to unveil the opportunity to play on national TV in the Meadowlands. "Tom, think of the recruiting boost this will give us," Dad argued. "We'd get national exposure!"

President Bartlett saw this opportunity quite differently and was initially against the idea. "Fred, that could backfire on us," he countered. "Rutgers is *really* good. We play them every year and they kill us." Bartlett shook his head. "We don't want that to happen on national television. It could be a huge embarrassment."

It was true that Rutgers had beaten Colgate badly in recent years. In 1974, Colgate lost 62-21, and in 1975, they lost 56-14.

Dad countered by saying, "I know that. But in the same years, we beat Rutgers when I was at Lehigh. I know their strategy and I know their personnel. And we are a lot better football team this year than Colgate was in the last two years." Dad exhorted his boss. "It won't be a slaughter; we will be competitive. I know our defense can play with them. We just have to come up with a plan of attack that gets us some points on offense."

The meeting ended. Bartlett reluctantly agreed to move the game to Thanksgiving night.

Taking the field in the Meadowlands—1976 Rutgers game

Colgate on Offense—1976 Rutgers game

Dad was right. Colgate was competitive. By the end of the first half, Colgate trailed 7-3. In the third quarter, the deficit had been cut to one point, 10-9. Both teams were playing hard, but neither team knew that controversy was right around the corner.

Late in the 3rd quarter, Rutgers was driving and had reached midfield. The Colgate defense stiffened, and Rutgers was forced to punt.

During the week before, while watching scouting films, Dad and his coaching staff noticed that the Rutgers center did a peculiar thing when he snapped the ball on punts. Because the snap was a full 15 yards back to the punter, the center "wound up" to snap the ball. An instant before he snapped it, he thrust the ball forward to increase his leverage.

The Colgate coaches knew that (technically) the play started when the ball moved. Dad therefore informed the officials before the game about this quirk in the center's routine, and he told the umpire his players would be acting on that first move.

For every one of Rutgers' punts in the first half, Colgate lined a player up right on the center. That Colgate player was instructed to swat the center's hand (and the ball) the instant the center began his motion. The strategy worked. It caused the Rutgers center to mishandle the snap. That distracted the punter, who found the balls coming back to him in every direction.

The center complained to the official, but the umpire had been prepared for this happening. The center's appeal was ignored.

On that late 3rd quarter punt, again Colgate had a player prepared to swat the ball. Dad had called a punt block play, where all of the Colgate players rushed the punter. He did this because our offense had been struggling, and, up to that point in the game, hadn't been able to sustain a long drive. Rather than set up for a punt return, which would give us the ball deep in Colgate's territory, Dad felt we needed to *shorten the field* by trying to block the punt and get the ball in Rutgers territory.

By this juncture in the game, the Rutgers center had lost all of his composure. The Colgate lineman was definitely in his head. The snap began. Our player again swatted him. And the ball bounced errantly toward the punter.

The punter had trouble handling the snap. This gave Colgate that extra split second of time to block the punt. Pat Horan rushed off the corner, leaped in the air above the punter's foot and blocked the punt.

The ball bounced backwards toward the Rutgers goal line. There was a mad scramble of Colgate players and Rutgers players chasing after it. Horan was chasing. Mark Murphy was chasing. And as the pursuit and struggle to recover the free ball ensued, the ball kept being batted toward the Rutgers goal line. There was pushing and shoving going on as both teams tried to get the ball.

Eventually, Colgate recovered the ball on the Rutgers 8-yard line. The punt block play had worked: Colgate had really shortened the field.

One problem. There was a flag on the play.

One of the officials called clipping on Colgate. The official saw a Colgate player push a Rutgers player from behind during the mad scramble for the ball after the punt was blocked.

On television, the announcers called it a "botched call" by the officials. Bud Wilkinson, the winningest coach in Oklahoma history (and the same man whom Dad had learned from at a football clinic he attended when he was in the Army), was one of the announcers that evening. Wilkinson was outraged. He explained to the national audience, "After a punt is blocked, it is a free ball—there can't be a clipping penalty because neither team is on offense or defense!"

No matter, the officials administered the penalty while Wilkinson continued his protest over the call. Unfortunately, the official's mistake got even worse. The officials took the ball all the way back to midfield (where the play had started), and then administered a 15-yard penalty. That gave Rutgers a first down and the ball was placed on Colgate's 35-yard line. It amounted to a change in possession and a penalty of 57 yards.

Wilkinson went crazy. "You've got to be kidding me!" he roared. "A clipping penalty is wrong. But even if you call clipping, the clip itself happened after the punt, way down in Rutgers territory. At worst, it should be Colgate's ball on the Rutgers 25-yard line. Boy, is Colgate getting the shaft."

The game stopped for a brief period as the officials tried to explain their rationale. They made their pitch to a relieved and delighted Rutgers coaching staff and a disbelieving, outraged Colgate coaching staff. When the game resumed, only a few plays later, Rutgers scored. It was now Rutgers 17, Colgate 9.

Colgate regrouped. Several offensive drives ensued with the players knowing they were still only one touchdown and a two-point conversion behind. Late in the 4th quarter, Colgate made a final attempt, driving to the Rutgers 20-yard line. But on fourth down, they came up short.

Colgate lost 17-9 that Thanksgiving night. They didn't lose by 40 points as the Colgate president had feared. It was a loss by eight points, after a controversial call.

During the days and weeks that followed, that controversy didn't die down. The botched call was aired on television the entire Thanksgiving weekend and was carried in newspapers all over the northeastern part of the United States. The officials were under siege by the media. Rutgers was seen as having been lucky to have won. And little Colgate, from the Chenango Valley, had captured the imagination of football sports fans across the country.

Dad grimaced many times over the years about how different that game might have turned out if Colgate had gotten the ball on Rutgers' 8-yard line. But the irony was that Colgate got tremendous exposure for having played on national TV. Colgate played a great game and was competitive with a stronger Rutgers team. And the controversy only increased the loyal following for the little school located in rural New York. Colgate became the David, able to take on the Goliaths. And that reputation would prove beneficial to Colgate in coming years.

Reflections Over Thanksgiving

When the game ended, Dad and Mom quickly drove Jessie and me back to Hamilton for what remained of the Thanksgiving weekend. Jessie was home from college and the four of us were reunited.

With the Rutgers game fresh in our minds, we talked at length about it over the weekend. Dad also talked about the rest of the season. The team had finished the year with an 8-2 record, beating many teams they had lost to in previous years.

While Dad felt good overall, he regretted losing the final two games and mentioned how we could have done this or could have done that to win the games. Dad was always about improvement. Rather than reflect on his successes, he was more fixated on what needed to be done better. And on that weekend, he was already thinking about spring practice and the start of next season.

I asked Dad why he thought Colgate had played so well that year, when the team had generally a .500 record for the previous 7-8 years. And I reminded him that Lehigh had beaten Colgate soundly the past three years while Dad was coach there.

Dad smiled and said, "The reasons are complicated. But they are also pretty simple. The 1976 season wasn't different because we had better talent than Colgate had in previous years. It was because there was a change in how the program was being run."

Dad talked about how there had been a dearth of leadership with the previous regime, and how Colgate had lacked discipline. "The offensive scheme in previous years lacked imagination," he said. "There needed to be more variety in their plays, using passing more often. I am doing the same things here that we did at Lehigh; the only difference is that I am starting out with much more talent than we had back in 1965."

Dad reminded me of his Team Rules regarding discipline, hard work, commitment to the cause, taking care of the little things, organizational structure and strong communication. "These foundations were largely absent at Colgate before I got here. The players at Colgate were always talented. All I did was give them a structure and a culture where they could then get the most out of their abilities.

"In past years, I observed Colgate from afar," he said. "Its program had more prestige than Lehigh's. We lost some good recruits to Colgate because of that." He shifted in his chair. "It always seemed like Colgate started their season off strong but then began to fade toward the end of the season. It was like they lacked a certain amount of character to get themselves through difficult situations. Wheelwright had talented players, but he never got out of the program what it appeared he could have gotten."

Dad continued. "Being around here for a year, I have heard a lot of stories about Wheelwright from the players. He was a smooth guy, a good recruiter and a knowledgeable football man. But evidently he was a bit of a Jekyll and Hyde. Hyde showed up when the kids came on campus.

"I heard stories about how he would scream at players and jump on top of them in practice, basically abusing them," he told me. "And I think that degree of inconsistency with a leader can lead to inconsistent behavior with the team. Maybe that is why Colgate lacked character over the years at critical moments."

Dad then told me a story that had been shared with him that year. There was a player named Dick Slenker who collided with the Colgate kicker during practice one day. The kicker was Jerry Andrewlavage, one of the finest kickers in Colgate's history. Jerry still holds many of the Colgate placekicking and punting records.

On that day, Slenker rushed in and tackled Andrewlavage. They both went down in a heap. Wheelwright rushed in and jumped on top of Slenker, putting his knees on his chest and screamed, "What the hell do you think you are doing? You don't hit *him*—he is a *real* football player!" Wheelwright then grabbed Slenker by the facemask and shouted, "You won't ever be a *real* football player!"

Dad felt that stories like that were an indictment on leadership. And he was certain that those events, if they happened with any frequency, worked against any sense of unity that was being fostered.

As an aside, Wheelwright was wrong. Dick Slenker later started as a wide receiver in both his junior and senior years. He was elected co-captain in his senior year and was a critical element to the Colgate offense in both years. He turned out to be a real football player, after all.

During that Thanksgiving weekend, Dad provided some other perspectives. He said, "There are other reasons why 1976 was easier than 1965. The Colgate kids bought in to my system immediately. We had beaten them three years straight and they knew I had already built a winning program at Lehigh. So they didn't question whether I was right."

Dad then compared that with his Lehigh days. "At Lehigh, I was an unproven entity. I was a new head coach and didn't have a track record," he reflected. "So I suppose there was more doubt back then about whether my approaches would really work."

Then Dad became quite serious. "Tiger," he said, "the other thing is that I am a better coach now than I was back then. If a person is truly honest with himself and open to self-evaluation, each year and each experience can make you better. It can shape how you will handle issues in the future, if you ever face them again."

Dad chuckled. "Hell, in 1965, I was a young man, full of piss and vinegar, and I probably was *less graceful* in the application of my methods." He laughed again. "I thought that building a program based on character was all you needed to do. I didn't realize you needed to win games, too, to keep your job." He was referring to the winless early years at Lehigh.

Dad was reflective and philosophical. From what he shared, it was clear that personal growth, development and maturity didn't just apply to children. They were things that should be pursued throughout life, at any age.

For me, this was a valuable lesson learned. Later in life, I recalled this discussion many times. Like Dad in his early years, my "bedside manner" as a manager evolved with each of my experiences. My more resolute tendencies as a younger man, through many experiences, matured into a delivery that I discovered accomplished the same objectives while avoiding unnecessary distractions or disruptions.

Learning never stops, I realized, if you allow it to happen.

Finishing Up at Hamilton Central School

With Mom inspiring me to work hard and Dad continuing to build Colgate into a football powerhouse, my goal was to enjoy my senior year at Hamilton Central School to the fullest.

That year passed by quickly. After football season, I played basketball for Hamilton and then in the spring, I participated in golf and track. Playing two sports in the same season took some logistical juggling. My golf coach, Gary Rider, allowed me to spend the bulk of my time on track (on practice and in meets), so long as I could break away and be available on days that the golf team had a match.

When I wasn't playing sports or going to school, I was heavily involved in filling out college applications. I applied to six schools (Colgate, Lehigh, Cornell, St. Lawrence, Franklin & Marshall and Bucknell) and therefore had six lengthy applications to complete.

Mom was a huge asset. She helped pull the compulsory personal data together and provided editing oversight for the written essays required for each application.

This was nothing new; Mom had mentored me for years, helping me refine my writing skills. Like so many Lehigh football players had done, I sat at our kitchen table with her and pored over my early drafts. Again, she used her Socratic style to prod me. "What message are you trying to get across, Tiger?" she would ask. "Do you think your choice of subject best matches what they are asking for in the application, or do you think we should select another subject?"

Beyond that strategic consulting, Mom also assisted with editing, refining the clarity of my sentence structure. She didn't edit my work directly. Instead, she nudged me with questions like, "Do you think that's the most succinct way to present that idea? Or is there a way to impart your message with fewer words and tighter sentences?"

I will freely admit that her *Socratic-ness* was frustrating to me at times. *This would go a helluva lot faster if you would just fix the sentences for me,* I often thought. But that wasn't how Mom tutored. She knew I would learn more by working through the project myself, even if that meant the project would take more time.

I toiled with the applications for weeks. Eventually all six were completed and mailed to the schools.

Mom was heavily involved in the selection of these choices. She didn't select them for me. Rather, she used her style to help me sort out what mattered most in a school. She asked, "Is that school strong academically? Would you be happy playing football for that coach? What else about the school is intriguing to you?"

On and on, Mom would ask questions without showing any personal bias to the colleges we discussed. The closest she came to signaling any personal opinion was when all six applications were complete. "I think you have a nice group of schools there, Tiger," she summarized. "Any one of them would be a good choice."

A few weeks later, I started receiving calls from various individuals at the colleges. The football coaches invited me to come for a weekend recruiting visit. Six weekends were spent that spring visiting these schools. The visits were great and I learned a lot about each school.

Typically, the visits worked as follows: A host, usually a current football player, was assigned to me when I arrived on Friday evening. His job was to escort me for the weekend and make sure I had a good time. The activities usually included attending a sports event (basketball or hockey), taking a tour of the campus, attending fraternity parties or just hanging out in one of the dorm rooms with the football players. I also attended one-on-one meetings with the head coach, and another with my prospective position coach.

Over the course of each weekend, I got a sense for the culture of the team. My senses were fairly acute since I had been heavily exposed to Dad's culture and approach to running a football program. Team culture was very important to me, so I listened closely to the comments made by players and coaches about what it was like to play there.

Most of my visits went very well, but there was one exception. During my trip to Cornell I was matched with a unique host. He was drunk when he picked me up, having arrived from a Friday afternoon beer bash. I wasn't offended by the drinking; most of my recruiting trips involved frat parties and I drank my fair share at those events. *But being hammered at 5 p.m.? When you are a host for a total stranger!* That surprised me.

As we walked to his car, my Cornell host told me he could only stay with me for a short while since his girlfriend was visiting campus later that night. He suggested that we grab a quick dinner because, as he admitted, "I need to sober up."

The host suggested Burger King, located in downtown Ithaca, New York. Before we left, he grabbed three of his frat buddies and told them to join us. The five of us piled into his small car and headed downtown.

It was customary for the host to pay for the recruit's expenses on these weekends. But that player hadn't gone to the coach's office to collect the weekend stipend. "I didn't want the coach to see that I was bombed," he explained before asking me to pay for dinner.

When the Burger King feast was over, we didn't return immediately to campus, since he and his buddies wanted to cruise around town. That wasn't usually part of the recruiting trip, but I wasn't in charge. As we drove around, I listened to the four of them talk. From what they said, it became clear that we weren't just cruising: they intended to steal batteries and hubcaps from parked cars.

When we stopped in parking lots, they walked around lifting hoods and prying off hubcaps. I stayed in the car, panicked that we were going to get arrested. After a couple hours and a few successful heists, we returned to the frat house. On the ride back to campus, I learned this was how the players made extra spending money—by stealing the car parts and selling them to service stations.

By the time we arrived at the fraternity, my host's girlfriend had arrived. They darted into his bedroom and as he was closing the bedroom door, he looked back at me and said, "Hey, just hang out with the other guys." Since they were in his room all night, both nights, I slept on couches in the basement of the frat house. I didn't see my host again that weekend. Needless to say, Cornell wasn't my college choice.

The final decision was between Colgate and Bucknell. I was interested in Colgate, for the opportunity to play for my father, but Bucknell had a good football program, too. Both were challenging academically. Both schools wanted me. And I had good recruiting visits at both colleges.

My parents had opinions about which college to choose, I was sure, but they were careful not to voice them. I believed they wanted me to choose Colgate. I would have been part of Dad's team and would have been close to home. But they could also see the benefits of my going elsewhere where I would be more independent and grow as a person.

Mostly, Dad and Mom wanted *me* to make *my* decision, separate and apart from the affiliation with Dad's program. They gave me space to assess the points of consideration and waited for me to reach a conclusion.

Advice was plentiful outside of my family unit. People admonished me that, "playing for your father can be difficult." They said, "It might be a better experience for you to play football somewhere else."

That concern became the deciding factor in my choosing Bucknell. When I discussed it with my parents, they were supportive of my decision and were excited for me. I called some of the Colgate players. When they heard the news, they were disappointed. We had gotten along well and they were convinced that I'd choose Colgate. But they understood my reasons, and we stayed friends in spite of it. "We'll kick your ass this fall when we play Bucknell!" they kidded me.

After I graduated from Hamilton, I spent the summer training for my freshman fall at Bucknell. I used the Colgate facilities for running and strength training. That summer, there were many Colgate football players enrolled in summer school classes. That was typical at Colgate. Students attended one summer school semester and then took one spring or fall semester off.

I hung with these guys throughout the summer, working out and drinking beer with them in the evenings. In 1977, the drinking age in New York State was 18. Being of age, I received *training* in alcohol consumption, too.

That summer at Colgate was great fun. My new friends prepared for Colgate football and I prepared for my start at Bucknell.

Leaving the Nest—August 1977

I BEGAN PACKING FOR COLLEGE in the middle of August. I was to report to Bucknell for Fall Camp two weeks before the general student body would arrive. Double sessions were commencing and this would be my first opportunity to play college football.

Mom helped me gather and pack my clothes. She also bought supplies for class work. That would begin two weeks later. Dad had been busy planning for his own season—coaches' meetings had been ongoing since the beginning of August. I had seen him each night during that month, but otherwise he was consumed with preparation for Colgate's double sessions.

On the evening before I left for Bucknell, Dad came home early so the three of us could have dinner together. The conversation centered on Bucknell, not Colgate. Dad wanted to hear my plans. We discussed my schedule for the next few weeks. I would be living offsite with the team, and rooming with Tom Hislop, my host on the recruiting trip. Tom was going to be a senior and had been elected football team co-captain.

Dad had not met Tom, but he was very familiar with him since Colgate played against him for three years. "He's a really tough kid," Dad told me. "He is one of their best linemen. And he must have strong leadership qualities if they elected him captain."

We talked for a while that night, and Dad gave me several pieces of advice. He felt a need to exhaust all of his wisdom on me as if he would never have another chance to share it.

I went to bed that night both anxious and excited about the drive to Bucknell the next morning. As I lay there in the dark, the moment felt eerily similar to my last night in our house on Willowbrook Drive. I was leaving and turning another major page in my life. My time spent in Hamilton had been considerably shorter than Bethlehem but I felt a similar sense of loss, leaving the Hamilton world behind.

What would I encounter at Bucknell? I wondered. *Would I be good enough? Would I like the school? Would I have a girlfriend?* All of these thoughts raced through my mind.

When I awoke the next morning, Dad was at home. It was 9 a.m. and he was still there—unusual for him. I ate breakfast and got ready to go. Mom was driving with me to Bucknell, a 4-hour journey to Lewisburg, Pennsylvania.

Curiously, when I walked downstairs, Dad still hadn't left the house. He seemed to be killing time waiting for me.

Then he asked, "Tiger, can you step into the living room with me?" He asked me to sit down. When we were both settled, he looked down, struggling with what he was going to say. He started to speak. And then stopped. Then he started again, only to halt himself.

Finally Dad began. "Tig, you know your mother and I love you." He stopped again. He looked up at me and abruptly changed the subject. "I'm wondering...do you have any questions about what we talked about last night?"

"No, Dad, you were pretty clear. And I appreciate it." I replied. "I think I am ready to go, or at least as ready as I am going to be."

Dad nodded and said, "That's good." He again started to appear uneasy. "You know your mother and I love you. And we are very proud of who you are and what you've become—a young man." More pause. He was struggling in a way I had never seen before. "You know how to reach me if you have any questions or need to talk to me about anything."

He *knew* I knew how to reach him, but for some reason he told me anyway.

"Tig," he said softly, "your leaving is really difficult for your mother. She is taking it very hard. You know that, don't you?" I really didn't. I knew she loved me, but she had seemed so excited for me. And she had been her typical energetic, pro-active self, organizing me for the move. *She was a good actor,* I thought, *if she felt as Dad described.*

"You are her only son," Dad continued, "and her last child to leave the nest. It's the end of her role with you as your mother. I just want you to be aware of that. It's going to be a tough ride home for her after she drops you off at Bucknell."

I understood what Dad said. Thinking that he was done, we moved toward the door and walked outside. When I approached the car, Mom was already in the driver's seat and the car was running. I hugged and kissed Dad, and I told him I loved him. And he did the same. I said goodbye and got inside next to Mom.

As she put the car in reverse to back out of the driveway, I looked at Dad, standing in the driveway watching us pull away. Suddenly he burst into tears. His shoulders shook as he sobbed. I yelled to Mom to stop the car and I got out and ran to him. He hugged me hard and he buried his head into my neck, weeping uncontrollably.

"I'm so sorry, Tiger," he said. It was hard to understand him through his sobs. "I'm sorry I wasn't a better father." I hugged him as hard as I could. "I was gone so much while you were growing up," he added. "And now you are gone, and I have lost so much. I can never get it back." Dad cried harder.

I hugged my father as hard as I could, while neither of us said anything. I hadn't expected this and I wasn't sure what to do. I had never seen my father cry. He was always a rock.

I just consoled him as best I could. I was also crying at this point. "Dad, you were a great father," I told him. "You ARE a great father. The best any kid could have." He cried some more, as we held each other. And then as he gathered himself, he kissed me again and told me I better get going.

When I got back in the car, Mom was a mess, too, having watched us through the windshield. She and I cried our way out of Hamilton and didn't really speak. We didn't have to—everyone understood each other.

It was quiet in the car for quite a while. As Mom drove, I pondered. I saw a side of my father that morning that had eluded me for 18 years. It was a softer side, an emotional side. The side of a man who always did what was right but now realized that came with a cost—that cost being his lack of time spent with his kids.

I didn't resent him for that—it was our *normal*, growing up in our home. And our normal was a great normal. Our normal came with two parents who loved us immensely and spent 18 years instilling in us great values and giving perspectives for conducting ourselves. Those values, I was sure, would guide us well through life.

I loved our normal. And I loved my mom and dad.

Fifteen years later, after I had become a father, Dad spent considerable time talking to me about it. I had taken on challenging jobs, demanding a lot of my time. Dad was concerned I might be falling into the same time trap he had experienced. I think he saw it as his duty to remind me to spend time with my kids while they were growing up. "It all goes by so quickly," he said.

To be certain, Dad, and of course, Mom, were valuable guides for me over the years. I did continue to pursue larger positions and they did place extreme demands on my time. But I think I did a good job of finding a lot of quality time for my children, just as Dad suggested. And spending time with my kids came to me naturally, as I will describe later.

The Bucknell Experience

There wasn't much time for slow, drawn-out farewells when Mom and I arrived in Lewisburg. The campus was empty because we were there two weeks ahead of the rest of the student population.

The welcome I received was probably comparable to what an enlisted man would receive as he begins boot camp. The coaches were pleasant enough to me and my mother, but the exchange was brief. I quickly said goodbye to her, and I hustled into the locker room. Inside was a line of players waiting to get their equipment. I gradually moved to the front of the line where I was fitted for football gear and given some practice jerseys and pants. I was then assigned a locker and told to head down the hall for a physical.

As I waited my turn, I could tell who the freshman were—the players in line who *weren't* talking. The other guys looked far more at ease. They kidded each other, talking about their summers and referring to things at Bucknell with a sense of authority. *These guys know their way around,* I thought.

When my physical was complete, I was given some bedding and a key to a dorm room. I was told to hurry there and get settled, but to be back in an hour for a team meeting. I scurried off, trying to avoid any chance of being late.

The team meeting was something familiar to me, after having sat through many similar meetings that my father conducted. Our head coach, whom I will call Coach Landry, spoke to the whole team and then we broke into smaller groups to meet with our position coach.

There weren't any introductions of players—it was all business. As I looked around at the players in the meeting, I wondered who they were and who I would be competing with for a starting position.

When the meeting ended, we were released to the cafeteria for dinner, and after that, to our dorm rooms for the rest of the evening. That's where I spent some time with Tommy Hislop. Being with Tommy was reassuring, because the coaches weren't nearly as friendly as they had been on the recruiting visit. I was starting to think of them more as prison wardens. And I was starting to think of myself as an inmate.

Having Tom to balance my reactions was great. He helped shape my expectations about what would transpire over the next two weeks. Double sessions, I knew, would begin in earnest the next morning.

I had a fairly successful Fall Camp. Though only a freshman, I made it onto the varsity travel squad as a second string defensive end, and I started on varsity special teams that year. I was delighted to be on the travel squad. I hated the thought of being left behind on campus while the rest of the team traveled to away games.

One thing about Fall Camp is that you get to know everyone very quickly. It's a closed environment where players are sequestered for 14 days with no outside distractions, while going through a physically grueling process. By the time the rest of the student body arrived, I felt like I had known my teammates forever—even the upperclassmen. They were strangers only a couple weeks earlier, but now we were well-acquainted.

Several upperclassmen invited some of the freshmen to their fraternity houses after double sessions ended. The drinks flowed abundantly as everyone celebrated the end of Fall Camp and the arrival of the 54 percent of the student body, best technically described as: WOMEN.

Life at Bucknell was great. I enjoyed my classes. I was making friends. The parties were fun and the girls were pretty. The downside was, unfortunately, the football experience. To be fair, I was in a peculiar situation since I was the son of another head football coach. I was not only related to the Colgate head coach, but I had been deeply invested in his program since I was six years old.

I had studied Dad's leadership and management style and had embraced his practice regimen. It had proven to be successful, and I believed in his methods.

As my freshman fall progressed, I continued to observe the manner with which Coach Landry ran his program and I naturally compared it to how Dad was running things at Colgate. The comparison wasn't a good one. There were few similarities and the differences were many.

Examples of basic differences:

Lack of organization at practice—the schedule kept changing, practices continued interminably; difficult for a new college kid to manage.

Lack of precision—segments of practice weren't consistent. They would be changed at the whim of the Bucknell coaches. My father ran everything with precision. Practice segments and pre-game activities were managed and run to the minute. A player never questioned where he needed to be or when he needed to be there.

Examples of more important things:

Demeanor—Coach Landry was emotional, a screamer. Contrastingly, I had grown up in the Land of "Less Is More." Landry berated players and coaches, like he felt he needed to remind everyone he was in charge.

Discipline—Coach Landry and his staff weren't firm with Team Rules and the rules weren't enforced consistently. Lots of threats were made, but the follow-through was erratic, which led players to question whether rules really mattered.

Inconsistency—Player treatment seemed to be based on how important the player was to winning. At times, the coaches treated less talented players worse than the better players. Sometimes it was more subtle, when they would pander to the better players while seemingly ignoring lesser players.

Academic importance—The coaches didn't show a significant interest in a player's academic performance. Dad and his staff monitored and emphasized academic performance as much as athletic performance.

Respect—Coach Landry's tirades and veiled threats made him unpopular and detracted from his credibility with the players. Some of the assistant coaches would even confer with players after one of Landry's tirades, telling the player to "ignore him" and "don't worry about it." Contrastingly, there was never a break in ranks with my father's program: respect was the most critical element to his leadership. It was mandatory with Dad's team and with his family.

It was clear, relatively early at Bucknell, that the players didn't respect the head coach. During the bus trip for our opening game at Rutgers, I grabbed a seat in the second row. The first row was reserved for Coach Landry. As the bus filled up, a junior named Mike Cosimano jumped into my seat to sit with me. Mike was a great guy and probably the funniest person I had ever met. He did stand-up comedy routines on campus. Everybody knew "Cozzy," our nickname for him. He had a wit and delivery like Robin Williams.

I liked Cozzy and looked forward to riding with him to Rutgers. It would be a boatload of laughs, I was sure. When the bus departed, Cozzy was in high gear, telling story after story. At one point, Coach Landry, apparently growing tired of Cozzy's manic series of tales, told him to quiet down and do some homework.

I grabbed my textbooks and started to study. Cozzy did the same. But a few minutes later, he elbowed me and smiled his devilish grin. Though he was silent, he had my attention. Cozzy had started tearing little pieces of paper from his notebook and carefully dropping them on Coach Landry's head as the coach sat reading a magazine. First one.

Then another. Then five more. Coach Landry didn't detect it, as the pieces of paper rested on his hair like the feathery feel of new-fallen snow. Pretty soon he looked like a guy who had been walking in a blizzard.

Cozzy continued. Meanwhile, across the aisle from Coach Landry sat my position coach. He saw what Cozzy was doing. Rather than stop him, he smiled at Cozzy and then turned his head and ignored what was happening.

We rode for another hour with Landry's head still covered with snow. I was panicked he would discover it since the only two players who could have done it were Cozzy or me. As the bus ride continued, more players noticed what Cozzy had done, and everyone had a good, but discreet, laugh about it.

Eventually, Coach Landry adjusted himself in his seat and paper pieces began falling in his lap. He then ran his fingers through his hair and more pieces fell in front of him.

Cozzy immediately took on the persona of being fast asleep, mouth wide open. Thinking quickly, I followed suit. Minutes passed without consequence. Yet I was afraid to open my eyes. After all, I thought, there might be a seething coach waiting a few inches from my nose.

Just then, Cozzy elbowed me. Opening my eyes, I could see that Coach Landry had gotten up and moved to the back of the bus. We had eluded a possible altercation and Cozzy was delighted with himself. I, on the other hand, only felt relief.

The image of Coach Landry with the paper on his head remains vivid to this day. As I sat beside Cozzy, frightened about being implicated, I was struck by the contrast between my father's football program and Landry's.

What happened on that bus would never have happened with my father's team. There was too much respect for him. If it ever had, the penalties would have been severe and the players knew it.

Disturbingly, at Bucknell, there wasn't respect for the coach. Perhaps even worse, the assistant coach didn't even step in to stop it. Respect was lacking everywhere, a fundamental breakdown of one of the most important Dunlap Rules.

Colgate Football—The 1977 Season

While Bucknell thrashed its way to a 4-5 season, Colgate had another strong season. Colgate's home opener was against Rutgers, and the sting from the prior year's controversial loss was hot on the minds of the Colgate players and coaches.

In the nine months since the Meadowlands game, I don't think the players or coaches had thought about anything but beating Rutgers. Throughout the off-season, the players salivated at the chance for a re-match. "We get to play them at home! We get to play them in the Kerr Dome!" they chanted.

The Kerr Dome was an affectionate nickname for Colgate's home field. The official name was Andy Kerr Stadium, named after a successful Colgate football coach from the 1930s and '40s. Most notably, Kerr was the head coach for the '32 team that had a perfect record (9-0). That team didn't allow a single point scored against them in the *entire season.* The 1932 team was undefeated, untied, unscored-upon, and uninvited (to a bowl game).

Impressive as Andy Kerr's record was, the Andy Kerr Stadium was diminutive. Given Colgate's rural location, the maximum capacity of the stadium was commensurate with the census count of the community: small.

Andy Kerr Stadium wasn't a dome at all. And it wasn't really a stadium.

It was a string of bleachers along each sideline with a maximum capacity of about 10,000. Many of the Colgate players had played in high school stadiums that were bigger and more impressive—which is why they poked fun at it.

Because nearby Syracuse University played their football games in The Carrier Dome, the Colgate team affectionately called their inauspicious home stands The Kerr Dome.

Also, because Colgate was situated in such a remote location and because Andy Kerr Stadium could accommodate so few people, many of Colgate's opponents were unwilling to play in Hamilton. They only agreed to play Colgate if the game was played on their home field. Consequently, Colgate played only 3-4 home games a year; the bulk of their schedule was on the road.

Though it was unusual, on a sunny September day in 1977, Rutgers made a rare appearance in Hamilton. Rutgers tended to recruit city kids, and they weren't pleased with having to travel to play in a cow town.

When Rutgers players ran onto the field for warm ups, many of them started "mooing" loudly, openly mocking the Colgate players and the meager state of the Kerr Dome. As they made fun of Colgate, what the Rutgers players didn't realize was that they would face a determined opponent that day, and the mocking only incensed the Colgate team more.

Following the kickoff, Colgate dominated Rutgers for a full 60 minutes. Offensive domination. Defensive domination. Domination by Special Teams.

The final score was a resounding 23-0 victory. With that win, Colgate was off to a fast start to their 1977 season.

Colgate Defense shuts down Rutgers—1977

Colgate Offense taking charge—1977 Rutgers game

VICTORY!—1977 Rutgers game in the "Kerr Dome."

Coach Dunlap conferring with QB Bob Relph (1977).

I knew when I decided to attend Bucknell that we would be playing against Colgate later that fall. It had been a source of banter between the Colgate players and me before I left for school. What I didn't know was that Bucknell would have a 3-4 record going into the match up, and Colgate would be 8-0.

Having eight straight wins was one thing, but *the way* Colgate had beaten its opponents was another. Colgate beat six of the first eight opponents by 17 points or more. Colgate's defense was as strong as the prior year's team, but their offense was vastly improved, averaging 35 points a game.

As luck would have it, Bucknell's starting defensive end got hurt on the day before we traveled to Colgate. With him sidelined, I would have my first starting assignment as a college football player against Dad's team. The Colgate players knew I was coming, but they weren't aware I would be starting. I hadn't shared that with my father. It wouldn't have been proper. After all, he was the enemy!

During the first quarter, it was clear that Bucknell was no match for Colgate. Their team jumped out to a big lead. The player across the line from me was Ed Argast, Colgate's offensive tackle. I knew Sugar Bear (his nickname) from the summer before.

At one point, I rushed the quarterback (Bob Relph) and Sugar Bear blocked me. As we slammed and pushed on each other, we went down in a ball of pads and cleats, and I ended up on top of him. As I started to get up after the play, I put my hand on his facemask and pushed him back down.

Sugar Bear reacted viscerally, thinking he was about to get in a brawl. And then he looked and recognized me, smiling and winking back at him.

I trotted back to my defensive huddle and waited for Colgate's next play. As I watched the Colgate offense in their huddle, I could see Sugar Bear talking animatedly with his teammates. All of a sudden, all eleven players turned around to look in my direction.

It was a homecoming of sorts, and you can believe that there was a fair amount of kidding and jousting going on for the rest of the game. Whenever Henry White set in the slot position across from me, he grinned and winked at me.

It was a memorable day, and though we played hard, Colgate sent us home to Lewisburg with a 49-17 loss.

Colgate was now 9-0, and after a convincing win the next week against Northeastern, the team was ranked 17th in the country in Division I-A. Colgate was being courted to play in a post-season game, the Tangerine Bowl. This was, of course, provided that Colgate could complete their undefeated season.

Between Colgate and the Tangerine Bowl, stood Delaware. The game would be played on the road, making the challenge of an undefeated season more difficult.

Because Bucknell's season had ended the week before, I traveled to Delaware to watch the Colgate game and to root for my friends and my father. As well as Colgate had played all year, their performance at Delaware fell far short of that. On a frustrating day in November, Colgate lost 21-3. With that defeat, it lost any hope of playing in a bowl game.

Despite the season's bitter ending, Colgate's 10-1 record was the second best record in its football history behind the 9-0 finish in the 1932 season. It was also the first time a Colgate football team had won 10 games in a season.

The team was named ECAC Team of the Year. Colgate was selected over outstanding teams like Pitt, Penn State, Syracuse, Boston College, Temple and Rutgers.

Coach Dunlap with Co-Captains Mike Foley and Gary Hartwig—1977 ECAC Team of the Year.

Dad was also given several honors. He was selected by the American Football Coaches Association as the District Coach of the Year. It was the second straight year he received that award.

Dad was also honored by the Walter Camp Football Foundation as "Man of the Year." Dad was humbled to see the list of past recipients, including NFL Commissioner Pete Roselle, Army's Doc Blanchard and Syracuse's Duffy Daugherty.

Little did he know that in the following years, the award recipients would include Roger Staubach, Merlin Olsen, Gale Sayers, Jack Kemp, Floyd Little, Bob Griese and John Elway.

Fred Dunlap receiving the 1977 Walter Camp Football Foundation "Man of the Year" Award. Presenting the award is Lewis A. Hurwitz, President of the Walter Camp Football Foundation.

Dad appreciated the awards, but he always gave credit to the players and the other coaches. For him, it was always about the team and about the pursuit of perfection. While that is the case, an excerpt from his acceptance speech for the "Man of the Year" Award on the following pages is revealing and describes Dad's philosophy about the journey he had chosen.

A Fortunate Man

I am a very fortunate man. I am being honored here tonight for my contribution to football. That's really ironic, for I have benefited immeasurably from my association with the game. I ***love*** *what I do for a living. And I guess the main reason I feel this way is that football is a game of* ***people****. We coaches deal in people as other businessmen deal in steel or plastics or chemicals.*

But a further distinction is necessary. The special people we deal with dare to compete. They test themselves physically, mentally and emotionally. They sacrifice. They endure pain. And they push themselves beyond their physical limitations. I think that's ***heroic.***

That's really what a coach's commodity is: ***heroes.***

These heroes come in all sizes and all shapes, and they manifest their heroism in many different ways. Some are public and obvious—you read about them in the newspapers, like these young men we are honoring tonight (the National All-America Team). But most of them are private, secret heroes—like the unheralded lineman, or the second-stringer, or the injured. They receive little recognition, but they are heroes nonetheless.

These are the tools of my trade—these special people—these heroes. It's a privilege to work with them. That's why I feel somehow guilty to accept an award such as this one for the work that I do.

I don't motivate these people to heroism. I don't lead them to heroism. They have that in them already. What I do is simply establish an atmosphere or environment that gives them the opportunity to discover their own latent potential for heroism. I feel this is the obligation of every coach.

We must provide these special young people with the best possible total experience. We must supervise and maintain its quality, and then stand back and watch them blossom. Their potential for heroism is already there. Give them the right opportunity and they'll find in themselves their own special brand of it. I am grateful and honored to work with the commodity that I do. I have dealt with heroes for 26 years now. ***I am a very fortunate man.***

This short excerpt is a succinct encapsulation of what my father believed, and what drove him each day to pursue perfection. The speech was eloquent. And yes, the speech was written by my mother. After all, she was a big part of the Dunlap Team, and a team sticks together.

Following the Walter Camp Awards, Mom and Dad returned to Hamilton. It was recruiting season. And in his mind, in spite of the accomplishments in 1976 and 1977, there was more work to do and more improvements to make.

A Reconsideration

THE REST OF MY FRESHMAN year at Bucknell passed quickly and soon I was back in Hamilton for the summer. Like the year before, many Colgate football players attended summer school and I spent time with them working out and socializing.

The head golf professional at Seven Oaks was Gilles Gagnon, who was also the assistant hockey coach at Colgate. He offered me a job in the golf shop—I worked long hours there that summer. Gilles was a great boss who permitted my hours to be flexible so I could train for football. He also took me to professional golf tournaments, where I caddied for him. As our familiarity with each other grew, Gilles took on a role of a big brother. The friendship we forged that summer resulted in an even closer friendship lasting to this day, 38 years later.

As the summer months wore on, I grew closer to the Colgate football players. I also thought more about my disenchantment with the Bucknell football program, and I began considering a transfer to Colgate.

I had listened to people who said, "It's tough to play for your father," but the more I thought about it, none were speaking from experience. It was only that they *imagined* it would be hard. Nobody considered the opposite perspective, that if I had spent a lifetime immersed in my father's program and I loved my father and respected his style, then it would be really hard to adapt to other styles and other programs.

Certainly, I recognized that there was a downside to each choice, Bucknell or Colgate. But there was an upside to each choice, too. I was convinced I would rather play in Dad's system, and I was willing to take a chance that it might not be as hard as the opinion-makers had forecasted. After all, I knew Dad's Team Rules and that was fine with me.

In June 1978, I spoke to my parents about a possible transfer. My mother was deliberate, deploying her Socratic method of drilling into my reasoning. As she did, I could tell Dad was excited about my possible transfer. He stayed quiet, letting Mom perform her surgical evaluation.

After walking them through my rationale, they both said, "Think about it overnight. There's no reason to rush into this." I told them I already had thought about it and I was sure a change was for the best. But they prevailed, and we agreed to freeze the conversation and wait until the next morning to talk again.

For the rest of that evening, we didn't discuss the possible transfer. Instead, Dad and I watched TV, but I could tell he was preoccupied with it. He was like a cat who knew he was going to the sardine factory the next day. He was salivating.

The next morning we resumed the conversation and this time I prevailed. I told them I wanted to transfer to Colgate. Dad couldn't suppress his excitement. He shook my hand and congratulated me. Though I am sure she was happy too, Mom was still in conversation control mode. She turned to Dad, prompting him, "We have some things to discuss with him, don't we?"

Dad tempered his enthusiasm for the moment. "Ah, er, yes we do," he said. "Tig, if you are really serious about doing this, we need to set some rules."

I looked at him intently, unsure where he was headed.

"We have been open with you and Jessie these last few years about some very confidential things," Dad began. "And we have shared them with you in order to seed your own development as young adults." He shifted in his seat. "But if you come to Colgate to play football for me… then you are coming to play as one of my players, not as my son." He let that thought hang for a moment. "I need to treat you no differently than I treat other players," he said. "Which means that I will not be sharing things about the team, about other players or about sensitive parts of our program."

Mom piped in. "And Tiger, the same goes for you. We don't expect… no, we don't *want* you sharing things about players that, as a player, you wouldn't be inclined to share. You should behave well because you are our son, but you shouldn't share anything with us *because* you are our son."

"That's right," Dad said. "That would put you in an uncomfortable position. An impossible position."

I thought about what Mom said for a minute. Suddenly the idea of transferring to Colgate became a bit more complicated. But that awkward moment was quickly replaced by enthusiasm. I filled out a transfer application and within a week the appropriate people at Bucknell and Colgate were notified of the change and I was accepted by Colgate.

When I told the Colgate players I was transferring, they were jubilant. By NCAA rules, I needed to sit out a year as a red shirt athlete. That was less important to me because I was now going to be a part of the Colgate football program. I wouldn't be able to play in the coming season, but I would be able to practice with the team for the next year, and I figured that year would go by quickly.

Restraint

AS THE SUMMER PASSED, I spent more and more time with the Colgate players on campus. It was natural, given that I was joining the program in September. I spent time with them during workouts and I also did things with them socially.

One early August night, a bunch of us finished working out and decided to organize a party, like the ones usually involving a keg of beer. On this occasion, however, an ample supply of Jack Daniel's also appeared. As the night progressed, I transitioned from beer to whiskey. Everyone was doing shots, and I did likewise. Things got fuzzy after that and I wasn't even sure when I left the party. It was probably around 4 a.m. Or was it later?

Suddenly I heard the words "What the hell are you doing?" whispered to me.

Then I heard them again, only much louder. And then I heard someone scream, "WHAT THE HELL ARE YOU DOING?"

I tried to pull myself out of my groggy, drunken state, but I was disoriented. It was daylight, and I was sitting in my parents' car, looking at a man, dressed in pajamas, standing in front of the car.

The man screamed again "WHAT THE HELL ARE YOU DOING?"

I was still trying to get my bearings. As I straightened up, I could smell and see vomit all over the car. There was another thing: I noticed that the car was leaning to one side. And the hood of the car was way up in the air. Was I dreaming?

Suddenly, the sound of the man's fist hitting the driver's side car window confirmed that this was no dream. He kept yelling the same thing, but I didn't respond. I was pretty sure I didn't know the answer to his question.

I started the car and tried to back it up but the wheels were spinning. I stumbled out of the car, trying to keep a safe distance from the angry guy. With the car being elevated, that first step was a big one and I nearly fell on my ass. "Whoa," I said out loud. "Whoa!"

Once outside of the car, I could see what had happened. And I also figured out who the angry man was. It was Professor Elgie, a Colgate professor. I had spoken to him before, but never when he was wearing pajamas.

I realized I was at the bottom of our hill on Spring Street, at the base of Spring Hill Road, and that somehow I must have fallen asleep at the wheel and missed the left turn. Instead, I veered to the right, taking out an entire row of hedges.

I remembered those hedges: they were 10 feet high. *Damn, those shrubs were big,* I thought. They were Sequoia shrubs. But now they were all lying crushed under my parents' car. *This explains why I can't free the car and back it up,* I realized. The car was suspended in air on top of them.

"I'm sorry," I said to Professor Elgie, without calling him by name. "I don't know what happened." That seemed like the right thing to say in my compromised state. But upon reflection, I am not sure how consoling that sounded coming from a guy who was wearing last night's dinner on his shirt and pants.

Professor Elgie stood looking at me. He was seething. "You ruined my front yard!" he shouted. "It's ruined!"

"I'm sorry," I said again.

"Get a tow truck and get that car off my property!" he yelled before he turned and stormed inside his house.

To call a tow truck, I needed to find a telephone. (Cell phones were still a decade away.) I looked to the left, figuring I needed to climb up the hill and make the call from our house.

Trudging up the hill, soaked in vomit, my sobriety had returned. After being confronted by the pajama warden, my adrenalin had fully kicked in and my Jack Daniel's buzz was now gone. At split-second speed, I began thinking about how I could somehow undo the problem I now found myself in. *Is it possible*, I wondered, *to deal with this without my parents finding out*?

Glancing down the hill at the car, it didn't look that damaged. *Sure, it's airborne*, I thought, *but a quick tow-job can fix that. And all of those shrubs jammed up in the motor? Heck, I was good at landscaping. I could fish all of that out of there.*

All I needed to do, I thought, *was to enter the house quietly and call the tow service. Then clean the car up and everything was solved.*

As my optimism grew, I took one more glance down the hill. Then reality set in, as I looked at the snow-plow job I had done on the Sequoia shrubs.

Aw shit! I said to myself. There was no way my parents wouldn't notice the absence of the hedges. Or question the Elgies about them. I hadn't been thinking clearly. There was no way I could undo this mess.

My focus then turned to my parents. Was this going to be round two of the "Dirt Bomb Caper?" Then worse things came to mind. I thought about how embarrassed my parents would be, especially now that I was going to be on campus. They were so proud of my decision to transfer to Colgate. Now they were going to be the parents of the famous bush jumper! I could see it now. "I'd like to introduce you to our son, Tiger," they'd say. "If you ever need to have some landscaping removed, call him. He works from 5 to 6 each morning."

Having reached our house, I was about to open the door when it opened for me. There stood Dad with his hand on the other side of the knob. In that split second, I realized that any damage control I might have planned was no longer possible.

Dad looked at me. I stood silently. "Where's the car?" he asked in a measured tone.

"It's at the bottom of the hill."

"Why didn't you drive it up?"

I was forced to drop the bombshell. "I tried, I couldn't," I said meekly.

Dad looked at me silently, measuring me curiously as he got a good sniff of my fragrance. It was a unique blend of Ode to Kentucky Whiskey and Essence of Pepperoni Pizza.

Dad sniffed again. "Is that *you?*" he asked.

I nodded.

Dad stared at me silently. "Go to the back yard and hose yourself off." He spoke quietly and firmly. "And then go up and take a shower."

Without objection, I went around the house and turned on the faucet. I didn't even feel the chill of the well water as it came out of the hose. I was still feeling some effects from the prior evening's libations. After drenching myself, I stripped and left my nasty-smelling, soiled clothes on the back porch before hustling upstairs to the shower.

Standing under the hot soapy water, I prepared for the second half of the reception committee. I assumed Mom was awake by now and would confront me in a few minutes.

With hesitation, I walked downstairs. Mom and Dad were sitting at the kitchen table. By the chagrined look on Mom's face, I knew Dad must have informed her. Mom sat silently with a grim look on her face. Dad told me he had already called a tow truck. He spoke in a business-like tone, but nothing else was said.

Sensing that this wasn't the best time to try to explain my actions, I meekly announced that I was going to walk down to the car and wait for the tow truck. Hearing no objection, I left the house.

At the bottom of the hill, there was our car, still suspended on the heap of brush, its nose in the air like a rocket positioned for takeoff. I figured I would have another 30 minutes to relish the view of this precarious perch before the tow truck arrived.

Hamilton was a small town. Everyone knew everyone. The tow truck guy was the father of one of my high school classmates. He gave me a curious look before surveying the situation. Then he surveyed me again. By the look on his face, I sensed he was getting a certain amount of amusement from this unusual assignment. "I can pull the car off," he said, "but first I am going to need to get under the car and cut away all of the bushes up front. They're stuffed up inside the engine."

Great, I thought, *I have to stand here and wait as he prunes the car bush.* And he did, chopping away as I stood idly watching him. By then it was about 7 a.m. and cars were slowly driving by, first looking at the *car rocket* and then at me. I figured it would only be a couple hours before everybody in town knew how I spent the previous evening.

When the car was finally freed, the truck operator towed it to his shop to assess the damage. As he drove away, I began my second march back up to the house that morning, to a meeting I could only assume would be a harsh one.

I walked into the quiet house. Then I heard voices upstairs. As I approached, I could hear my parents in their bedroom, showering and getting dressed. Rather than interrupt them, I elected to go downstairs. I sat at the kitchen table awaiting my hearing.

Dad's familiar footsteps could be heard first. "Let's get in my car and go down to the shop," he said before he hit the bottom step. I jumped up at his suggestion. Nothing was said on the short ride to the shop. When we arrived, I was told to stay in the car while Dad talked to the mechanic. As I peered over the front dashboard, I watched them walk around the car. There were still pieces of shrub stuck in the side mirror.

Dad got back in the car and we headed toward home.

"What did the guy say?" I asked.

"He won't know until later today." Dad responded without looking over at me. This was followed by more silence as we drove home. As we approached Spring Street, Dad said, "We're going to stop here so you can apologize to Professor Elgie." Dad stood next to the car and watched as I scaled up and over Mount Bushmore to get to the front door.

Professor Elgie appeared immediately after my knock. He was much calmer than before. *Whew!* I thought. I apologized and assured him I would fix the damage quickly. As I tried to make amends on his front porch, I imagined my father's reaction. How embarrassed must he be, to experience such a spectacle caused by his son?

When we arrived home, Dad suggested I use his car that morning to get supplies to fix the bushes. I spent the next couple hours at the hardware store and the lawn and garden store, buying things that were needed. When I got back, the first thing I had to do was unearth the bushes. These were mutant bushes. And they had mutant roots!

Over the next two days, I cleared the brush and removed the wire fence I had demolished. On the third day, I planted new shrubs and installed a new fence. Those three days seemed like an eternity. I had plenty of time to think about my mistakes and the embarrassment I had caused my parents. I felt awful.

Finally, the work was completed. And with that, I resumed my normal summer activities. My parents never confronted me again about the incident. And there was no grounding that came with it. We moved forward as if nothing had happened. Which made no sense to me—but then it did.

I realized that my parents didn't punish me or scold me because they knew I was already beating myself up over it. They knew *that I knew* I had made a mistake, and rather than berate me, which in some ways might have punctuated the incident, they decided it was better to let me deal with my own conscience over it. And that proved to be very effective. I certainly was beating myself up over my stupidity and lack of sensitivity for how my actions could hurt or embarrass others, especially my parents.

In effect, Mom and Dad were exercising the leverage of 19 years of parenting. They believed that if it had been good parenting, then I would self-scold to an appropriate level. And they seemed willing to put that to the test. Their restraint that week was the ultimate example of "Less Is More." Punishing me was unnecessary, they concluded, if they had done their jobs well as parents. And they had, for sure.

When I walked into Reid Athletic Center later that week, I was met by a bunch of the Colgate players. Several had been with me that drunken evening. They all had heard the news and some of them were worried I might have implicated them with my parents. I reminded them that my parents and I had an agreement not to share information like that. The guys were relieved.

And then the kidding started. I was no longer called Tiger. Instead, when I walked into a room, I heard, "Hey guys, here comes the Shrub Jumper!" Or, they'd ask, "How ya doin', Bushman?" The guys were merciless.

The kidding eventually died down a couple weeks later. It was time for the start of Fall Camp.

1978—A Red Shirt Year and Bringing Out the Best in His Players

DURING FALL CAMP AND THE football season, I participated with the team in every respect, despite being ineligible to play. I missed being in the action, but hey, I had accepted those terms when I decided to transfer.

Most of my time was spent playing for the Scout Squad during scrimmages. It consisted of players who were neither starters nor second string. The job of the Scout Squad was to learn the plays of the upcoming opponent and then run them in practice against Colgate's starting lineup. It was a way to give the starters a simulation of what they would face on the following Saturday.

Most of the Scout Squad was made up of freshmen who hadn't yet been able to pierce the starting lineup. We spent a great deal of time together and I came to know them well. They were like me in other ways, too: we were all new on Colgate's campus. We ate at the same cafeteria, lived in dorms together, and collectively learned how to navigate academics, dormitory parties and the Fraternity Rush ritual.

My three closest friends that year were Dave Moules, Marty Schuff and Brian Plunkett. Marty and Brian lived in my dormitory, on the lower campus right off Whitnall Field. We were busy with football and with class work, but when there was free time, Marty, Brian and I would hang out in the dorm social room.

Invariably, in those kinds of settings, players talked about why they chose to come to Colgate, what other schools they had considered and where their high school friends went. I remember one night talking to Marty, affectionately called Schuffy.

He explained to Brian and me that he had been anguishing over the decision as to college choice, given that he had a number of attractive options. When he finally decided on Colgate, he called my father on the phone to tell him the news. Schuffy admitted to us that as he waited for Dad to answer, he still had some misgivings about whether he was making the right choice.

When my father answered, Schuffy walked through his thought process and then told Dad he had decided to attend Colgate. He said my father exclaimed, "That's GREAT news, Marty! I am so happy to hear that!"

Schuffy then told me, "Right then, Tiger, I could hear your mother's voice in the background. She asked your dad what the call was about. Your dad told her, "Marty's coming," Schuffy explained further. "He didn't say *Schuff,* but just 'Marty's coming.'"

Schuffy smiled. "Then all I could hear was your mother screaming, "Marty Schuff! From Brockport! Whoo-hooo!"

"After that happened, I just knew I had picked the right school. For the wife of the coach to know *that much* about recruits, to be *that* tuned in to the program...I knew I had picked the right place."

Marilyn D.!

The 1978 season was marginal. Colgate had come off the great '77 season, but many of the best players had graduated. There were good players behind them, yet the newer players had difficulty establishing themselves as reliable performers. Colgate lost the first four games, and had trouble performing consistently on offense. There were some good moments, but too many mistakes at critical times thwarted the ability to score points.

That year, Colgate lost to teams that were inferior. But inexplicably, Colgate was able to upset two of the four toughest teams on the schedule.

In the fifth week, Colgate traveled to Philadelphia to face Villanova which had a strong team with great athletes. Their roster included a defensive lineman named Howie Long, later an NFL Hall of Famer with the Oakland Raiders. That day, Colgate upset the Wildcats, 20-14.

With a dose of momentum, Colgate used that win to re-start its season. The following week, Colgate traveled to New Jersey to play Princeton, one of the teams Colgate was favored to beat. But lack of consistency resulted in another poor performance and a loss, 13-12.

After a loss to Army and a win against Lafayette, Colgate's record was 2-6, with three games remaining: Bucknell, Delaware and Rutgers. The best chance to win was at Bucknell. The games against Delaware and Rutgers would be much more difficult.

The Bucknell game was marked by good defense and missed opportunities by the offense. Colgate's offense drove the ball inside Bucknell's 10-yard line on three different occasions and came away with no points. We lost 7-0 that day. The team was thoroughly frustrated.

A few years after I graduated, Dad told me a story that he had been unwilling to tell me earlier. He reminded me, "We had an agreement back then not to discuss confidential matters while you played on my team."

Coming home from the 1978 Bucknell game, Dad sensed that his quarterback was steadily losing confidence as the season progressed.

As the team bus made its way to Hamilton, Dad replayed the missed opportunities of the Bucknell game in his mind and he thought he spotted a troublesome trend.

In Red Zone situations, Dad had called plays allowing the quarterback to have a run or pass option. Dad concluded that his QB, John Marzo, had run every time. Dad could recall on a few of the plays that a couple of receivers had been open in the end zone.

Marzo met with Dad the next day to review the game films. As they watched, Dad stopped the film to show Marzo examples of where it would have been a better decision to pass the ball rather than run. More examples followed. Finally, Dad stopped the reel and looked at Marzo and said, "You are running every time we call that play. And there are guys who are pretty open. Why aren't you throwing the ball?"

Over the next few minutes, Marzo explained that he didn't want to make a mistake. He had thrown an interception earlier in the game and didn't want to throw another one, especially when Colgate was deep in the opponent's territory. Dad interrupted him. "Yeah, but your choice to run didn't work either. That was fourth down, John; not making the necessary yardage is a turnover, too."

Dad studied his quarterback. He realized that Marzo was putting too much pressure on himself and trying too hard to be perfect. After a brief silence, Dad launched, "Listen, John, you are trying so hard *not* to make a mistake, that you aren't able to make a play, either. The reason you are playing quarterback for us is that you are the best athlete we have and we trust that you can do the job and help us win. That doesn't mean that I expect you to be perfect. It means that I expect you to use all of your athleticism, not just a conservative piece of it."

Marzo and Dad talked at length about that aspect of John's play. Dad recalled telling him, "I want to see you going all out, playing aggressively, and playing to win. Don't worry about mistakes. I will gladly accept them, because the great things you will do will far outweigh them."

The following week, Colgate played at Delaware against a very talented team. Colgate lost the game 38-29 in a high-scoring affair, but they played well that day. John Marzo played aggressively, trusting his coach and his own abilities and athleticism. He threw for 482 yards that day, which (at the time) set the all-time NCAA record for passing yards in a game.

With Marzo again discovering his comfort zone and rhythm, Colgate played Rutgers in the season finale. Rutgers was a heavy favorite but Colgate beat them 14-9. The odd season of miraculous wins and dubious losses was over. Fortunately, my year of ineligibility was over, too.

The story about John Marzo and my father stuck with me as I grew older. Many times I was confronted with challenges in business over the years. There were a few hard situations that caused me to have some self-doubt and to display some tentative behavior. It's easy to allow that to happen if you are hard-working and self-critical by nature, since you become your own hardest critic. John Marzo was that way in 1978. And I was too, in later years as I persevered through my business career.

As an adult, I often reflected on Dad's "trust yourself" speech as a stabilizing force to keep me aggressive and self-confident amid many of life's struggles.

John Marzo graduated from Colgate and then medical school. He ultimately became the team physician for the NFL Buffalo Bills. Later in life, if he encountered similar struggles like the one during his Colgate playing days, I bet he relied on Dad's counsel, too.

The Entrepreneur Heads to Alaska

MY FIRST YEAR AT COLGATE flew by, and before I could blink, it was May. Most students returned home for summer; the 1970s were an age when summer internships (as they are defined today) didn't exist.

Moreover, the quality and sophistication of a student's summer job wasn't scrutinized heavily by recruiters for post-graduation jobs. Most kids looked for more basic summer jobs like being a lifeguard at the local pool, waitressing in a restaurant, working construction or mowing lawns for a hometown landscaping company.

I had worked a construction job in 1977 and in the golf shop during the summer of 1978. But I was looking for something different, something more challenging, perhaps something that gave me an opportunity to make a lot of money.

As my spring 1979 semester was nearing the end, I happened to speak to a Colgate student named Bernt Killingstadt. I was somewhat acquainted with him since he had tried out briefly for the football team that year. I'd also occasionally see him around campus.

On that day, we bumped into each other in a bar in downtown Hamilton. He asked me what I was going to do that summer. I hadn't figured out a plan yet, and I told him so. But I went on to say that I was looking to do something different. Bernt told me about what he had done the previous summer: he worked in a fish cannery in Alaska. As he described it further, I became more intrigued and we talked longer.

Over a beer (or ten) at Hickey's Tavern, I must have asked him a hundred questions. *Wow,* I thought, *the job is in Alaska...on one of the Aleutian Islands...the land of the midnight sun.* Did that ever sound cool!

The pay Bernt described was more than double what I could make at home, and I was hell-bent on expanding the size of my bank account.

Also, I had warm memories from our family trip to Wyoming and Montana. I loved the adventure of seeing those places. There was a part of me that yearned to see even more.

Alaska! I considered with a smile. *That was the Rocky Mountains on steroids!*

I collected all of the facts and approached my parents about the concept. With no vehement protests from them, I began booking a flight to Kodiak Island.

Fortunately, I managed to convince Doug Curtis, defensive captain on our team, to come with me. He had been a four-year starter and was my roommate the last semester. Doug was just graduating and hadn't yet figured out what he wanted to do after college. The job I described in Alaska sounded intriguing.

Kodiak Island was not Malibu Beach. It was a barren island with one town on one side of the island—that town being Kodiak. It existed for one reason: to serve the fishing industry. There were cannery factories for two miles lining the rugged shores of the island.

When we arrived, the taxi stopped in front of the fourth cannery in the row: Alaska Pacific Seafoods, Inc. We lugged our belongings to the main office. Doug and I signed our employment papers at the front desk and were directed to the stairwell, which led up two floors to a makeshift bunkhouse where some of the workers lived. Each room had bunk beds and lockers. There were gang bathrooms, one for men and the other for women.

Alaska was part of the United States, but you couldn't tell that by the population on Kodiak Island. The majority of inhabitants were from Korea, the Philippines or Vietnam. This was not Hamilton, New York. Caucasians were a small minority.

The terms for living in the bunkhouse were:

- A bed, a locker and access to a bathroom
- Three meals a day
- Total cost: $10 a day

There were no welcome receptions or orientation tours. Doug and I were put to work immediately, roughly 60 minutes after we stowed our luggage in our lockers. We were assigned to a shop foreman, and he directed us to our first task.

The weird thing about being in Alaska in the summer was that the sun was visible 22 hours a day. The sun didn't rise and set; it went *around* each day, about 20 degrees above the horizon. When we finished work that first day as the sun went just below the horizon, it didn't occur to us that it was 2:30 a.m. Or that we had worked 12 straight hours.

Doug and I were easy to identify in that cannery. We were the only humans taller than 5 foot, 6 inches. And we were football players. I'm sure the workers who were a foot shorter thought we were superheroes. In a factory reliant on manual labor, we became rock stars. The foremen loved us. We could work harder and carry more weight, and we weren't shy about working overtime when asked to do it.

As the resident Number Nut, I quickly caught on to an opportunity. I talked to Doug one night about their calendar. Alaska Pacific Seafoods (APS) tracked its workweek beginning on Mondays.

We had been there three days and had already worked more than 40 hours in that shortened week. The foreman had casually mentioned to me that the few hours we worked above 40 hours would be paid as overtime, which meant that our wage would be multiplied by 1.5.

I shared that information with Doug as we sat at dinner on that

Sunday evening. "Dougie, tomorrow starts another fresh week. That means if we crush it for seven straight days, we can get paid a crap-load on the hours above 40." I was on a roll. "And do you know what the foreman also said?" I continued. Doug watched and waited, chewing his dinner. "If we get above 80 hours a week, we get paid twice our base wage!"

Doug looked at me, wondering if I was insane. But I continued my unrelenting delivery. "Shit, we worked 14-16 hours a day these last three days. These guys love us. We don't work like the other folks who live here," I said, referring to the smaller workers.

I had Doug's attention as I added, "If we keep that pace, we are gonna blow through 80 hours by the fifth day of the week!" Doug laughed nervously but he still seemed supportive of my grand plan.

During the next few days, we worked 16-18 hours a day. We carried salmon into the sharp freezers—40 degrees (F) below zero. We also unloaded halibut as the fish poured off the massive vessels.

The halibut weighed between 10 and 250 pounds, and the job we were given was to "catch the fish" as they slid quickly down a giant metal chute and then toss them into huge bins on wheels. There was a bin designated for the 10-40 pound halibut, another for the 40-80 pound halibut, another for the 80-150 pound halibut, and the closest bin was for any halibut over 150 pounds. Grabbing and throwing these huge fish was exhausting—especially when we did it for 8-10 hours at a time.

The foremen had quickly figured out that the only two guys on the island strong enough to do this were the two guys from Colgate. We had created a demand for our services. And the number of hours that we worked soared.

Around us, the other workers supported us, waiting for us to fill the bins. Then they would wheel them off to another part of the factory for processing.

As I walked toward the bunkhouse one night, I laughed to myself. We had only been there a week and already were controlling and influencing our work pace. The demand we were creating in Alaska, I reflected, was not too different than the demand I had created as a caddie at Saucon Valley, running around the golf course with two bags on my back.

By the end of the first full week, we logged more than 100 hours.

By the end of the second week, we eclipsed 110 hours.

By the middle of the third week, we were again cruising toward a new weekly record until I was stopped in the shipyard by the foreman's boss. "Hey Dunlap, come over here," he ordered. I walked toward the manager. "We need you and Curtis to come into the office *right now*."

Doug had been called earlier to another part of the cannery so he wasn't around. I followed the manager into his office, unaware of why he wanted to talk to me. "We're getting some shit coming at us from corporate down in Seattle," he said, beginning his explanation. "Seattle is asking *who these guys are* that are getting paid crazy amounts of overtime. It's you and Curtis they are talking about." He looked at me like I had done something wrong. I just smiled and shrugged my shoulders and said, "You guys said you needed the help."

The manager said, "I know, I know. But corporate said that they don't have that kind of money in the budget and they want it to stop."

I explained that we were only doing what the foreman asked us to do.

"Yeah, I already talked to him. Hey, he and I aren't against it, but Seattle wants it to stop. They said it was okay if you worked up to 80 hours a week. But they are dead set against paying double your wage." That meeting put an end to my get rich quick strategy. But only for a week.

At the end of the next week, the Halibut fishing season had closed and it was now shrimp season. Fishing seasons were controlled and specified by the government. With this change, all of the deep hull transport boats suddenly began providing ferry service to the shrimp boats. The shrimp boats would stay out at sea, fishing, and as they filled their boats, they would transfer their catch to the transport boats. They would, in turn, ferry the catch to the cannery.

In some respects, Doug and I had become celebrities (or freaks of nature?) on that island that summer because of our imposing physical stature. By this time, the ship captains knew about us, and some of them even called us by name.

The transport boats were only doing ferry work in the summertime for extra income. They were actually crabbing vessels, and their primary business was fishing for king crab and tanner crab. Those seasons ran from November through February up in the Bering Sea.

Summers were their off-season, when the transport boats owners and operators could make a few extra bucks running the catch back and forth from the fisherman to the canneries—all while they caught a suntan.

One day, a ship captain pulled me aside to talk. "I heard you guys got your hours clipped?" he began.

I confirmed his suspicion.

"How would you two like to make some extra money?

"How?" I asked.

"If you guys work for the cannery during the days," he explained, "up to your max hours, then you could work nights for me, unloading my boat. It usually takes two days to unload it. But if you guys worked nights getting the shrimp unloaded, I could get back out there a day faster."

The captain looked for my reaction and we discussed a few details. We had a deal.

Whenever he came into port, we would work through the night unloading his boat. And for that, he would pay us each $100 cash. Plus, he would make sure his deck hand supplied us with coolers full of beer that would last us the entire night.

It was a great deal for him, *and* for the two Colgate guys. We were pumped. Three times a week, the captain arrived in port and we stayed up all night unloading his boat. And we got a helluva beer buzz to boot!

When he and his crew came into port and disembarked, they would wave to us as they walked across the street to a bar for the evening. Kodiak was a frontier town; guns, booze and women were necessities. People carried handguns like we carried wallets.

The captain and his crew spent their evenings at the bar enjoying the leisure summer season. They would drink until late at night, and then walk up to the second floor where the prostitutes waited for their money and attention.

In the morning, they'd stumble back across the cannery yard to their ship. With the hull now empty, they were ready to cruise back out to the shrimp boats that were waiting to transfer more of their catch.

Doug and I ended up making more money with the new deal than we had made in the early weeks when we were working 110 hours with APS. With our working only 80 hours a week for APS, the corporate office in Seattle seemed content that their budget crisis had passed. And we were content, spending a summer making more money than the two of us could ever have imagined.

Soon it was early August, and I needed to return to Hamilton to prepare for Fall Camp. As I gazed out the window on my flight home, I smiled at the summer's developments. Similar to my days as a caddie, I had once again found a way to differentiate my product—that product being *my services*. And the result of having created that differentiation was a better business for me. Differentiation had worked on the fairways of a swanky country club, and it appeared to be equally effective in an Alaska boomtown.

My parents always preached that hard work and making the most of an opportunity were important ingredients to becoming successful. Dad had taken chances before, and with hard work, he became successful. I had taken a chance by going to Alaska with no guarantee of a job. But I worked hard and became successful, as well.

As I flew over Alberta and Saskatchewan toward upstate New York, I concluded that there must be something to this idea of differentiation. *And if I ever go into business*, I thought, *these experiences will be beneficial later in life.*

The 1979 Season—The Best of Times and the Worst of Times

WHEN I RETURNED TO THE Chenango Valley and Hamilton, the routine of preparing for Fall Camp awaited me. Some of the players had already returned to Colgate and together we lifted weights and performed running drills, preparing for the upcoming season.

Being home was grand. I spent time with my parents and was also able to catch up with high school friends and Colgate players. Everyone wanted to hear about my summer in Alaska. It felt odd to me, sitting in Hickey's Tavern, telling stories about the fishing industry. I had only been back for a week, and yet the frontier world of Kodiak Island already seemed so far away.

Since this was my second year at Colgate, I felt more at home. I was fully familiar with the university. I had joined Delta Upsilon (DU), an athlete fraternity comprised of football and basketball players. We had a number of wrestlers, too.

Schuffy and Brian joined DU, and Dave Moules did, too. We lived in the DU house that fall, in the back wing of the 3rd floor. Dave and I roomed together and Schuffy and Brian were right across the hall. It was a great set-up, and we looked forward to a fun year.

The Colgate experience was turning out well and I was glad I had made the decision to transfer. But not everything about the change was easy. My parents and I had agreed that we would never share information about players or the team. Although we honored that pact for the full time I was at Colgate, it didn't mean that other players fully trusted it.

In college, lots of stuff happens. Kids do things that are funny, hilarious, goofy and stupid. These silly moments become fodder for great stories later in life when alums gather. This said, at the time these things happen, college kids are concerned about information flow. They don't want their parents to know what occurred. And they certainly don't want the football coaches to know, either. This is where my Colgate experience became a little awkward.

Just because *I knew* I was not going to share any college secrets with my parents did not mean that other players were as sure. I found myself at times being shielded from certain things. On one level, I could understand the players' reluctance to include me. But when that happened, it became a constant reminder that I wasn't just another player or just another college kid. I was Coach D's son.

Another reminder of that status was the reaction at times from some of the student body. Like many other college kids, I did some stupid, funny, hilarious things at Colgate, too.

Delta Upsilon had a basement tap room called Fred's Place (no connection to me or my father). The DU brothers loved to spend time there before, during and after parties. Drinking games were abundant, with the taps always flowing.

It was not uncommon for a bunch of us to take a dare and chug a pitcher of beer. If this was during a DU Disco party, it ended up happening in front of a crowd of people. It was all in good fun, but periodically, when I engaged in this, I might hear some kid I didn't even know, say, "Holy shit! That's the coach's son! I bet his dad would be pissed to see that!"

This didn't happen all the time, but it happened enough that I became conscious of it. I felt like I was being held to a different standard. And it made me watch my actions more than I would have if my Dad weren't the coach.

Another complicated aspect of playing for your father relates to an on-the-field issue. During my 1978 red shirt season, I practiced as an offensive center. When 1979 spring practice began, the coaches moved me to offensive tackle. My friend Marty Schuff was also an offensive tackle. With my position change, Schuffy and I were then competing for the same starting position.

Schuffy was a talented player—a standout in high school in Brockport, New York. And he had become even better as a college player. He had quick feet and great balance. The two of us competed in the spring and again in Fall Camp. As we headed into the first game of the season, the coaches selected me for the starting job.

I was excited about the opportunity, but felt badly for Schuffy. He was a great player, and I wished there were some way for both of us to play. It was an awkward situation and it strained our relationship.

One of the tough things about making the starting lineup when your father is the head coach is that it leaves open the question as to whether you legitimately earned the position, or are the subject of favoritism. I could sense both feelings at times that September, and it placed more pressure on me to perform just to remove any doubt.

I'm unsure whether Schuffy experienced any of these conflicted emotions. I couldn't blame him if he did. This would seem a fairly normal human reaction when dealing with losing a starting position to anyone.

No matter, I felt squeamish at times. I longed for invisibility and some form of non-affiliation with my father. It would have been a simpler existence, I concluded, if I were just another player and not the coach's son.

In truth, I felt like I was in a spotlight and being judged, and that my accomplishments at times seemed to carry an asterisk with them. It was the *coach's son asterisk*. And I had lost a close friend over it.

I was in the starting lineup for the first four weeks of the season, but during the fourth game, against Yale, back spasms forced me to leave the game. My back had been troubling me since the start of the season. During the weeks that followed the Yale game, none of the medical staff could figure out what was wrong. X-rays were inconclusive, and none of the physical therapy and stretching exercises improved my condition. I couldn't practice—heck, I couldn't even bend over.

A couple months later, I was driven to Syracuse for a new, advanced X-ray procedure. It was an early, crude version of what is now an MRI. The doctors discovered I had three fractured vertebrae.

The stress fracture was due less to impact and more to a gradual weakening of the back. We later concluded that my spending the previous summer throwing 200-pound Halibut around was likely the cause.

My football season was over. Doctors recommended a spinal fusion, an attempt to rebuild and support what had been damaged in my spinal column. The surgery entailed grinding up the bone in my hip and then packing the bone fragments against the damaged vertebrae, the goal being to calcify as one continuous bone. To assure that the calcification took hold, I would need to spend four months in a body brace. With no other viable alternatives, we moved ahead quickly to schedule the operation.

Dumb and *impetuous* are words that are often used when describing young people. They fit me perfectly since part of my interest in having surgery as soon as possible was that I wanted to try to make a comeback and play football. *The sooner the surgery*, I thought, *the sooner the four months could begin (and end), giving me more time to get ready for the next season.*

The doctor who performed the surgery disagreed with my plan to play football again. He pointed out to my parents and me that the operation was designed to permit me to live comfortably for the rest of my life—NOT to prepare me for more football.

Predictably, Mom and Dad were both concerned about my playing again, but they reluctantly left the decision to me. It was an easy call for me. My identity at the time was as a football player. My friends were football players. I wasn't comfortable hanging up my cleats. I had just gone through a year of ineligibility, due to my transfer, and didn't fancy ending my football career just yet. Added to that, our opening game in 1980 was against Penn State. I had dreamed of playing them, and my goal was to be suited up for that contest.

For four months, I couldn't bend at the waist. I was therefore either lying down or standing up. I got good at both. I continued taking college classes, even though I didn't attend them. Mom went in my place, listening to the lectures and taking notes that she brought home to me.

Four months later, I said goodbye to the back brace and began training for the upcoming football season. I was weak from the inactivity but that weakness gradually dissipated as we neared Fall Camp.

Through two weeks of double sessions, my back held up fairly well. I felt like I was fully recovered. However, during the Saturday scrimmage before the Penn State game, I collided with another player as I ran downfield to block and my back seized up. After X-rays were taken, it was determined that I had pulverized the newly formed bone in my back.

I had made a deal with my parents and the doctor when I had the operation. They agreed to my attempting a comeback with one condition: I would be allowed to play football as long as I had no pain and did not have any possibility of future setback. On that Saturday scrimmage before the Penn State game, one hit ended my college football career.

Picking Up the Pieces

After an ample amount of remorse over the next couple weeks, I focused my efforts away from the football field. I attended classes and lived in the fraternity house, and of course, rooted for my teammates.

With football behind me, I became just another college student, trying to pass my exams and work toward graduation. In some ways, it was easier and a simpler life. But being away from the football program was difficult, too. I felt disconnected from my friends and from the mission my teammates and Dad were pursuing.

Since the transfer to Colgate made me ineligible for a year, I had planned to stay for a fifth year of college in order to use my full athletic eligibility. Now, without football in my schedule, I abandoned the idea and accelerated to graduate with the 1981 class. If I couldn't play football, I was determined to get the best education possible and ready myself for career opportunities in the future.

At the start of my junior year, I chose English as my major. It had been an erratic path getting to that point. I had studied civil engineering at Bucknell but changed to math when I came to Colgate. A semester later, I changed to geology until I realized it required classes in chemistry and soil mechanics. Chemistry? Soil Mechanics? What was I thinking?

Like many college students, I really didn't have a clue what I wanted to do in my adult life. My erratic choices of majors was evidence of that.

During my junior year, I sought refuge in English. I probably settled on that subject because it was very much in concert with the training Jessie and I received from Mom over the years. She taught us well, and that education gave me a command of the language that made college class work relatively easy.

During my final two years of school, I really got engaged in English. I enjoyed writing the papers and short stories that were requisite with that major.

I even mused at times about becoming a writer after graduation. I thought about living on some island where I could conjure up the creativity to write short stories and novels. The idea sounded so seductive.

Regardless, as I neared graduation, I listened to the excitement of my peers as they planned to start their adult lives in business. I became curious, then excited about that possibility, thinking that I, too, could be a businessman. As for the writing, that was something I could do in my free time, I rationalized. Now, more than 30 years later, I am doing just that.

When I look back at my Colgate experience, there were periods of awkwardness that at times made me question whether the transfer from Bucknell was worth it. But there were so many great things about my Colgate experience outweighing the fewer difficult moments. Colgate is a special university, attracting students who are talented and intelligent, but also regular and humble.

One of them was Schuffy. Fortunately, he and I reconnected over the years and have built a lasting friendship. We have talked about that awkward period when we competed for the same spot on the team and both acknowledged how hard it was.

In hindsight, what happened back then was pretty small. We focus now on the good times we had and are still having. He is still the great guy I knew back when we had so many memorable discussions in the dormitory. That was an innocent time for us, a time when we were both exploring who we were as people.

Some 30 years later, on fairly close inspection, I think we both turned out alright.

Taking Chances—The Dawn of the Calabria Era

> "There are times as a leader when you have to make decisions that are unpopular. But if you are convinced they are right, you need to be true to your instincts in spite of any potential fallout."

Through the years, this statement of Dad's resonated with me on a continual basis. Never was it more true than during the 1981 Colgate season.

That year, the Colgate team reported for Fall Camp with a focus on the first game against Rutgers. Colgate had two senior quarterbacks who were vying for the starting position. They had paid their dues during earlier years, playing behind starters who had since graduated. Now they were competing for the starting job. Fall Camp was filled with intrigue as the rest of the team observed the two during daily practices.

When the first Friday of the season arrived, the team boarded the buses, prepared to ride to New Jersey to face Rutgers. One of the quarterbacks had been selected to start, but the other was told to be ready in the event that he was needed.

The game was a defensive struggle in the first half; neither offense was productive. The score was an unusual 5-2 as the closing minutes ticked down in the second quarter. Dad played both quarterbacks during the first half and neither had shown an ability to move the offense.

Years later, Dad told me what was going through his mind. "We had the ball with a couple minutes left in the half," he said. "But we had been really shaky on offense to that point, and because of it, I was afraid to call pass plays that were too aggressive for fear they might result in an interception. I began calling conservative plays just to avoid making a critical mistake. And then I realized what I was doing in this first game of the season." He added, "I was playing it safe because I didn't have the confidence that our first two quarterbacks could execute effectively. Suddenly, the whole upcoming season flashed before my eyes and I realized that if I didn't make a change, we would be hostage to this style of conservative play for a whole season." He paused. "And I wasn't going to do that. Because we couldn't win with that strategy."

As the team jogged toward the locker room at the half, Dad continued to think about his two quarterbacks' performance. After conferring with the defensive coaches about any changes they felt should be instituted, he headed to where the offensive assistant coaches were huddled. They had been conferring about which plays had worked and which needed to be scrapped, or changed.

Dad's top offensive assistant coach was Chris Palmer, who later became head coach of the Cleveland Browns. As Dad approached, Palmer began summarizing what the offensive coaches felt were the best strategies for the second half. Dad stopped him in mid-sentence. "Guys, that stuff is secondary to us at this point. I want to talk about changing quarterbacks. And I want to do it now."

The assistant coaches assumed that Dad meant changing to the second quarterback. "No, I'm talking about playing Calabria," Dad insisted. "I want to start him in the second half."

The assistant coaches looked at Dad blankly. "Over the last three weeks of practice and today," Dad continued, "we have sputtered on offense, and we aren't getting what we need out of the quarterback position. Our second quarterback isn't that different from the first guy." He looked at them intently. "We need to find a quarterback we can win with. And we can't win with these two guys." He looked over his shoulder to where Calabria was sitting. "We need to reassess which plays will work with Calabria in the second half. And I need to communicate this news to the team right now."

Steve Calabria was a freshman, the third string quarterback behind the two seniors. But in Fall Camp, he had performed impressively. Dad announced to the team that Calabria was going to start the second half. There were a fair number of vacant stares in the locker room.

The team ended up losing the game 13-5. But Calabria had been indoctrinated and had done some good things in the second half.

During the entire bus ride home, Dad sat with Chris Palmer, redesigning the offense. They discarded the offensive strategy they had prepared for the 1981 season, and moved toward an offense complementing what Calabria could do.

Years later, Dad explained, "We were running a Wing-T offense that year, which is complex and takes some time to learn. With Calabria being a freshman, I thought it was too much for him to master at that early juncture. So we changed to something simpler—an offense operating out of an I-formation, which would allow us to run Sprint Pass, Sprint Draw and Sprint Counter. That gave us some misdirection on running plays but it also made it easier for Calabria to execute on passing plays."

With Calabria at the helm, Colgate won the next three games and lost only two of the remaining games that season, to Temple and Syracuse. The team finished 7-3, and Calabria finished his first of four seasons as the Colgate starting quarterback. It was the beginning of a career where he re-wrote the Colgate record books.

Some doubted Dad's selection of Calabria to lead the team on that September day at Rutgers, and his abrupt decision did cause a certain amount of fallout. But he felt a greater obligation to the team to make the hard decision. "I watched how we moved and reacted offensively during Fall Camp," he told me, "and I wasn't comfortable with how potent we could be. But I had a lot of respect for both of the senior quarterbacks, and so I resisted my own instincts to look past them to the freshman."

Dad added, "I really wanted the senior quarterbacks to prevail, given how long they had supported the program. But during that first half at Rutgers, I could see failures that I had tried to rationalize away during Fall Camp. And I realized that it wasn't their effort that was the limitation—it was their ability to make things happen that *we needed to happen*."

Most importantly in terms of lessons learned for me, Dad said,

"After the first half at Rutgers, I watched the players in front of me jogging toward the locker room. Many of them were seniors, too. And I realized that if I didn't make the change, I was *limiting their chances* for success. And I wasn't going to allow that to happen."

What did I learn? Whether it's a football coach or a businessman, the clarity of Dad's move that day has universal application. I had moments later in my business career where I was similarly conflicted due to loyalties. I had to make tough, sometimes controversial decisions so that the entire business team could prosper.

As Dad did that day, I learned it's essential to be willing to question and challenge your own thinking and to be willing to admit when things are going wrong. Then it's important to have the courage and gumption to take chances in order to radically improve the chances for success.

A Lesson Not Worth Learning

The lessons I learned from my parents transformed me from a child into an adult. In so many ways, they prepared me for the future. But there was one area, candidly, where my parents were not omniscient.

My father was a career football coach. My mother was an English teacher and then a homemaker. Mom took care of the family business but neither she nor Dad had any exposure to the outside business world. When I decided during my senior year at Colgate that a career in business was my goal, I had to look outside the family for guidance.

My parents knew many business people, including the successful alums who came back to the school for reunions and football weekends. While they were friendly with these people, they didn't know their business or how business people work.

Like many of my classmates during our senior spring semester, I signed up for on-campus interviews held in March and April. In 1981, many companies visited Colgate's campus, attempting to recruit talented graduates into their firms. Most recruiters arrived the night before and held a group informational meeting. Then they would conduct a series of one-on-one interviews the next day with interested candidates, each of those sessions lasting 45 minutes.

Colgate had a career planning department to help guide and advise graduating students toward companies matching their specific interests. But at 22 years old, most college seniors weren't sure what their business interests were. Most hadn't been in the business world before to know what would be exciting or fulfilling. The exception might be students whose parents were in business, providing some mentoring to them along the way.

Since my parents weren't business-oriented, no mentoring was possible. The closest I had been to developing any sort of business acumen had been in Alaska, and that exposure was from the hull of a boat shoveling raw shrimp into a bucket.

Making matters more complicated, I was oblivious to things like business dress code or what was known as "dress for success." Mom was equally unseasoned. Nevertheless, she was an energetic, proactive sort, telling me, "Tig, we need to get you some business clothes so you can knock 'em dead during interviews!" So we bought a suit. It was a *polyester* suit. It was a *brown* polyester suit. *With bell bottoms.* And to go with that: brown penny loafers.

Complementing the suit (everything couldn't be brown), we purchased a white shirt and an orange tie. Why orange? Because Mom remembered how good brown and orange looked together when we were at Lehigh. She said, "That accent of orange on the Lehigh football uniforms really looked sharp!"

With her positively charged nature now at full speed, Mom added, "The brown suit matches the color of your eyes, and makes your eyes sparkle."

Was the white shirt to be professionally dry-cleaned? Not a chance. We were still living in the Land of "Waste Not, Want Not." To save expenses, she bought a *polyester* white shirt that was wrinkle-free. "Just throw it in the wash and it comes out perfect," she said with a satisfied smile.

In hindsight, that shirt didn't need to hang in a closet. It probably could have stood by itself against a wall! Regardless, I was dressed for success. I had my fancy wardrobe in hand and was ready to go. Or so my mother and I thought.

I failed miserably in the on-campus interviews. I was zero-for-infinity. Sure, our choice of garb was a bit misdirected, but there were other failures, too. My performance in the interviews was shaky: I was nervous. It was an unfamiliar environment for me. And so I started to perspire. Sometimes a lot.

My biggest problem was being off-balance. When the interviewer was trying to make small talk, I was too serious. When a different interviewer was stiff, I was trying to make small talk. I couldn't seem to select the right radio frequency. Worst of all, my nervousness caused me to say dumb things. I underestimated how much research I should have done on a particular company before the interview. When the recruiter asked me, "Why are you interested in working for XYZ company?" my answers were vague and sometimes incongruous. If an interviewer asked me what I wanted to accomplish in my career, I replied, "I want to be CEO of your company." That sounded like a good answer to me—I figured it would give the impression that I was ambitious. The reaction appeared to be just the opposite.

Reflecting back on that experience, I have cringed many times. There I was, sitting with a mid-forties guy, whose career to that point was doing on-campus interviews. And then some cocky 22-year-old with clammy hands was sitting across from him bragging about doing a *fly-by* to the executive suite!

Needless to say, the battery of campus interviews in 1981 did not make my lifetime highlight reel. When graduation rolled around, most of my classmates had already locked down jobs. They were ready to leave Colgate and pursue the exciting world of business. I, on the other hand, had not yet been given an offer. As they left college for the working world, I left graduation to drive three miles away to my parents' home. It was easier to get to, but a lot less impressive.

Nevertheless, adopting Mom and Dad's never-give-up attitude, I spent the summer calling companies, writing letters and sending out my resume. I found that most of the companies had already filled their openings for incoming college graduates. Occasionally, I would be invited to an introductory interview, but none of them panned out. The interviewers typically said something lukewarm, like, "It's been a pleasure to meet you and get to know you, but as I said, we don't have any openings right now. We will keep your resume on file in case that changes." It was nebulous feedback at best.

When I wasn't trying to get a job, I worked on the maintenance crew at Seven Oaks Golf Club. As I drove the gang mowers up and down the fairways, I had plenty of time to imagine what I was missing in the working world. My friends were all busy with their new careers in new cities, while I was cutting grass and still sleeping under my parents' roof.

Five months passed and my interview losing-streak was still intact.

In October, my father bumped into Russ Buchanan, an old college buddy, at one of the Colgate alumni meetings. Dad had been asked to speak to the gathering and, after his speech, he had a chance to spend some time with his friend.

In the course of their chat, when Mr. Buchanan asked Dad how Jessie and I were doing, Dad explained that I was still looking for a job. Buchanan took it upon himself to make some calls on my behalf. Within a couple weeks, I had an interview in northern New Jersey with Prudential Insurance Company. The job was in their Group Insurance Department, based in Parsippany.

A few days after that interview, I received an offer and, desperate to get going, I accepted it immediately. I was grateful to Mr. Buchanan for extricating me from my stagnant situation. I was also grateful that Dad was the kind of guy, who had friends willing to help out his wayward child.

Russ Buchanan's influence must have been significant. After all, it trumped any potential objections that might have been generated by brown polyester suits and sweaty hands. And really nice loafers.

The Business World

To this day, I am thankful to Russ Buchanan for finagling a job opportunity for me. It wasn't a glamorous first job, and it didn't pay very well, but it was a start, and I was relieved to have it.

In 1981, the going wage for my college classmates who secured their jobs from on-campus interviews was $20,000-22,000 a year. If they were sales jobs, the new hires also received a company car with all expenses paid.

My job with Prudential was as a group insurance underwriter, a desk job and a financially oriented position. Starting salary: $14,300 per year. I knew I would be financially strapped...but hey, I had a job.

The first thing I needed to do was buy a car. John Morris, who owned the Chevrolet dealership in Hamilton, assessed my needs and my means. When I walked out of the dealership, I was the proud owner of a brand new Chevy Chevette Scooter.

The Scooter was no Mercedes. Let me describe it. It was brown (naturally). And yes, my mother declared that the color of it matched my brown eyes. It had NO air conditioning. NO electric windows. And NO glove compartment. Was there a nice sound system? Well, it had an AM radio. No FM, no tape deck. The car was the civilian's version of an Army surplus vehicle. But, hey, it was the cheapest thing on four wheels. I paid $4,100 for it. I put $300 down, and car payments would be part of my life.

That November, I packed my few belongings and left Hamilton in my nifty Scooter armed with the $3,000 I had earned from summer jobs. Destination: New Jersey.

Where was I going to live? Where was this executive of the future going to stay? A young singles apartment complex? Nope. I rented a room in the basement of a house in Dover, NJ. The family had just remodeled it, hoping to take in a few bucks. I was their first tenant at $300/month—just my speed.

Ever supportive, Mom followed me to New Jersey in a small U-Haul truck loaded with a sparse assortment of furniture and furnishings. She had refurbished a desk, a dresser, and a kitchen table, and we bought a mattress and box spring. She bought bedding and towels. Other than that, my furniture consisted of a bean bag and two fold-out lawn chairs, and a little plastic table for my TV.

Was it a new color TV? No. The "Waste Not, Want Not" queen

had located an old 13-inch black-and-white television set for a pretty cheap price through a newspaper ad. The seller was willing to throw in a rabbit-ear antenna for free. What a deal!

I got moved in and Mom headed back to Hamilton. As she drove away, my life in Hamilton left with her. I was no longer Tiger Dunlap. I was in business now, and I would be Fred Dunlap from that day forward.

I started work the next day. Due to my shaky financial status, I developed a very basic routine that included working or watching a lot of television in the apartment.

When the four available channels had nothing worthwhile to watch, I read books and magazines. Or I slept. I learned that sleeping late in the morning wasn't part of my rental agreement. During their renovation, the family neglected to insulate the ceiling; I could hear every footstep and voice above me as the family began their day.

What about food for a growing boy? Steak dinners at fancy restaurants? Lobster bisque? Nope. I cooked most of my meals. Mom gave me her recipes for the meals I loved the most. Before we departed for New Jersey, Mom spent a week teaching me how to make each dish.

Sundays were my organizational days. I tuned in to the NFL football games—there was always a double-header on Sundays. While watching the games on my fuzzy TV set, I did laundry, ironed shirts and shined my shoes.

Cooking also was part of organization day. I would make several of Mom's dishes, let them cool and then stick each tasty dish in Tupperware containers to go into the freezer. That made them easy to thaw and heat-up on a work night when I was too tired to cook something from scratch.

Besides food and shelter, there was one other need this healthy

22-year-old had: nightlife, with eligible women. After a few weeks, I had gotten to know many of my co-workers, and we sometimes went to bars after work. We all did the same work, which meant we were all on a tight budget. So the places we could afford were not, shall we say, the hot spots.

We usually went to small, dive bars where the beers were cheap. These places were filled with smoke from the nasty habits of the other clientele. Dart boards and pool tables were plentiful and we kept ourselves amused playing both games late into the evening. Being good at pool, I generally was able to make a few bucks by betting my opponents. This helped pay for my beer.

We drank Pabst Blue Ribbon in those days. I can still remember the label on that bottle: "Since 1844…Selected as America's Best in 1893…" Yep, I thought, rated highly back when Grover Cleveland was in office. But worthy of a massive hangover in 1982.

What about women? These bars weren't a huge magnet for young, attractive women. The cute girls I wanted to date were at the upscale nightclubs where they didn't need to play pool to pay for their drinks. The men around them took care of that.

It's not that there weren't women in the bars we frequented—there were. But from my quick assessment, they weren't what I was looking for. And upon closer inspection, I surmised that they hadn't signed up for very good dental plans.

Generally, in 1982, I worked and spent time at my apartment. And I occasionally played pool and drank beer with my work friends. Six months went by very fast.

Beers on the Porch in Coraopolis

I was recruited to another company in May 1982 when Equitable Life offered me a sales job in Pittsburgh, Pennsylvania. It wasn't for much more money—$1,700 to be exact, raising my yearly income to $16,000. A company car wasn't part of the deal, but I didn't care. It was a job in sales, and I couldn't wait to get started.

The increased income permitted a move to a one-bedroom apartment where my TV, bean bag and lawn chairs fit perfectly. Best of all, there were no footsteps or voices to hear up above at 6 a.m.

The apartment complex was located in Coraopolis, a suburb west of Pittsburgh. It wasn't an upscale apartment village, but it was clean and it was a reasonable commute to the office. Coraopolis was a residential area filled with young parents and small kids. It wasn't a trendy place, where women my age would live. So I figured I would have to look for female friends in other parts of the city. *There will be plenty of time for that*, I thought. *First, my focus needed to be on making a good impression at Equitable Life.*

At Prudential and now at Equitable, I employed the same methods that had served me well as a caddie and in Alaska, each method an extension of what my parents had taught me. This meant differentiating myself by my work ethic. It included working nights and weekends during the early months, trying to develop a good reputation with my bosses. The sales field was a perfect fit for me, but the products we sold were very technical, so I spent a lot of time with other salesmen, learning the details of the business.

From time to time, I'd speak to Mom and Dad on the telephone, catching up on both ends. Words of advice continued to filter my way, especially when a fresh perspective was necessary to get me through any predicaments.

After a few months, my parents decided to pay me a visit, making the seven-hour drive down from Hamilton for a weekend.

For some reason, I felt much more established in Pittsburgh than I had in northern New Jersey, perhaps because I felt I was on a career path now vs. a first job out of college? Maybe it was that I was living in a real apartment instead of a cave under another family? But it might just be that I had been out on my own long enough now that I felt more in command of my life, more self-sufficient? Whatever it was, as I prepared for their visit, I felt better about my situation in life.

When my parents arrived, I wanted to show them everything—my apartment, my office, the whole city of Pittsburgh. We had a great time touring my new world. We didn't go out to dinner; I cooked them dinner. I could tell my mother was impressed that I had become somewhat accomplished with running my life.

After touring with my parents in the morning, we sat in the sunshine on that Saturday afternoon. I lived on the bottom floor of the apartment building. The only benefit to that was that I had a sliding glass door that led out to a cement porch and a grassy area.

We took the lawn chairs and bean bag onto the lawn, and I provided the beer. My parents have never been big drinkers. *But hey, they are in my town now,* I thought. *We were on my turf, and we would play by my rules!* We sat in the sun and downed a few cold ones. And then we downed a few more.

We talked about Colgate and things going on in Hamilton, but the majority of our time was spent talking about my new world. I explained in detail the things I was doing in the new job, and I described the different people I was working with, inside and outside of the company. They listened with great interest and asked a lot of questions.

I also wanted to explain *how* I was working, to make sure they knew I was employing many of the things I had learned from them over the years. I wanted them to know that their principles were working well in my new environment.

I spoke about the fundamentals: work ethic, attention to detail and relentless follow-through. I reminded Dad that, like him, I was being fanatical about preparation so I would have a command of every variable that could come into play.

We also talked about complex issues, like dealing with favoritism in the office or having a manager who wasn't enforcing rules consistently among sales people. We compared those issues of mine to some of the challenges Dad dealt with over the years at Lehigh and then at Colgate. I explained how I was perceiving these same issues in my office and how I planned to address them.

As Mom and Dad listened intently, I talked about the future and gave them a prognosis of where I thought my career was headed. I also explained why I was confident that this was a viable path for me to invest my time.

By the time the sun began to disappear on the horizon, we had talked for hours. It was a thorough discussion, an exhaustive session. But it was a *different* discussion than we had ever had. I certainly wasn't the "intelligent pet" anymore, but rather an adult talking to my parents as peers or colleagues. That day was the student's chance to give his mentors an update on how their lifelong pupil was doing.

It was apparent that my parents were watching me with wonder as I described the adult world in which I was embroiled. Their eyes were warm and their smiles broad with the look that speaks of their happiness for what they created.

I will acknowledge the possibility that some of Dad and Mom's reflective appearance might have been due to the beer, too. I had never seen my parents drink more than they did on that sunny afternoon in Coraopolis. But the novelty of their alcohol intake was no more novel than their impressions of my new world. It was a special day for the three of us.

When darkness set in, we retired back inside my apartment and brought the chairs with us. And that night, after watching some television on my fuzzy screen, my parents went to sleep in my bed, while I slept in the living room on the bean bag.

When Life Isn't Fair

COLGATE FOOTBALL WAS ON A roll coming into the 1982 season. Steve Calabria was in his sophomore year and he had a strong offensive supporting cast with players like Rich Erenberg and Tommy Rogers. The defense was potent too, led by Jeff Knight, Curtis Thompson, Dave Wolf and Danny Arment.

The season began with wins against Connecticut, Lehigh, Cornell and Dartmouth. Heading into their fifth game, the team was 4-0 and ranked nationally in Division I-AA. The next game was against Holy Cross, also undefeated and nationally ranked.

Because of increased interest in the game, Dad was contacted by an official at ABC Sports. He told Dad the network wanted to televise the matchup. However, because the World Series was being aired that Saturday afternoon, ABC asked that the Colgate/Holy Cross contest be moved to a twilight game so it didn't compete with baseball. Andy Kerr Stadium didn't have lights, but ABC paid to have temporary ones trucked in for the game.

It was a hard-fought game, but Colgate ultimately prevailed 21-17. Colgate was now 5-0 and their national ranking improved further after the big win.

1982 Colgate/Holy Cross game—ABC Sports comes to Hamilton, NY.

RB Rich Erenberg runs wild on Holy Cross under the lights.

While things were going well on the football field, trouble was brewing off of it. More specifically, trouble was brewing in the Colgate president's office.

During the week before the Holy Cross game, the *New York Times* published an article titled "Colgate's Effort to Change Image Upstaged by Success in Football."[3] Also during the same week, Austin Murphy, a Colgate football player and later a superb writer for *Sports Illustrated*, had written an article for the student newspaper. Murphy praised the football team and predicted that it was destined for the Division I-AA playoffs at the end of the season.

The confluence of the *Times* article and the student paper's mention of the playoffs rattled George Langdon, Colgate's president. He replaced Tom Bartlett as Colgate's president in the late 1970s. Though Langdon

3 Lyons, R.D. (1982, October 9). Colgate's Effort to Change Image Upstaged by Success in Football. *The New York Times*. Retrieved from http://www.nytimes.com.

had been supportive of Colgate athletics, he was an academic at heart. His bias was to attend to the needs of the professors and their academic departments above other university functions. The following events and discussions were recounted to me by Dad years later.

On the Tuesday before the Holy Cross game, Langdon called Dad, requesting to meet immediately. Dad recalled Langdon hurrying down the hill to Huntington Gym and into Dad's office where Langdon asked, "Have you seen the articles?"

Dad had seen both but wondered what the fuss was all about. "All of this emphasis on football is hurting our reputation," Langdon barked. "And what's this about going to the playoffs? I never said we could go. No Ivy League team is going to any playoffs."

Dad countered, "Listen, George, you've been aware of this all along. When we moved to Division I-AA this year, the playoffs were part of that change. Every athletic team strives to be national champion. Why should football be any different?"

Langdon looked puzzled. "I don't remember hearing any of that," he said. "But playoffs make no sense. Participating in them would compromise our exam schedule and it would hurt the players' academic performance."

"The success we are having in football has nothing to do with Colgate's academic reputation," Dad protested. "We fully support the academic requirements of the university and we always have." Dad leaned forward. "There is no reason why we can't have academic excellence *and* athletic excellence."

Langdon remained unconvinced. "But that's not how it looks. Those articles don't talk about academic excellence. All they talk about is football. Fred, we *can't* go to the playoffs—it would damage Colgate's academic reputation."

Since Dad had to start football practice, the discussion ended. While pleased with the start of his season, Dad was suddenly preoccupied by this disagreement with his boss over the playoffs.

He and the team had put much work and preparation into the season and Colgate's football prowess. It was actually giving Colgate immense exposure with alumni and prospective students.

How can Langdon, Dad thought, *be so influenced by the professors? And have such a myopic view on this?* Dad felt violated and betrayed. He had done nothing but instill the importance of Colgate's academic standards in every player and every recruit. He had extolled the virtues of academic excellence while doing the same with athletic excellence.

Moreover, Dad knew many professors who were strong supporters of athletics and Colgate football, and he knew they weren't the cause of this rebellion. He realized that the source of the problem was a *fanatical few*. They were a small group of outspoken professors.

These people are the source of the problem, Dad thought. *They have no understanding for how the alumni and the students feel about the school or athletics.*

Colgate's next opponent was Rutgers and the game would be played at their New Brunswick stadium. A normal week of practice and preparation for the game was interrupted by Langdon's need to continue the debate. Dad was unyielding. "George," he said, "I have recruited this team and coached them by setting expectations that if the players work hard and perform well, there will be an opportunity for us to play for the Division I-AA national championship. I made that commitment to the players with your support. It would be wholly unfair to suddenly take that away from them."

Langdon was partially sympathetic. "I know it won't be easy," he said, "but the players respect you—you can convince them. And after all, in the end, they will be graduates of Colgate University, and its academic reputation will be more important to them especially when they are trying to get jobs after graduation."

Dad was unwilling to engage. Langdon then told Dad the real reason behind his displeasure with the football team competing in any playoffs. "Fred," Langdon pleaded, "what would the faculty think? This playoff issue is being discussed everywhere on campus. We could have protests by our professors. They might even resign!"

Langdon believed those points would influence my father, but it wasn't the first time that the president misread Dad. Again the meeting ended in a stalemate, and the football team headed to New Brunswick.

Rutgers beat Colgate 34-17 but Colgate's team still remained ranked second in the Division I-AA standings, because the loss was to a Division I-A team. Meanwhile, back on Colgate's campus, the other battle was just beginning. Dad had two big issues confronting him in the next week—a game against Syracuse in the Carrier Dome and a crisis on campus over the playoff issue.

During that following week, Langdon suddenly notified the NCAA that "Colgate's football team will not participate in postseason playoffs because of a conflict with final examinations." Langdon had evidently sided with his academic bias, and buckled under the pressure from his university professors. But he had also acted without even discussing his intention with Dad, his athletic director and head football coach.

Furious, Dad read Langdon's quote in the *New York Times*[4]: "I was compelled to rule out Colgate's participation in the playoffs because the four-game schedule, and especially the semifinal and championship games, coincide with Colgate's reading and final examination period. The

4 Exams Bar Playoff, Colgate Declares. (1982, October 26). *The New York Times.* Retrieved from http://www.nytimes.com.

practice, travel and emotional involvement in championship play would come at the times of the most intense academic pressure." Langdon further went on to say that the playoff schedule was "excessive" and that it "flies in the face of the academic priority of NCAA member institutions."

Given this surprise announcement, Dad met with the coaches and players immediately. They were incredulous and then unruly. As news of Langdon's decision circulated, alums began calling, angrily protesting the decision. Players threatened to transfer, including Steve Calabria and tailback Stacey Hall.

Later that evening, one of the very supportive alums met with the football captains separately and suggested to them that the players' rights were being violated. After getting the consent from the captains to pursue a legal complaint, the alum contacted Rocky Willard, an attorney and former Colgate football player, to represent the team.

Rocky immediately arrived on campus and met with the players. Coaches were asked not to attend the meetings. The meeting resulted in a formal complaint against the university and the president, and a demand via subpoena that president Langdon appear in a Syracuse, New York courtroom.

In what can only be described as delusional, Langdon called Dad and pleaded for him to step in and convince the players and Willard to withdraw the complaint. Langdon's actions that month had been detrimental to the football program and disrespectful to Dad, yet he somehow thought he deserved Dad's assistance. My father calmly explained to his boss that he was not party to the lawsuit, and therefore could not intervene.

Wanting to avoid getting embroiled in the legal mess, Langdon reversed his decision due to a different, unexpected type of pressure. Langdon had underestimated how vehemently the alumni, players and coaches would respond. The news of this reversal was noted in the *Times.*

In his effort to do damage control, Langdon met with the team the next evening. Dad was quoted in the *Times* as saying Mr. Langdon had "a good exchange of information" with the players.[5]

The crisis had passed, the team remained eligible for the playoffs, and the Colgate football team returned to preparing for future opponents. The team finished the year at 7-3 and was awarded a berth into the Division I-AA playoffs. In their first game, they beat Boston University 21-7 and advanced to the quarterfinals. However, the next week, Colgate again faced their perennial nemesis, Delaware, and Colgate's season ended with a 20-13 loss.

The drama of "Playoff-gate" resulted in the creation of the Patriot League a few years later. It was Langdon's idea as a suitable solution to give the players something to play for (Patriot League championship) while also allowing Langdon to remove Colgate from I-AA playoffs. Colgate would only play one more time (the following year) in those playoffs during the Langdon Presidential Era.

Eventually, Langdon retired from Colgate. Soon after his departure, the Patriot League universities unanimously announced their desire to participate in I-AA playoffs. Langdon's worries in 1982 turned out to be unwarranted. In future years, when Colgate received a bid, the playoff games didn't unduly compromise the academic schedule and the decision to renew playoff eligibility didn't denigrate Colgate's academic reputation.

More importantly, the football team continued to get good grades and the players graduated on time.

Imagine that.

---

5 Colgate Shifts Playoff Stand. (1982, October 27). *The New York Times.* Retrieved from http://www.nytimes.com.

Colgate Football—1983 through 1987: The End of Invincibility

SINCE I LIVED IN PITTSBURGH and was focused on building my business career, my first-hand perspectives on Colgate football became fewer as Dad's team played during the mid-1980s. I saw as many games as possible, but Pittsburgh was distant from many of the venues where they competed.

The 1983 team finished 8-3 and received another invite to the Division I-AA playoffs. Of three losses that year, only one was by more than three points—an away game at the University of Wyoming.

The playoffs began with an exciting match-up at Western Carolina, with the Catamounts heavily favored. Colgate built a commanding lead in the first half, but Western Carolina rallied to win 24-23.

The following year was complex. The 1984 team started with a win at Connecticut but got trounced by Army the following week. Dad wasn't pleased with the team's performance, later telling me, "We were 1-1 but we weren't playing good football. I met with the team the day after playing Army and told them we weren't executing effectively and we weren't disciplined in the most basic fundamentals."

Feeling a need to shake things up, Dad explained his intention after the loss. "I told the players we were going to spend the week before the Lehigh game going back to the basics. And I told the offense that we were going to run the Toss Sweep[6] every play in the Lehigh game

6 "Toss Sweep" is a basic offensive play designed to gain yards by running toward either sideline. The quarterback takes the snap and tosses the ball to the tailback as he starts running to one side (or the other). At the same time, the backside guard and tackle pull to lead the play, with the fullback and quarterback also blocking. It is designed to overpower the defense by putting more blockers out front as compared to the number of defenders in that area of the field. On TV, the announcers often refer to this play as "Student Body Right" or "Student Body Left."

until we could prove to ourselves we could run it." He continued. "So all week long, that's all we practiced. And when we got to Lehigh on that Saturday, we drove them crazy running Toss Sweep. Barry Chubb and Kenny Gamble ran wild on Lehigh, and we won 40-35."

The 1984 season produced mixed results (5-6) but 1985 was another good year for Colgate. The team finished 7-3-1 with two losses by a field goal or less.

The Patriot League debuted in 1986 but nothing on the field was as memorable as what happened off the field. I was in Pittsburgh working when I got a call that still haunts me to this day. In mid-September, Mom told me Dad had suffered a heart attack and been rushed to a Rochester, New York hospital.

Immediately, I headed for the airport. When I arrived at the hospital, Mom said doctors had performed double bypass surgery. The closest I could get to him was the small window into the Intensive Care ward. Mom and I sat together that evening. She looked weary and uncertain; her "knowns in life" were now suddenly unknown. I'd like to think that I did a good job of consoling her, but truly I don't remember much about those late evening hours.

The next morning, I was allowed into Dad's Intensive Care room provided I stayed a few feet away from him. He was unconscious and hooked to a respirator. I watched him and whispered, quite aware that he couldn't hear me.

Dad's body trembled with the rhythm of the respirator. It was an eerie scene. I studied his body and then his face. I looked at his hair as it quaked with the motion of the machine.

For the first time in my life, I thought my father looked old. Suddenly I could see lines on his face—lines I had never noticed before. And his gray hair—it looked grayer to me.

I stood silently, looking at this dynamo of a man who now looked so fragile. He had been invincible but now was clutching to life.

When Dad regained consciousness later that day, we talked for a short while, but I quickly left Mom alone with him. It seemed like the right thing to do.

A day later, when he had stabilized and when Mom was more settled, I returned to Pittsburgh. They stayed in Rochester at the hospital for another two weeks before returning to Hamilton.

Ever the warrior, Dad missed only two games that season (Cornell and Yale). For the Holy Cross game, he managed to participate from the press box. It became his perch for the remainder of the season until the last game when he convinced team doctors to let him return to the sidelines.

Though he didn't announce it until a year later, 1987 would be my father's final year as head football coach. He did some reflecting after the 1986 season and was committed to returning for at least one more year. He wanted to finish his coaching career on a high note. He wasn't going to end it with the drama of his recent illness.

Dad's 1987 team had a good season, finishing 7-4, with a schedule that included Duke, Syracuse and Army. Following the last game, Dad met with the team and notified them that he would relinquish his coaching position but retain his job as athletic director. He tapped his long-time assistant coach, Mike Foley, to replace him as head coach. Mike had been a player and a coach under my father and he provided great continuity after Dad's departure.

When Dad announced his plans, there was a mix of sadness and shock from the players and assistant coaches. There was also a sense of shock and sadness from the wives of the coaches for the presumed loss of my mother being a part of the football program. Mom had provided leadership for the coaches' wives: they were a dogged group who supported the team in many ways.

A letter written by Ann Marie Callahan, wife of defensive assistant coach Kevin Callahan, best portrays the impact my mother had on the football program.

January 1988

Dear Marilyn,

I have put off writing this because I was not sure how to express myself. Thanks is not enough. Yes, thank you for always being a big part of my life, for always putting me on your level and for always showing me the ropes in this wonderful world of football. But it goes far beyond football.

Marilyn, you've made things so comfortable for me. You've shown me so many things about being a wife, not just a 'football wife.' Most importantly, you've given me a beautiful relationship, one that goes beyond football.

Colgate football will change without you at the helm, but in my mind, you are Colgate football, and nothing can change that.

You and Fred are so special to Kevin and me. I'm sure you realize what a loss it is to Kevin, but also what an incredible opportunity it has been to work for Fred. If at some point Kevin and I have our own football program, and can generate the enthusiasm and spirit that you have, we will be a success because of your success as a couple (as a team).

I guess the bottom line here is that I hope you know how much I love everything about you and how grateful I am for all you have given me.

Love,
Ann Marie

Dad, with Mom's blessings, continued as athletic director for another four years before officially retiring. Over those four years when we would talk, he privately mentioned his regret for having given up football coaching. After his heart attack, many advised him to relinquish the coaching position. They argued it would be less stressful for him to be the AD than the football coach. Dad followed the advice but he found that he didn't enjoy the AD role as much. He encountered bureaucracy at times with the AD job, which he found frustrating. What he longed for was to be on the practice field and in the locker room. He missed being in the war—that war being the combat missions each week taking on a different opponent. He missed his players and he missed the coaches. More than anything, he missed the intensity of being with a close-knit group committed to putting everything on the line.

With his career as AD winding down, Dad was pleased to appoint Mark Murphy as his successor. Mark played for Dad in 1976 before an impressive career as safety for the Washington Redskins. Off the field, Mark had also been a leader for the National Football League Players Association (NFLPA).

Dad was confident that Mark would be an exceptional athletic director, given his close affiliation with Colgate and the experience gained since graduating. Dad's instincts were good. Mark served well as Colgate's athletic director for nearly 12 years before moving to Northwestern University in 2003 to perform the same role. In 2008, Mark accepted the position as president and chief executive officer of the Green Bay Packers.

The news of Dad's retirement drew interest from many reporters and publications. By that time, Austin Murphy had become a prominent writer for *Sports Illustrated*, and he asked to meet with Dad to write an article on his retirement for the *Colgate Scene*, the Colgate alumni newspaper. An excerpt reads:

> According to Dunlap, Marilyn has been a great asset to his career. 'She has been supportive of all of my endeavors and has brought-up our children to be team players, as well. Her interest and insight into the complexity of my jobs, especially since my first head coaching position, have been invaluable. Whatever I brought to coaching and administration has been polished and improved by her perspective and wise counsel. She tutored players as well as me—I never delivered a serious written proposal or speech that I didn't seek her guidance for form and development. On top of that, she has been the love of my life and my best friend.'

When Dad retired in January 1992, he arrived home to a wife of 40 years who had been anxiously waiting for that moment when she could have him all to herself.

Congratulations, Marilyn D.!

September 1994—Dad is inducted into the Colgate University Athletic Hall of Honor (Award presented by Colgate Athletic Director Mark Murphy).

November 3, 2012—Marilyn and Fred Dunlap are honored by the Inauguration of the Fred '50 and Marilyn Dunlap Endowed Coaching Chair for Football. (Photo by Alice Virden-Speer)

Coach and Mrs. D. are recognized by Tom McGarrity '79 (President of Colgate's Maroon Council)—November 3, 2012. (Photo by Alice Virden-Speer)

PART IV

The Test of the Teachers: The Pupil Implements the Playbook

Getting Ahead

While Dad was finishing his career as football coach and athletic director at Colgate, I spent the 1980s furthering my career. When I first got the sales job in Pittsburgh, it was an entry-level position in a big sales office. Equitable's product suite was Group Insurance. We sold to corporations and managed their employee benefit programs (life, health, dental and disability insurance).

Being the newest and youngest member of the team meant that I was starting at the bottom. Yes, I had the same job as the senior salespeople but the quality of sales leads that were bequeathed to me were... shall we say...suspect. This was to be expected since I was 10-20 years younger than some of the other salespeople, and seniority was the fair way to distribute sales assignments. Having no experience and no seniority, I was given the state of West Virginia as my sales territory. Yes, West Virginia.

One of the best salesmen in our office was Stan Clymer. He handled many of the big accounts and large sources of new business. He was a real pro, and he also had a quick wit. He'd saunter into my office, cigarette in hand, and say, "Freddie, how goes it down in Death Valley? Have you taught those hicks how to read yet? Ha! Ha!"

Stan busted my stones constantly, which was all in good fun. Though he wasn't the manager of the office, he took it as his responsibility to teach me the business. He dedicated many hours to showing me the ropes and mentoring me about all of the important things that were not covered in the company training manuals. He was fun and he liked to drink beer. So we had some things in common, given that I was a 23-year-old fresh out of the frat house.

My fellow salesmen had admonished me about the West Virginia territory, about how difficult it had been historically to generate sales from that market. I could see eyes roll at sales meetings whenever I mentioned rejuvenating the sources there. I guess I was too naïve to understand how untenable that assignment was, but I was determined, convinced that I would be *that guy* who could pull off a miracle.

During the next three years, I traveled each week to different parts of that rural state—Charleston, Parkersburg, Martinsburg, Beckley and Bluefield. I knew every exit on Interstate 79 as it slithered its way through the mountainous terrain. I learned that the West Virginia state flower was the satellite dish. And I learned how to add syllables to the words I had learned in school, like: "Hey they-er!" which is how the folks in West Virginia said hello.

Selling insurance plans in West Virginia was hard. Really hard. And like my father's early years, when I started my job at Equitable, I had a number of *losing seasons*. But, like him, I toiled there for three years and gradually made some sales. My results weren't stellar, but they were much better than any before me.

The sales I did make were relatively small because the corporations in West Virginia were relatively small. And the sales commissions I received matched the size of the sales: relatively small. I wasn't getting rich, but I took solace for having created some new traction in Death Valley.

Despite being new to the business world, I was a veteran at understanding leadership and management techniques. I had spent my life thus far closely observing how my father managed his football operations and I had watched how my parents managed the family. With these baselines in place, I was highly sensitized to spot any differences. Those differences were striking when comparing Coach Landry at Bucknell and my Dad, and I could see them now with my Pittsburgh sales manager, whom I will call Bill.

Bill was a reasonably polished guy and generally looked the part. But he lacked substance and self-confidence, a deadly combination for a person in charge.

Why? A sales office is a competitive environment. The salesmen are competitive with each other. They chafe over who gets the sales lead or who deserves the commission on a sale. It's a spirited place. To keep order requires a strong leader who can deal with conflict and resolve issues fairly. Without firm leadership, jealousy and infighting can swell. Bill was not that guy. He was weak and the whole sales team knew it, which accentuated the amount of negative office discourse.

To make matters more awkward, Bill wasn't authentic. I was fairly certain he knew his weaknesses, but he tried to mask them by putting on an air of charisma. Bill read books incessantly about management, leadership and strategy and regurgitated what he read in the weekly sales meetings.

Bill spoke to us as if he were reading from a success manual, spewing corporate buzzwords. He closed each meeting by pounding his fist on the table, conjuring some form of an inspirational message like a coach would do in a pre-game speech. "You guys are destined for greatness!" he would say. "Nobody can beat this team! In our office, we have the greatest sales team in the industry!"

Each week, Bill used the same lines, trying to inspire us. But it got old, the same message over and over. As I listened to Bill, I often wanted to say, "Really, Bill? The best in the industry? If that's the case, why are seven other sales offices kicking our butts this year in sales?"

While Bill tried to motivate us, Stan usually kicked me under the table. Right after meetings ended, Stan would walk into my office, close the door and mock our sales manager, "Freddie, you are the BEST."

To which I would counter. "No, Stan, you are the BEST."

"No, Freddie, it's true," he continued mocking Bill. "I am f---ing unbelievable, but you have an edge on me, you f---ing sales stud, you!" I would then mimic some other absurd thing Bill said in the meeting and we would both buckle over in laughter.

While Bill was trying his best, the sales team had little respect for him. Unfortunately, that lack of respect also permeated other parts of the organization. This was problematic since some deals required organizational concessions in order to secure the sale. Concessions included things like softer contractual terms or operational flexibilities, or profit margin reductions.

Getting these accommodations approved internally required Bill to make a dogged effort to convince his peers in Operations and Finance that without the concessions, the deal was dead. Winning that appeal required fierce determination, but Bill was intimidated by those he needed to convince.

Bill was afraid of many things. He was afraid of his boss. He feared that members of his sales team might be trying to take his job. And he was afraid to go to bat for his salesmen on deals. The problem was that going to bat for us *was his job.*

Having Bill in my corner was especially important since I was trying to breathe life into Death Valley. I needed his support to overcome a palpable level of internal skepticism over West Virginia, where there was no track record of sales to justify the wisdom of making concessions. But Bill couldn't do it. He got run over by everybody.

Bill had difficulty managing people, too. He couldn't deal with conflict and instead chose to avoid it. If there were disagreements between salespeople, he couldn't mediate.

Bill was equally absent when it came to dealing with non-performance, and there were a few salespeople who weren't performing. One was a salesman we called "Old Joe" who had never carried his weight. But he had never been put on performance warning. We called him "Old Joe" not because of his age (40), but because he walked around the office like he had a handful of marbles in his underwear and was afraid with each step that one or two would slip out.

Bill fawned over Old Joe and gave him many of the hottest sales prospects. But Joe couldn't close a sale if his life had depended on it.

This dynamic was bad for office morale and there was significant resentment, including mine, over Old Joe's preferential treatment. Joe's leads were in cities that had electricity and running water, not in West Virginia where they were still celebrating the invention of the fried egg.

A disturbing quality of the handling of Old Joe was that it affected the performance of other salesmen. Since Joe wasn't confronted about poor results, other performers and non-performers began to relax. It was like, "If Old Joe isn't on the hot seat, then I must be totally safe." Even the high performers tended to pull back some out of disgust for the "Old Joe situation." This lack of management was affecting everyone. Guys stopped coming into the office on weekends to catch up on work. Happy hours started earlier on Fridays. Things like that.

There were only a couple of exceptions: Stan and his protégé (me). Stan was my compass in those early years. We continued to put in long hours, working nights and weekends, persevering in spite of the office issues.

Having inherited Dad and Mom's spirit for hard work, I continued to travel each week to West Virginia, chasing after low-percentage sales opportunities. As time passed, I began going around my boss, directly to his corporate peers, to plead my case on each deal. If Bill wasn't capable of backing me, I needed to fight for myself.

My situation in Pittsburgh was similar to my father's situation at Lehigh. Though Bill wasn't malicious in his role as a boss, both Dad and I had bosses who provided little help or support. As such, we needed to find a way to achieve our goals in spite of our bosses.

Assessing my situation in Pittsburgh and the failings of my manager, I was struck by the contrast with how Dad had operated. Dad was strong, decisive, and supportive. He was able to confront things and people and he dealt directly with conflicts. He was everything my sales manager wasn't.

Without question, the dysfunctional elements in the sales office provided me with a valuable learning experience. I was learning how *not* to manage and Bill was my teacher. As inept as he was, he provided abundant case examples for learning. To make sure I never forgot these examples, I began to document them.

In the early 1980s, Dictaphones were the rage of new technology and a means for improved work efficiency. While driving to West Virginia each week, I would use my Dictaphone to record a variety of letters on cassette tapes. They could be internal correspondences to various departments in the company. Or they might be thank-you letters to customers or new producers whom I had just met. When I got back to the office, I would hand the cassette to my secretary who typed the letters for my review. Dictaphones made driving time more efficient.

Until one return trip, when I began dictating the "I Would Never" tape. This was a tape I dictated to myself, and kept to myself, about each example of Bill's management incompetence. I called it the "I Would Never" tape, because it documented events and actions I would never do.

Watching my father manage his football teams over the years, I had always dreamed that someday I might be fortunate enough to become a manager and have the opportunity to lead an organization. And should that good fortune ever come my way, and should I ever have such great responsibilities to others reporting to me, I would never do what Bill did.

The episodes I described soon took on the style of book chapters, documenting the details of each of Bill's latest mistakes as a manager. As each management stumble occurred, another chapter was added. Soon there were multiple tapes. As I drove down Interstate 79, I would listen to them to refresh my memory, while also considering how I would have handled the situation better, from the lessons I learned over the years while watching and listening to my parents.

I continued to dictate even in later years while working for other companies and other managers, when I encountered another poor management approach. And I often played the tapes again as a means for grounding myself and renewing my vigilance to not make the same mistakes these managers made. As I advanced in management, those tapes guided my actions and also the actions of managers under my command, since I would not permit this type of behavior.

Substance Over Style

DURING MY YEARS IN PITTSBURGH, I learned something valuable from my friend, Stan. It was the lesson of "Substance Over Style."

I had learned that lesson from my parents throughout the years. However, in my early tenure in business, I sometimes wondered if the formula for success in business would be different than the approaches for football or the rules on Willowbrook Drive.

For instance, when I first noticed how Bill managed as compared to how my father led his football program, I wondered whether the requirements for business were different from sports—whether the disciplines Dad instilled were only applicable to sports or football. I wondered if it was impractical to run businesses that way. Did the unbridled intensity of Dad's organization have any place in the business world? And, is it unrealistic to think business people can be motivated to make that level of commitment?

It didn't take more than a year for me to realize Bill's approach wasn't the right equation for building winning teams in business. But what was the right approach? These questions remained with me in my early years in business as I observed how various managers ran their organizations. As my observations continued and I was given leadership roles, the answer became blatantly clear: EVERYTHING that applies in sports (and is learned in sports) has transferability and relevance in the business world.

While I was grappling with these questions in the early years, Stan Clymer was my first point of validation in the business world that substance mattered far more than style. When I started my job in Pittsburgh in the early 1980s, most sales training focused on presentation skills. We presented using wallboards and handouts. Projection screen technology was still a few years away.

When we attended offsite training seminars, Equitable's trainers spoke about "presentation style," emphasizing the use of eye contact, hand gestures, moderation of speech tone, and employing tactics from the Xerox Professional Selling Skills program. Praise was handed out for how accomplished each presenter was. At the national sales meetings, it became a bit of a beauty contest when different sales people presented. Without a doubt, presentation skills (style) were seen as essential to sales success.

Stan was the exception, since he was not an accomplished presenter. In fact, when he had to present, his voice quivered and his hands shook. He sweated his ass off. There was perspiration dripping out of pores I didn't even know existed.

Fortunately, what Stan lacked in presentation polish, he made up for in knowledge of the business. Stan studied every aspect of Equitable's operation so he was prepared for any question any prospective customer might ask. His mastery of the business made him highly credible with potential clients because most of them were looking for someone who could engineer a sophisticated solution to their problems, not a flashy sales guy whose best skill was selecting vintage wine from the menu at a business dinner.

Stan was the highest achieving salesman in the office because, bottom line, people bought from Stan. They did so because they were sure he could deliver. His presentation skills became an endearing part of who he was, both with customers and within our company.

I remember one occasion when Stan returned to the office from a sales call. Seeing him pass by my office, I asked him how it went. Stan exclaimed, "It was excellent! The guy shook my hand at the start of the meeting and said he had heard great things about "The Sweater."

Then Stan smiled. "When he got done shaking my hand, his hand was drenched, and he knew he had found me!"

This was vintage Stan. He was blunt, sometimes callous, but always truthful. He and I spent countless hours in the office working on sales proposals, fixing operational issues and discussing strategy. He often invited me to his house after work to drink beer and talk about the day. I was single at the time and loved spending time with him, his wife Gail, and their young son.

Stan's bluntness was endearing and part of his matter-of-fact style. He'd chug his first beer as soon as he got through his front door just to get a buzz started. And sometimes he'd chug a second one before the sermon started.

Stan talked about business incessantly. This was much appreciated since I was still figuring out how to navigate the Equitable system. I'd listen intently to every word, every bit of advice, just as I had done when Mom and Dad gave me lessons on how to live my life. But this was business and Stan was my mentor. As he pontificated, he paused occasionally to belch. The belch was distinctly a *Stan burp*, where the force he applied was as if he wanted the neighbor down the street to hear it.

Gail chatted with us now and then, but it was really just Stan and me discussing and solving issues of the day. Then, when it was time for me to leave, Stan would call out, "Gail, have you taken a shower yet?"

From the other room, Gail replied "Yes, Stan, I took one earlier."

"Okay, then, go get ready for me," he shouted, as he turned back to face me. He belched one more time and said, "Freddie, I have loved having you here tonight, but it's time for you to go. I need to go now and have animal sex with my wife."

And that was how our evening would end, each time I visited there. Vintage Stan.

For Stan, it was all about business and his family. I appreciated his friendship and tutelage more than he will ever know. But his lasting impression on me, more than any other, was his pursuit of substance over style. I learned that knowing your business deeply and being a student of the business are essential traits to becoming a respected businessperson. Like Stan had done, I became fanatical about it for the rest of my career.

Interestingly enough, as I ascended to higher levels in business, the jobs didn't require that I have that detailed knowledge. In those loftier positions, it wasn't expected that I know every detail. Peers would tell me, "That's because we have people who are supposed to know that."

Regardless of this advice, that is precisely why I chose a contrarian path…Stan's path. I chose not to defer knowledge to subject-matter experts (SMEs) below me. Instead I forced myself to stay current with the details of whatever business I had chosen. It made me more relevant to the tasks at hand and a better decision-maker on key issues at critical moments.

It became something unique about me, as compared to my peers, who repeatedly chose to defer to the SMEs. It was another point of differentiation and a key to later success. Most of all, it made me a better executive and I owe that instilled discipline to my friend Stan Clymer.

I owe that to Fred Dunlap, too. Even as a head coach, Dad made sure he was fully conversant with what every coach and player was doing, on or off the field. Through my time with Stan Clymer, I started to see that the approaches that led to success in business were far more consistent with my father's methods than I could ever have believed they would be.

An Attempt at Leadership

HARD WORK AND CONSIDERABLE TIME spent beyond conventional business hours generated more sales for me at Equitable. And through both, I had become fully knowledgeable of the inner-workings of our company at all levels.

Fortunately, by 1985, Bill had been replaced by another sales manager. Within a few weeks, my new manager had surveyed the office and decided to rescue me from West Virginia. He assigned me to the largest prospective sources in the Pittsburgh market. With better leads and now being a more experienced sales executive, I made huge sales for the next three years.

With that prosperity, I retired the 13-inch TV set, the lawn chairs and the bean bag. And alas, I retired the Chevy Chevette Scooter, too.

Those weren't the only changes. I bought a house on Kind Drive in McCandless, a northern suburb of Pittsburgh. My first house wasn't grand—it was actually quite modest, but it sat on an acre of wooded land. Following the example from Mom when she improved our home on Willowbrook Drive, I began making improvements on Kind Drive. I didn't build massive rock walls, but I did construct landscaping walls around the house using railroad ties. Mom and Dad visited and helped me with this project.

In the back yard, I cleaned up my own "back forty." It had everything we had on Willowbrook Drive except, of course, dirt bombs.

Life was good on Kind Drive. As I worked on project after project, I had time to think about things. Business was good. Succeeding seemed easier now that I was out of West Virginia and had established a good reputation with the people in Equitable.

From time to time, I thought about how difficult my first years out of college had been, about how frustrating they were. I reminded myself about how little money I had and how tight things were for me. I thought about the job at Prudential and about the many nights spent in dive bars paying for my beers with a pool cue. Those were hard times, I thought, and I had come a long way.

During these times of reflection, I thought about my father and the feelings he shared with me 15 years earlier about the hard times during the early years at Lehigh. He said that *the hard times become the best times* and create the most rewarding memories. "For while times are better now," he said, "you remember how difficult it had been, how hard you had worked, and how many sacrifices were made in order to succeed."

Dad would say, "Success without having first experienced failure is less fulfilling. Until you have examined the emotional depths of failure, you can't really appreciate the good times appropriately. Those who have failed, but then persevered through the obstacles, they learn to appreciate success fully. They find success to be far more gratifying."

Dad's words resonated with me as I sat on the Kind Drive lawn pulling weeds and trimming shrubs. I was in a better place now, but I still cherished the memories of harder times. The struggles during the early years weren't negative memories. Prudential and the West Virginia years were part of a process, part of my grooming, and though hard, I had warm feelings for the battles I fought and frustrations I felt. This had led to a genuine sense of gratification for the successes I was now experiencing.

In 1988, that success triggered a chance at management when I was approached by the regional sales VP. He asked me to consider a sales management position in the eastern Pennsylvania/southern New Jersey market, based in Philadelphia.

The position was open because Al, the previous Philadelphia sales manager, had taken a less stressful job where he would only manage certain large accounts. I was fairly familiar with the sales team in the Philly office since both the Pittsburgh and Philadelphia sales offices were in the east central region.

The Philly sales team was a complex group of people who had earned a bad reputation internally within other company departments (operations, finance and legal). I had observed this while in Pittsburgh because we worked with many of the same employees. Those people weren't shy about stating their displeasure with how the Philly team treated them, with descriptors surly and demanding used. The Philly sales team ignored many of the company policies and made commitments to customers that weren't standard or acceptable. If the operations people ever balked at it, they would complain and threaten, "The customer will leave if the company doesn't accommodate the request." Generally, these people bullied their way internally to get non-standard things approved.

In contrast, I had been taught by Stan to operate in a collaborative way with operations and finance. They were my partners, and I took it as my responsibility to influence my customers *toward* our standard offerings. That wasn't difficult if the benefits of standardization were explained properly to customers, especially if our prices might be lower and our service delivery would be more consistent. I had built a lot of trust with the internal regional departments in the six years I worked in Pittsburgh, and as rumors circulated about my becoming sales manager, the internal teams were counting on me to improve the sales team's behavior when I got to Philadelphia.

The new job excited me because the Philly sales office was one of the largest in the company and I was yearning to become a manager. It was certainly a promotion but more important to me was the chance to lead an organization and try to impose many of the leadership methods I had observed as a kid on the sidelines.

During my interview for the position, my new boss told me that Equitable needed new leadership in Philadelphia. As I prepared to take the position, I understood that one of the bigger tasks was to improve the office culture. The sales executives in the office didn't like each other; they were jealous and didn't work well together. If there were ever any sales failures, they blamed the loss of a sale or a customer on the operations department or the legal team or finance. Anyone but themselves.

During my first few weeks in Philadelphia, much of what I had observed or heard from afar was validated. The salespeople had an air of superiority. They expected other company departments to support whatever they demanded. They had little respect for the roles others played, and if the internal teams resisted, they expected me as sales manager to simply support them and override any objections.

About a month in, my first confrontation happened. It involved one of the senior salespeople, a guy whom I will call George. He was a smart man and a hard worker, but he had an abrasive way about him, and for a salesman, little ability to understand how he was being perceived. He was condescending to nearly everyone, speaking as if he was convinced he was always the smartest guy in the room.

Our confrontation was the result of George making certain commitments to a customer that were detrimental to our company. He had been reckless in his assurances, disregarding some very important company policies.

When I confronted George, he was outraged that the operations team wouldn't support him. I explained that I wouldn't support what he had done either, and I told him he needed to call the customer and revoke the commitment. George was shocked and began raising his voice. I cut him off using Mom's Cobra Treatment. I went on to explain what I would and would not condone. I also told George that his boorish behavior was creating a poor relationship with the regional support teams.

Moreover, I told him that it wasn't my job to approve exceptions. Rather it was *my job* to make sure he abided by company policies and treated all parties internally with respect. And that it was *his job* to be a better salesman and convince his customers to accept willingly the standard products we could deliver.

A similar run-in happened the next day with the most senior salesman whom I will call Tom. The meeting went similarly. By the surprised look on his face, I could tell he wasn't used to being confronted.

Having seen enough evidence of poor salesmanship, poor behavior internally and a growing potential for a mutiny with the new manager (me), I decided I needed to re-clarify the office rules. To do so, I called the entire sales team into our conference room and used the George and Tom situations as examples while explaining how they should be handled in the future.

Further, I pointed out that those actions would not be tolerated and I reinforced the ways we would conduct ourselves, both with customers and with internal partners. I told the sales troops that respect and trust were critical to building healthy business relationships, and that our conduct to date was combative, limiting any potential for building trusting relationships.

The room was quiet, but I could read body language pretty well. It ranged from a silent protest to controlled enthusiasm. The two men whom I had confronted weren't pleased, but they didn't voice objection.

Perhaps it was because they didn't believe I would really enforce my rule. Other salespeople remained silent in the company of the two senior salesmen, but I could tell they agreed fully with my points.

Driving home that evening, I replayed the meeting in my head. I had made the right points, I concluded. But from the visible dissent from the two senior people, I was sure I had more work to do. It was clear to me that the previous manager really had not managed; he allowed his people to act poorly and it had been going on so long that the salespeople weren't even aware of how unreasonably they were behaving.

Another Challenge to the Culture— A Generation Later

Within a week, another incident occurred with George. I was sitting in my office preparing for a meeting, but I could hear him ranting on his speakerphone, talking to the finance team in the regional office. He was so loud that I couldn't concentrate. I walked into his office and abruptly put his call on mute. He looked shocked. "End the call," I said briskly. "We need to talk."

George hung up the phone and I closed his office door. "Didn't you hear me last week?" I demanded in a controlled voice. "THIS is exactly what I was referring to. You are berating our internal people."

"I wasn't berating her," he replied. "I was explaining to her what she was too stupid to understand."

"George, I meant what I said last week," I said sternly. "If this ever happens again, I will fire you on the spot." He looked at me vacantly as I asked, "Do you understand?" He started to make excuses, but I cut him off with "DO YOU UNDERSTAND?" He nodded. I got up and walked back to my office.

Over the next few weeks, I spent long hours mentoring the younger sales people while joining them to meet the key market people (brokers, consultants, key clients). Soon, we were making progress as a team using the new rules I had imposed.

Meanwhile, George had his tail between his legs and was doing his best to re-invent himself internally and externally. He was no longer a dissenter. He actually sought me out, wanting my counsel on how he should handle issues and people. We were making progress there, too.

Tom, however, was rarely in the office. When I called him on the phone, I always got voicemail, and his return calls weren't prompt.

When Tom came into the office later that week, I cornered him and asked where he had been. He said he had been with clients. His predicament was that, by that time, I had met most of his clients, and I was getting the sense he wasn't being very attentive.

Tom held to his story, so I pressed him for details. "When were you with him? Who else was there? What did you discuss?" Within the next week, I managed to find a reason to call some of the clients Tom had mentioned and, without causing an awkward situation, was able to discern that most of what he had said was crap. I wasn't sure what he was doing with his time, but one thing was sure: he hadn't met with those people and we weren't getting the right amount of sales from his brokers and consultants.

As the senior salesman, Tom had been given the most lucrative sales leads. Al had granted them unevenly to him, which was a source of frustration for the other salespeople. I had heard complaints of favoritism from my seat in Pittsburgh.

When I arrived in Philadelphia, I had a suspicion that we weren't getting the best results from the big brokerage firms. On the surface, it looked like a dominating portion of market sources were assigned to Tom, but I didn't want to rock the boat during my first few weeks. Instead I chose to observe things for a while. Two months into my tour, I had seen enough and heard enough that it was time to shake a few things up.

I called Tom and asked to meet with him. A few hours later, he showed up and came into my office. I explained that we needed more results from his sales contacts and I asked him to explain what he planned to do to increase our sales. His answers were vague. I then questioned how hard he was working and I told him that unless I could see a significant amount of effort and improvement, I was going to pull some of his assignments and give them to the younger salespeople.

Tom was a difficult guy to read. He didn't seem angry, but he also didn't show the vital signs of someone who was going to kick into gear. The meeting was short and I ended it by scheduling to meet with him every other day to review his progress. He had never been closely managed or monitored and I wanted to see how he would respond to a dose of micro-management.

The next morning, Al appeared at my office doorway. In his new role, he still worked from our offices though he was no longer involved in the affairs of the sales office. I had expected his visit, given how close he and Tom were.

Al had been manager for many years, and it was suspected that the reason he moved to the account management job was more his boss's decision than his. Al was older and wasn't an active manager; he delegated everything and monitored nothing. While he seemed to have a close relationship with Tom, it had been widely rumored that Al was intimidated by him. This, most believed, led to him giving Tom the most attractive sales contacts.

"Fred, do you have a minute?" Al asked. I nodded. "Hey, I got a call from Tom last night," he began. "He said you two had a discussion yesterday, and he's pretty worked up over it." I played it cool and asked him to explain. "Tom said you are concerned about his sales production." Then he shrugged. "Yeah, I guess he hasn't sold much lately, but I think he's trying real hard."

"Al, he's not working hard," I began "He's not even working. He shows up here a couple hours a week, then he's gone. Where he is, I don't know. But he's not with clients. I have talked to them and they haven't seen him."

Al shifted in his seat; he looked uncomfortable. "Fred, I can't argue with you on that. But I like you and I thought I better explain something to you...because I am concerned!" As I watched, I had no clue where he was headed. "You see, Tom is a *different* guy." Al hesitated. "He's hard to read, but he has an angry streak." He gestured. "Fred, he has guns. A lot of guns. And he can be hot-headed.

"You see, Fred, I think you are doing the right things here in Philadelphia," Al said. "And I like you. But I just want to make sure you are careful with Tom...you know...." He gestured again.

"So you are warning me not to push him to do his job," I suggested.

"No, I didn't say that," he replied. "I guess you just shouldn't push him too hard."

Al's innuendo was obvious. I smiled at him and said, "Everybody around here thinks Tom is treated in a more privileged way than anyone else. From what I see, they are right." I stood up. "For me to perpetuate that would be unhealthy, and I won't do it. We need to improve the culture and teamwork here, and treating people inconsistently would be a barrier to progress."

"Fred, you can do what you want," he said. "But I like you, and I wanted to alert you." Al got up and walked out.

As I drove home, I thought about the odd meeting that day. It was a Friday and my parents happened to be in town to visit that weekend to see the new house in Philadelphia and help with some home improvements.

On Saturday, I was refinishing an old bedroom set in the garage. It was messy work, but hey, I was still operating in the Land of "Waste Not, Want Not." Off and on during the day, I added more coats of shellac to the woodwork and Dad helped me. It was just the two of us working in the garage, and that gave me a chance to update him on my new job. I talked about personnel, about the challenges with getting sales results improved, and eventually we talked about my situation with my senior salesman. I explained his lack of work ethic and I described the inconsistencies existing in the office, which had been created by the previous sales manager. Dad listened as I described the environment.

"That's a tough situation," he said, "and I know what you are trying to do—create a healthy, fair environment. But unless you address that issue, you won't get the respect of the other people in your organization. If you don't move decisively, you will appear weak." I knew that, but it was good to hear Dad confirm my assessment of the situation.

We talked about Tom's guns and any risks associated with disciplining him. Fresh on my mind was an incident aired on television the week before where a boss and his employee had quarreled and the employee shot the boss. I was certainly committed to dealing with Tom but I wondered if it was worth getting killed over it.

Dad understood the risk, though it was remote, but that didn't soften his strong position on what needed to be done. "Tiger, I don't think you have a choice," he explained. "You need to confront the situation directly and keep the heat on this guy to perform."

I sensed some of Dad's wisdom and he didn't disappoint me. Laying his paintbrush to the side, he said, "I have a rule around this sort of thing. If someone is causing me anxiety, and it's their fault, then I owe it *to myself* to make that person feel an equal or greater amount of anxiety." We looked at each other in silence as I soaked up his words.

The next week I met with Tom and continued to pressure him to perform. After repeated meetings every other day for two weeks, he decided to resign. I then reassigned the sales contacts immediately to salespeople deserving of them. The sales team was elated; the contacts were redistributed and more fairly apportioned. While they were happy to get expanded assignments, they realized that they needed to cultivate those sources quickly. The pressure was on all of us.

During the weeks after Tom's departure, I met with many of the brokers and consultants who had worked with him. After meetings, they pulled me aside. "We wondered when you guys were ever going to figure Tom out," one of them told me. "Tom was the laziest sales guy in the business and we weren't ever going to award a piece of business to him."

The news wasn't surprising. It confirmed my suspicions about Tom and confirmed my decision to take action.

Similar to my father's challenge to his culture in 1965, when one of his top players resisted the Team Rules, I had taken a risk by removing one of the top people in my department because he wasn't willing to adhere to my rules. I would have been weakened as a leader if I hadn't held Tom accountable to the same requirements as the rest of my team. That was Al's downfall as a manager and was the reason he was removed from the position: he didn't set a consistent set of rules, and that led to anarchy and lower results.

Like my father, I made some mistakes during my early leadership years. But some good decisions made a difference, as well. Over the next two years my colleagues and I built a strong sales organization in Philadelphia. Progress came from holding the team to a higher set of standards and working some long hours mentoring and coaching the team in areas where they were deficient.

Early mornings and evenings were dedicated to one-on-one training. Those were times that wouldn't impede our ability to be out in the marketplace during standard business hours. The mentoring sessions with the young sales execs began to pay off. They were hitting their stride and our sales production was reaching a crescendo.

Everything was improving until one day when I was asked to join a conference call chaired by the top officers at our corporate headquarters. The presenters informed us that the company was being sold to CIGNA Healthcare.

My status with the new company was in jeopardy since CIGNA had a talented and well-respected Philadelphia sales manager. But CIGNA liked me, too, and officials at CIGNA asked me to relocate to Phoenix to run the sales office in the Arizona market.

My sales office in Philadelphia had about a dozen people. The Arizona office had nearly 70 sales and service reps. Moving was inconvenient, but it was a bigger job and paid a lot more money. I was gone within a week.

Heading to the Desert

With two years of management experience already under my belt, the early days of getting oriented in Arizona were easier. The seasoning I had gained in Philadelphia made me a more decisive manager on issues I may have hesitated on two years earlier. At the same time, managing a team of 70 people presented its own set of complexities and I had to make some adjustments in my approach.

The hardest part of the move to Arizona was that I was working for an acquiring company (CIGNA) instead of working with the internal people at Equitable's east central region with whom I had built trusted relationships. That trust had been built carefully over eight years. I could easily get concessions on deals, because they trusted that I would protect the company's interests. Now, in Arizona, I would be working with CIGNA operations and finance people from the Connecticut home office, who didn't know me. I needed to start over, building trust with them. And I was sure this would be burdensome.

Further complicating the situation and making the "trust proposition" harder, I discovered that the CIGNA people generally didn't respect anyone at Equitable. They rationalized that since they bought our company, somehow that made Equitable workers inferior and a lower life form.

Worse, the CIGNA people in the home office were East Coast oriented. They were prejudiced against *their own* CIGNA salespeople on the West Coast. This attitude stemmed from the CIGNA home office folks believing that business generated on the East Coast was of better quality than business sold in the west. This new world of mine was far more complicated than anticipated. I was experiencing a set of prejudices I hadn't expected.

It also soon became apparent that CIGNA home office departments had a controlling mentality, meaning no sales action could be taken without first getting the consent of the home office. This was a huge change for me. Having built trust at Equitable, I had been given substantial latitude to make my own business decisions.

Adding to the difficulty, we discovered people in the CIGNA home office departments were unwilling to work flexible hours to support us. They worked 9 to 5 EST. Arizona was in the Pacific Time Zone during the summer, which created a three-hour difference.

But that wasn't the worst of it. When we needed access to these people, they always seemed to be unavailable. They reserved their morning hours for the East Coast sales offices and spent their afternoons in staff meetings.

This frustrated my Arizona sales team who had dealt with this encumbrance for years. I was astounded by how unyielding the home office people were. How was I to get their sign-off if they wouldn't even respond to our requests?

After being stonewalled for a week, I managed to get the home phone number of the top finance person and called him late in the evening. He was pretty unhappy to get my call at home and I was pretty angry that he was ignoring us.

Following a heated exchange, our tones became more reasonable. His excuse was that he was busy in the afternoons (our mornings) and couldn't be available to us. I asked him, "How's your schedule from 7 to 9 a.m.?" He hesitated, somewhat startled, before saying, "Well, it's okay, but that won't do you any good, given the three time zones between us."

Determined, I asked him again, "So you are free between 7 and 9 a.m.?

"Er, ah, yes, but..." he replied. I cut him off quickly, by interjecting, "Then we'll take that slot each and every day."

"But that's 4 a.m. in Arizona," he responded incredulously.

"I know," I replied. "We'll call your office at that time each morning. I look forward to speaking to you then." I hung up the phone.

The following day, I shepherded my sleepy-eyed sales people into the office at 3:30 a.m. so we could prepare for the call. We did that for the remainder of the week. And the following week, too. Given the home office's schedule inflexibility, it was the only way we could effectively get the decisions we needed to run our business. At that hour, the home office snobs had no excuses to duck us. They had to attend to our needs.

By the end of the week, my sales team was dragging and sleep-deprived. I imagined their spouses weren't happy with me, as they watched them leave their homes each morning at 3 a.m. But the tactic worked as I had hoped, and eventually the home office people cleared their schedules so we could get access to them during *our* business hours.

A few additional benefits came out of that early morning adventure. Initially, through our daily interactions, we were able to build a rapport with the home office people. They were amazed that we would come in that early, and we gained their respect from our doggedness. It shamed them into giving us more access and at more reasonable hours.

The second benefit was more self-serving, since I had gained a bit of a reputation as the crazy guy (I would have preferred "innovative") in Arizona who would work at any hour. I was seen as being extreme—but it was "crazy" in an unrelenting, intense way, a "willing to go to any extremes" way. It sent a clear message that we would not be deterred. So it was a "we better give this guy what he wants" type of crazy. Privately I smiled and thought, this was a *really good* kind of crazy.

The support we received from the home office dramatically

improved. It was collegial. It was respectful. And it was very responsive. It was the way it should have been all along.

I was still a new guy in a big new company. People can get lost in big companies, but it's hard to get lost and go unnoticed when you are *that 3 a.m. guy*. Without a doubt, my navigation skills inside CIGNA quickly became very efficient. Differentiation, once again.

With the home office support teams becoming more responsive, my credibility soared with our sales people. They had never received this level of access to the home office before and were more effective in the market because of it. Despite this improvement, I realized the home office's concerns about my sales team's competence were partially warranted.

My salespeople were good service people, but they weren't financially and technically knowledgeable. They were ardent in servicing customers, but weren't skilled negotiators, since they had never been properly trained. As I evaluated each deal with them, they and I could see how deficient they were. But with a new coach having arrived, my salespeople saw an opportunity to improve, and they thirsted to learn.

I agreed to train them, realizing that doing so would take a great deal of time. I consented, provided the training occurred outside of normal business hours, since those hours needed to be reserved for clients and prospects.

To make sure there was dedication on both ends, I told the sales team I would invest my time training them as long as they made an investment, too, by committing their personal hours to the task. Most agreed and the training sessions were held from 5:30 a.m. to 8 a.m., five days a week. Promptly at 8, we'd adjourn to our respective offices and start our workday. The rigor of this schedule wasn't easy on anyone, but there were few complaints and the employees learned quickly. Best of all, sales results improved significantly.

Part of our success in Arizona was driven by a change in attitude, a change in culture, and a change in expectations. Higher expectations. We conducted post-mortems as a sales team, dissecting successes and failures alike, and debating our methods and techniques.

To instigate discussion, I asked, "If we could go back in time and start this particular deal over again, knowing what we know now, what would we do differently?" In cases where we had been successful, I'd say, "It's great that we won the deal, but if you had it to do all over again, what other steps would you take to make the result even better?"

These discussions, shared with the entire team, helped to enhance their overall business IQ. It also made them think bigger. It made them think about how they could re-invent their approach to become more effective.

These were approaches I had learned from my father. Dad always preached about self-improvement. He implored his troops to think big and to pursue perfection. Dad's stated commodity was people. And people, he knew, are imperfect by definition, but he believed that to get maximum performance from his commodity, he needed to reshape their mentality to view perfection as the goal.

In pursuit of perfection, his people, football players, would have the greatest likelihood of beating the competition and achieving their goals. But most fulfilling to Dad was to see one of his players discover in themselves a level of performance previously assumed to be impossible. Quite similarly, my sales team in 1991 was experiencing a similar kind of awakening.

Another of Mom and Dad's Rules dealt with commitment, and I drew upon that important edict, as well. My parents had both been "all-in" with recruiting by investing themselves in the players and their families. Like they had done, I was investing (first at 3:30 a.m. and later at 5:30 a.m.) in the development of my salespeople.

To be sure, none of my actions were compulsory in accordance with my job description. I was doing it with a sincere desire to help my people improve themselves. And they realized my efforts to help them get better was *my commitment to them.*

It created a magnetic field pulling the sales team together with a strong allegiance. Our overall performance then took on greater meaning to them. They wanted to be a part of something bigger. They embraced my results as being their results and they became more heavily invested. It had worked for my parents and now it was working for me.

I was a businessman, not a football coach and his wife. But in my third year managing a business operation, I was quickly becoming convinced that the methods should be the same. My commodity was people, too. Amid my team's imperfections, there was an opportunity to improve and an opportunity to motivate. In those 5:30 a.m. sessions in Arizona, I watched a group of people pursuing perfection in earnest. And through that experience, I became emboldened to employ all of my father's approaches in the business setting.

A year went by quickly before I was called into the regional president's office. The purpose of the meeting was to discuss promoting me to senior vice president of sales for the entire Western Region. I accepted his recommendation and began my new role. I was 32 years old and now responsible for 9 offices in 13 western states and 400 sales people.

As I drove home that night after receiving the promotion, I did the math. It had only been 15 months earlier when I was managing a staff of a dozen sales people in Philadelphia. And only three years earlier when I was a sales person myself, living in Pittsburgh. So much had happened in such a short amount of time.

I thought about the promotion and I was thankful for the

opportunity. I had worked hard over the years to become successful, and I took some credit for having earned it. But I also appreciated how fortunate I was to be selected for the position. There were many other talented executives who could have been chosen.

The trite phrase "The harder I work, the luckier I get" came to mind on that drive home. That quip seemed particularly applicable that night. I was excited, but mostly I felt satisfied.

The previous year had been grueling; the acquisition created a lot of upheaval. Change brings uncertainty and change brings volatility. Some people were being promoted quickly, such as me, but there were also people who lost their jobs as the merged company began to consolidate operations. I thought about the amount of change that the old Equitable team had endured after being acquired by CIGNA. So many of the middle management had been laid off. So many good people had their careers rocked. Many of them were my friends and most were older than me.

Several of them were in their late 40s and early 50s. They had kids in high school. Those kids would be in college soon. *Would these people be able to get new jobs?* I wondered. *Would they be able to replace their previous income? And if not, had they saved enough to be able to pay for life's expenses? Or to put their kids through college?* I couldn't imagine the stress they must be feeling while scrambling to stabilize their careers.

The upheaval in 1990 and 1991 convinced me of one thing: the business world was becoming a young man's game. Why had I gotten the promotion over a bunch of other qualified people who had 15-20 more years of experience? The answer was clear: I was young and had 15-20 *more years* to contribute to the company's future while others were in the sunset of their careers.

My being frugal was a mindset that Mom had impressed on me. I was making a significant amount of money—more than I could ever have imagined—and for that, I was thankful. But I realized that evening that while I was a coveted employee today, there could be a day when I would be as vulnerable as the others.

Aware of that potential, I committed to myself that I would not allow myself to be *that guy*. I wasn't going to wake up at 49 years old to learn that my job was gone. I wasn't going to be sitting at home calling people for a job while my kids sat on the other side of the kitchen table filling out college applications.

I concluded that job risk wasn't a question of *whether*—it was a question of *when*. Why? Because there was always going to be someone younger or better who could fill my shoes.

In order to take all risk out of play for *when* that happened, I decided I needed to get financially bulletproof as soon as possible. *When I get outplaced in the future*, I thought, *I want to have enough money already put away so the moment of departure doesn't rock my world or those closest to me.*

In 1991, I was fortunate to make a lot of money, but I also had an opportunity to dictate how much of the money earned would be saved, not spent. I re-committed myself that evening to a level of spending frugality that would increase my savings as quickly as possible. Was this an over-reaction? Maybe. Was it a somber way to spend an evening celebrating a promotion? Most likely. But I didn't like the picture I was watching with my outplaced Equitable friends, and I was going to do everything possible to avoid the same thing happening to me.

I went to bed that night, happy and satisfied about the promotion while being determined to take my good fortune and make the most of it.

The Dunlap Clan Expands

I BECAME A FATHER ON September 13, 1991. Chelsea Jane Dunlap arrived and my life would never be the same. As much as my parents had prepared me, I couldn't have imagined how exciting it would be to watch her grow up. Chelsea was a happy baby and she seemed to grow and develop continually. Each week there were new expressions, new movements, and then new words.

Chelsea Jane Dunlap at your service!

When Chelsea could crawl and then walk, nothing was safe. Her exploratory marine park was the toilet; splashing water was a fascinating pastime for her.

Nineteen months later, Chelsea got a sidekick, Tyler Frederick Dunlap, born April 17, 1993. Though still less than two years old, Chelsea was gentle with her little brother. Years later she would discover that he was a competitive threat to her domain, not too different than the dynamic had been between Jessie and me.

Our home bordered the third hole at Desert Highlands Golf Club in Scottsdale. When they were three and two, I'd take Chelsea and Ty out onto the fairway in the evening after the golfers had left and kick a soccer ball to them. Up and down the fairway they chased the ball, kicking it to me or to each other.

Sometimes I'd grab a beer and walk out to the third green and practice chipping and putting. While I did, the kids played in the sand bunkers, making tracks in the sand and then dragging the rake behind them to fix the mess they had made.

My maintenance crew.

Chelsea and Ty with Coach D. Playing soccer?

Having kids, I tried to apply what I had experienced with my parents and Grampa when I was a child. I had seen the camp counselor spirit in them and I longed to create some of the same fun-filled activities for my kids. Though Chelsea and Ty were quite young in Arizona, there were plenty of adventures for them. They were active all day long, every day, and they used every ounce of energy getting the most out of their days.

In the evenings, after dinner and a bath in the kitchen sink, the two youngsters put on their fuzzy pajamas and curled up on the couch before bedtime. They would lie against me, sprawled on my chest. I loved to watch the slumber slowly apprehend their senses as we stared at the television. Gradually, the yawns arrived. Then they nuzzled more as if they were boring a hole in my chest. And then the breathing became heavy and rhythmic, and their arms and legs went limp.

Heading off to their crib or bed, it was like carrying a wobbly sack of potatoes until they were carefully lain into position and covered with a small blanket.

Rub-a-Dub Dub, two kids in a tub.

Zzzzzzzzzzzzzzzz.......

The look on Chelsea's and Ty's faces was always the same—it lacked of any concerns at all. No worries. No frustrations. Just the desire to rest so they could do the same things the next day.

While the kids slept, I returned to my laptop to re-engage with the work pressures I had set aside earlier in the afternoon at the office.

The Emergence of Another Head Coach

WHEN I WASN'T AT HOME with my new family, I continued to be a student of the business. Stan and Dad had emblazoned that discipline in me. However, it was becoming increasingly hard to do in my new, larger role. My workdays were taken up with conference calls, strategy sessions and travel. I used the edges of the workweek to reinforce my knowledge of every operational and financial aspect of our business.

As a senior vice president (SVP), this curriculum was self-inflicted. It wasn't compulsory.

I was one of four SVPs across the country and none of the other three SVPs were inclined that way. Each of us had broad jobs, big territories, and many direct reports, but the other executives simply didn't find enough time to stay in touch with the details of the business. In order for me to do so, I traded sleep hours to invest in staying conversant on CIGNA's internal workings.

My reasons for going the extra mile, all the time, were based on the belief that I needed to be current in order to be relevant and to make astute decisions. I often sat in strategy sessions in Connecticut with the top officers of the company, including my three counterparts. When certain issues were debated, I had a head start, since I was up on the details, permitting me to impact the direction of decisions. While I'd drive the discussion toward a practical solution, my counterparts sat quietly and observed. It became another form of differentiation that set me apart from the others.

While my main responsibilities were in the sales arena, I also worked on solving problems at the lower levels of our operations. Most large companies encounter service issues from time to time. To get them resolved, people in positions of power are needed to authorize changes and corrective measures to remedy issues and assuage the angst that customers are feeling. With this in mind, I took it as my responsibility to identify and arrest known service issues. Those service areas weren't my direct responsibility, but I knew that if those issues were left unaddressed, they could plague our sales effort or put in peril our existing customer relationships. And those *were* my responsibility.

I believed that my job was to do everything possible to enable my people to be successful. I needed to fix the potholes and clear the boulders from the street so my race car drivers could drive better and faster. Like Dad had done, I was taking steps to create an environment conducive for my people to be at their best.

There was a third reason for staying current with the elements of CIGNA's business. I was managing 9 different sales offices across 13 states and 400 sales people, and one of my jobs was to evaluate whether we had the right people in the right jobs. How could I effectively do that unless I knew what they were supposed to know?

Staying current with the details of the business gave me a very sensitized "Bullshit Meter." Sales people are very social and some are pretty cagey. Given the size of my territory, I could only visit each sales office periodically. That didn't allow much time to get fully acquainted with the entire sales team or to assess their competence.

With this limitation in mind, I concluded that the only way to decipher whether my people were adequately qualified was if I could speak about the details of the business as well as any of them. If my people, the ones embroiled in business details each day, weren't as knowledgeable as I was, then I had the wrong people.

In sales, you are either *the hunter* or *the hunted.* It's a very competitive arena. And I had concluded that the quality of the people entrusted with growth goals would determine which end of that slogan refers to us.

Taking a Risk

IN 1994, CIGNA WENT THROUGH another re-organization. Many of the top officers were removed, including the regional president I reported to on a daily basis.

CIGNA had a tendency to re-organize every year. They treated it like a sport. It was disruptive and created a lot of tight ass-cheeks. Every employee worried about keeping his or her job during those periods of organizational turmoil. This caused the decisions that senior leaders made to become very cautious.

I became frustrated with the growing bureaucracy and ever-changing nature of how CIGNA ran its business. I became fixated on another thing, too.

I was 35 years old and had reached the top regional sales job in one of the largest companies in my industry. Essentially, I was at the top of my *elevator shaft.* The only floor higher was my boss, the national head of sales, and I was pretty sure he wasn't going anywhere soon.

I had spent the last 13 years being a student of every aspect of our business. I knew operations and finance about as well as the people who ran those units. With this in mind, I asked myself a question: "If I know every aspect of our business because I have made it my business to do so, and if those areas all interact with me on a daily basis and take my instruction for how to serve our clients, then how much different could it be to actually be a CEO?"

In reality, I thought, *I had already been doing the job of a CEO.* But my resume was still a sales resume. It didn't scream: "This guy can run companies."

I called my parents to talk about my quandary. As they always did, Mom and Dad were good listeners. They asked many questions and they allowed me to vent about the inconsistent environment existing at CIGNA. They let me talk about my desire to leave sales to run companies. They knew I loved Arizona and they knew I had a good job at CIGNA. So they took quite seriously the fact that I was willing to leave that all behind for a chance to run a company.

Dad said, "You sound a lot like me, Tiger, back when I took the job at Lehigh." Dad had been an assistant coach for years but longed to have an opportunity to oversee all areas of a football program. He wanted a chance to drive the culture of the organization, and being a head coach was the logical next step.

Being in charge of sales was in many ways like being an assistant coach. I didn't control the culture and I wasn't able to dictate the overall direction of the company. Dad had been a defensive coordinator at Cornell, but, like me, he had gained experience on the offensive side of the ball, too. He was therefore familiar with all facets of the game, but he was still an assistant coach, until he became the head coach at Lehigh. Like he felt at age 35, I wanted my shot.

Timing is everything, and a month later I got a call from an executive at United Healthcare (UHC), headquartered in Minneapolis, Minnesota. He asked to meet and discuss my joining United to run some of their smaller specialty healthcare companies with the title of CEO at each one.

At the time, United Healthcare was a $3 billion company with a very entrepreneurial spirit. There were only two negatives accompanying the offer: I would need to move from Arizona to Minnesota while taking a 60 percent pay cut.

At the time, salaries were low at United. They had an incentive-pay philosophy and much of my pay would involve stock options. This meant my personal savings strategy would need to take a hiatus, since the salary was barely large enough to cover our family expenses.

Though those negatives were significant, I figured it best to make some short-term sacrifices to jump to another elevator shaft since the *CEO elevator shaft* had many floors above it. I accepted United Healthcare's offer and our family moved to Minneapolis.

My hunch was fairly accurate. The requirements on a CEO were not very different from what I had been doing at CIGNA. In fact, the demands of the position were very much in line with the rigor I had forced upon myself in previous years. But that didn't mean everything went smoothly. It took some time to acclimate to the policies and procedures of a new company.

The best part was that even though I was working for a larger company, and therefore part of a larger culture, United Healthcare fostered an environment of entrepreneurial thinking. The company encouraged its CEOs to run their own business units independently, and with that, establish their own cultures.

A Brand New CEO (With 30 Years of Mentoring Under His Belt)

What I liked most about my new job was having the freedom to set the pace, the expectations and the healthiness of the work environment. For my four specialty companies, I was able to develop the culture. My field manual included all of the things I had learned from Dad and Mom, many of which I had already incorporated in previous management roles.

The specialty companies were mostly fledgling concepts, some of which were start-ups. They were early-stage companies where much of the corporate infrastructure didn't exist or needed to be fortified. Two of them had been stalled out; they were turnaround situations. With limited operational history, much of our time was spent with "sleeves rolled up," figuring how we were going to structure or re-structure the organizations and how we were going to grow the business.

This came naturally to me, as I had the strong predisposition for learning the business's details. During the next two years, I worked with a close-knit group to build these businesses. But more than that, we developed strong cultures that would drive strong performance in the ensuing 10 years.

While I was working at United Healthcare, my father suddenly came out of retirement. His long-time assistant coach, Dick Biddle, became head coach at Colgate in 1996 and he asked Dad to become his Offensive Coordinator and help revive Colgate's football program. Dad was glad to help Dick get started as head coach. After a year as Offensive Coordinator, Dad moved to coach the quarterbacks in 1997, when Mike Foley returned to Colgate as the Offensive Coordinator. Following the 1997 season, Dad returned to retirement. Dick Biddle went on to become the winningest coach in Colgate history.

Coach Dunlap with QB Ryan Vena—1996

Back in Minneapolis, I was busy growing the specialty companies. When I got away from the office, I had a great time being a father. Chelsea and Tyler were now four and two, and on March 8, 1995, their sister, Kathryn Jordan Dunlap, was born. The house was full of diapers and fast-moving twerps.

Raising kids in Minnesota wasn't easy. The frigid weather limited playing with them outdoors. We had to make the most of the short summers and take advantage of any reasonably warm days during the other seasons.

Taking after my mother, I invented games out of chores. The trees in our yard would shed their leaves in the fall and Chelsea and Ty helped me rake them. Even Katie participated in her own way—as a wobbly little 18-month tike. Toting an oversized diaper, she staggered around us, trying to join the effort.

As I raked the abundant leaves in the cool autumn air, on either side of me, the *midget battalion* imitated my actions using Little Tikes tools. They felt like contributors to the cause, though I am not sure how many leaves they actually gathered.

For them, the treat came at the end when the leaves were all in a pile. Before stuffing them in garbage bags, the kids jumped on the giant piles and buried themselves underneath. I played Mr. Monster and searched through the leaves for little children to eat. As I poked through a pile, I could hear the sound of giggling children. That made Mr. Monster even more hungry!

"Thanks for the help, Katie."

Minnesota winters were long and cold, but the kids loved to play in the snow. Wearing snowsuits, they helped me shovel the driveway with plastic shovels. Of course, with their little bodies and little tools, along with little attention spans, they tended to push the snow around more than off the driveway.

Did we fool around? Yes. I piled up snow banks on both sides of the driveway, I tossed them on top, and they slid down. How many times? Countless.

I also introduced them to the concept of a snowball…and a target. When Ty was bending over to pack another snowball, Chelsea took delight in hitting him right in the butt!

My snow shoveling assistants…

At the ages of four and three, Chelsea and Ty learned to ski. I can still feel the burn in my thighs as I skied down the slope with each of them between my legs. Over the winter, they actually progressed well. Chelsea was able to ski independently from the top of the small slope to the bottom. Ty did okay, too, but his favorite part of skiing was riding on the lift. He'd say, "Daddy, I like riding on the swing!" as he pointed overhead at the chairlift.

"This isn't hard at all."

"I can't move my feet."

"You've got me, right?"

When warm weather hit Minnesota, which wasn't often, the kids played outdoors. During the summer of 1996, before she was five, I took the training wheels off Chelsea's bike. A little cautious at first, she got the hang of it. I ran alongside her, holding onto the seat as she found her balance.

Then Chelsea pedaled faster. I was at an open gate, trying to stay with her. I couldn't keep up as she rode around the corner and started down a slope. But...she hadn't...learned how...to stop yet...CRASH!

A few tears and a scuffed pair of hands later, Chelsea mounted the bike again and started back toward the house. She rode a little slower so her sweaty father could run next to her.

A month later, her 3-year-old brother convinced me that he, too, was ready to lose the training wheels. Ty was a risk-taker. I learned very early that my #1 job as a father was to keep him alive long enough for him to realize how foolish his daring moves were and how reckless he was. The kid lived to be airborne. Jumping everywhere: off the couch, off the back porch, off the diving board. Off of everything. At three, he hadn't yet learned the concept of gravity, or that gravity causes you to collide with hard objects.

I wasn't surprised when he pleaded with me to take the training wheels off his bike. He wanted to ride fast to keep up with his big sister. Those burdensome training wheels were slowing him down.

Off we went down Silver Lake Trail with my hand on his seat. The only comfort I had was that, at three years old, he was small. Therefore his bike was small. If he fell, the distance he would fall would be smaller. But that pavement was hard, so I stayed close to him, honoring my #1 job as a father. He tried to go faster, but I held him back. I didn't need to see a sequel to Chelsea's maiden voyage.

Thirty minutes later, Katie and I sat on the front lawn watching

Chelsea ride by with her little brother in hot pursuit. The bike milestone had been surpassed—the kids were growing up. I shook my head and smiled at Katie as they passed by. *Two kids down and one to go,* I thought.

During the two years in Minnesota, while raising kids and running the specialty companies, United Healthcare had been on a buying binge, making many acquisitions across the United States. In 1995, it acquired MetraHealth, and in the ensuing nine months, there were signs of cultural stress fractures between the employees at United and MetraHealth. The integration of the two companies had not gone smoothly, and in some parts of the country, the market-based personnel refused to work with each other. The Florida market was one such place.

Leaving Minnesota for Florida

DURING THE SUMMER OF 1996, United Healthcare's Executive VP Jim Carlson called and asked to meet. He was responsible for all of United's operations nationally. At the time, it was an $8 billion business.

Jim asked me to move to Orlando to run the Florida operations, a billion dollar business at the time. The integration of the MetraHealth business wasn't happening as expected. Each company was running separate businesses in the same markets. Worse, there was fighting across the respective company units and the discourse was causing confusion in the markets.

Florida was a huge United Healthcare operation. Four thousand employees worked there, but despite $1 billion in revenues, the company was losing $100 million a year.

After some debate, and again consulting with Mom and Dad, I

accepted the offer and we moved to Orlando. And I began a hard job, straightening out the confusion caused by an acquisition that had not been handled with grace or precision.

A Knack for Turnarounds

In September 1996, I arrived for work in Orlando. My family wouldn't be moving until the following January. I used the time alone there to throw myself head-first into the business. Every waking hour was spent working on the problems with the Florida markets.

United had a business presence in Tampa, Orlando, and Jacksonville and an even bigger one in south Florida. The managers of those operations were all a bit skittish over the arrival of their new boss. That was not surprising because the Florida company was losing money every day due to bad contracts, mispriced business, and inefficient operations. Bad contracts were ones where commitments were made to deliver services the company couldn't practically provide. Mispriced business was where the prices charged were lower than the cost of delivering the service, causing the company to lose money. Inefficient operations meant that we hadn't integrated United and MetraHealth back-office activities. With both company offices still active, we had multiple teams doing the same work. This was costly and led to confusion with our customers.

Further complicating things, we had a blended sales force made up of people from both companies. Because the integration had never really taken place in a proper way (management hadn't yet finalized the assignments to certain brokers and consultants), people were undercutting each other as they competed for sales leads and sales sources. It was a volatile situation.

There was one other dynamic trumping all of these issues. The company was in trouble with the Florida Insurance Regulator. United was a healthcare company, but our method of delivering services was through an insurance product where our corporate customers purchased a group insurance product covering their employees and their dependents. Through this insurance product, United Healthcare managed the healthcare needs of the insured employees and dependents.

Group insurance is a heavily regulated industry and to be gainfully in business, the state's financial and legal requirements must be met. When I arrived in Orlando, we had 62 products offered across the state of Florida, and 54 of them were out of compliance with regulations. The State Insurance Commissioner was threatening to shut us down.

Jim Carlson had braced me for these problems when he offered me the job. But as clear as he was with me about the concerns, my employees in Florida were equally oblivious to the problems. They were fixated only on protecting their positions in the internal company turf war.

Immediately upon arrival, I realized the Florida United job would be a real challenge. I was sure of that by the second week, as I sat in my hotel room one night and assessed the multitude of problems. I thought about my past work experiences and the challenges I'd faced before. And then it dawned on me that all of my past jobs were challenging. All the companies had needed fixing. And they all had needed a revitalization of their culture.

I had worked in many jobs to this point in my career and had many different titles, but the common denominator was an obvious one. I had become a "turnaround expert," a re-builder, just as Dad had rebuilt the football programs at Lehigh and Colgate. We were both turnaround guys. What he did in sports, I was doing in business.

The turnaround skill was to quickly fix a division or department that was not performing in the way the bosses wanted. Maybe it was a business that couldn't seem to grow or was losing money, but before the owners decided to sell it or shut it down, they made one last attempt to fix it. I had become the fixer, the guy they handed it to. I then was the guy who inherited the dying dog of a business, the guy who'd try to breathe some life into it and save it from demise.

Who was I, really? My job titles over the years had changed, but basically, with every job, I was "Vice President of Screwed-Up Things." In each situation, I employed the methods and approaches I had learned from my father. Those methods had worked for Dad and they were working for me.

As I sat in the hotel room one night in Orlando, I reflected on my batting average on reviving troubled businesses, and it was pretty good. I went to sleep that night with a mixture of thoughts. I was troubled by the extent of complicated problems facing me in Florida. But I was comforted by the knowledge that I had dealt with tough situations before. And like I did in those cases, I would just need to persevere in Florida in the same way.

The Task of a Turnaround Pro

"SO, FRED, WHAT *EXACTLY* IS it that you do?"

I have been confronted with this question countless times. At cocktail parties, at my kids' school functions, at my daughter's dance recitals, and by the neighbors down the street.

Over the years, I have tried many ways to explain what a turnaround guy is and what a turnaround guy does, but the look of confusion on people's faces told me I wasn't describing my working world very well.

I was at a party one time and a buddy asked this question of me. He was a businessman, and he knew I was a businessman, so he was a bit embarrassed that he had to ask. But he also sensed that the work I did was quite different from conventional business (whatever that is). When my friend posed the same question, I suddenly found the metaphor best describing what I did.

"Well, Mark," I said to my friend, "the businesses I get assigned aren't the best." Conjuring up some suitable visuals, I said, "They aren't the prettiest girls at the dance and they aren't the first boys picked for the softball team." Then the best descriptive hit me.

"Mark, imagine you and I are attending a college basketball game. We have good seats, center court. We haven't seen each other for a while and we are catching up on things while we watch the first half." Mark nodded politely, wondering how in blazes this had anything to do with his question.

"While we are talking," I said, "the home team is getting beaten badly in the first half. It's almost over, and they are already trailing by 20 points."

Mark nodded again. "At halftime," I continued, "the teams head to their respective locker rooms. The cheerleaders take the court, ready to entertain the home crowd—a crowd which hasn't found the first half to be very entertaining.

"Now," I said, "You and I are hanging out in our seats, eating popcorn and all of a sudden, some guy approaches us and interrupts our conversation." I pause. "He looks at me and introduces himself as the athletic director of the home team's school. He informs us he has just fired the head basketball coach and he wants me to take the job." Mark was now probably regretting he asked his question altogether. "I accept and the AD tells me that my job is to rally the team, somehow find a way to recover the deficit in the second half and miraculously win the game. He hands me the coaching whistle and wishes me good luck."

I looked Mark square in the eye and added, "So now I am the coach of a team that's behind by 20 points and I have only a 20-minute half to find a solution."

Next I asked Mark rhetorically, "So to be successful, what would I need to do?" I answered my own question: "First, I would immediately leave you sitting here eating popcorn and hurry to my team's locker room. On the way there, I would try to recall any impressions I had about the first half."

Looking at him, I said, "In spite of your distracting stories, Mark, I did notice a few players who looked promising. But my lasting impression from the first half was that this team lacks talent, isn't playing well together, and are playing a formidable opponent."

Mark's face indicated he was still with me. "When I get to the locker room," I said, "I need to quickly assess the talent and determine my starting lineup for the second half. It may be that I will need to remove some players and I may even ask some to play other positions. And any of those players might not like my decisions."

"Okay, sounds good," Mark commented.

"But this all needs to be done with split-second speed," I continued, "because the second half is starting soon.

"Next I need to evaluate the team's plays," I said, "and figure out which ones are worth keeping. Also, as a somewhat knowledgeable guy about basketball, there are a few plays that have always proven to be helpful, so I quickly need to teach those to the starting lineup."

"Makes sense," Mark commented. He now wished he had asked a question about bass fishing.

"I am nearly out of time before the start of the second half. I have a brief moment to assess the overall situation. We are behind by 20 points and have only a 20-minute second half to recover the deficit.

"In order to save the day, I would need to run a full-court press defense for the entire second half. We would need to play aggressively at all times, but we'd need to avoid causing any unnecessary fouls. We would need to avoid turnovers and I would have to use my time-outs efficiently. We would need to make every free throw and hit a very high percentage of our field goal attempts. And above all, we would need to play well together as a team, with energy and tenacity."

Mark's neck was probably sore from nodding. "If we were able to somehow do all of those things with perfect precision," I said proudly, "we could recover the 20-point deficit and win the game."

Again, I looked at him and said. "Mark, *that's* what I do for a living as a turnaround guy!"

What Makes a Great Manager?

I had never abandoned the "I would never" tapes I compiled during my first few jobs. I routinely listened to the thoughts I had then on how "not to manage" and tried to learn from them.

During my business career, I had many bosses. Like Dad had done in the 1950s and early '60s, I observed my authorities closely, picking up on their effective approaches and noting those approaches I would never replicate.

Those approaches were management styles and methods. They were ways of dealing with people.

When Dad gave his speech at the Walter Camp Foundation after having been named "Man of the Year," he referred to people as being his commodity. He contrasted that to businessmen who, he believed, worked with commodities of steel or plastics or chemicals. Given that I was a businessman, I suppose Dad would have suggested that my commodity was healthcare.

I think my father was wrong about that.

In each business situation I encountered, there were different problems and different challenges. None were identical; each required unique steps to resolve them. But the approach to solving each problem relied on the same management methods. It was about ways to relate to people, individually and collectively. People were my commodity, too, in the best sense of the word. And if the managers in steel and plastics companies were doing their jobs well, I think they would say their commodity was people, as well.

The tenets for building a winning business culture include excerpts from the Dunlap Rules:

Building Trust—Dad talked about the "little things taking care of the big things." The little things were all about building trust and building commitment. It's not about giving a great speech or making a great transaction happen. It's about the way a manager conducts himself or herself each day. That consistency creates a sense of nucleus across an entire organization whether it's 80 football players or 4,000 healthcare workers in Florida.

Being Unselfish—Dad said, "Leaders have to be willing to give to their people unselfishly. They need to commit themselves fully to their people with energy, intensity, enthusiasm and a genuine interest." In the Army, Captain Morgan made a lasting impression on Dad because he showed an interest in his people and let them get to know him. By doing so, his people became committed to him more emotionally, triggering their willingness to work hard for the captain.

The Value of Emotion—Does emotion have a place in business? I have always thought so. Emotion certainly plays a huge role in sports, bringing out the best performances. And since my commodity was people, too, I made a leap to assume that if I could get people to commit their emotion to their work, it would bring out their best performances. I found that to be true in Philadelphia and especially in Phoenix, where it became undeniably clear each day at 5:30 a.m. I saw the excitement in the eyes of my salespeople as they realized they had a boss who cared about them.

Willingness to Invest in People—Great managers have limitless borders. They don't define their role by the job description of their position. Instead they assess their people's needs and are willing to step in and help, providing mentoring, no matter how unglamorous the work is. Their presence with their people provides wisdom and tutelage, but most critically, it shows they care.

I mentioned that I had a very close-knit group in the Specialty Companies in Minnesota. But I didn't mention what caused us to be so close. When I got there, a number of issues needed to be addressed, and it's fair to say that many people weren't properly trained for their positions. To eradicate the problems and identify weaknesses in personnel, I had to dive deep into the organization and make assessments. Management and the line-level employees were shocked that I would engage with them so openly. They had never had a CEO who was willing to get directly involved.

Immersing myself in the most granular levels of the business, they marveled that I showed such concern and in turn, were pleased to educate me on issues that needed to be resolved. More amazing to me, the management folks and line-level employees were flattered that someone at my level would show a genuine interest in them as people, not just as employees.

Experience has shown me that most senior executives really like being senior executives, meaning they like not having to get into the guts of the business anymore. They rationalize that since they had worked hard to achieve senior executive status, the last thing they are going to do, now that they are a big shot, is go back into the bowels of the business, thinking: "I spent years doing the shit work, and now that I'm in the corner office, I ain't going back!"

Such a state of mind is why many top executives are referred to as "sitting in the ivory tower." Doesn't that sound isolated? Doesn't it sound exclusionary?

Most people at some point have worked for somebody who did just that. When bosses delegate the shit work to those under them, they lose a huge opportunity to know their people and to get them engaged.

Why? Because when people feel ignored or are made to feel inferior, they become disillusioned and detached. They don't care as much.

Over the first 20 years of my life, I watched Mom and Dad live their adult lives by being willing to dive in and help, to coach and mentor, to lead by example and to invest in people to help them get better. In so doing, they got to know the people around them and they allowed those people to know them. The result of that philosophy was that it engendered strong loyalty and lasting commitment. People wanted to be part of what Mom and Dad were creating and those people were then willing to extend themselves emotionally and physically to the cause.

My parents were always firm in their convictions. They always had high expectations and they demanded excellence from those around them. They weren't easy bosses. But amid those lofty requirements, they cared about people and they were committed to help them become great.

During each of my management assignments, I followed their recipe, the lessons learned from my early upbringing. It was not a common recipe in business, which, in turn, made it another point of differentiation.

Since my first management assignment, I employed these same approaches in many different companies and businesses. Through all of those varied situations, I've noticed one thing that has been common in every experience where I have led an organization: If you are honest, sincere and open with people about good news or bad news, you can capture their attention and get into their minds, because they become willing to trust you. And if you show a personal interest in them and help them improve, they will become committed to what you are trying to accomplish. If you reinforce that by helping to remove other roadblocks that are thwarting their ability to be at their best, they respect you, and you can get into their hearts. If you can get into their minds and hearts, people will begin to care more deeply. They will become emotionally connected and committed to the cause.

Finally, if people truly care, they can do amazing things. They will find in themselves a level of performance unknown to them before. And while they are astounded and proud of their loftier accomplishments, their satisfaction will not be only with themselves, but it will be shared and mixed with those around them...because they feel like they are part of a team...because they feel like they are part of something bigger.

Doing all of that for employees seems like a lot of work, doesn't it? Who has time for all of that? That is exactly my point. Very few leaders make the effort to extend themselves that way: they don't walk the talk. Sadly, they miss the opportunity to motivate and they aren't able to connect with their people emotionally. They squander an opportunity to create a special experience and a special closeness with people.

I have found, time after time, that there is the potential for greatness in every employee. The problem is that most employees have become deflated by the "Ivory Tower syndrome," which depletes their willingness to extend themselves emotionally for a cause. That potential for greatness exists in all people but it takes the right surgeon to extract it from within and bring it to life.

Yes, it's true, I had ambitions to become a CEO long before I became one. Underlying that was my curiosity and desire to test Dad's formula. I wanted to create an environment that was conducive for success using the same principles he used in sports, but infusing them into business. If the truth be known, while my title was a CEO, I never really thought of myself as a CEO. I thought I was just a guy who was working hard to help other people have more fulfilling work experiences. Sure, given my authority level, my decisions had greater consequences, but what I loved most was spending time with people, no matter what their pay grade, getting to know what they needed and then trying to help them get it. I wanted to know them and I wanted them to know me.

I had my share of bad bosses and I used the "I would never" tapes to document their foibles. I had some great bosses, too. And the defining element for the best bosses was their willingness to engage in the business and with the people. Two of the best were Dave Devereaux and Jim Carlson.

Dave was CIGNA's regional president when I worked in Arizona. He was deeply knowledgeable of the business, and he showed a constant willingness to dig in and help resolve issues.

A high-energy person, Dave had an insatiable desire to problem-solve in order to help his people have an improved work environment. He was also a risk-taker—it came to him naturally, because he had a strong command of the business. He took a risk hiring me in 1990, and he took a bigger risk by promoting me to the top regional sales job a year later. I was 32 years old and the other three senior VPs were in their late 40s or early 50s. It would have been much safer for Dave to appoint a veteran or a CIGNA employee to the position, but he took a chance and picked me.

In 1994, Dave was also instrumental in introducing me to the people at United Healthcare. He convinced them that I had the potential to make the transition from sales to CEO. For all of these reasons, I am indebted to Dave Devereaux.

Jim Carlson was my boss when I worked in Florida, and as noted, the United Healthcare Florida company turned out to be a bigger mess than either of us expected. We had to make some drastic decisions to save that business, including significant personnel and product changes. Without Jim's support, we never would have been able to make the progress we made especially in such a short time. My problems in Florida weren't Jim's only problems—there were many issues in other regions of the company, as well. He had a massive job responsibility with many other distractions but somehow found a way to be available to me whenever I needed his help.

Jim was a passionate person and a dedicated advocate for his employees and managers. As strong a leader as he was, he was also very compassionate, and perhaps best of all, a good listener. He almost played the role of a therapist for me when the pressures were extreme.

Complicating the challenge of turning around the Florida operation, another problem emerged shortly after I arrived in Orlando. The United Healthcare division in Puerto Rico began losing business and losing money. The problems in Puerto Rico made the issues in Florida look easy. With this development, Jim called and asked me to take that operation over at once, and run Florida and Puerto Rico simultaneously.

On that beautiful island, we discovered fraud and graft stemming all the way to the top government officials. Predictably, my arrival there was not appreciated by local officials. As I systematically identified costs that were really conduits for bribes and political contributions, those sources of funds were shut down. In response to my actions, calls filtered into my Florida office and my home threatening physical harm if I were ever to return to the island.

Those threats didn't deter me and I continued to travel to San Juan. However, upon hearing of the threats, Jim Carlson immediately employed an armed bodyguard who accompanied me when I traveled to Puerto Rico. My security guard was an ex-FBI agent who served as my cab driver, office assistant, and hotel companion. No matter where I went in Puerto Rico, he flanked me.

This degree of threat was highly irregular for our industry and something Jim and I would not soon forget. Hiring a gun-carrying bodyguard 24/7 was very expensive, and not a typical United Healthcare expense. But there was nothing typical about Jim Carlson. He knew I was working in a dangerous environment and, like always, Jim had my back.

Both Dave and Jim are giving people—they were leaders and mentors to me. During difficult times, they were both patient with company progress and cool in a crisis.

Most importantly, when we required extraordinary help, they were willing to drop everything to provide the troops the reinforcements needed.

I was lucky to have worked with them. Their influence impacted greatly how I developed as a leader.

An Impossible Balance—Working and Parenting in the 1990s

LIKE MY FATHER BEFORE ME, I spent an enormous amount of time working. Turnarounds are excruciating and they take twice the effort of a typical CEO position because of the rebuilding required.

Dad and I were from two different generations, but I found his leadership methods to be timeless, and I emulated most of his approaches consistently and successfully during my business career.

Our generations were less similar when it came to parenting. For his, it was customary for the father to work and provide for the family, and he wasn't expected to be ever-present with family activities. Also, there weren't as many family activities in the 1960s and 70s. Kids spent most of their time outdoors where they made up games and created their own fun.

My adult generation was different. By the time I was in my 30s and a parent, youth activities were far more structured than they had been when I was a kid. My children didn't routinely play pick-up games in the neighborhood—everything was organized and supervised. There were youth sports teams, dance classes, and school functions.

By the 1990s, society imposed other responsibilities on the breadwinner. In addition to keeping a job and earning a livelihood, the breadwinner was also expected to be omnipresent with the activities of the children.

Further complicating things, "keeping up with the Jones" in the '90s meant inundating your children with as many activities as possible. You weren't seen as a vigilant parent unless you had every schedulable calendar block filled with something for your kids to do. With that influence, it created more demand on parents to attend those events.

By the time our family settled in Orlando, the kids were ages five, three and one. Within a few years, all three kids were immersed in many activities. They were headed everywhere at every waking hour. Some of this evolution was a good thing. Dad had implored me to be an involved parent and I was totally committed to that. But the magnitude of kid activities was so great that it was impossible to be at every event.

If I had been a postman or a teacher or a dad who worked any standard 9-to-5 job, it would have been much easier. Then I probably could have found a way to attend the majority of activities. But I didn't have a standard job and I wasn't earning a standard wage. Instead, I had high-pressure, complex jobs requiring long hours and travel, and it was therefore impossible for me to be in two or three places at one time.

The demands on the work front were significant, but I loved being a father, too. So I had to juggle things. I had to make some sacrifices and use some creativity. Here is what I would do.

When I wasn't on the road, in spite of the crisis du jour, I'd try to leave the office to be at home with the family for dinner. After dinner, I'd spend the evenings with the kids, playing games or helping with homework. When it was bedtime and they were settled in, I'd retreat to my home office and re-engage with the work issues I had set aside earlier. My work associates were battling the same logistical pressures with their children, so we'd schedule conference calls late in the evening or at absurdly early hours in the morning.

On weekends, I awoke very early and worked until I heard the pitter-pat of little feet coming down the stairs. I then spent the whole weekend with the kids except for Saturday night. After they fell asleep on Saturday nights, I usually retreated to the home office and rejoined the stressful issues. There were many in this turnaround world in which I was engaged.

Sunday morning was a repeat of Saturday morning, where my work stopped when one of my three little alarm clocks came running into my lap.

During those years, I juggled three things in my life: work, family and sleep. For more than a decade, sleep got slighted in order for me to participate in as many work and family activities as I could. How much sleep did I get? Perhaps four to five hours a night for 10-15 years.

Travel took me away from the family more than I preferred. But like Dad, when I returned from a trip, I raced home so I could trade my dress-for-success clothes for a t-shirt and gym shorts. There was a lot of fun ahead for me with the little people I loved so much.

I Had "a Lot of Clark" in Me

Similar to my business approach, I was a clone of my parents with my personal life, too. I especially modeled myself after Mom and Grampa.

As a father, I was strict with my children. There were rules. They were the Dunlap Rules and, like my parents had done with me, I made them clear to the kids and they understood them. If the rules weren't followed, there were consequences and the punishments didn't get appealed.

I didn't raise my voice and I didn't rant at the kids. I used "Less Is More" and the "Cobra Treatment," and they responded as effectively as Jessie and I had done 30 years earlier. There was one dreaded word: "Hey!" I used that word when they got out of line, and the sound of it stopped them in their tracks. I didn't need to say anything else. But they were good kids and those "hey" moments were infrequent. Most of our time together was filled with fun and laughter as we played one game after another.

Like the Clarks, I tended to set aside my children's formal names and give them nicknames. Chelsea was "The Bug." Tyler was "Wally Burger" or "Super Lou." And Katie was "The Moose."

Everyone wanted to know why in the world I called a cute little girl, "The Moose." First of all, the name itself had precedence in our family, given that I had an Uncle Moose. But secondly, Katie was bigger than life. She had a huge personality as a little kid and made us laugh a lot. She had her own unique style, her own swagger, and though she was the youngest, she made a prominent impact on our family social circle.

Katie could also be strong-minded at times—even tempestuous. All together, based on her personality and our history, it seemed to me that this little dynamo should be called "The Moose."

Cute Moose.

Zany Moose.

Tempestuous Moose.

How did Katie like being called "The Moose?" She loved it. She would strut into a room and announce, "Daddy, I am Da Moose!" After she ate a big meal or drank a lot of water, she'd stroke her distended tummy and declare, "Daddy, I am plump!"

As time passed, the kids' nicknames evolved into hybrid names. "The Bug" became Buggy, Buggo, Buggable or Buggalooga. "Wally Burger" became Wally, WB or Double-U (or as my father called him: Du-Bul-Yah). And Super Lou morphed into Lou, Louie or Luigi. And of course, "The Moose" became Moosey, the Mouse, or Moosible.

I am at a loss to provide a more coherent set of explanations for the nicknames or the morphing of them. I suppose it was the zany moments and their vibrant personalities that provided the impetus for the loving/goofy names I gave them.

When we were together, there was always something going on. We'd play in the pool or in the yard. But it wasn't just playing for me: it was physically taxing. In the pool, I was a one-man catapult, tossing the kids into the sky, listening to their screams as they floated through the air before making a splashing reentry into the water.

A flying Bug.

A suspended Moose.

Taking a break.

The playing and the games didn't stop when we left the pool. Riding bikes around our Cypress Point neighborhood was a favorite, as was playing basketball in the driveway and football in the front yard. Because Katie was the smallest, she was always on my team. She and I would play against the Bug and WB. When my parents were in town, they played too. Watching the two generations around me compete with each other was a thrill. Who won? You guessed it: Mom didn't like to lose.

While my parents were called "Coach and Mrs. D." by those closest to them, as grandparents, they were "Ninny and Da" to my children.

The football team.

When I was in town and away from the office, the activities never ceased. We played all day, every day. I was like a camp counselor, shepherding my offspring around to different sources of fun. When their cousins were in town, we played the same games but the teams had more players. With Kevin, Kirsten and Amy around, we had six twerps running at all times.

When the kids were young, we vacationed at the beach with their cousins each year, either in Massachusetts or North Carolina. I loved being with the six-pack of kids, building sand castles, throwing the Frisbee, playing horseshoes and racing each other on the beach.

New games were even invented. The favorite was "Hot Ball." The six twerps surrounded me in a semi-circle and I tossed the ball quickly to one of them. If they caught it, they were still in the game. If they dropped it, they were out. It was essentially a game of musical chairs except that the ball served as the music.

The game triggered laughs, giggles, cries and, on occasion, temper tantrums. This was a very competitive group! But then there was Kirsten. She had good hands and quick reactions and always seemed be there at the end after others had dropped the ball and been eliminated. That made her happy, and sometimes made the others jealous. Nevertheless, it was all fun, and the six of them tugged at me each day to start another round of Hot Ball.

The Six Pack—Cousins get together at the beach.

The Bug with her cousin, Kirsten.

After a long day at the beach.

After the sun set, it was time for the arrival of Mr. Monster! The kids hid and I growled, snorted and grumbled around, searching for little children to eat. As I trudged around in the darkness, I could hear their giggles as Mr. Monster got near to them. Then the squeals, giggles and shrieks filled the air as Mr. Monster reached under a bed or a blanket and grabbed a scrumptious leg.

As the grandson of my prankster Grampa, it was only a matter of time before I started playing pranks on the kids.

My kids loved to ride with me to the store—it didn't matter what we were buying. Even a trip to K-Mart was an adventure to them. When they were younger (age six, five and three), I told them I had special powers. As we approached the K-Mart front entrance, I told them I had a magical way of opening the door. I'd gather them a few feet outside of the sliding doors and say, "Abra-cadabra, open sess-a-me!" Then I'd lurch forward (just enough to activate the motion sensors) and the doors opened.

The kids went bananas. "Daddy is magical!" I heard them shout. As we walked through the aisles of the store, Ty stopped strangers and pointed toward me to say, "Did you know my daddy is magical? He can open doors without even touching them."

Another prank happened inside our home. Just as Jessie and I had fought a turf war in my childhood household, my three kids vied for their rights. Saturday mornings usually included some time where the three kids watched cartoons. After eating their breakfast, they'd sit in the family room sprawled out on the couches watching their favorite shows.

They didn't always agree on which show was worth watching. As I cleaned the dishes from breakfast, I could hear the sounds of their democratic debate. It was a household version of *Lord of the Flies*.

Most important to this debate was "clicker control." More specifically, the child who held the TV remote control, by possession, had veto rights on any given show.

For some reason, the Bug and the Moose always ceded clicker control to their brother Ty. Or maybe he just took it? Anyway, he'd hold onto it like a prized possession, never letting it out of his sight. The clicker even made trips to the bathroom with him.

As I put the breakfast dishes away, I could hear protests whenever

Ty might switch the channel away from whatever the girls wanted to watch. What the kids didn't know was that I had a second, identical clicker.

One Saturday morning, they were watching cartoons and were getting along fine—a rare, quiet, congenial moment. As they sat quietly, watching a show, I stood in the kitchen and pointed my clicker at the TV and changed the channel.

"Ty, we were watching that show! Put it back on," Chelsea yelled.

Ty looked at them startled and somewhat bewildered. "I didn't change it," he replied defensively.

"Yes you did. Put it back on," Chelsea roared.

Ty fumbled with the clicker in a hurry and returned the TV to the original show. A few moments later, the TV again mysteriously changed to another channel. "Ty! Stop it!" Chelsea yelled. Ty fumbled again while professing his innocence.

At that moment, I walked in and said, "Come on, kids, you need to quiet down. You are getting too loud."

"Dad," Katie said, "Ty keeps changing the channel on us. Tell him to stop it."

"Ty, is that true?" I asked.

"No, Dad, I didn't do anything."

"Okay, kids, you all agree on what you want to watch?" They all nodded. "So just sit here quietly and watch it," I said. "I don't want any loud noises this morning."

The kids settled in and I returned to the kitchen. A moment later, I discreetly pointed my clicker and turned the volume WAY UP. The sound was deafening.

"Ty, turn it down. It's too loud!" Chelsea implored him.

I came into the room. "Ty, what did I say?"

"Dad, it wasn't me. There's something wrong with this remote."

I stood there (with the second clicker hidden behind me) and said, "Let me see if I can fix it." As I waved my free hand, I said "Abra-ca-dabra, volume please turn down!" The kids watched as the television volume signal appeared on the screen and the volume returned to an acceptable level.

Katie looked at Chelsea and Ty and said, "See, guys, Daddy really is magical!"

This little form of amusement went on for a few weekends until I unveiled the presence of a second clicker. Was I a tease? Sure. Did I get a kick out of it? You bet. But that was our dynamic, the kids and me. I was always playing the kook and was being silly. Chelsea always laughed and said, "Oh, Daaaad! You are such a silly daddy!"

My kids did have a silly, goofy father, and his humor was at times corny. My goofy, playful Grampa was to blame.

The kids and I shared other fun moments, as well. On a cold day, when we were outside playing, I'd declare: "Boy, it sure is chilly today, but it's gonna be hot tamale!" The kids eventually memorized most of my goofy quips.

For instance, I'd blurt out: "So I said to the girl on the beach..." and Chelsea would shout: "Sandy!"

I'd follow that with: "Soooo, I said to the girl with the loafers..." and Ty would shout: "Penny!"

"Soooooo, I said to the girl on Christmas..." and Chelsea would shout: "Mary!"

"Sooooo, I said to the girl with the wooden leg..." and Katie would cry out: "Peg!"

"Sooooo, I said to the girl with the limp..." and they would all yell: "Ei-Leeeeeeeeeen!"

We had many lighthearted times in those days, but there were also serious and more instructive times. When she turned four, Katie joined her siblings by taking the training wheels off her bike. She was cautious at first, and didn't want me to take my hand off her seat. But she soon gained her confidence and rode her bike everywhere.

A mobile Moose.

We also focused on other sports for all three kids, including soccer, basketball and T-ball. I coached Ty in a T-ball league. Those five-year-olds didn't hit the ball very far, but they sure had fun and learned the baseball basics.

Given my inclination for the sport, I started teaching the three kids to play golf at a very young age. We belonged to Bay Hill Club, where I taught them the basics. I am sure we were a spectacle on the driving range as golfers drove by in their carts. There we were—three little kids lined up hitting balls, with me strolling back and forth instructing each of them. As they developed and became more accomplished, I took the kids to the Charger Course, a smaller nine-hole course built next to Bay Hill's championship course. It was ideal for new and developing golfers.

A hole in one?

Is that a future professional golfer?

Taking a break from the putting contest.

The kids played nine holes and I shepherded each of them, shot by shot. They were ages four to seven, yet they were really progressing well. To give them a sense of competition, I'd create little games: putting contests, chipping contests, things like that, which would keep their attention and help them get better.

We spent hours at Bay Hill each weekend. The ritual included hitting balls and playing nine holes and then finishing with a putting contest. It was Katie and me against the two older kids. A prize each day awaited them at the halfway house. We sat outside at a table with an umbrella and ate the famous Bay Hill tuna sandwiches. If they had behaved well that day, the kids were rewarded with a Slurpee at 7-Eleven on the ride home.

The four of us had fun and each of them was getting better. But there was one big problem: his name was Tyler.

The girls were doing well and showing a lot of promise, but Ty was an exceptionally good golfer. The kids were competitive with each other, and though the girls were progressing nicely, they were bothered because their brother was better than they were.

Ty made matters worse by his post-game commentary. He'd sit with the scorecard after we finished each round, analyzing each hole and each shot. And then he'd report, "Chelsea, did you know that I beat you on eight out of nine holes today?" He'd then look to his younger sister and say, "And Katie, did you know that your score was more than two shots worse than my score on every hole?"

The girls didn't appreciate this reporting. Tempers flared and the girls began to see golf as a reflection of their deficiencies, rather than their progress. I tried to get Ty to tone it down, but I was starting to lose the girls' interest. To revive the enthusiasm, I offered a reward system. Okay, it was a bribe.

I agreed to pay each of the girls 10 cents for each double bogey, 25 cents for each bogey, 50 cents for a par and a dollar for any birdies. This lifted their interest at first.

With Ty, however, I made the reward system tougher since I couldn't have him raking in the dough. If he amassed a lot of cash, I could see his weekly reporting to the girls changing from a review of the scores to a review of the size of his piggy bank. That might incense the girls even more.

To even things up, Ty would only get 10 cents for a bogey, 25 cents for a par and 50 cents for a birdie. He was outraged. "Dad, that's not fair!" he protested. "Why do the Bug and the Moose get more than I get?"

Despite Ty's protest, my "Golf for Greenbacks" continued. This kept all three kids interested for a while but eventually the girls decided not to play golf, and moved on to other activities.

A visit to Hamilton to see the grandparents ("Ninny & Da"). Coach and Mrs. D. like taking pictures on "Big Whitey" in the front yard.

Halloween in Orlando. Coach is there, and "Spot" also makes an appearance.

We didn't have leaves to rake in Florida and there wasn't any snow to shovel, but there was another job that constantly needed to be tackled since everything grows at a rapid rate in the hot, moist Orlando climate. Our back yard was consumed with vines that seemed to grow by the hour.

With each house we lived in, I was ever in hopes of creating another "back forty" like I had as a kid. To do this in Orlando, I cleared the vines to make our back yard more expansive. It was a big undertaking and a dirty, sweaty job, and I needed some company.

To get the kids excited about this dubious task, I pulled them together to rally their interest. Like I did with all chores, I made a game of it. "Kids, there are vines out back that are growing everywhere," I began. "They are taking over our yard. We need to stop them! And I need your help." They looked at me wide-eyed as I portrayed the vines as a threatening beast. "I am going to start a Vine Patrol and I will be the leader. Who wants to be a part of the Vine Patrol?"

The kids were fascinated and ready for battle. For the next three days, I hacked the vines and they pulled them out of the thicket and dragged them to the curb so the garbage man could take them away. Back and forth the kids marched, carrying sticks like they were swords. I had my little military unit and we had a lot of fun doing that nasty chore. The reward at the end of each day was a big splash in the pool to cool off and rinse the sweat and dirt from our bodies.

I might have sold the Vine Patrol as being more glamorous than it was. But the kids worked really hard and, as we worked, we talked about all kinds of things. We talked about school and about their other activities. We laughed about things like the clicker prank and they asked me about serious things, too. These discussions reminded me of many I had with Mom and Dad, only my role had switched to parent. I was fascinated by their curiosity.

That summer, the kids had made some money playing golf and they had gotten birthday money from their grandparents. They talked about what they wanted to buy with their money, but I also explained to them the value of saving money. We discussed compound interest and the concepts of banking just as Mom and Dad had done with me decades earlier.

As I answered each of the kids' questions, I wondered if it was time to open bank accounts just as Mom had done with Jessie and me. I discussed it with them and they were interested.

With the Vine Patrol mission nearing its end, we took our daily swim. As we splashed around, I told them I wanted to meet in the kitchen afterwards and that they should bring all of their money with them. A while later they each appeared with their pile of money and we sat at the table and counted each pile. With the kids sitting around me, I described a new type of bank. It would be a private one called the Dunlap Investment Bank (the DIB).

I explained that I would be the Chairman of the Board and they would be the only three depositors. If they deposited their money (gave it to me), I'd record their deposits. I'd then pay them 1 percent interest per month and give them monthly statements reflecting how their money was growing.

One percent was a high interest rate then, but I figured it would make it simpler for them to calculate. Plus, that lofty rate provided an extra incentive to save vs. spend money.

The Dunlap Investment Bank began in August 2002. As the kids grew older, I continued to accept deposits and continued to pay them interest and provide statements. Like my experience as a kid, the DIB reinforced the values of saving and being conservative with spending.

During the summer of 2014, after 12 years of banking and with the three kids in college, I closed the Dunlap Investment Bank and returned the money to my three customers. Through disciplined saving and attractive interest payments, I returned thousands of dollars to each of them.

Looking back on that time, being a parent during my generation was a challenge with all of the expectations society imposed. I had spent 15 years juggling work and personal demands. I didn't make it to all of my kids' events, but I attended as many as I could. And when

I was home, I made the most of the time I had with them. Did my kids miss me when I was gone? Yes they did. Is it possible they were disappointed at times and wondered why I couldn't be at every one of their events? From their young naïve perspectives, I would guess that they probably had some of those feelings.

Time is a perspective-maker. Chelsea graduated from college and is an investment banker in New York City, working for the Global Healthcare division of one of the larger banks.

A hard worker, Chelsea routinely works 80 hours a week, trying to meet the requirements of her challenging career. She works every weekend, and during the week often doesn't reach her apartment door until after midnight. It's a demanding environment for her, but amid the rigor, it gives her a new appreciation for the pace I kept during my working life. I'm sure she wonders how anyone could balance work with raising kids and spending time with them like I tried to do during my career.

Moving to Texas

BY THE YEAR 2000, SEVERAL developments had affected my career. In Florida, we managed to restore United Healthcare's compliance with the Insurance Commissioner. We integrated the company. We improved the financials and we grew our business by 100 percent. It was now a $2 billion business and instead of losing $100 million a year, we were now earning $150 million. Things in Florida were good.

During the same time, United Healthcare continued to make more acquisitions. These acquisitions created some confusion and some problems organizationally, and to arrest those issues, United started to impose restrictions on decision-making, adding unwelcomed bureaucracy. Gone was the entrepreneurial environment I had relished so much in 1994. Bottom line: it was starting to feel like CIGNA, all over again.

Based on these developments, I assessed my career path again just as I had in 1994 when I left CIGNA. After several discussions with my parents, I decided privately that it was time for me to leave United. I was 41 years old and at an inflection point. I had earned enough money to retire and strongly considered it.

At the same time, I was becoming more aware of the private equity (PE) industry. It's just that: privately invested assets. These are privately held firms that solicit money from pension funds or other private investors. In turn, these firms deploy those investable assets by purchasing companies. They then appoint management teams to run them. The goal of private equity firms is to buy a company at one price, improve it (via good management) and then sell it at a higher price, thus returning the gain/proceeds to investors.

Most private equity firms are forward-thinking and very aggressive. They are therefore very entrepreneurial. With that being the case, I thought, private equity seemed to be the last bastion of an entrepreneurial world, where there was ultimate accountability and total freedom to devise strategies and create a vibrant culture. I found it to be alluring, and I wanted to give it a try.

Taking Another Risk

Leaving United Healthcare to work in private equity meant that I was trading the security of a big successful company for the prospects of finding an entrepreneurial habitat. Private equity was more risky, I recognized, but it would give me the ability to operate without encumbrance. I had seen bureaucracy present its own set of risks at CIGNA and then United, and I concluded that I would rather have the freedom to make decisions and drive an organization than be hostage to a lumbering organization whose risks are of inertia and decisions *not made*. I was ready for a change, and this ultimately led to the family moving to Dallas, Texas.

Several job offers had appeared but the one I accepted was president of a large healthcare company in Texas. It was the #2 ranking job, reporting to the CEO, in a 10,000-employee company. During the interview process, the CEO and the PE investors explained to me that the company had been struggling to grow and, in their estimation, wasn't as profitable as it could be. They were creating the president's position (under the CEO) to add senior management in the hope that the company's performance could improve.

It was here that I met *my own* Leckonby, the same type of person Dad had encountered when he coached under the Lehigh athletic director. My Leckonby was a guy I will call Joe, who was the CEO and my boss.

During my early days working with the company, our relationship was good. At Joe's suggestion, I came in and approached the challenge in the same ways I had always done, using my father's methods.

Within a year the company was showing signs of growth in revenue and earnings. I had imposed a lot of changes and the most notable was a culture change.

The company had some areas where the work ethic had lagged. Addressing that issue, we imposed firm accountabilities and breathed some excitement and spirit into the ranks. We were driving a higher degree of vigor across the company, and, consequently, our company meetings started to feel more like pep rallies than business sessions.

People were getting excited.

Unfortunately, there was one person who wasn't getting excited: Joe. The cultural renaissance was starting to bring into question "who was really running the company," and rumors were surfacing that I'd replace Joe. This had never been my agenda but that didn't stop our management team from speculating.

Predictably, Joe became paranoid and felt threatened. He began to subterfuge me within the organization. When I found the evidence, I confronted him directly. He dismissed my points as being invalid, but the evidence was too great. I no longer trusted him.

I approached the PE investors and told them we had an untenable situation and that I would be leaving the company.

In the aftermath, I pondered how this could have happened. I had gone there and worked my ass off to accomplish exactly what the CEO and investors said they wanted, and it was working. The people in the company were excited about the changes. Everyone except the CEO, who saw the cultural changes as a threat to his existence. I realized then that there is no substitute for being in charge. A culture is something very personal. It's the way that the *top person* wants it to be.

I was now not working. I talked to my parents about the situation, and as usual, they provided valuable perspectives. Dad was struck by how similar my situation was to his own situation with Leckonby. "Tiger," he said, "that's what Leckonby's issue was all along. He viewed the changes in culture that I was making as being something threatening to him. He saw my culture putting his culture into question."

Over the following weeks, as I dwelled on the bizarre developments, I vowed that, should I ever work again, I would only take a job where I could control the culture. The top person in any organization, I considered, is the person who *owns* the culture. Whether it's a good or bad culture, the CEO owns it and steers it. The culture resembles his personality. Never again, I thought, would I put myself in a situation where I was tasked with changing the culture, but was not ultimately in charge.

"The Clark in Me" Takes Charge

While I had made that pact with myself, I had other philosophical thoughts going through my mind that were quite different. I had spent more than 20 years pushing the envelope in business and it had worked out very well. I had enough wealth that I didn't need to work anymore.

It was 2004 and I was 45 years old. I had kids ages 13, 11 and 9, and they were a blast to be around. While I had found a way over the last decade to be very involved in their lives, I realized that any future jobs would continue to limit the time I could spend with them. I reflected on their ages; they were only going to be in the house for a few more years. I loved being a parent and a camp counselor, and I contemplated retirement...again.

Retirement, I thought, would allow me to dedicate all of my time to the family. I could do what most people can't do because they still need to work. I had already had a fulfilling career, but now I had a chance to do something rare: have a full-time parenting role, too. So in late 2004, I retired.

My work friends were shocked by this development. They claimed my retirement wouldn't last. My private equity colleagues thought I had gone soft. Some said, "Fred is too intense to do that. He's never gone less than 1,000 mph in his life!"

While I heard those observations, I moved forward with my version of retirement. I was still the Type-A guy I always was. It's just that I would now devote my Type-A-ness to my kids.

To be certain, my new pursuits weren't all that sexy to the Wall Street gazelles I had worked with, but they were sexy to me. My new life included things like cooking breakfast for the kids before school, making peanut butter sandwiches for their lunchboxes, and driving carpool. It also involved swinging by school for little presentations that my kids would periodically make to their classmates. It was me and all of the other moms sitting in the back of the classroom.

I was able to help Katie as she managed the 4th grade Pet Club. For me, this mostly amounted to cleaning the fish tank. Boy, can those fish poop!

After school, I coached the kids' sports. I worked with Chelsea on basketball. I worked with Ty on football, basketball and golf. And I coached Katie's basketball team.

Later in the evenings, after dinner, I tutored them in English and math. I tried to help with science, but I quickly remembered how lousy I was at that subject when I was in school. As for Spanish, my complete command of the language was limited to "Cerveza, por favor." That had worked just fine for me, but it wasn't going to help my kids get a passing grade.

The Advent of Social Calculus

TUTORING AND MENTORING CAME IN other forms, too. My kids were approaching the awkward teenage years, and like my shocking introduction to junior high school back in the 1970s, Chelsea was starting to encounter some of the same complications of adolescence. She was in 7th grade in the spring of 2005 and the simple math of elementary school was abruptly being replaced by the social calculus of middle school.

One evening, she and I were reviewing some of her homework. During a break in the study session, she mentioned to me that she was troubled by how some of her friends were behaving. She shared examples that were very familiar to me. Hearing this and realizing the same would soon confront Ty and Katie, I asked Chelsea to pause and I called the other kids into the room.

The Moose was the first to arrive. "What is it, Dad?" Katie asked. Ty was right behind her.

"I want to talk about middle school," I responded. Each of the kids watched me, not sure where I was headed with the discussion. "First of all," I said, "you kids are all good kids. Your mother and I are very proud of you. You all have friends, right?"

They each nodded.

"I have *more* friends than Ty does!" Katie interjected.

"No you don't, Katie. I have *way more* friends than you do," Ty replied, glaring at her with disgust.

It is fair to say that Ty and Katie were quite competitive with each other at that age. Chelsea smiled at me and said, "Guys, Dad is trying to tell us something." Chelsea wanted them to be quiet. After all, she was in need of some perspective.

"So, you all have friends, a lot of them. But I want to talk to you about *why* they are your friends. There are four reasons." I began to explain, while holding my left hand up with four fingers extended, as they watched with anticipation.

Pointing to the first finger, I continued. "Let's see, they like you because you are a nice person and you treat them nicely." Pointing to the second finger, I said, "They like you because you are a good student. They admire you for it." Pointing to the third finger, I said, "They admire you because you are a good athlete. And fourth, they might think you are pretty or handsome and they find that to be impressive, too."

Ty glanced at Katie and said, "Dad, that fourth one doesn't apply to Katie!"

"Ty, why are you so mean?" Katie replied, "Dad, make him stop!"

It took a moment to settle the little suburban disturbance. All three kids were tracking me to this point.

"When you get into middle school," I told them, "things are going to get more complex. There will be people who still like you, but there will also be people who won't like you and won't treat you nicely." Three pairs of wide eyes watched me intently.

"Your friends will like you," I continued, "for the four reasons I just mentioned." I kept my left hand up with four fingers in the air. Then I put up my right hand with four fingers extended, and said, "but there are four reasons why some people *won't* like you."

Katie looked scared, unsure of what I was going to disclose, and not liking the sound of it. Pointing to each finger on my right hand in succession, I said, "There are people who *won't like you* because you are a nice person, because you are a good student, because you are a good athlete and because you are pretty or handsome."

Chelsea appeared to be grasping what I was inferring. Ty's face was blank. But Katie looked at me like she had a dad with a suddenly diminished IQ. "Dad," she scoffed, "you just said the *same things*." Katie didn't suffer fools well, and as she gazed at me, she might have thought she had discovered a new one.

"I know I did," I replied.

"But that makes no sense!" Katie interjected. She stared at me with incredulity.

"Katie, it *will* make sense in a few years," I suggested. "You are in 4th grade now, and your world in school is a simple one. When you get to middle school, like your big sister is now, things won't be so simple." Katie still seemed confused. "What I am saying," I explained, "is that people will start to become competitive. They will start to compare themselves to those around them.

"There will still be people who appreciate you for those four reasons. But there will be other people who will become jealous or envious of you. They will view your four positives as a threat to them. They will see them not as a credit to you, but as something that points to their own deficiencies."

Pausing for effect, I added, "And to make themselves somehow feel better, they may put you down or treat you in a mean way. Human beings are capable of that: they can put others down in order to make them feel better about themselves."

Katie and Ty looked bewildered and afraid. Chelsea was thoughtful.

"Your big sister is learning that now," I said to Ty and Katie. "There are some of her old friends who suddenly aren't being as nice to her." I held both hands up with four fingers extended. "*This* is the dynamic causing that."

Katie still seemed frightened. "But when will that stop?"

"It will be that way for the rest of your life," I said to my shocked children. "It's part of life. You can only control *your actions*. You can't control the actions of others, which is why I wanted to talk to you about it—so you would be prepared." I stopped for a moment to let them absorb the point.

Continuing, I said, "So let's talk about what you should do about this. About what you can control. Should you change how you are behaving? Should you stop being a nice person, a good student or a good athlete? No, you shouldn't.

"But when you encounter someone who is treating you poorly, I want you to think about *these*." Again, I held up both hands, and they stared at the four fingers projecting from each hand.

"You can't prevent their behavior," I explained, "but you can choose with whom you will spend your time and who will be your friends."

I then summarized. "Remember one of the most important Dunlap Rules: Treat people the way you want to be treated, and then expect that they return the favor out of respect and care for you. But if they don't, you should recognize it for what it is, and then move on to better people."

This had turned out to be an eye-opening discussion for three kids. We talked about it again many times during the following years when each encountered something or someone who fit with the theme of our discussion. Over time, our discussions became shorter and the messages more abbreviated. Oftentimes, one of the kids would just hold both of their hands up, with four fingers extended, and say, "Ya know, Dad, I know why this guy acted that way. It's just a case of *this*."

Mentoring sessions like this one were the reasons I cherished early retirement. Being there for the kids full-time put me in a position to help them when they needed it.

One of the other benefits of my being retired was that we were able to take long vacations. Five weeks in the Rocky Mountains visiting the national parks. Three weeks in Alaska. Three weeks in Peru, down in the Amazon Valley and up in the Andes. As I stood at Machu Picchu, gazing at the spectacular views, I appreciated how these moments would have never happened if I were still working full-time.

Though the kids were now getting a little older, we still had the same spirit of playfulness, and the camp counselor was still in full stride. I was having a blast with my version of retirement and the kids were loving it, too. I didn't miss work and I didn't miss the stature that came with important positions. Work was what I had done to keep the family secure. It wasn't who I was.

What I was doing in my version of retirement was cooler than anyone could imagine. I was closer and more connected to my kids and their friends than I was to their parents. Imagine being a fly on the wall (carpool driver) and taking in the chatter of the social network of a bunch of 12-year-olds. It was very informative...and shocking at times.

My kids loved having me around, but I am pretty sure that, at their age, they weren't able to comprehend how unique that circumstance was. All they knew was that Dad had time to be with them and they liked it.

My wife at the time didn't share the enthusiasm for my being at home. She felt I needed to go back to work and make more money. She wasn't nearly as entranced as the kids were with my camp counselor antics, and it became clear that she didn't want a second decision-maker in the house. I tried to ignore the problem for a while, but that didn't last. She wanted the "Disney Dad" era to end and for me to go back to work.

In order to appease her and still stay closely connected to my children, I started a one-man consulting company. I could work for some of my former private equity (PE) colleagues, assisting in turnarounds that were needed with some of their portfolio companies. I figured I could work when the kids were in school and take off when they were on school breaks and during the summer.

These consulting gigs were as short as a few weeks when I assisted a PE firm with due diligence on a prospective deal, or as long as three months when I provided interim CEO services while they conducted a search for a permanent CEO. Whatever the task, I made sure it ended before summer break. I wanted to be around full-time when the kids were out of school.

What was the name of my company? BWM Ventures LLC. A peculiar name? Well, not so peculiar, when you consider that those three letters are the first letters for Bug, Wally and Moose.

The consulting gigs went on for nearly two years. I worked for several PE firms on a number of portfolio companies. I was also doing a fairly good job meeting my wife's requirements while still satisfying my requirement of quality time with the kids.

During the fall of 2007, I was consulting in South Florida when I received a call from a senior partner at MatlinPatterson, a large PE firm from Manhattan. I had never worked with them, but they had heard of me through other industry connections.

MatlinPatterson (MP) had recently made a new investment in XLHealth Corporation, a company based in Baltimore. They were calling because the company's results weren't meeting MP's expectations. They had invested in XLHealth only a few months earlier, and since then, the company had missed many of its forecasts.

Missing forecasts that early after an investment was unusual and because of that, MP wasn't sure that the CEO was being forthcoming with them about the degree of the problems.

The partner at MatlinPatterson asked me to go to Baltimore and spend 90 days reviewing and assessing all phases of the company. My obligations to my client in South Florida were winding down in November so I accepted the offer and committed to start at XLHealth after Thanksgiving weekend.

The XLHealth Years

IT WASN'T MANY DAYS AFTER my arrival at XLHealth that I noticed some strange methods of managing a healthcare company. The CEO wasn't overjoyed to see me. He saw my presence as a threat and a sign that his investors' confidence in him might be waning. But he was professional nonetheless and gave me access to anything I requested.

He was polite and proper at all times. He had never run a healthcare insurance company before XLHealth but he dismissed that fact as being unimportant. He fancied himself as an entrepreneur and felt that industry knowledge was secondary to creativity, good instincts and a great education.

The CEO had an MBA from a prestigious business school. Why is that worth noting? Because I heard about it in every meeting I had with him with his standard line being, "Fred, when I was in business school, we learned that..."

He assumed the business school reference, by itself, made the next thing he was going to say irrefutable. I, on the other hand, never went to business school. Formally, that is. I attended a different type of business school. I graduated from Street U. It's a curriculum taught just outside of that window over there....on the street.

For the entrepreneur he claimed to be, my Street U assessment was that the CEO was surprisingly structured and inflexible. He had 13 direct "reports" and, as told to me by those people, he typically met with them individually. Because of this, there was very little communication fostered across functional areas.

For example, the sales people didn't adequately understand the needs of the operations people. The operations people didn't know to provide essential information to the finance team. There wasn't enough cross-pollination of information or market intelligence. It was an insular company where critical information was shared within functional silos. And the merging of those silos only occurred (and was shared) with three people: the CFO, an executive VP and the CEO.

The company was losing money in 2007. A lot of money. With revenues of $600 million, they had incurred more than $100 million in losses. The company's reserves were being depleted and the insurance commissioner was calling for more statutory capital, the financial backstop needed to assure that the company was solvent.

I spent the first 30 days working with every discipline in the company, attempting to discern the extent of problems in each area. My experience told me that knowledge couldn't be gained simply by meeting with the senior manager of each department. When things are going poorly, there are usually problems that the senior managers don't know about, but their people *do know*. So while I met with the functional heads, I met with their people, too. In each meeting, I relied on my "Bullshit Meter," which was a highly sensitive portable meter lodged in my head, calibrated by 25 years of industry experience and nearly 50 years of exposure to my parents and the lessons they bestowed on me. If there were any organizational dysfunction, I would identify it pretty quickly.

To cover as much ground as possible as quickly as possible, I scheduled meetings from 7 a.m. until 8 p.m. After that, during most evenings, I participated in calls with the investors at MatlinPatterson to unveil any new findings.

The list of company ailments grew with each week of my review. And with each call to the investors, it became apparent to me that their confidence in the CEO diminished. After I had been there for five weeks, they elected to remove the CEO and name me as interim-CEO.

I was fine with that. It was similar to other roles I had played with BWM Ventures.

With the CEO removed, it actually made it easier for me to navigate the company. Senior managers were more willing to be open since they no longer worried about protecting their previous boss.

To instigate sharing more information across operational areas, I scheduled a meeting that included the heads of each functional area. We called it the "Tuesday Group" since the first time we met was on a Tuesday, and we met every Tuesday thereafter.

As the team learned of issues in different functional areas, the collective group became more aware of how badly the company was performing. Importantly, people also became more aware of how their actions might impact other parts of the company.

As the days passed, we were starting to interact in a more productive way, but the company was still in deep trouble. Most vexing to me was that the company's financial results had *never* been shared with anyone other than the CEO and his two top officers. The rest of the management team was kept unaware of how dire things were.

Following five weeks of 12- to 14-hour workdays, I now knew the management team very well and they knew me. Morale was growing and the group's collective business IQ was improving.

At this point, I reflected on the management team and the departed CEO. There were some executives at XLHealth who weren't competent, but there were some really talented people, as well, although many of those people needed better training. They had been stuck in their silo for too long.

My assessment of XLHealth in early 2008 was: there were a lot of good athletes who had gotten on a bus which was driven into a ditch. The XLHealth employees were victims of the CEO's underestimation of the complexity of the healthcare industry. He didn't appreciate how truly complicated it was to run a health insurance company and how valuable industry experience could be to his position.

Two weeks later, the investors contacted me and asked me to take the permanent CEO position. I had been working with the management team for seven weeks at this point. Without my knowledge, the investors had contacted many of the managers to seek their input about offering me the job. Management had embraced me and wanted me to be their CEO. The investors wanted me, too.

I was flattered, but I declined the offer. I was happy with how my consulting work with BWM Ventures allowed me to stay involved with my kids. I knew that a permanent position in another city far from my home in Texas would interfere with my ability to be with them in the summer and on school breaks.

I continued as the interim CEO and offered to help the investors recruit a permanent CEO. A month later, as I was nearing the end of my assignment, the investors had not been able to find a suitable replacement. Then another problem arose. The insurance commissioner demanded that the investors infuse another $100 million to shore up the company's statutory capital. The deadline to do so was the end of February.

Soon thereafter, I received a call from David Matlin, president of MatlinPatterson. He asked me to come to New York for a meeting. I had been to their offices, but I had a feeling this meeting would be different from any before. After greeting me and exchanging a few pleasantries, David got to the point of the meeting. "Fred, we really appreciate what you have done for us with XLHealth. The management team really respects you, and we would love for you to take the CEO position on a permanent basis."

I thanked him for his words, but politely said that I was committed to my consulting lifestyle.

"Fred, I know you love your kids and I respect you for that." David leaned forward. "But I thought I should also share with you our position." I listened intently. "This investment hasn't gone the way we wanted. And this call for another $100 million is really problematic. If we fund the capital, it could be *good money thrown after bad money.* Without a bankable CEO in place, I wanted to let you know that I have decided not to put the money into the company."

I looked at him, fully comprehending what he was saying—that the company would effectively be dissolved.

"I am sorry to hang this on you," he said, "but the only way I will agree to invest new money in the company is if you take the CEO job. We trust you and we will invest in *you*. But I am not going to invest more money without knowing I have a solid CEO in place."

This said, David watched me as I grimaced at his comments. "I am not pressuring you to take the job," he said, "I just thought you deserved to know the consequences to XLHealth if you don't take it. And if you don't take the job, we're not going to be upset with you. This was our problem, not yours—you have been consistent all along about not wanting a permanent position. But if you choose not to accept this, I'd like to talk to you about extending your consulting contract another 90 days so you can help us wind this company down."

My mind was racing at this news and I was conflicted. I asked David if we could break the meeting for a short while and I left his office. Instead of staying in the building, I took a walk. I rode the elevator 35 floors down to the lobby. I walked out onto the sidewalk, where people were passing me in a hurried fashion. It was nothing new, just a bunch of New Yorkers walking past a stranger, intent on where they were going and preoccupied by their own worries.

What these people didn't know was that the stranger they were passing that day was worried about hundreds of good people in Baltimore and three special kids in Texas. As they brushed past me, they were unaware of the consternation I was feeling and unaware of the difficult proposition I had just received. It was a crowded sidewalk, but I somehow felt alone, isolated in thought.

Up and down Madison Avenue I walked, thinking about the options. I loved my freedom to be at home with the kids when they were around. But during the prior 90 days, I had gotten to know well the people at XLHealth. They were good people trying hard to fix the company's problems. Many of them weren't performing the right way yet, but they were showing a willingness to learn and get better. They had become excited about the progress we had been making. Their enthusiasm was so evident.

As I walked, I imagined them working in Baltimore at the same moment, trying to finish some of the projects before their CEO, me, returned from New York. But amid their exuberance, they were certainly unaware of how tenuous their working careers were as I strolled around Manhattan that day.

I examined my options, sure of a few things. I was sure that if I *didn't* take the job, more than 500 people would lose their jobs, and more than 500 families would be shaken. I was also pretty sure that if I *did* take the job, I would lose a lot of quality time spent with my kids.

As I deliberated over the two choices, it dawned on me that I was completely sure my wife wanted me to keep working—*that* pressure wasn't going to stop. This made me concede to the reality that I would be working somewhere anyway, not at home with my kids. And if that were the case, I figured it was better to choose XLHealth where I knew my choice would save hundreds of jobs, held by many employees I had already grown to admire.

I walked back into the MatlinPatterson offices and resumed the meeting with David. A few moments later, I accepted the position and we began discussing the radical steps needed to turn around the company. On February 29, 2008, MatlinPatterson funded the capital that was needed to keep XLHealth solvent and I began preparing a massive restructuring of the company.

Hard Decisions and Straight Talk

XLHealth was spending money at an inordinate level. The previous CEO had authorized hiring scores of people to perform functions that had questionable returns on investment (ROI). These people were working on nebulous, esoteric activities, and to an industry veteran like me, this seemed superfluous and excessive. The company couldn't afford to keep many of these people. Sadly, there were talented people working in these functions. They weren't bad employees—the trouble was that their skills were in areas which weren't critical to the company's recovery.

"There are times as a leader when you have to make decisions that are unpopular. But if you are convinced they are right, you need to be true to your instincts in spite of any potential fallout." My father's advice was very relevant in March 2008.

During that month, I worked confidentially with management to restructure XLHealth. Three weeks later, we laid off nearly a third of the company employees. More than 150 people had their positions eliminated. The move was disruptive and risky, but we needed to do it. If we didn't, the company wouldn't have survived. In order to preserve the most talented and most vital employees, we had to part with those keeping the company from being at its best.

In many ways, this decision was analogous to Dad's decision in 1981 when he, in effect, "fired" two Colgate senior quarterbacks and put Steve Calabria into the starting quarterback position. Dad made that hard decision because he realized that *not doing it* would hurt all of the other seniors on the team. I was doing something similar at XLHealth, because not doing it would put our most vital people's jobs in peril.

The news shocked the employees, including those who weren't dismissed. Over the previous three months, they had gotten to know me and trust me. But I imagined their comfort with me now might be shaken as they watched the guy they trusted remove 30 percent of the workforce, many of whom were their friends. I figured they had never seen a company make such a drastic move and they might wonder if this was the beginning of more drastic steps. I needed to get out in front of this to communicate the reasons for the layoffs in order to stabilize the remaining employees.

I organized a meeting for later that week to include all employees. It would be a town-hall-style meeting, offsite for an entire day. There would be some presentations featuring a few improvements we were making, but the main presentation was mine and I reserved more than two hours for my slot.

I opened the meeting without much fanfare. The looks on 350 faces were a mix of fear, anger, distrust and sadness. It was what I expected.

I addressed the group. "Thank you all for coming today. I want to talk to you about the recent layoffs. I know it was sudden and I want to explain to you why it was done. I want you to know what I know. Without that level of transparency, I couldn't possibly expect you to agree with or understand why it was done."

I proceeded to share with them the truth about how XLHealth was doing. I shared the company financials. As I did, the looks of shock on their faces remains vivid to me today. They weren't aware that the company was losing money, much less that the company was in deep trouble.

"Now that you know what I know," I continued, "I am going to ask you a couple of questions. Did each of you get a raise last year?" All heads nodded. "Did you get a raise this year?" Again they nodded. "And did you get bonuses each of the last two years?" After some hesitation, all heads nodded a third time.

I started walking up and down the aisle to get closer to the people sitting in the back of the room. "Now we are going to play a game," I said. "I want you to imagine yourself as CEO of XLHealth. If you were CEO and you were aware that the company was losing this much money, would you have given *you* a raise or a bonus? Would you think that it was in the best interest of the company to dole out pay increases that might further threaten the company's existence?" Many people shook their heads. "No, you wouldn't. You wouldn't do it because you have a responsibility to take careful steps at all times to protect the company's well-being."

I surveyed the room. "Well, that's what I am doing, which is why the layoff earlier this week was necessary. I am taking care of the company's well-being. Inherent in that statement is that I am taking necessary steps to protect the best, most talented people in the company. And those people sit before me today."

I went on to explain the business. I talked about what we needed to do to recover and stabilize the company. Occasionally, people asked questions. Some were good questions, but some were not very sophisticated. Amazing to me, most of the line-level employees didn't really understand what we did or why we did it. I needed every employee to understand the strategy. Without that, I couldn't expect them to engage.

I told those gathered that the company was in a tenuous state. I needed them to know the extent of our troubles. "You need to know how big the problem is," I said, "or you won't know what remedy is needed. And you won't know the level of urgency that must be applied." I looked around the room. "I want you to imagine that this company is your home. That it's your house. If I were to tell you that I smell smoke in the kitchen, you would be concerned and would go investigate it. But if I told you that the back half of the house is in flames, raging out of control, you would naturally move with much greater intensity.

"Well, I will tell you honestly that our situation at XLHealth is the latter." Wide eyes stared at me. "And to arrest the fire, we will need an intense effort from everyone in the room bringing water to the fire as fast as possible." The metaphor was serving its purpose.

I was asked why this information wasn't shared with them before. And I was asked why they were given bonuses and pay increases if the company was in shambles.

"I can't answer that," I explained, "and the CEO who authorized it is no longer here. But I know one thing. In order for us to put out the fire, and save our house, we need an air of frankness and honesty across all of our family. Otherwise, how can I expect you to appreciate the extreme requests that I will be making? How could you appreciate how fast you need to bring water unless you are aware of the true size of the blaze?"

I let that thought resonate for a moment. Then I changed the subject. "I am not a CEO. And I don't work for the investors." I blurted that out suddenly and then scanned the room. There was a look of confusion on the faces before me. "Sure, my title is CEO," I continued, "but that's not who I am. I am just a guy trying to help a good bunch of people try to be successful. As for the investors, they are my bosses and they can fire me. But they aren't who I work for.

"I work for the best people in XLHealth. Not all of them—only the best." I scanned the room again. "The best people are the people who are conscientious and working hard on things that are vital to making this place great. They are the people who are willing to go to great lengths to make good things happen."

I followed this with a question. "Have you ever worked with someone who was lazy or incompetent?" Heads nodded. "I call that guy *Old Joe*. Didn't that make you angry at times? Didn't it make you wonder why your boss hadn't spotted Old Joe and made him more accountable? And didn't you imagine how much better your group could perform if you weren't weighed down by that lack of performance?" Many heads nodded.

"Imagine that we are in the business of racing. We have great technicians, we have the finest cars, the strongest engines and the most skilled drivers. Then imagine on the morning of the big race, as we push our car into position for the start, the official comes up to us and tells us to open our trunk. And then three men pile a dozen cinder blocks into the trunk of our racecar. Will that make the car go faster? Will that increase our chances of winning? No, it won't. It will reduce our chances for success. It will impede our chances for an optimal performance.

"In business, unnecessary costs or non-performing people or activities are the *cinder blocks in our trunk*. And that is why I took the difficult steps with the layoff this month—to get the cinder blocks out of our trunk, so our team can drive faster, so we can perform at a more optimal level."

The somber looks were now gone. Instead faces were quizzical as they perhaps had never heard business portrayed this way. But I wasn't finished. "I work for the *best people* at XLHealth—no one else. I am driven to do everything possible to remove barriers and fix potholes in our road, so our racecar drivers can navigate optimally and have the best chance to succeed." Signs of acceptance were apparent as heads began nodding.

"To that end," I said, "I am going to try every method to repair our company. But I am just one guy. I can't do it alone. I need help." I looked around the room. "I can't guarantee we will succeed. But what I will guarantee is that we will do everything we can. And I will also guarantee that I will be honest and open with you every step of the way, keeping you informed on how the company is progressing."

There was a mix of nods and blank stares. "Now I need a guarantee from you," I asked. "I need to know whether you will commit yourself with intensity to help bring water to the fire. I fully recognize that many of your friends were terminated this week, and that this new guy, me, might have looked a lot less foreboding last week than I do now. But last week was a myth. Last week you thought you worked for a successful company: that was a lie.

"What I bring to you today is the truth because I think you deserve to know the truth. What I need from you is *also* the truth. I need to know if you will engage with me in a difficult pursuit, a job of stabilizing this company so we can be assured of a future of prosperity.

"Before you answer, I want you to play one more game with me. I want you to close your eyes." They looked at me quizzically, but gradually everyone closed their eyes. "I want you to think quietly about something personal, something special you just love to do, more than anything else. It may be a sport or it may be spending time with friends or family. It may be something you do with your church or an outside organization. The thing you should be thinking about is the thing that, when you are doing it, you are doing it all out, where you extend and exert yourself willingly. It's the thing that brings you inspiration and joy. It's the thing you look forward to the most—the thing you can't wait to do and the thing that brings you sorrow when it's over."

A minute went by, maybe a bit more, before I went on. "Think about that thing, and don't tell anyone around you what that is. Do you have that thing in your mind?"

Three hundred people sat quietly around me with their eyes closed. Their heads were nodding. "Okay, you can open your eyes now."

With their attention on me, I resumed. "Now that you have that in your mind, I want you to think about how much time you really get to spend doing that thing you love. It's relatively small, right? It's only a small fraction of your waking hours or your waking month, right?" All heads nodded.

"Well, why is that?" I asked. "Why is it that this thing you love to do—this thing you throw all of your energy into—is limited to only a small amount of time?" I let that soak in. "It's because the majority of your living, waking hours are spent at work! That's right, it's because you need to work, because you need to pay bills and you have responsibilities, right?" Heads nodded and they began to smile.

"Let's face it, you spend 80 percent of your waking hours on this planet either working or worrying about work. I know I do." Smiles and laughter seeped through the faces that had seemed worried and perplexed only a few moments earlier. "So if you are going to spend that much of your waking lifetime working or worrying about work, shouldn't it be in a place where you get that special thrill? Shouldn't it be in a place where you can extend yourself emotionally, with a group of people for whom you have great regard? Why wouldn't you want to make that massive portion of your waking lives extraordinary, too? Why would you limit the euphoria you feel when you are doing that special thing to those few hours you can do it? Why wouldn't you want *all of your waking hours* to have that potential for happiness and satisfaction?

"That's what I do. With every work assignment and with every personal pursuit. I learned that from my parents. They taught me to *filter out* the things that don't matter and to focus my time intensely on the things that do. And when I made those choices, they taught me to commit myself to them fully and with passion. They taught me to throw every ounce of energy I had toward making that chosen pursuit spectacular."

Redirecting, I continued. "A wise man once told me that "Life ain't no dress rehearsal," and that each day is either maximized or squandered. Each day is an opportunity to do something spectacular. I think he had it right."

I had their full attention. "That's what I am committed to do here—throw myself forcefully and emotionally toward fixing our house. It's our house and it matters to me. *XLHealth has made it through my filter.*"

Looking directly at several employees, I said, "And I would ask you whether you are capable of making that commitment, too." Then I shifted my gaze to another group of employees. "If you aren't able to commit yourself to XLHealth with the same intensity that you apply to your private special thing, then I would urge you to leave the company immediately and go find a different job where you are happier and can willingly commit yourself." They stared at me. "After all, life ain't no dress rehearsal. We get older each day, and we should treat preciously those days and spend them in a place that can bring lasting satisfaction." I peered into yet another group of faces, challenging them. "So if this place isn't for you, you should move quickly to find a better place."

"For those of you who want to engage with me, we will build a culture here based on openness and trust. It will be a culture that is active, energetic, aggressive and urgent—*because minutes matter*. In business, like in sports, you are either the hunter or the hunted, and we will not be the latter. We will make games out of things that were formerly considered to be drudgery and we will find ways to make things easier and more efficient. We will test your endurance and you will learn and grow in the process. We will applaud each success and we will pick each other up after any failures. And amid the effort we will collectively make, we will have FUN."

Then I summarized. "I can't predict the future, but what I can guarantee is that you will have an experience here which will be unlike any other work environment you have experienced. It will be memorable."

I gave them a thoughtful smile. "These are the things that I promise and the things that you can count on."

As I walked to my apartment that evening, I realized some people in the audience may have been scared by my speech and the impending cultural change, but we didn't have the luxury of time. We needed a radical shift and a quick one.

"Speed" Can Be a Differentiator—"Because Minutes Matter"

Over the next few months, we did lose some people and we had to remove some others who weren't performing, but the vast majority of the Town Hall attendees bought into the new culture and committed themselves to our cause. They worked nights and weekends to address the company problems.

Similar to my experiences in the Philadelphia and Phoenix offices, there were people at XLHealth who needed training and mentoring.

To provide that, we typically worked 7 a.m. to 10 p.m. daily. And it was not unusual that we were in the office for entire weekends.

This was due to having a company full of broken processes, broken systems and broken services. Fixing them was hard and the work required wasn't always glamorous. Regardless, everyone pitched in, including the guy with the CEO title. It was like having Vine Patrol in a business setting.

Because of contractual commitments made by the prior regime at XLHealth, we continued to lose massive amounts of money throughout 2008. We had been given the needed statutory capital by MatlinPatterson, but those funds were rapidly being depleted and our financial condition remained in peril. We were in a race against time to fix our operational and contractual problems before we would again face insolvency.

Keeping my pact with employees, I continued to report the financial results each quarter. The results were dismal and the outlook was foreboding, yet I used each of these presentations as a chance to educate our people collectively. It was an opportunity to teach them and motivate them. In many ways, I became a business evangelist, extolling the postulates by which we needed to behave and perform. I was deploying The Dunlap Rules.

A couple months after the first Town Hall meeting, in one of my business evangelism meetings, I talked to the employees about *speed* being one of the most under-appreciated forms of differentiation. Once again, I relied on a metaphor to reinforce my message. "Imagine that we are in the bread delivery business." By now, my strange metaphors no longer surprised employees—they knew that somehow it would relate back to what we did at XLHealth. "We *don't make* the bread. We just deliver it.

"We get the bread products from the same source as our competitor does, so our base product is the same as his. So how do we compete with our adversary if we both are selling the same product?" Rhetorical once again. "We could lower our price...but that would only lower our profits. And we aren't going to do that. So how do we differentiate the product we sell to the end consumer?" I answered my own question. "We find a way to get it to them faster than our competition can deliver it.

"Let's examine how we could do that. We could tune up our trucks so they could drive faster and perform better. We could train our drivers so they handled the trucks like racecars. We could also analyze the routes our trucks take for delivery to ensure we are using the shortest routes. We could employ GPS models and test-drive each route every hour, assessing any predictable traffic delays.

"We might explore new forms of transportation. Maybe helicopters?" I smiled at them as they digested my extreme example. As I looked around the room, I recalled images of a sweaty boy running across fairways with golf bags on his back. I also thought about a young man who worked all night unloading shrimp from the hull of a ship. "Even if it's the same product that we offer, if we can devise ways to deliver it faster, then we have differentiated our service in the eyes of our customer. Speed can be a differentiator. In fact, we must make speed one of our differentiators." I scanned the crowd one more time. Referring to our competition, I said, "We need to find ways to outrun the other guys. And therefore, minutes matter. And a sense of urgency is critical to getting the most out of every minute."

This was just one of my business coaching sessions to our people. These talks were frequent, and they served to revive our spirit during difficult times. They also helped reinforce a sense of team unity, which was needed for our difficult turnaround.

We did make speed a differentiator. Everything we did was done with urgency. We weren't reckless; we moved with precision, but as fast as possible. Speed led to efficiency, as we fixed our company's operations. Speed also led to quicker designs on product enhancements. And finally, speed gave us a sense of confidence that, even if we had setbacks or made mistakes, we could move quickly to fix them and still deliver the enhanced product by a sooner date.

The inaugural Town Hall meeting was followed by more Town Halls. We also initiated company-wide video conferences and company-wide newsletters. The goal was transparency and creating open communication with all employees. I met with employees continually, whether it was in scheduled brown-bag lunch meetings or just shooting the bull in the hallways. It was a way to keep me grounded in the details of the business and a way to ensure that I knew the people and that they knew me.

In the same way my mother felt about attending football practices, I felt I needed to swing by our service offices, even if only for a few minutes. I had been doing this for a while, and like the Lehigh and Colgate players expected Mom, the service people expected me.

The service teams and I had an unwritten and unspoken code between us. When I entered the call centers, before me stood a field of cubicle stations filling the vast open room. In each cubicle sat a call center representative, busily attending to the needs of a customer on the phone. In this open-air room, I could be seen from a distance. They knew I was there.

As I walked past each cubicle, a hand would go up expectantly. I would slap it as I went by. It was a "high five" method of recognition for their conscientious work, a silent way for me to say "thank you" without interrupting their discussion with the customer. And they were counting on it.

This became a tradition. And then it became more playful. The high fives became "low fives" as reps leaned over and held their hand just above the floor. I suppose I looked ridiculous, crouching and stumbling my way down the hallway, slapping hands at my ankles.

But it was *our way* of communicating and infusing some fun into an otherwise serious workday. Truly, it was our way of letting each other know they were appreciated. It was our way of telling each other we had their back.

As much as I loved spending time with my management team, it was the time spent with the line troops that I cherished the most. There were young people who yearned to learn more. They were like me when I was young, working in lesser positions, but trying to improve their standing.

There were also older people in these jobs who had seemingly spent a career performing entry-level work. Their jobs weren't glamorous. Their tasks were banal and sometimes tedious.

They ended up in those careers for a variety of reasons. They might not have had the education to choose other occupations. They might not have had the benefit of the mentoring I had growing up. They might not have been supported or challenged to do more due to their life circumstances. But like my father had done with Jose at Lehigh, I treated them well and showed a lot of interest in them—because they were good people.

Through the years, I had seen so many leaders ignore people in these positions. Recognizing this, I paid particular attention to these people. I needed them to know they were valued and that their work was critical to our being successful. So I made a point to visit those areas regularly.

As with any company, there were times when we had service difficulties. To resolve the issues, there was often a need to take extraordinary steps to assuage the customer service problems. Often that involved the need to work around the clock. In those situations, when we communicated the problems to our service people, they willingly volunteered for the duty and together we worked through the night to meet our goals.

When this happened, senior managers alerted me to any of these "work sessions," because they knew I wanted to be there with the troops. It was important to me that these employees knew their sacrifice was being recognized by the whole company and that they and their work mattered to me.

When Defense Turned to Offense

THE ENSUING TOWN HALLS BECAME more like pep rallies. At one of the 2009 meetings, a certain CEO started the session by sprinting down the aisle and doing a flip onto the stage. The employees were stunned and went bonkers. It was a spontaneous move, and disarming, but it fit with my theme of a work hard, play hard attitude. I wanted to foster a casual, fun atmosphere void of any caste system. And, alas, my flip onto the stage routine became expected by the employees for every Town Hall after that.

Also reflecting our fun atmosphere, the majority of XLHealth people didn't call me Fred. They called me Dr. Deeeee. To be clear, I am not a doctor and to be more clear, that spelling is not a typo. It's how I signed my letters to employees, whether it was about a company update or an invitation to an after-work celebration.

How I got this name is a long story, but what matters most is that everybody had a good time with it. And the ease of our interface at all levels of the organization was, at its core, driven by deep trust and respect...and a boatload of affection for each other.

Reflecting back on my time in Baltimore, I have immense respect for the people at XLHealth. During the early years, they were undaunted by the uncertainty of our future and worked tirelessly to fix the problems in the company. Many of them weren't properly trained back then, but they showed a willingness to work hard and learn and adapt to new methods. They were committed to our cause, and for all of that, **they are my heroes.**

Four years later, after a lot of flips onto the stage and a tireless commitment by many wonderful people, we essentially created a new company. We fixed the problems by making work into a game and we outran the *other guy*. We differentiated ourselves against our competition by creating new products and services, and we grew significantly.

The relatively small group of 350 people who attended the first Town Hall grew to 1,600 employees. The company with $600 million in revenue and huge losses morphed, by the end of 2011, into a $2 billion company earning more than $200 million a year in profits.

Because of our success, we became a target for acquisition. In February 2012, XLHealth was acquired by none other than United Healthcare, which since my departure in 2000, had changed its name to UnitedHealth Group. The leaders at United admired XLHealth's products and culture, and believed many of our innovations could make UnitedHealth a better company.

"Don't Stay Too Long"

THE ACQUISITION BY UnitedHealth brought a mixed reaction within the XLHealth team. The employees understood that our private equity owners would eventually sell the company, but the news of the sale nevertheless caused sadness and nervousness with employees and managers.

Uncertainty always produces anxiety. The XLHealth employees were curious to know how United might deal with them since they had little knowledge of the *United way* of doing business. The employees wondered whom they would report to or, worse, whether they might lose their jobs. There was also some sadness since they identified so strongly with the culture we had formed and had a great affinity for the XLHealth way of getting the job done.

From the moment the merger was announced, I reassured the employees that I knew the leaders at UnitedHealth well, and that, if there was going to be an acquisition, United was the best possible parent company. Also, during the course of the sale, United officials made it clear that they admired the XLHealth culture and wanted to foster it across their company.

Some comfort was evident to the XLHealth employees when I informed them that United management intended for me to take on a much larger role at United after the integration of XLHealth had been completed. This news was reassuring since I'd presumably have a much stronger influence regarding future company decisions.

Out of the Mouths of Babes

Two months into the integration of XLHealth, I happened to be back in Texas for a weekend. Ty was home from college on break. As we drove around town, he quizzed me about the XLHealth sale and how it might affect me. When I told him about the potential expanded role at United, he asked, "Are you going to take it?"

"Well, United is a good company," I replied, "and if I end up in a larger role, I can help ensure that the XLHealth people get treated well after the integration is completed."

"But Dad, is that really what you want to do?" he asked, shaking his head. I was intrigued and asked him to go on. "You have worked your ass off," he asserted. "You saved your company from bankruptcy, tripled the size of it, and then you sold it for a boatload. You've done your job."

I tried to explain that there was more work still to do.

"I don't get it, Dad. I am sure you could be successful at United. I'd bet that if you stayed there another 10 years you could even end up running the whole company. " He looked at me emphatically. "But you are 53 years old. You are healthy and you have more than enough money. You could do anything you want with the rest of your life. And your most healthy years are the next ten." He had my attention.

"Dad," he continued, "you could spend those 10 years on conference calls and in boardrooms, or you could spend them with us. Heck, you could play more golf and get that low handicap back again."

Ty's thoughts swirled around in my head during the next few days. *Smart fellow*, I thought to myself.

Ty's comments also reminded me of a discussion he and I had seven years earlier. After I left the job in Texas, I had admitted to Ty the problems I had with the CEO. I had explained the nuances of corporate culture and told him that I would never work in someone else's culture again.

Now, seven years later, I realized I was on the verge of breaking my rule, by taking a job in someone else's culture—United's.

During the next couple months, the integration started to become complex. The responsibilities for that task had been delegated from the senior United people to their middle management. Something got lost in that translation.

With United's middle management now in charge, they began dismantling XLHealth, placing each functional area under their United counterpart. Moreover, they began to preach the United culture to XLHealth employees in sharp contrast to what the senior United officers had intended.

After XLHealth people complained to me, I contacted the senior United officers to complain directly to them. They assured me that forcing the United way on XLHealth was not their intention. Nevertheless, the integration moved forward through the vision of the middle managers.

I had committed to my XLHealth team that I would protect their interests under the new owner, but now none of my people reported to me. I therefore had little ability to impact decisions affecting them. My team was disgruntled and I was, too.

Fortunately, my parents happened to visit during that period. As always, they wanted to hear all about my life and the conversation naturally included a discussion about XLHealth. They heard about my growing frustrations with the integration. They listened carefully and asked many questions, but they weren't quick to offer their opinions. It was another vintage Marilyn and Fred session.

After I had given them a full description, Dad offered some advice.

"Tiger, make sure you don't stay too long" he said. I asked him for more clarity. "Cultures are complex. They are invisible and intangible. They are almost undetectable, but they are also very strong. You have built a strong culture that you and your team believe in. But United has its own culture and its people believe in that culture, too. The problem is that they bought your company which means they hold the trump card."

We talked more about my frustrations and some of the disagreements I was having with the United middle managers. "Tiger, that's what I am talking about: you are going to lose that fight. And you are going to get more frustrated and you will continue to lose your cool. I would hate to see your reputation get tarnished because of it. That's probably inevitable if you stay too long."

Over that evening and the next couple days, I thought a lot about those conversations. They were lessons learned from two Dunlap generations, my son and my parents.

I wasn't going to be able to change the United culture and I *was* growing more frustrated. If I accepted a new position with United, I might squander my remaining healthiest years in a losing effort, trying to contend with a big company's cultural differences.

Instead, as Ty suggested, I had an opportunity to spend time with family and friends and explore other interesting things. All of that would have been impossible if I accepted the United promotion.

During the following week, I contacted United senior officials and notified them I would be leaving. Over the next two months, they assigned one of their experienced veterans, Kevin Ruth, to work with me to transition my remaining duties to him. I had made an exit in as elegant a way as possible.

Leaving was difficult given all that we had accomplished at XL-Health. Most of all, I knew I would miss the exceptional people who had made XLHealth such a special place to work. We were a close group driven by the experience of working hard and saving a company in a dark moment. My band of brothers (and sisters) had pulled off a miracle and we were forever changed, because each of us would never forget the experience.

A couple months later, I was driving into Baltimore to have dinner with a couple of my work friends, a reunion of sorts after having been gone. What I didn't anticipate as I entered the familiar restaurant were the other 150 people waiting for me at a surprise retirement party. But the surprises kept coming: my parents were there, too. They had driven down from Hamilton, New York, to be a part of the celebration.

It was a very special time. It was also a rare time where my parents could experience being in *my* locker room. They could be in *my* huddle and meet *my* players.

One special moment happened when Dad pulled me aside during the party. In an excited voice, he said, "Tiger, this is like a pep rally! I never knew business could be like this. And your mother and I have met so many nice, impressive people here tonight. There is so much love and closeness in this room. And, Tiger, they just adore you."

I replied, "No Dad, we adore each other."

Coach and Mrs. D. with me in *my* locker room.

Some of the many heroes at XLHealth.

PART V

Enduring Lessons and Perpetual Values

The Dunlap Curse—
A Bar Set Very High

By attending the retirement party, my parents were able to meet a special group of people and witness firsthand the product of *their work*. They got to see the way I had implemented the lessons they had taught me so many years ago.

Along with those important lessons came high expectations. While I felt privileged to have been their son, at times it was difficult trying to live up to Mom and Dad's standards. The vessel by which they navigated life created a significant wake for young tugboats like Jessie and me who were being pulled behind it. Measuring up turned out to be a daunting proposition.

I had watched two people accomplish many things in their lives. I then spent the majority of my life trying to live up to what they accomplished, to make them proud of me. I was trying to reach a bar that had been set very high.

What I failed to realize was that the bar wasn't being set by them but by me. It was my desire to do something worthy of their being proud of me.

I remember sitting with Dad a number of years earlier in Orlando. The kids were 7 to 11 years old at the time. Dad and I talked early one morning on the back porch while the rest of the clan was still asleep.

It was the last day of my parents' visit and we had already covered all of the family updates the day before.

So we ventured into a different discussion. I gestured openly that I was still looking to do something impressive and meaningful, something that was comparable to what Dad had accomplished. "Dad, I want to do something that makes you and Mom really proud of me," I suddenly said.

It should be noted that my parents had always been loving and always showered Jessie and me with compliments. But in my constant effort to please them, I discounted their accolades along the way, thinking that their source was more out of politeness than sincerity. And with that mindset, I always felt the pressure to do more.

Dad was startled by my comment. "Tiger," he said, "what are you saying? Your mother and I are very proud of you. We listen to you talk about business, about fixing these companies, dealing with problems, and it boggles our minds. We don't know how you do it—you are able to juggle so many things and still manage them all so effectively."

Dad sat forward. "My work wasn't nearly as complex," he said. "It wasn't nearly as stressful. And any stress I had was for three months a year. You have it all year long."

As a blind, somewhat deluded over-achiever, I again tried to diminish his compliments as I had become so adept at doing in the past. But Dad wouldn't let it go. "Is that really how you feel?" he asked. "That you haven't done enough already to measure up to what Mom and I have done?"

I hesitated and nodded, looking at my lap.

"Whew!" Dad said. "That's not right. We marvel at what you have done and wonder who you could have learned it from. It wasn't us. You are still a young man, and yet you've accomplished more than I did in an entire career."

I started to object, but Dad cut me off. "And let's not forget about your role at home. Somehow, amid all of the work demands, you have found a way to be a big factor in your kids' lives. You have been a great dad. You are so much more involved with your kids than I ever was. And they love you for it and they are so close to you. We can see it in their eyes when they see you come through the door."

After thanking him for the comments, I explained that what drove Jessie and me in life was the desire to measure up to him and my mother. It was a self-induced drive, the pressure to make them proud of us.

"You shouldn't feel that way," Dad said. "You don't owe us anything. We couldn't be prouder of you than we are, with all that you have done here at home or at work."

To be certain, my parents had set high expectations. But those were expectations *for themselves*—it was what fueled their efforts throughout their lives. And on that humid sunny morning in Orlando, I realized that I had done the same thing, inflicting expectations *on myself* with those high bars driving me each day.

I suppose then that it's not surprising that those tendencies also flowed down to my children. At the risk of appearing to boast, it's important to describe my kids, in order to make this point clearly.

Chelsea is an investment banker, working in Midtown Manhattan. She graduated from Yale University and was captain of the Yale swim team. Before college, she was an outstanding student in high school, graduating 12th in a class of 700. She was also captain of her high school swim team.

Ty is a professional golfer, playing currently on the PGA Mackenzie Canada Tour. In high school, he played football, basketball, track and golf. He was the captain of the golf team and the Texas state golf champion in 2011.

In track, Ty was a member of the 4x200 relay team that broke the state record. Academically, he was named a National Merit Scholar. In addition to receiving the National Merit Scholarship, he received a golf scholarship at Texas A&M, a team ranked perennially in the top 10 in the country.

Katie was an outstanding student in high school, too. She played volleyball and was captain of the high school team. She received a volleyball scholarship to play at Louisiana State University and an academic scholarship at LSU, as well. Currently, she is beginning her junior year at LSU.

Like my parents have been of Jessie and me, I am very proud of my children. They have each outperformed me at this juncture in life. Did they make mistakes over the years? Sure they did. But to date, to the best of my knowledge, they haven't mowed down a row of hedges with a car. So I guess they are ahead of me in that regard, as well.

The reason I am providing this background on my children is to lay the groundwork for something that happened during summer 2014.

Ty became a professional golfer in May 2014. He spent that summer trying to qualify for tournaments around the U.S. and Canada. I accompanied him on several trips and caddied for him.

In July, we were in Thunder Bay, Ontario, a small town on the northern shore of Lake Superior. Ty played that day in a qualifier and lost in a playoff. Afterwards, we were back in the hotel room. He was disappointed and wanted to talk about it.

Like most 21-year-olds, Ty was impatient for success. He wanted to make progress quickly and move up the ranks of professional golf. I, on the other hand, was counseling him about becoming too anxious and putting too much pressure on himself.

"But Dad, I have a lot to live up to," he countered. I was puzzled by what he was inferring. "It's not easy being your son," he added. "That's a high bar to match."

I was shocked by what he said. "I hope I haven't put pressure on you," I replied. "That certainly isn't my intention."

"No, Dad, it's not you," Ty said. "It's me. I am putting pressure on myself. I don't want to be the *loser Dunlap*. I want to make you proud of me." I told him that he was already better than I ever was at that age. And I told him I couldn't be more proud of the person he had become.

Despite my assurances, that over-achieving drive in Ty will continue, I suspect, just as it had with me. My over-achieving nature was triggered by the example my parents had set and the demands they put on themselves. There is a generational trend in effect here...or so it seems. My girls have never directly said anything like what Ty shared with me, but it's entirely possible that they feel the same way, too. They may pressure themselves in the same way.

The truth is that all three of my kids have accomplished more in their young lives than I ever accomplished at their ages. I am proud of them and love them very much.

An Unexpected Gift

AS MENTIONED, I HAD NOT wanted to work after 2004. But sometimes things happen for a reason. Had I gotten my way and not gone back to work, I never would have had the experience of knowing the extraordinary people at XLHealth. And I never would have met Andrea Burchell.

Andrea was one of the senior executives at XLHealth. She was a Pharm D, a Doctor of Pharmacy, and she ran the XLHealth pharmacy program. Andrea had worked in the hospital setting for many years, handling the most severe and complex medical cases before coming to XLHealth in 2005.

When I first arrived as a consultant to XLHealth in 2007, I was given a briefing on each of the executives. Andrea was described as a smart, spirited person who worked hard and could overcome any obstacle. She was described as tenacious and driven, no matter how hard the task.

I learned later that one of those obstacles was breast cancer. Andrea was stricken with that dreaded disease shortly after joining XLHealth. At the age of 38, she underwent all of the rigorous treatments and operations to fight the disease. But even with the toll that chemotherapy took, she continued to work each and every day throughout the ordeal, determined not to let the affliction control her or impact her team at XLHealth.

By the time I arrived in Baltimore, her immediate health crisis had passed. She was willing to talk about it, if anyone asked, but she treated it as something in her past, something no longer significant. On a day-to-day basis, working with her, no one would have known she had endured that ordeal. She was always enthusiastic, positive and cheerful, full of energy and full of personality.

One lingering element to her ordeal was the outlook that breast cancer gave her. She once said to me "Hey, I have survived cancer. I appreciate every day. And I treat each day like it might be my last."

After one of our Tuesday Group meetings, most of the attendees had returned to their offices. A few of the executives were hanging around, still discussing some current issues. This wasn't unusual—it was part of our culture of exchanging information across functional areas.

In the course of those impromptu discussions, I generally circulated, listening in on the topic matter and tossing in my opinions. While I was doing this from one group to another, I happened to overhear a discussion Andrea was having with a few others. "I don't mind traffic jams anymore," she said. "I used to hate them, thinking about the inconvenience of sitting still in traffic. But after cancer, I was sitting in traffic one day and I thought, *hey, I could be dead right now. But I am not. I am sitting in traffic, but I am still alive.* And I was never bothered by those traffic jams again."

Andrea's experiences, dealing with the threat to her life, made her unique in our group. I grew to appreciate that many of what I would call 'my worries' paled in comparison to what this woman had endured. It was good medicine for my perspectives.

Andrea was tenacious, spirited and even dogmatic at times. Frankly, she frustrated the hell out of me sometimes as she stubbornly fought for things she felt mattered.

While I felt periodic frustrations, her doggedness was far more an asset to the company than a liability. XLHealth benefitted greatly by having Andrea Burchell on our team. She made many huge contributions to the renaissance we were creating.

When she wasn't fighting hard for something she believed in, Andrea was a catalyst for office morale. She was funny, animated, and engaging. Everyone knew Andrea, no matter what department they worked in or what job level they performed. She was probably the most socially outgoing person on our team and she had the highest attendance at company gatherings. She participated in everything. Concerts, bowling leagues, dance parties—at every function, she was there.

And then there were Andrea's famous shoes. She had more shoes than a shoe store, and she flaunted them playfully with her associates each day. "So, how do you like my shoes?" she would announce with a smile and a strut. And everybody would kid her about it.

Andrea's playful style and self-deprecating nature were popular with our team. This was particularly valuable in the early XLHealth years; 2008 through 2010 were very uncertain times and there was a fair amount of nervousness across the team. Her presence helped to break that tension. She provided an enthusiasm and vivaciousness that was infectious.

Though we hadn't expected it, the sale of XLHealth to UnitedHealth changed our company forever. Our management structure got systematically dismantled by the United middle managers, and with that, our culture got dismantled, too. Everything was different. And with that, other things became different too. I began dating Andrea.

Having known Andrea through a work environment for years, it was an interesting transition when we began a personal relationship. I had known a tough, resilient, dogged executive who would fight for what she thought was right and would defend her people as if they were her children.

As our personal relationship grew, I saw a different, softer side of Andrea. I saw someone who was vulnerable and wanted to love, be loved and be cared for. Her tough business side was replaced by a sensitive, loving demeanor.

As for Andrea's dogged, unrelenting nature, that's still in play. But she channels it in the pursuit of making our relationship more special every day. She is the most positive person I have ever met. She is full of life and full of joy, and she has made me happier than I have ever been.

Each morning I wake up to a smiling face and those familiar words: "Good morning, Baby! I love you!" And as I look at that beautiful face, I can't believe I was so fortunate to get such an unexpected gift.

My unexpected gift.

"I Am a Fortunate Man"

When Dad retired, his ideal day included playing golf early in the morning with the "Dew Sweepers" group at Seven Oaks, followed by lunch with my mother, followed by helping Mom with different afternoon tasks, followed by a nice dinner, two beers, and a healthy dose of *ESPN* in the early evening. But Marilyn had different plans.

After spending a lifetime working and raising two kids, Mom wanted to travel, and she wanted the love of her life to be with her on each trip. Dad was happy to go with her, though he would miss his *ESPN*.

In the 23 years following their retirement from Colgate, my parents traveled to 69 different countries! Each trip and every detail was orchestrated by the master planner, Marilyn. Mom and Dad managed to work their trips around their other commitments—those being obligations with their kids and their *other kids.*

What's an *other kid?* I've mentioned that my parents cared about those around them and took a special interest in people. They made an impact on so many of the football players and alumni over the years, teaching *them* life lessons, too. Those people maintained close relationships with my parents long after college. Because of this, my parents have been invited to hundreds of weddings over the years and have been included in family functions with their *other kids.*

Dad spoke to me about these relationships. "Your mother and I have *kids* all over the place. They are kids who are now as old as 75 or as young as 42! They include us in their lives and consider us as part of their family." He then mentioned a number of people he had seen or talked to in the recent past before adding, "It's so great to see how they have matured. I am a fortunate man to have so many high-quality people in my life."

My parents are timeless. Most people tend to narrow their focus as they get older. They become self-centered and concerned mostly with their own needs and activities. They can become more negative about life, and they can become less connected and less interested in the things that matter to those around them.

My parents have never been that way. Even in their 80s, they are filled with excitement and a desire to care about other people. They have an inexhaustible curiosity and interest in others and they remain wildly positive in their outlook on life. These are the reasons why younger people continue to seek them out as frequently as they do.

As a son blessed with their guidance along the way, I've spent a lifetime in business attempting to create the same emotion, the same determination and the same sense of close teamwork as they did in the college sports environment. Those efforts have made for some very lasting memories and close ties with the people who were part of each experience.

Like them, I still stay in touch with many of those people, even 30 years later. Also like my parents, in my retirement, I have invested my time heavily in younger people, those in their 20s and 30s. People of all ages have needs and ambitions, and I now devote a great deal of time to helping, coaching and mentoring people who reach out to me for guidance on business or personal matters. I am glad to help. It doesn't pay well (at all, really), but it sure is gratifying. My energy toward this type of service was guided by my parents' example. It was another life lesson they provided to me.

"The evidence of a life well-lived is the quality of the people who want to spend time with you."

That's a very succinct statement, isn't it? And it says it all.

In many ways, it goes with, "If you take care of the little things, the big things will take care of themselves."

That isn't a coincidence, because both statements came from the same person. He was the best man in my wedding.

A Final Lesson Learned

The lights sparkled off the chandeliers, and a faint glimmer of their reflections could also be seen dancing off the petals of the flower arrangements perched on each table at my wedding reception. My father had said enough about me. The notes in his hands crackled as he paused to look at them. Then he transitioned to talk about Andrea.

November 1, 2014

"When our son was alone and separated, our constant prayer was that he would find someone he loved and respected, and someone who loved and respected him, and that in his remaining years, he could have the fun that we have had for almost 63 years. And our prayers have been answered. Andrea, you are a beautiful person. And we love you."

The audience applauded, and he and Andrea embraced before he returned to the mic. "I just want to say a few things about her, before I present the toast. Our acquaintance hasn't been too long, but we have gotten well-enough acquainted that Marilyn and I have noticed some things about her. Besides being a beautiful lady and being warm and loving, she is thoughtful and poetic. If you get an email from her, she has a quote at the bottom from Elisabeth Kubler-Ross. It says a lot about how she thinks and feels toward others and I want to read it to you."

My father recited the words, speaking about people who have dealt with challenges, known suffering and struggle, but have found their way from those deep places. And that they have a unique appreciation for good things in life and that those challenging experiences fill them with compassion and gentleness. Knowing Andrea's struggles with cancer, Dad felt these words were especially meaningful.

Dad looked up from his notes. "We took a trip with them once," he said, "and afterwards, she put together a book of pictures to memorialize the trip. It was so considerate. And on the back of it, she put a saying: 'Don't cry that it's over, be happy that it happened.' Andrea is a very sensitive person and we love her for it. And we know that she is right for our guy." Applause engulfed the room as he smiled at us.

Referring again to the lyrics in "Moon River," he began: "As I finish this toast, I want to say this: How great it is that these two drifters are off to see the world. And I could wish them nothing better than what is happening to them today. And I want to take a glass now..." Dad turned to me. I had been holding his champagne. "My toast is to the bride and groom. We hope that they have a long life of beautiful love together. And we love you both."

Everyone raised their glasses, and the shrill sound of glasses colliding could be heard throughout the room. He hugged and kissed us both. Then he returned to his seat to receive an embrace from the other half of "we."

Andrea and I spent most of the wedding reception on our feet, hopping from table to table to greet our guests. As dessert was being served, we could hear the band gearing up for a big performance.

Our guests began to move to the dance floor, and the band played our wedding song. As I held her close, I whispered to Andrea how lucky we were—lucky to have found each other and lucky to have so many special friends with us on that day.

When the song ended, I moved toward the bandleader and he handed me the microphone. "Can I have your attention?" I began. The throng gradually quieted. "That was our song, and it is very special to us.

"But there is another song that is very special to us, as well. It's a beautiful song with very special lyrics. Andrea and I think it says a lot about who we are together as a couple." I paused and scanned the crowd. "But this song also tells the story of who my parents are together. It's about who they are as a couple, now for 63 years. And I'd like to ask them to come forward and dance to their song. It's a song written and performed by Clint Black, and it's called 'Something That We Do.'"

My father led my mother carefully onto the dance floor as the music started.

As they danced slowly, they listened to the words of the song, so similar to how they live together. They live each day as if their relationship is new. They are close, yet they can be independent too. They are strong. And loving. They are so enmeshed that they don't know where one ends and the other starts. For my parents, love isn't something that they share, it's something that they do.

A little while later, my parents left the reception to head to the airport to fly home. They had accomplished their objective: to be with us at this special moment. As they stepped into the sedan, I hugged my mother and thanked her for being there, just a few days after her hospitalization. "I wouldn't have missed it for the world," she said. Then she shook her head and added, "It wasn't that hard. I'm just so happy for you two."

Before she closed her door, Mom looked at Andrea. With a wink and a smile, she said, "Good night, Mrs. Dunlap."

Andrea and I watched as they drove away, the red taillights disappearing down the drive. Standing there in the dark, we could hear the sounds of our festive crowd inside, dancing to a very good band. We silently held each other. It was the first moment we had that evening when we weren't talking to someone. We didn't need to speak to each other, either. We were in a quiet sanctuary—a brief respite from the excitement inside.

My parents' car was no longer in sight. Inside their car, I imagined that not much was being said, either. Mom had to be exhausted, and I figured the car ride to the airport was their own quiet sanctuary to catch their breath, just as Andrea and I had done, standing silently in the cool November air.

I had been taught all my life to give it my all and to persevere through hard times. I had learned to tackle conflicts and to have the courage to deal forcefully with confrontations. I had also been taught to be compassionate and to appreciate others. And I had been taught to appreciate the simple things. The good things. And to always keep a positive outlook on life.

On that cool November evening when I was beginning my new life with Andrea, I learned that those lessons don't stop. As I watched my 84-year-old mother drive away with her 86-year-old husband, I realized that there is no expiration date to life's lessons. I realized that The Dunlap Rules live on, through my parents' actions and their love for the people who matter most to them.

For my parents, it has been a lifelong commitment to virtues that don't ever retire. And I realized that those special people would continue to be a guide for me, even in the autumn of their lives.

I am truly a fortunate man.

Coach and Mrs. D.—May the birdies be many and the hazards be few. We all love you both very much.

AFTERWORD

I HOPE YOU HAVE ENJOYED reading this book. Writing it has been a labor of love. Whether or not you have a direct connection or affiliation with Dad, Mom, Andrea or me, I hope you could feel the sense of appreciation and love I have for my parents and the immeasurable effect they have had on me and others.

Writing this book has taken more than 2,000 hours over eight months. This has included countless talks with my parents to ensure that events have been documented accurately. In the course of my research and writing, Andrea and I have taped many of those conversations. They were priceless and we will save them forever.

My parents were very moved by this project for a number of reasons. The frequent interaction with Andrea and me invigorated them. It has enlivened their memories of times and people from their past and it has made them think about many people who may read the book. Moreover, the project caused my father to revisit and ponder his career from a variety of perspectives: as a coach, as a teacher, as a leader and as a father to two children who loved and revered him.

As this project moved forward, Dad became so actively engaged that I was receiving calls from him at all hours, wanting to prompt me on one detail or another. And one late night, while my mother was sleeping, he felt compelled to commit to writing what he thought was his purpose in life. It was his summary of what drove him for the 40 years that he pursued his version of greatness. It was his depiction of what mattered to him and what he strived to achieve as a coach.

Here are Dad's words, special in every way.

February, 2015

Dear Tiger,

As I told you in the conversation at Christmastime, 2014, the biggest influence on my coaching style was Capt. Patrick Morgan, US Army. Everything from his bearing, dress, action and command was direct, honest and reasonable. He made me want to earn his respect and to please him. This influence was made on me in the short period of 12 weeks, which was "basic training." Then, as I told you, I did see him with his family 1-2 times during the following 8 weeks of Leadership School. He took an interest in me and counseled me regarding Leadership School and then subsequently, Officer Candidate School (OCS).

As I try to crystallize what I felt was my mission as a coach, I definitely feel that my forte was my leadership ability, which was not showy or overt, but was solid and purposeful. A person must be themselves and "be true to himself," not something that they are not. It's important to be authentic.

I grew up with an inherent, hard-working ethic—I would not be out-worked. Hence, I tried always to be well-prepared or even over-prepared. That was an obligation I had to the players, to put them in the best position to use their skills and to succeed.

So even though I feel that I was reasonably good as a tactician, and did things that helped us to succeed, I feel that my best strength was my influence on the players and my leadership ability, which was probably a "quiet influence," one that often went unrealized. But that's OK. Time has shown me that I have helped a lot of kids. Some realized it later in life, some sooner.

As a coach, I tried always to help make my players into better players, or to help them improve as players. Also, I tried to make them better people, or to enhance their self-value. As a coach, I have always had an unwritten or spoken bond with all my players, regardless of their abilities. If I am needed, or can help, I am there for ALL of them, and I continue to this day to try to be "the coach." Some kids stay in touch and continue our relationship. Some, I reach out to in times of trouble. But I feel the same about all of them and I am there for them, even the ones that I rarely (or never) hear from.

My greatest satisfactions when coaching came from individuals who accomplished something that exceeded their expectations. It might be making a great play, sometimes this was accomplished in practice, sometimes in a game. This was true also as a team, when we made some great play or pulled off a great upset. Records are important, but as a coach, sharing in the emotion of the young people exceeding their expectations—for me, that was the greatest!

Now as a "retired coach," my thrills and satisfaction come from the good lives and successes that my players are having after football.

These were my objectives. These were the things that drove me.

Love,

Dad

APPENDIX I

Some Things Speak for Themselves

THOUGH THIS BOOK IS WRITTEN from a son's perspective, it's only appropriate to include comments from some of my parents' *other children.* Below are some of the letters sent to them over the years by people whose lives they have influenced both on and off the football field. Also included is an excerpt from an article in the *Colgate Scene*, the Colgate alumni newspaper and one letter written about them.

October 30, 2010

Coach Dunlap,

It's hard to believe that this fall marks the 35th anniversary of your last season as Lehigh's Head Football Coach (and also mine as a student-athlete!). Your legacy at this institution lives through so many of us who were fortunate to play for you. I hope the reunion event held today serves as a small reminder of the influence of your leadership and the friendships you formed.

Personally, I can't overstate the impact on my life of your decision in 1972 to invite me to visit Lehigh and subsequently to become a part of the Lehigh Football Family. I arrived here in August of 1972 and haven't left yet! While a lifetime at Lehigh was never part of the plan, it sure has been a profoundly impactful and richly rewarding experience....

More important than the opportunities you provided me and ultimately my family, is the football experience as part of your program that was so central to my time at Lehigh. I learned to compete, I learned to line up in other positions, I learned toughness, I learned to be patient (well, at least I learned I don't like being patient), I learned the cerebral aspects of football and the importance of preparation, and I learned to make the most of the opportunities that are presented.

Those experiences have shaped my life for the past 34+ years. Today, I remain intensely competitive in all that I do. I've confronted a wide range of challenges that have required mental toughness, patience, and resourcefulness in order to achieve desired outcomes. I've had to "play" different positions here in my career, and I've learned from all of them in ways that make me better at what I do. And, I think I've done OK for a still skinny kid with mediocre abilities but also the willingness to work hard, plan intensely, and come ready to play every day. Again, I have you to thank for all of that.

As I look back on the early 1970s and the state of Lehigh Athletics and Lehigh Football relative to all that is available today, I find myself appreciating more and more all that you were able to accomplish. You built the modern era of Lehigh Football, virtually from nothing, and because of that foundation, the Lehigh Football experience is better for all of the student-athletes and coaches of today. So on behalf of all the current generation of Lehigh Football players and coaches, I thank you.

Finally, I can't close without thanking you for your wife! As I tell many people, but also as I hear others come back to tell me after having met you and your wife somewhere in the world, SHE SAVED MY LIFE! Maybe not literally, of course, but I don't think I would have survived 6 weeks during the football season of not eating solid foods while my jaw was wired closed, without the Dunlap blender! I'm also certain that after 6 weeks of cafeteria food being liquefied in your blender that you never got to use it again!

Thanks for being such important parts of my life and the life of my family.

With great respect and affection,

Joe Sterrett
Class of 1976
Director of Athletics, Lehigh University

8/28/15

Coach and Mrs. D.,

After reflecting on last weekend, I want to send you a short note of thanks for all you've done for me and for so many others in the Dunlap family. The fact that Tiger and the two of you have now put the Dunlap Rules in a book is a gift that will last the ages.

Saturday afternoon with the two of you and Tiger was such a special day. Seeing the love each of you have for one another on Saturday was a reminder of the example the two of you have set for all of us over the years. Hearing Tiger's motivations for writing the book was a reminder of how profound an impact the two of you had on his life. And for me, our time together reminded me of how much you've influenced and shaped my life.

I, and so many others, are thankful to have you in our lives. God bless you both!

Hope to see you soon.

"Buck"
Todd Buchner
Class of 1988

Fall 2009

In an article published in the *Colgate Scene*, Dan Hurwitz was being interviewed as the new member of Colgate's Board of Trustees. He was asked to name a key Colgate person who influenced him for the rest of his life. Hurwitz responded:

> "Fred Dunlap, Class of 1950. Coach Dunlap was more than a coach who taught us football. He was a mentor who taught us about life. He required us to understand that we were all a part of something bigger than ourselves, that we represented our families, our school, our fellow classmates, and with that, came a responsibility of conduct at the highest level."

Dan Hurwitz
Class of 1986
Trustee, Colgate University

11/4/91

Coach and Mrs. Dunlap,

I have so much to thank you for. Coach, thank you for being an inspiration, father figure and for demanding 100% in everything. Mrs. "D," thank you for reading over so many poorly written papers, taking care of Coach, and for an unexpected phone call to my "soon-to-be" mother-in-law. And thank you both for being an example of a truly loving, caring and supportive couple....Thanks again to both of you for not only teaching us to go the extra mile, but for also living that extra mile.

Sincerely,
Jeff Crowell
Class of 1988

10/22/91

Dear Coach,

It is with great admiration and respect that I write to congratulate you and Mrs. Dunlap on such a storybook career together. It is, and always will be, an honor to not only have known both of you personally, but to have played for you during the early 1980s.... Coach, you have always exhibited a class that few people even aspire to in this life. You are a nationally known figure, yet you have always had time for anyone who wished a moment to speak with you. Even after numerous years have passed, you have made the effort to speak and spend time with those of us from the past. That kind of character is rare, and ever so cherished by anyone who has crossed your path during this illustrious career.

I believe it goes without saying that anyone who knows you, or has known you, regards the experience as not only a privilege, but an honor. It is an honor to know you, and an even bigger honor to have played under you with the great teams in the early '80s. I wish both you and Mrs. Dunlap the most relaxing and enjoyable retirement there could ever be. Please remember that you are both always welcome to stay and visit in beautiful Harrisburg, PA anytime you may be passing through.

With deepest regards,
Robert Kuntz
Class of 1984

October 2010

Coach,

Let me first offer my sincerest congratulations for an enviable career that spans decades.... Few have achieved so much!

Perhaps it is appropriate at this moment to share a few thoughts and memories:

My Lehigh football experience ranks in my very few top life experiences. I did not come to Lehigh with the All-Star credentials like many others....Thanks for having the confidence to recruit a skinny kid from Bethel Park...You and John Whitehead were technicians of the game—and taught me how to "play" football.

I left Lehigh as a confident young man, ready to tackle the business world. I had one issue though—I needed a job. Thank you again for recommending my candidacy to John Winchester and Jack Zapf. Both Roger McFillin and I spent 28 great years with Baker Chemical. Utilizing some of your leadership style, coupled with a lot of hard work (perhaps a work ethic learned on the gridiron) and some very good mentors, I rose to lead a division of more than 1,000 "teammates".... For me, it could only have been achieved as a result of a terrific Lehigh education, the work ethic and teamwork I learned on the football field, and the leadership that was taught by you, John Whitehead, and my mentors. Thank you, again.

Bottom line, my experiences with Lehigh football and with you have made me a better football player, a more effective business leader, and a better husband and father. Thank you again.

I'm proud to have been a member of Fred Dunlap's team. Thanks for giving that skinny kid from Bethel Park the opportunity.

Congratulations again. Best wishes to you and Marilyn as you continue to enjoy the years ahead.

My best, always…
Dan Mulholland (Class of 1974) (and #76 in your program!!)

October 2010

Dear Fred,

It is with great pleasure and an honor for me to be able to take part in the day honoring you at Lehigh. My football experiences in the 1971-1974 era were clearly the highlight of my time at Lehigh and helped me form a solid foundation for the future.

One particular highlight I have always remembered was when we made the trip to West Point to play Army. As we were about to leave the locker room and take the field, you addressed the team and you made the following comment: "If you go out and beat Army today, everyone in the country will know it!!" For me it was, and continues to be a very motivating comment and one that has stuck with me over the years. It says everything about exceeding expectations and buckling your chin strap to give it your best.

Fred, best wishes on this special day.

Kind regards,
Mike Chieco
Class of 1975

7/26/91

Dear Coach D,

I recently read in the Colgate Scene that you have decided to retire in the near future. Congratulations.

I would like to take a moment to thank you for giving me the opportunity to attend Colgate University, participate in a first class collegiate football program and receive an education that is second to none in the country.

I can recall as if it was yesterday my recruiting trip to Colgate. After an adventurous Friday evening at D.U. (of which I later became a fraternity brother), all of the recruits were to meet bright and early Saturday morning at Huntington Gymnasium. As the numerous recruits were entering the gym, the coaching staff was busy greeting and talking with all of the prospective players. When my parents and I entered the building, you personally took the time to introduce yourself, knowing my name, my hometown, etc. and we talked as if we had met several times before. My parents and I were extremely impressed by your honesty, sincerity and gentlemanly manner. Although this was one of the little details that you and your coaching staff did, it made a lasting impression in my mind. Now, as the years pass on and I reminisce about my Colgate days, I realize the significance of my experience in the Chenango Valley.

Coach D, once again, congratulations on your decision and I wish you and Mrs. D. much happiness.

Best regards,
Joe Kozak
Class of 1984

11/9/91

Dear Coach D,

To describe in detail the impact you made on so many people is not possible in a short note. Let me just say that you have been a great coach and friend. Your dedication and discipline have been an inspiration to me.

I wish you and Mrs. D. a happy and healthy retirement. Good luck!

Sincerely,
John Grabaritz (Grabs #52)
Class of 1986

....

10/31/91

Dear Mr. Joyce,

It is with great regret that I will be unable to attend the dinner in honor of Fred Dunlap on November 9th. However, I would like to share with you, Coach and Marilyn some thoughts regarding the Man of the Hour.

There were, no doubt, many key factors contributing to my growth as a quarterback at Lehigh University in the early 1970s. But I am certain the key element to my selection as the Atlanta Falcons' 3rd Round selection was my relationship with Fred Dunlap.

Coach Dunlap (to this day, I have never called him Fred—I feel more comfortable keeping him on hallowed ground) spotted something in me that most recruiters did not recognize. Back in the lean years of Lehigh football, it was the way he had to build the program. He had to recognize hidden talent and cultivate it. And he had to fend off restless alumni and insensitive administrators while he was developing Lehigh's road to success. It was an uphill climb all the way. But Coach was relentless and never wavered.

In my sophomore season, we realized a dream come true—Coach's first winning season at Lehigh (8-3). It was a big year, marred only by

Delaware, Penn, and yes, Colgate.... By the end of our senior year, Coach had Lehigh on track for a Lambert Cup and an invitation to the first NCAA Division II Playoffs.

Lehigh went on to achieve many great victories under Coach Dunlap and he was the catalyst for the development of many great careers. But to me, there will always be a special attachment to that first winning season and the Coach's perseverance. He was a man on a mission and led us to the pinnacle of success.

Coach's success centered on discipline, creativity, mental toughness and cigars... My evenings during the season were spent in Coach's office viewing films and applying Visine! By the time I graduated, I had learned how to read defenses, audible at the line of scrimmage, and breathe without inhaling...

But it was all worthwhile because playing QB for Coach Dunlap was the highlight of my career. He is the finest coach and teacher I have experienced. Quite simply, he made a difference in my life. I congratulate him on a great career and salute him on this fine evening. Thanks Coach—thanks for everything.

Warmest regards,
Kim McQuilken
Class of 1974

October 2010

Dear Coach,

After 45 years, it is great to reflect back to the fall of 1965. My senior year of Lehigh football was highlighted by a victory over Lafayette in the 101st game.

Over the years it has become evident that being a member of your first football team as the head coach at Lehigh has helped to establish and validate the solid and lasting foundation of your incredible coaching career. An old locker room phrase "You done good" is certainly worthy of you as the football coach, and you as a quality person.

I know both Hal Yeich and I are proud to have served as your 1965 Co-Captains. Whatever leadership skills we were able to provide to you and the team have been a small measure of the athletic/life skills and values your coaching techniques have contributed to our growth and successes as adults.

To know you and call you COACH Dunlap is a true honor.

Bob Draucker
Class of 1966

October 2010

Fred,

I cannot believe 45 years have passed since your first year at Lehigh. I do not think either of us will ever forget your first of many victories at Lehigh. It was too bad we had to wait until the Lafayette game, but we did build a lot of character that first year.

I knew that the fortunes of Lehigh football would change if the Alumni would give you a chance. How right I was…you should be proud of what was accomplished over the years.

Here is wishing you and Marilyn well as you continue to enjoy retirement.

Hal Yeich
Class of 1966

October 2010

Dear Coach Dunlap,

While more than 40 years have passed since were together at Lehigh, I wanted to take this opportunity to let you know that over the years, your leadership and management style was often the model for me during my career in the US Navy and later in a civilian capacity with NATO. Your early years at Lehigh certainly were difficult ones if the won-loss record is any indication.

Nevertheless, it was clear to me as well as many others that even though you may not have had the quality players that you had in your later years at Lehigh, you had a vision of what it would take to build a winning organization. Through those first losing seasons, we could still look like winners, thanks to your leadership. The confident, business-like manner in which you directed the football program in those early years left no doubt in my mind that with your perseverance and vision, winning football teams at Lehigh would eventually become a reality.

Over the years I have found myself in challenging situations, probably not so different from what you initially experienced at Lehigh. More than once I was confronted with an organization that had not been adequately managed, staffed or funded. Inspired by what I had observed under your leadership at Lehigh, I consistently maintained a winning attitude right from the start....As I now begin the next phase of my life (retirement), I would like to think that the leadership and management style that I learned from you went a long way towards my success in life, and for this I am indeed grateful....I wanted you to know how much I appreciated the chance to be part of a Lehigh team coached by you...I wish you and yours all the best in the future.

Warm regards,
Ted Stewart
Class of 1967

October, 2010

Coach Dunlap,

I was delighted to learn yesterday of Lehigh's intention to honor you at next weekend's game....I am sorry that I am unable to be there to honor you with my presence. Because this is the case, I did want to take a moment to share some thoughts and reflections on this "long ago time" (1967/8 seasons).

Through 7 football seasons between high school and Lehigh, I never experienced the exhilaration of playing on a winning team....it is said that you learn more from losing than from winning. In reflecting on my life...I find this to have been the case. The character that it took to show up for practice on Monday after losing on Saturday... has served me well in life....

While specific techniques that you may have taught us over the years are long since forgotten, what cannot be forgotten is the lesson of your example. While I would love to take credit for the character described in the preceding paragraph, much of it rubbed off from observation of you and our coaching staff. No matter how dismal our loss, you never appeared to give up hope on us....you had helpful suggestions as to ways in which we could correct the shortcomings that led to our loss....they were always couched in a positive and constructive way that built us up, rather than tear us down. And if you had doubts as to our ability to succeed that week, they were never apparent.

And the thing that stands out most in my memory...is that you never asked us to do anything that you were not prepared to do.... while not consciously aware of it at the time, I imbibed this critical important lesson about management and true leadership.

I do want to say thank you for the important role that you played in a formative part of my life, and I wish you every success and happiness in the long life that I pray lies before you.

Respectfully yours,
Reginald Jennings
Class of 1969

12/12/14

Coach "D" and Mrs. "D,"

Every year at this Holiday time, I take the opportunity to reflect on all of my good fortune. Without hesitation, every year, Colgate U. and the Dunlap name are at the top of my 'gratitude list'. Mrs. D., I tell my daughters how you helped me with my writing when I was a struggling freshman. And Coach D, your outstanding leadership and strategic planning have become even more evident to me as I get older.

Thank you both for making my Colgate experience so special. Those four short years were incredible! Merry Christmas and Happy New Year!

Love,
"Chubber"
Barry Chubb
Class of 1987

12/13/14

Dear Coach and Marilyn,

I am now in my 21st year with the SEC. I cannot help but think of your collective impact on my life, especially with the law school admission recommendation.

Warm regards,
Nicholas Panos
Class of 1988

October 2010

Dear Coach,

I am thrilled that I was able to have the idea to put together a Reunion in your honor and that so many of your players have returned to meet with you once again. I believe that so many have returned or sent messages as a way to express their respect and affection for you, while also recognizing your influence and impact on our lives. And it is that way for me too.

By the calendar, it is 44 years since our 1966 season and that is indeed a long time. But yet, there are parts of the season and certain games that I remember as if almost yesterday. I was not recruited by you, but I do believe that it was my good fortune and privilege to play for you. As much as I am a forward-looking person, even now, I look back to our 1966 season and wish I could go back to do more to have put some games in the "win column." Nonetheless, there were great lessons embedded in that season, such as effort, discipline, sacrifice, courage, and your favorite, I believe, to act and carry oneself as a winner, without regard for the score.

So, now through the prism of time, I look back on our last year on the field with great fondness, its difficulties notwithstanding, and I am so very glad that I had the opportunity to play at, and for, Lehigh and you....

So in closing, Coach, Lehigh was good for me and you were good for me, and I want to thank you. Over the course of the past four decades, I have met some truly wonderful, great people from all walks of life, but you have always remained in the very top group. I hope this Reunion will provide you with many wonderful memories. I hope too that you and Marilyn continue to enjoy many more years of good health and happiness.

With appreciation and warmest regards,
Mike Glasheen
Class of 1967

June 2014

Dear Coach Dunlap,

As the song goes, "It's not the breaths you take, but the moments that take your breath away."

On Monday night, Coach, you took my breath away! Seeing you walk through the door to Brad's viewing was more than a thrill. It was an example of what I have known for many years—you are a man of class, of grace, who will always be our head coach.

Thank you for the huge effort to pay your respects to a fallen teammate. It meant the world to Brad's family and the world to us "old Colgate ballplayers." To be sure, it was one of the proudest moments as a Colgate alum. While it is hard to put into words what your presence meant, I had to give it a try!

My love to Mrs. D., too. I hope she is feeling better.

Thank you for reminding us of the importance of what we shared. You are an amazing man.

Love and respect,
Bill Cullen
Class of 1984

October 2010

Coach,

Once, while I was walking on campus, you passed by, noticed I was looking at the ground and told me to always keep my head up. I've never forgotten that and have passed it on to my children. Thanks for the opportunity to play for you.

Denny Clayton
Class of 1971

October 2010

Dear Coach Dunlap,

I remember vividly the time that you and Coach Whitehead came to Reading just prior to my sophomore year. I needed guidance at that time in my life and you were there to help. I also remember how you helped me get back on track after my senior year, enabling me to eventually graduate. I needed support at that time of my life and you were there again to help. You were much more than a coach to me, and I will always be thankful for the positive impact that you have had on my life!

Sincerely,
Thad Jamula
Class of 1971

October 2010

Hi Coach!!

First of all, thank you for being a big part of my life!

It is hard to believe that it's been 43 years since I first stepped on Lehigh's campus as a wide-eyed, undersized quarterback (and Tiger was our ball boy). Your confidence in me to play and compete at the college level has left an indelible mark on my life. I am sure that you took a big chance when you decided to offer me a grant in aid to play for you at Lehigh (not many coaches were willing to recruit a 5-foot, 6-inch QB). I tried very hard to never let you regret that decision.

While our overall record during the '68-'70 seasons was not what we hoped for, there were some very special wins that I will never forget. Wins over Lafayette in '68 and '69. Wins over Rutgers in '69 and '70, and a certain game in Taylor Stadium in '70 where we got the attention of the whole East Coast when we upset Delaware when no one gave us a chance! (It is incredible how people still talk about that game.)

Please know that you and Marilyn have a special place in my heart. You gave me support and guidance when I needed it most. Your influence has been a major contributor to a successful life after Lehigh. I know that during your time at Lehigh and Colgate many others have been fortunate enough to benefit from being coached and taught by you.

Best wishes!

Jerry Berger

Class of 1971

October 2010

Hello, Coach Dunlap!

We have many fond memories of you from our time at Lehigh....we thank you for the example you set as a true gentleman and a fine coach during Bill's years on the Lehigh Football Team (1970-1974). We remember you and your wife so very kindly attending our wedding at Lehigh in 1975....Life has treated us well and you played a role in making that so.

Bill Schlegel
Class of 1974

October 2010

Dear Coach Dunlap,

I just want to take the time to let you know how much I respect you, both from the perspective of a player and now as an adult. You always conducted yourself in a manner which gave us confidence.... you were also influential in my life because you didn't allow me to quit football after my freshman year to concentrate on basketball. The next three years playing for you are now highlights in my life and my football teammates are still some of my closest life friends....

I have always thought that the best testament to a coach is what his players accomplish in life AND their post-playing relationship with the coach. If those are the criteria, then you are one of the extremely successful coaches.

Congratulations and Thank You.
Warm Personal Regards,
Norm Liedtke
Class of 1974

October 2010

Coach Dunlap,

Thanks for the positive memories, the life lessons learned, and for being an honorable, good guy. The best of health and happiness for you, Mrs. D., your son, your daughter and the rest of your family.

Sincerely,
Dan Hoerig
Class of 1970

October 2010

Hey Coach,

My father was not a man of many words, but there was never any doubt of his position. So when I was looking at colleges, he made it very obvious that Lehigh took the lead after meeting you. To him, associating with good people and obtaining an education was the priority, football was secondary.

You certainly proved him right. I have always considered myself lucky to have chosen Lehigh because of the people I was fortunate enough to meet there, especially you, the other coaches and my teammates. A sincere thank you for all the coaching, mentoring and friendship during school and over the years. You always provided a good example of how to act in both victory and defeat....

Best wishes and continued good fortune to you and Mrs. D.

Rod Gardner
Class of 1977

APPENDIX II

The Dunlap Family—Year by Year

April 18, 1928	Dad's birth date
August 31, 1930	Mom's birth date
June 1950	Dad graduated from Colgate University
November 1950	Mom and Dad got engaged
December 1950	Dad reported to Fort Jackson, SC (Basic Training)
December 1950–March 1951	Basic Training (Fort Jackson)
April 1951–May 1951	Leadership School (Fort Jackson)
June 1951–December 1951	Officer Candidate School (OCS) in Fort Riley, KS
December 22, 1951	Mom and Dad married in Utica, NY
December 51–May 1952	Armor School Training (Fort Knox, KY)
March 1952	Mom graduated early from St. Lawrence University (left for Kentucky to be with Dad)

June 1952–December 1952	Basic Flight School in San Marcos, TX (Gary Air Force Base)
December 1952–June 1954	Tactical Flying, Flight Instructor in Lawton, OK (Fort Sill)
Fall 1954	Assistant Football Coach (Hudson, NY)
Fall 1955	Graduate Assistant Coach—Colgate University
1956–1958	Assistant Coach—University of Buffalo (Buffalo, NY)
March 14, 1958	Jessie's birth date
January 2, 1959	Tiger's birth date
1959–1964	Assistant Coach—Cornell University (Ithaca, NY)
1965–1975	Head Coach—Lehigh University (Bethlehem, PA)
June 1971	Mom graduated from Lehigh (MA in English Literature)—She graduated 1st in her class.
1976–1987	Head Coach and Athletic Director—Colgate University (Hamilton, NY)
1988–1991	Athletic Director—Colgate University
January 1992	Mom and Dad's Retirement

ACKNOWLEDGMENTS

To my wife, Andrea: Thank you for loving me. Thank you for your inexhaustible enthusiasm and help to make this book as good as it could be. And finally, thank you for being patient and supportive this year, allowing me to take this hard, long journey of writing the book. And now that it's over, "Baby, I am back!"

To my parents, Fred and Marilyn Dunlap: Thank you for being the special people you are. Without that, there wouldn't have been the inspiration to complete this massive project. But with it, the task was effortless. I love you very much.

To my kids: Thanks for making your Dad proud of you every day. The memories you have given me will satisfy me for a lifetime. This story about Ninny and Da is also about you because you are a part of the Dunlap Team.

To Mark Murphy: Thank you for your eloquent contribution in the Foreword. But also thank you for being one of the many *other children* of my parents and keeping them close to you through the years.

To my Colgate friends: A special thanks to Vicky Chun and Ann-Marie Guglieri for their staunch support for this project. You helped spread the word to the Colgate Nation and provided me the operational support needed to get the books to the people who want them. And thanks to Bob Cornell for scouring the archives for pictures which make this book even more meaningful (Heck, where do you keep all of those pictures, Bob?). And finally, thanks to Debbie Rhyde and Cindy Chamberlain, the people who make everything at Colgate run on time.

To Joe Sterrett: Thank you for rallying interest with the Lehigh alumni and friends. And thanks for giving me so many pictures which bring distant memories back to life (Jerry Berger and Roddy Gardner still look pretty damn good, don't they?).

To my editors, Mark Shaw and Heidi Newman: Thank you for your critical and constructive input. You made a good book and a great story even better. And to Mark personally, thanks for helping a new author understand the maze of the publishing business. I was blind without your guidance. And now that I understand how complex and sometime convoluted this industry can be, I think about the 30 years you have been doing this. Are you nuts?

To my other friends and loved ones: Thank you for willingly reading the early drafts, giving me critical input, clarifying certain facts and providing Endorsements for the book. To my niece, Kirsten Hunter, and my son Ty, thanks for proofreading the book many times. By now, can you recite it in your sleep? Finally, to all of you: As Dad says, "The evidence of a life well-lived is the quality of the people who want to spend time with you." I am humbled and grateful to call you my friends.

—Fred "Tiger" Dunlap